R. Gupta's®

Popular Master Guide

BMRC

Bangalore Metro Rail Corporation Ltd.

Maintainers

Recruitment Exam

by
RPH Editorial Board

2020
EDITION

Ramesh Publishing House, New Delhi

Published by
O.P. Gupta *for* Ramesh Publishing House

Admin. Office
12-H, New Daryaganj Road, Opp. Officers' Mess,
New Delhi-110002 ① 23261567, 23275224, 23275124

E-mail: info@rameshpublishinghouse.com
Website: www.rameshpublishinghouse.com

Showroom
● Balaji Market, Nai Sarak, Delhi-6 ① 23253720, 23282525
● 4457, Nai Sarak, Delhi-6, ① 23918938

Book Code: R-1244

ISBN: 978-81-7812-942-6

HSN Code: 49011010

CONTENTS

| **YOUR SPACE** |

Bangalore Metro Rail Corporation Ltd.
BMRC–Maintainers 2016

1. What is the minimum age for eligibility to vote in India?
   A. 21 years
   B. 20 years
   C. 18 years
   D. 19 years

2. In Metric system 1 H.P. is equals to
   A. 746 watts
   B. 735.5 watts
   C. 1000 watts
   D. 746 k watts

3. An optical fibre is a transparent rod usually made of ____.
   A. clear plastic
   B. glass
   C. copper
   D. silica

4. The United Nations Organization (UNO) has its headquarters in ______ city.
   A. Washington D.C.
   B. Geneva
   C. Berne
   D. New York

5. The 200 kVA Transformer is operating on 440 V, 0.85 power factor, then the rating of Transformer in "kW" is
   A. 2.2 kW
   B. 170 kW
   C. 88,000 kW
   D. 235.29 kW

6. Which of the following is a term used in Cricket?
   A. Bull's eye
   B. Fine leg
   C. Love
   D. Ace

7. What is the maximum number of steps in one flight?
   A. 18
   B. 15
   C. 20
   D. 12

8. Who is the Chairman of the Lok Sabha?
   A. The Speaker
   B. The President
   C. The Prime Minister
   D. The Home Minister

9. The portion where we place our foot while ascending and descending is called
   A. Riser
   B. Tread
   C. Nosing
   D. Blocks

10. The algebraic difference between the maximum limit to the basic size is called
    A. Lower deviation
    B. Upper deviation
    C. Actual deviation
    D. Mean deviation

11. A JFET consists of
    A. Source, Drain and Gate.
    B. Anode, Cathode and Gate.
    C. Base, Emitter and Collector.
    D. B1, B2 and Emitter.

12. The maximum temperature of class "E" insulations is
    A. 180 °C
    B. 120 °C
    C. 105 °C
    D. 90 °C

13. For speed control of D.C. motors, the field control method gives the speed
    A. Above the rated
    B. Below the rated
    C. Remains same
    D. Becomes zero

14. Ammeter is always connected in
    A. Parallel to supply
    B. Series with load
    C. Across to load
    D. Series–parallel connected

15. For riveting a round head rivet hammer used is
    A. Cross peen hammer
    B. Sledge hammer
    C. Ball peen hammer
    D. Claw hammer

16. Working principle of micro meter is
 A. Sliding system
 B. Bolt and Nut system
 C. Cam system
 D. Rack and pinion

17. Which is not the property of a coolant?
 A. High cooling capacity between tool and work.
 B. Clear visibility between tool and work.
 C. Effective to skin and work.
 D. Increase the life of tool.

18. Lubrication is done in the machine to reduce
 A. The friction of sliding parts or Mating parts.
 B. The raising temperature between tool & work.
 C. The free movement of the sliding parts.
 D. None of these

19. The median of the data : 26, 31, 33, 37, 43, 38, 42 is
 A. 37   B. 26
 C. 43   D. 35

20. A temporary pier made in the river bed is called ______.
 A. Pillar   B. Parapet wall
 C. Caisson   D. Cribs

21. The L.C.M of $a^2b + ab^2$ and $a^3 + a^2b$ is
 A. $a^2b(a + b)$ B. $a^2b^2(a + b)$
 C. $a^2b(a - b)$ D. $ab(a + b)$

22. The circuit used to get a purer DC output from a rectifier is known as ______.
 A. converter   B. commutator
 C. inverter   D. ripple filter

23. Simplified value of $(1 - \sin^2 A)(1 + \tan^2 A)$ is
 A. 1   B. −1
 C. 2   D. 0

24. Bay window projecting in building is ______.
 A. Inward   B. Outward
 C. Backward   D. Proportional

25. The teeth of hacksaw blade are bent
 A. Towards right
 B. Towards left
 C. Alternatively towards right and left
 D. May be bent in any direction

26. A tower stands vertically on the ground from a point on the ground, which is 50 m away from the foot of the tower, the angle of elevation to the top of the tower is 30°, then the height of the tower is
 A. 50 m   B. $\dfrac{\sqrt{3}}{50}$ m
 C. $50\sqrt{3}$ m D. $\dfrac{50}{\sqrt{3}}$ m

27. The choke of fluorescent lamp is an example of
 A. Resistive load B. Capacitive load
 C. Inductive load D. Electrical load

28. Name the only Kannadiga to have become the Prime Minister of India
 A. Deve Gowda H.D
 B. S.M. Krishna
 C. Ramakrishna Hegde
 D. B.D. Jatti

29. The ratio of ON–time of a pulse to the OFF–time of the pulse is known as ______.
 A. PRF   B. Duty cycle
 C. Time cycle   D. ON cycle

30. Which one is *not* an A.C. motor starter?
 A. D.O.L. Starter
 B. Star–delta starter
 C. Rotor resistance starter
 D. Three point starter

31. Value of $^7P_3$ is
 A. 35   B. 840
 C. 630   D. 210

32. A bridge rectifier consists of
 A. one diode
 B. two diodes
 C. three diodes
 D. four diodes

33. The most populous state of India is ______.
 A. Andhra Pradesh
 B. Uttar Pradesh
 C. Bihar
 D. Madhya Pradesh

34. The ratio of diameter of driver and driven pulley is called
A. Module
B. Pitch circle diameter
C. Ratio of tension
D. Velocity ratio

35. In Construction of R.C.C. Roof slab, the proportion is ______.
A. 1 : 2 : 6   B. 1 : 2 : 4
C. 1 : 4 : 8   D. 1 : 2 : 8

36. Nobel Prize is not given in the field of ______.
A. Physics   B. Medicine
C. Economics   D. Mathematics

37. Sound travels the fastest in ______.
A. Gas   B. Solid
C. Liquid   D. Vacuum

38. The time period of an Astable Multivibrator output is given by the expression
A. $T = RC$
B. $T = 0.707\ RC$
C. $T = 0.69\ RC$
D. $T = 1.38\ RC$

39. All electrical measuring instruments measures only
A. RMS values
B. Peak values
C. Average values
D. Maximum values

40. What is the use of seasoning of timber?
A. Decrease the volume and weight of the timber
B. Decrease the strength of timber
C. Decrease the hardness of timber
D. Decrease the stiffness of timber

41. To remove more material the file used is
A. Smooth file
B. Second cut file
C. Dead smooth file
D. Bastard file

42. One bag of cement consist of
A. 10 kgs   B. 100 kgs
C. 50 kgs   D. 45 kgs

43. The property of a material due to which it breaks with little a permanent distortion is called
A. Brittleness   B. Malleability
C. Ductility   D. Plasticity

44. 18 : 4 : 1 high speed steel contains
A. Vanadium 4%, Chromium 18%, Tungsten 1%
B. Vanadium 1%, Chromium 4%, Tungsten 18%
C. Vanadium 18%, Chromium 1%, Tungsten 4%
D. Vanadium 1%, Chromium 18%, Tungsten 4%

45. Which of the following is the national game of India?
A. Kabaddi   B. Cricket
C. Hockey   D. Football

46. 2's complement of 11100111 is
A. 11100110   B. 00011001
C. 00011000   D. 00011010

47. Claw Hammer is used to remove the ______.
A. Nails   B. Screw
C. Nut   D. Bolt

48. Normalising of steel is done to
A. Refine the grain structure.
B. Remove the strains caused by cold working.
C. Remove the dislocations caused in the internal structure due to hot working.
D. All of these

49. Wood Turning Lathe used to
A. Turning the wood
B. Moulding the wood
C. Square the wood
D. Ripping

50. Which of the following is called the "Pink City of India"?
A. Udaipur   B. Raipur
C. Jaipur   D. Manipur

51. Annulary rings helps to Count the ______ age.
A. Tree   B. Table
C. Chair   D. Leaf

52. A couple closed roof can be used the span upto _______ metres.
- A. 2.5
- B. 4.5
- C. 6.5
- D. 8.5

53. Which among the following is the lightest gas?
- A. Hydrogen
- B. Oxygen
- C. Nitrogen
- D. Carbon dioxide

54. The Members of the Lok Sabha are elected for a period of
- A. 6 years
- B. 4 years
- C. 5 years
- D. 10 years

55. Suppose A and B together can do a job in 12 days, while B alone can finish it in 30 days, then time taken to finish the same job by A alone is
- A. 21 days
- B. 42 days
- C. 20 days
- D. 18 days

56. Mortise gauge is used to mark _______ lines parallel to face.
- A. Two
- B. One
- C. Four
- D. Three

57. The full form of SMT
- A. Surface Mount Technology
- B. Solder Mount Technology
- C. Surface Method Technology
- D. Surface Mould Technology

58. The electrical safety demands a
- A. Good connection
- B. Good earthing
- C. Good cleaning
- D. Good fixing

59. The popular food item "PIZZA" originated in the country ______.
- A. Spain
- B. Italy
- C. Portugal
- D. France

60. When the shaft is not aligned in a axis, then the bearing used is
- A. Deep groove ball bearing
- B. Thrust bearing
- C. Roller bearing
- D. Self aligning bearing

61. The sides of a right angled triangle containing the right angle are 5 cm and 12 cm, then the hypotenuse is
- A. 13 cm
- B. 17 cm
- C. 7 cm
- D. 169 cm

62. Name the highest award for bravery in India
- A. Ashok Chakra
- B. Mahavir Chakra
- C. Vir Chakra
- D. Param Vir Chakra

63. Product of $\left(\sqrt{6}+\sqrt{2}\right)$ and $\left(\sqrt{6}+\sqrt{2}\right)$ is
- A. $8-4\sqrt{3}$
- B. 8
- C. $8+4\sqrt{3}$
- D. $12\sqrt{3}$

64. The number of flip–flops required to construct Mod–10 counter is ______.
- A. 2
- B. 4
- C. 3
- D. 5

65. LED TV receivers are ______.
- A. LED screen with no need of backlighting.
- B. LCD screen with fluorescent tube backlighting.
- C. LCD screen with LED backlighting.
- D. LED screen with LED backlighting.

66. In the tail stock offset method if D = 30, d = 20 and length is 300 mm, then the offset should be
- A. 25 mm
- B. 10 mm
- C. 12°
- D. 5 mm

67. Ring gauge is used to check
- A. Hole
- B. Shaft
- C. Flatness
- D. Hole and Shaft

68. A dice is rolled once, then the probability of getting an odd number is
- A. 2
- B. $\dfrac{1}{2}$
- C. 3
- D. 6

69. The unit of conductance of conductor is
- A. Mho
- B. Henry
- C. Farad
- D. Ohm

70. Scarfed joints used to increase _______.
- A. Length
- B. Width
- C. Thickness
- D. Angle

71. The unit used for specifying the thickness of copper foil on a PCB is _____.
A. ounce per square foot
B. micron
C. milli–inch
D. nano meter

72. On solving linear equation $7x + 5y = 10$ and $3x + y = 2$, the value of x and y are
A. $x = 2$, $y = 0$
B. $x = \dfrac{10}{11}$, $y = \dfrac{-8}{11}$
C. $x = 0$, $y = -2$
D. $x = 0$, $y = 2$

73. The 2016 Olympic Games was held in which city of Brazil?
A. Brasilia
B. Buenos Aires
C. Santiago
D. Rio De–Janeiro

74. The medicine "quinine" is extracted from _____ plant.
A. Hibiscus
B. Tulsi
C. Neem
D. Cinchona

75. For finishing operation to produce a bevelled surface for already drilled hole is
A. Counter boring
B. Spot facing
C. Reaming
D. Counter sinking

76. The popular dance form of "Kathakali" originated in which State of India?
A. Karnataka
B. Kerala
C. Tamil Nadu
D. Andhra Pradesh

77. The language spoken by the largest number of people in the Indian sub–continent is _____.
A. Bengali
B. Punjabi
C. Hindi
D. Urdu

78. Who among the following is a vocal exponent of classical music?
A. Bhimsen Joshi
B. Praveen Godkhindi
C. Pt. Shivakumar Sharma
D. Pt. Ravishankar

79. Which amplifier has highest efficiency and distortion?
A. Class 'A'
B. Class 'B'
C. Class 'C'
D. Class 'AB'

80. Which country is known as the "Gift of the Nile"?
A. Sudan
B. Libya
C. Egypt
D. Ethiopia

81. The power factor $(\cos \phi)$ of A.C. circuit is
A. $\cos \phi = \dfrac{\text{Real power}}{\text{Apparant power}}$
B. $\cos \phi = \dfrac{\text{Apparant power}}{\text{True power}}$
C. $\cos \phi = \dfrac{\text{Reactive power}}{\text{Real power}}$
D. $\cos \phi = \dfrac{\text{Reactive power}}{\text{Apparant power}}$

82. Who is known as the "Flying Sikh of India"?
A. Manmohan Singh
B. Khuswanth Singh
C. Navjot Singh Siddhu
D. Milkha Singh

83. The diameter of a cone is 14 cm and its slant height is 10 cm, then the curved surface area is
A. 440 cm^2
B. 220 cm^2
C. 220 mm^2
D. 220 m^2

84. Co-ordinates of the mid-point of the line joining the point $(-3, 10)$ and $(6, -8)$ is
A. $\left(\dfrac{9}{2}, 9\right)$
B. $\left(\dfrac{-3}{2}, -1\right)$
C. $\left(\dfrac{3}{2}, 1\right)$
D. $\left(\dfrac{3}{2}, -1\right)$

85. What is the formula to find output load of an UPS?
A. Volt × Current
B. Current × Load resistance
C. Load resistance × Voltage
D. Volt ampere × Power factor

86. Name the present Vice-President of India.
A. Hamid Ansari
B. Zakir Hussain
C. Najma Heptullah
D. Krishan Kant

87. Which of the following is the largest Public Sector Undertaking in India?
A. Roadways B. ONGC
C. Railways D. Airways

88. The function of a diode can be compared with a
A. switch B. fuse
C. inductor D. relay

89. Factors of $x^2 + 7x + 12$ are
A. $(x - 3), (x - 4)$ B. $(x + 3), (x + 4)$
C. $(x + 3), (x - 4)$ D. $(x - 3), (x + 4)$

90. A chopper is a circuit that converts
A. AC to AC B. DC to DC
C. DC to AC D. AC to DC

91. Smoothing plane used for giving _____ finishing.
A. Rough B. Fine
C. Very smooth D. Very rough

92. FM signals are generally propagate by _____.
A. ground waves
B. sky waves
C. direct waves
D. ground reflected waves

93. In A.C. pure resistive circuit, the power factor is
A. Unity B. Lagging
C. Leading D. Zero

94. The words "Satyameva Jayate" which is inscribed below the base of the National Emblem of India are taken from _____.

A. Mahabharatha
B. Manduka Upanishad
C. Taittarya Upanishad
D. Ramayana

95. Name the first Indian ever to win the Nobel Prize.
A. Sir C.V. Raman
B. Mother Teresa
C. Amartya Sen
D. Rabindranath Tagore

96. Which is the surface sources of water?
A. River B. Sea
C. Well D. Infiltration well

97. The filament of Electric bulb is made by
A. Lead B. Tin
C. Copper D. Tungsten

98. If U = {1, 2, 3, 4, 5, 6, 7, 8, 9},
A = {1, 2, 3, 4} and B = {2, 4, 6, 8}
Then $(A \cap B)'$ is
A. {2, 4} B. {1, 3, 5, 6, 7, 8, 9}
C. {5, 7, 9} D. {1, 2, 3, 4, 6, 8}

99. Simple interest on ₹ 20,000 for 3 years is ₹ 4,800, then the rate of interest per annum is
A. 12% B. 4%
C. 24% D. 8%

100. One kilo–ohms can be expressed as
A. $1 \times 10^3 \, \Omega$ B. $1 \times 10^{-3} \, \Omega$
C. $\dfrac{1}{1000} \Omega$ D. $10,000 \, \Omega$

ANSWERS

1	2	3	4	5	6	7	8	9	10
C	B	*	D	B	B	D	A	B	B

11	12	13	14	15	16	17	18	19	20
A	B	A	B	C	B	C	A	A	C

21	22	23	24	25	26	27	28	29	30
A	D	A	B	C	D	C	A	B	D

31	32	33	34	35	36	37	38	39	40
D	D	B	D	B	D	B	D	A	A

41	42	43	44	45	46	47	48	49	50
D	C	A	B	C	B	A	D	A	C

51	52	53	54	55	56	57	58	59	60
A	B	A	C	C	A	A	B	B	D
61	62	63	64	65	66	67	68	69	70
A	D	C	B	C	D	B	B	A	A
71	72	73	74	75	76	77	78	79	80
A	D	D	D	D	B	C	A	C	C
81	82	83	84	85	86	87	88	89	90
A	D	B	C	D	A	C	A	B	B
91	92	93	94	95	96	97	98	99	100
B	C	A	B	D	A	D	B	D	A

EXPLANATORY ANSWERS

19. Arranging data in Ascending order.

26, 31, 33, 37, 38, 42, 43

$\because \qquad n = 7$ (odd)

$\therefore$ Median $= \left(\dfrac{n+1}{2}\right)$ th term

$\qquad = \left(\dfrac{7+1}{2}\right)$ th term

$\qquad = $ 4th term $= 37$

$\therefore$ Median $= 37$.

21. LCM of $a^2b + ab^2$ and $a^3 + a^2b$ is

LCM $\{ab(a + b), a^2(a + b)\}$

$\qquad = (b)(a^2)(a + b)$

$\qquad = a^2b(a + b)$

23. $(1 - \sin^2A)(1 + \tan^2A)$

$= \cos^2A \times \sec^2A \qquad$ [$\because$ In Trignometric

identities $\sin^2A + \cos^2A = 1$

and $1 + \tan^2A = \sec^2A$]

$= \cos^2A \times \dfrac{1}{\cos^2 A} = 1$

26.

Let the height of tower is 'h' m.

Then,

In $\triangle ABC$,

$\tan 30 = \dfrac{BC}{AB} = \dfrac{h}{50}$

$\dfrac{1}{\sqrt{3}} = \dfrac{h}{50}$

$h = \dfrac{50}{\sqrt{3}}$

$\therefore$ Height of tower is $\dfrac{50}{\sqrt{3}}$ m.

31. $^7P_3 = \dfrac{7!}{(7-3)!} = \dfrac{7!}{4!} = \dfrac{7 \times 6 \times 5 \times 4!}{4!}$

$= 7 \times 6 \times 5 \qquad \left[\because \ ^nP_r = \dfrac{n!}{(n-r)!}\right]$

$= 210$.

46. 1's complement of 11100111 is 00011000

$\therefore$ 2's complement of 11100111 is 00011000

$\qquad\qquad\qquad\qquad\qquad +1$

$\qquad\qquad\qquad\qquad\overline{\ 00011001\ }$

55. A + B, together can do a job in one day $= \dfrac{1}{12}$

B, alone can do a job in one day $= \dfrac{1}{30}$

8

$\therefore$ A, alone can do a job in one day $= \dfrac{1}{12} - \dfrac{1}{30}$

$$= \dfrac{5-2}{60} = \dfrac{3}{60} = \dfrac{1}{20}$$

$\therefore$ A, alone finish the job = 20 days.

61. We have,

   Height (h) = 5 cm

   Base (b) = 12 cm

$\because$ From Pythagorus Theorem,

$(\text{Hypotenuse})^2 = (\text{Height})^2 + (\text{Base})^2$

     $= (5)^2 + (12)^2$

     $= 25 + 144 = 169$

  Hypotenuse $= \sqrt{169}$ = 13 cm.

63. $\left(\sqrt{6} + \sqrt{2}\right)\left(\sqrt{6} + \sqrt{2}\right) = \left(\sqrt{6} + \sqrt{2}\right)^2$

$= \left(\sqrt{6}\right)^2 + \left(\sqrt{2}\right)^2 + 2\left(\sqrt{6}\right)\left(\sqrt{2}\right)$

$= 6 + 2 + 2\sqrt{12}$

$= 8 + 2\sqrt{12}$

$= 8 + 2\sqrt{4 \times 3} = 8 + 4\sqrt{3}$

68. Favourable case = {1, 3, 5} = 3

Total outcomes = {1, 2, 3, 4, 5, 6} = 6

$\therefore$ Required Probability $= \dfrac{3}{6} = \dfrac{1}{2}$.

72. We have,

   $7x + 5y = 10$ ...(i)

   $3x + y = 2$ ...(ii)

Equation $(i) - 5 \times$ equation (ii), we get

   $-8x = 0$

$\therefore$ $x = 0$

Put $x = 0$ in equation (i), we get

   $7 \times 0 + 5y = 10$

   $y = 2$

$\therefore$ The value of x and y are 0 and 2 respectively.

83. We have,

  Diameter of a cone = 14 cm

$\therefore$ Radius of a cone (r) = 7 cm

and   slant height (l) = 10 cm

Curved surface area of a cone $= \pi r l$

   $= \dfrac{22}{7} \times 7 \times 10 = 220 \text{ cm}^2.$

84.

$$\left(\dfrac{x_1 + x_2}{2}, \dfrac{y_1 + y_2}{2}\right)$$

A $\bullet$————————$\bullet$————————$\bullet$ B

$(-3, 10)$ $(6, -8)$

$x_1 \ y_1$ x_2, y_2

Co-ordinates of mid-point

$= \dfrac{x_1 + x_2}{2} = \dfrac{-3+6}{2} = \dfrac{3}{2}$ and

$= \dfrac{y_1 + y_2}{2} = \dfrac{10-8}{2} = \dfrac{2}{2} = 1$

$\therefore$ Co-ordinate of mid-point is $\left(\dfrac{3}{2}, 1\right)$.

89. $x^2 + 7x + 12 = x^2 + 4x + 3x + 12$

      $= x(x + 4) + 3(x + 4)$

      $= (x + 3)(x + 4).$

98. $A \cap B = \{2, 4\}$

 $(A \cap B)' = \cup - (A \cap B)$

    $= \{1, 3, 5, 6, 7, 8, 9\}$

99. We have,

  Principal (P) = ₹ 20,000

  Simple interest (SI) = ₹ 4800

   Time (t) = 3 years

$\because$ $SI = \dfrac{P \times r \times t}{100}$

   $4800 = \dfrac{20,000 \times r \times 3}{100}$

   $4800 = 600 \times r$

$\therefore$ $r = \dfrac{4800}{600} = 8\%$

Hence rates of interest per annum is 8%.

GENERAL AWARENESS

NATIONAL SYMBOLS

NATIONAL EMBLEM

State emblem of India is an adaptation from the Sarnath Lion Capital of Ashoka. It was adopted by the Government of India on January 26, 1950. In the adapted form, only three lions are visible, the fourth being hidden from the view. The wheel (Dharma Chakra) appears in relief in the centre of the abacus with a bull on the right and a horse on the left.

The bell-shaped lotus has been omitted. The words ''Satyameva Jayate'' meaning ''Truth alone triumphs'' are inscribed below the Emblem in Devanagari script.

NATIONAL FLAG

The National Flag of India is a horizontal tricolour of deep saffron (Kesari), white and dark green in equal proportion. In the centre of the white band there is a wheel in navy blue colour. It has 24 spokes. The ratio of the length and the breadth of the flag is 3 : 2. Its design was adopted by the Constituent Assembly of India on July 22, 1947.

NATIONAL ANTHEM

Rabindranath Tagore's song 'Jana-gana-mana' was adopted by the Constituent Assembly as the National Anthem of India on January 24, 1950.

Jana-gan-mana-adhinayaka jaya he, Bharata-bhagya-vidhata
Punjab-Sindh-Gujarat-Maratha-Dravida-Utkala-Banga
Vindhya-Himachala-Yamuna-Ganga Uchhala-jaladhi-taranga.
Tava subha name jage, Tava subha asisa mange, Gahe tava jaya gatha,
Jana-gana-mangala-dayak, jaya he Bharata bhagya vidhata,
Jaya he, jaya he, jaya he, Jaya jaya jaya, jaya he.

NATIONAL SONG

Bankim Chandra Chatterji's 'Vande Mataram' which was a source of inspiration to the people in their struggle for freedom, has been adopted as National Song. It has an equal status with the National Anthem.

Vande Mataram
Sujalam, suphalam, malayaja-shitalam,
Shasya shyamalam, Mataram
Shubhrajyotsna,pulkita yaminim,
Phulla kusumita drumadalashobhinim,
Subhasinim sumadhura—bhashinim,
Sukhadam, Varadam, Mataram.

National Bird and Animal of India: Peacock and Tiger; **National Aquatic Animal:** Dolphin; **National Flower:** Lotus; **National Game:** Hockey; **National Calendar:** It was adopted on March 22, 1957. It has 365 days in the year and the first month of the year is Chaitra.

NATIONAL CALENDAR

It is based on the Saka era with Chaitra as its first month and a normal year of 365 days. It was adopted from March 22, 1957. Dates of the national calendar have a permanent correspondence with dates of Gregorian calendar as Chaitra I falls on March 22 in a normal year and March 21 in a leap year. In official communications, both Saka and Gregorian calendar dates are written. Months of the national calendar are Chaitra, Vaishakha, Jaishtha, Ashada, Shravan, Bhadra, Ashvina, Kartika, Margashirsha, Pausha, Magha and Phalguna.

NATIONAL ANIMAL

The magnificent tiger — Panthera tigris (Linnaeus) is the national animal of India. Tiger is found in several parts of the country and is known for its grace, strength, agility and enormous power. 'Project Tiger' was launched in 1973 to check their dwindling population in India.

NATIONAL BIRD

The Indian Peacock — Pavo Christatus (Linnaeus) is the national bird of India. It is a colourful, swan-sized bird with a fan-shaped crest of feathers on its head and a long-slander neck. The male species is more colourful with blue breast and a spectacular bronze-green train of around 200 elongated feathers.

National Flower—Lotus

National Tree—Banyan

National Fruit—Mango

National Currency—Rupee '₹'

(One Rupee = 100 Paise)

National Aquatic Animal—Dolphin

BOOKS AND AUTHORS

Name of Book	Author	Name of Book	Author
Ain-e-Akbari	Abul Fazal	Mother (Maa)	Maxim Gorky
Anand Math	Bankim Chandra Chatterjee	Mother India	Katherine Mayo
An Unknown Indian	Nirad C. Chaudhuri	My Experiments with Truth	Mahatma Gandhi
Arthshastra	Kautilya	My Presidential Years	R. Venkataraman
Coolie	Mulk Raj Anand	Neeti Shatak	Bhartrihari
Das Kapital	Karl Marx	Nehru and His Vision	Dr. K.R. Narayanan
Discovery of India	Jawaharlal Nehru	Old Man and the Sea	Ernest Hemingway
Eternal India	Mrs. Indira Gandhi	One World	Wendell Wilkie
Godan	Prem Chand	Panchtantra	Vishnu Sharma
Gitanjali	Rabindranath Tagore	Paradise Lost	John Milton
Gora	Rabindranath Tagore	Ramayana	Valmiki (in Sanskrit)
Geet Govinda	Jayadeva	Raghuvansham	Kalidas
Harsha Charit	Bana Bhatta	Rajtarangini	Kalhan
Hindu View of Life	Dr. S. Radhakrishnan	Ram Charit Manas	Tulsi Das
India Wins Freedom	Maulana Abul Kalam Azad	Abhijnan Shakuntalam	Kalidas
Jobs of Millions	V.V. Giri	Satanic Verses	Salman Rushdie
Jungle Book	Rudyard Kipling	Saket	Maithili Sharan Gupta
Kamayani	Jai Shankar Prasad	Speed Post	Shobha De
Kadambari	Bana Bhatta	The God of Small Things	Arundhati Roy
Life Divine	Sri Aurobindo	Treasure Island	R.L. Stevenson
Last days of Netaji	G.D. Khosla	Twelfth Night	William Shakespeare
Les Miserables	Victor Hugo	Train to Pakistan	Khuswant Singh
Mahabharat	Veda Vyas	Uttara Ram Charitra	Bhava Bhuti
Macbeth	William Shakespeare	Vanity Fair	W.M. Thackeray
Mein Kempf	Hitler	War and Peace	Leo Tolstoy
Meghduta	Kalidas	Wealth of Nations	Adam Smith
		Wake up India	Annie Besant

INVENTIONS AND DISCOVERIES

Geographical Discoveries

Discovery	Discoverer
America	Columbus
Brazil	Cabral
North Pole	Robert Peary
Everest (Conquered)	Tabie Junko
Planetary Motion	Kepler
Hawaiian Islands	Captain Cook
South Pole	Amundsen
Solar System	Copernicus

Chemistry and Physics

Discovery	Discoverer
Atom Bomb	Otto Hahn
Atomic Theory	Dalton
Atomic Numbers	Moseley
Cosmic Rays	R.S. Millikan
Dynamite	Alfred Nobel
Electrons Theory	Bohr
Electricity (current)	Volta
Electric Telegraphy (Code)	S. Morse

Discovery	Discoverer
Gravitation	Newton
Gas Light	Murdock
Oxygen	J. Priestly
Photography	L. Daguerre
Printing for the blind	Louis Braille
Radium	Madame Curie
Telegraph	Samuel Morse
Television	J.L. Baird
Telephone	Graham Bell
Wireless	G. Marconi
X-rays	W.K. Roentgen

Mechanical

Discovery	Discoverer
Aeroplane	Wright Brothers
Bicycle	Macmillan
Computer	Charles Babbage
Dynamo	Michal Faraday
Diesel Engine	Rudolf Diesel
Engine (Railway)	Stephenson
Fountain Pen	Waterman
Gramophone	Edison
Locomotive Power of Steam	James Watt
Helicopter	Brequet
Life Boat	Henry Greathead

Discovery	Discoverer
Microscope	Z. Jansen
Printing Press	Gutenberg
Revolver	Colt
Sewing Machine	Elias Howe
Thermometer	Fahrenheit
Transistor	W. Shockley
Typewriter	Sholes
Telescope	Hans Lippershey
Tank (Military)	Swinton

Medical

Discovery	Discoverer
Antiseptic Surgery	Lord Joseph Lister
Bacteria	Leeuwenhock
Circulation of Blood	William Harvey
Homoeopathy (Discovered)	Hahnemann
Insulin	F. Banting
Penicillin	Alexander Flemming
Malaria Parasite	Dr. Ronald Ross
Stethoscope	Laennec
Vitamins	Funk
Anti-Rabies Treatment	Pasteur

General

Discovery	Discoverer
Nylon	Carouthers
Science of Geometry	Euclids

WORLD'S GEOGRAPHICAL SURNAMES

● City of Sky-scrapers—New York ● City of Seven Hills—Rome ● City of Dreaming Spires—Oxford ● City of Golden Gate—San Francisco ● City of Magnificent Buildings—Washington D.C. ● City of Eternal Springs—Quito (S. America) ● China's Sorrow—Hwang Ho ● Cockpit of Europe—Belgium ● Dark Continent—Africa ● Emerald Isle—Ireland ● Eternal City—Rome ● Empire City—New York ● Forbidden City—Lhasa (Tibet) ● Garden City—Chicago ● Gate of Tears—Strait of Bab-el-Mandeb ● Gift of the Nile—Egypt ● Granite City—Aberdeen (Scotland) ● Hermit Kingdom—Korea ● Herring Pond—Atlantic Ocean ● Holy Land—Jerusalem ● Island Continent—Australia ● Islands of Cloves—Zanzibar ● Isle of Pearls—Bahrein (Persian Gulf) ● Key to the Mediterranean—Gibralter ● Land of Cakes—Scotland ● Land of Golden Fleece—Australia ● Land of Maple Leaf—Canada ● Land of Morning Calm—Korea ● Land of Midnight Sun—Norway ● Land of the Thousand Lakes—Finland ● Land of the Thunderbolt—Bhutan ● Land of White Elephant—Thailand ● Land of Thousand Elephants—Laos ● Land of Rising Sun—Japan ● Loneliest Island—Tristan De Gunha (Mid-Atlantic) ● Manchester of Japan—Osaka ● Pillars of Hercules—Strait of Gibraltar ● Pearl of the Antilles—Cuba ● Playground of Europe—Switzerland ● Quaker City—Philadelphia ● Queen of the Adriatic—Venice ● Roof of the World—The Pamirs, Central Asia ● Sugar bowl of the world—Cuba ● Venice of the North—Stockholm ● Windy City—Chicago ● Whiteman's grave—Guinea Coast of Africa ● Yellow River—Huang Ho (China) ● Sickman of Europe—Turkey

CAPITALS AND CURRENCIES OF COUNTRIES

Country	Capital	Currency
Afghanistan	Kabul	Afghani
Algeria	Algiers	Dinar
Angola	Luanda	New Kwanza
Argentina	Buenos Aires	Peso
Armenia	Yeravan	Dram
Australia	Canberra	Dollar
Austria	Vienna	Euro
Azerbaijan	Baku	Monat
Bahrain	Manama	Dinar
Bangladesh	Dhaka	Taka
Barbados	Bridgetown	Dollar
Belgium	Brussels	Euro
Bhutan	Thimphu	Ngultrum*
Bolivia	La paz	Boliviano
Brazil	Brasilia	Cruzeiro
Bulgaria	Sofia	Lev
Byelorussia	Minsk	Zaichik
Cambodia	Phnom-Penh	Riel
Canada	Ottawa	Dollar
Chile	Santiago	Peso
China	Beijing	Yuan
Colombia	Bogota	Peso
Congo	Brazzaville	Franc
Croatia	Zagreb	Kuna
Cuba	Havana	Peso
Cyprus	Nicosia	Euro
Czech Republic	Prague	Crown
Denmark	Copenhagen	Krone
Egypt	Cairo	Pound
Estonia	Tallinn	Kroon
Ethiopia	Addis Ababa	Birr
Fiji	Suva	Dollar
Finland	Helsinki	Euro
France	Paris	Euro
Georgia	Tbilisi	Lari
Germany	Berlin	Euro
Ghana	Accra	Cedi
Greece	Athens	Euro
Guatemala	Guatemala City	Quetzal
Hong Kong	Victoria	Dollar
Hungary	Budapest	Forints
Iceland	Reykjavik	Krona
India	New Delhi	Rupee
Indonesia	Jakarta	Rupiah
Iran	Teheran	Rial
Iraq	Baghdad	Dinar
Ireland	Dublin	Euro
Israel	Jerusalem	Shekel
Italy	Rome	Euro
Jamaica	Kingston	Dollar
Japan	Tokyo	Yen
Jordan	Amman	Dinar
Kazakhstan	Akmola	Tenge
Kenya	Nairobi	Shilling
Korea (S)	Seoul	Won
Korea (N)	Pyongyang	Won
Kyrgyzstan	Bishkek	Som
Kuwait	Kuwait City	Dinar
Laos	Vientiane	Kip
Latvia	Riga	Lat
Lebanon	Beirut	Pound
Libya	Tripoli	Dinar
Lithuania	Vilnius	Litas
Malaysia	Kuala Lumpur	Ringgit
Maldives	Male	Rufiyya
Mauritius	Port Louis	Rupee
Moldavia	Chisinau	Leu
Mexico	Mexico City	Peso
Morocco	Rabat	Dirham
Mozambique	Maputo	Metical
Myanmar (Burma)	Yangon (Rangoon)	Kyat
Nepal	Kathmandu	Rupee
Netherlands	Amsterdam	Euro
New Zealand	Wellington	Dollar
Nigeria	Abuja	Naira
Norway	Oslo	Krone
Oman	Muscat	Rial
Pakistan	Islamabad	Rupee
Philippines	Manila	Peso
Poland	Warsaw	Zloty
Portugal	Lisbon	Euro
Qatar	Doha	Riyal
Romania	Bucharest	Leu
Russia	Moscow	Ruble
Saudi Arabia	Riyadh	Rial

Country	Capital	Currency	Country	Capital	Currency
Slovakia	Bratislava	Euro	Turkey	Ankara	Lira
Spain	Madrid	Euro	Turkmania	Ashikabad	Manat
Sri Lanka	Colombo	Rupee	Uganda	Kampala	Shilling
Sudan	Khartoum	Dinar	Ukraine	Kiev	Hyrvna
Sweden	Stockholm	Krona	United Arab	Abu Dhabi	Dirham
Switzerland	Berne	Swiss Francs	Emirates		
Syria	Damascus	Pound	U.K.	London	Pound
South Africa	Capetown	Rand			Sterling
	(Legislative)		U.S.A.	Washington	Dollar
	Pretoria		Uzbekistan	Tashkent	Som
	(Administrative)		Vietnam	Hanoi	Dong
Tajikistan	Dushanbe	Somoni	Yemen	Sana'a	Rial/Dinar
Taiwan	Taipei	Dollar	Zimbabwe	Harare	Dollar
Tanzania	Dodoma	Shilling	Congo (Zaire)	Kinshasa	Zaire
Thailand	Bangkok	Baht	Zambia	Lusaka	Kwacha

INDIAN CITIES AND THEIR RIVERS

City	State	River	City	State	River
Agra	U.P.	Yamuna	Kanpur	Uttar Pradesh	Ganga
Ahmedabad	Gujarat	Sabarmati	Ludhiana	Punjab	Sutlej
Allahabad	U.P.	Confluence of the	Lucknow	Uttar Pradesh	Gomati
		Ganga, Yamuna,	Nasik	Maharashtra	Godavari
		and invisible	Patna	Bihar	Ganga
		Saraswati	Srinagar	J & K	Jhelum
Alwaye	Kerala	Periyar	Surat	Gujarat	Tapti
Kolkata	West Bengal	Hooghly	Tiruchirapally	Tamil Nadu	Kaveri
Cuttack	Odisha	Mahanadi	Ujjain	Madhya Pradesh	Shipra
Delhi	Delhi	Yamuna	Vijayawada	Andhra Pradesh	Krishna
Haridwar	Uttarakhand	Ganga	Varanasi	Uttar Pradesh	Ganga

WONDERS OF THE WORLD

Seven Wonders of the Ancient World: (1) the Pyramids of Egypt, built in approximately 2700 BC; (2) the Hanging Gardens at Babylon; (3) the temple of Artemis at Emphesus; (4) the statue of Zeus at Olympia; (5) the tomb of Mausolus at Halicarnassus, built in nearly 350 BC; (6) the Colossus of Rhodes, built in nearly 280 BC; (7) the Pharos Lighthouse at Alexandria.

Seven Wonders of the Medieval World: (1) the Colosseum of Rome; (2) the Great Wall of China; (3) the Porcelain Tower of Nanking; (4) the Mosque at St. Sophia (Constantinople); (5) Stonehenge; (6) the Catacombs of Rome; (7) the Leaning Tower of Pisa.

Seven New Wonders of the World: (1) Taj Mahal of Agra (India); (2) Pyramid at Chichen Itza (Mexico); (3) Machu Picchu (Peru); (4) Statue of Christ The Redeemer (Brazil); (5) Great Wall of China; (6) Roman Colosseum, Italy; (7) Ruins of Petra, Jordan.

STATES OF INDIA (CAPITALS, PRINCIPAL LANGUAGES)

States / Principal Languages	Capitals	States / Principal Languages	Capitals
■ Andhra Pradesh *Telgu and Urdu*	Hyderabad	■ Meghalaya *Khashi, Jayantia and Garo*	Shillong
■ Arunachal Pradesh *Monpa, Adi, Nissi etc.*	Itanagar	■ Manipur *Manipuri*	Imphal
■ Assam *Assamese and Bengali*	Dispur	■ Mizoram *Mizo and English*	Aizawl
■ Bihar *Hindi and Maithili*	Patna	■ Nagaland *Naga, Assamese and English*	Kohima
■ Chattishgarh *Hindi*	Raipur	■ Odisha *Odiya*	Bhubaneshwar
■ Goa *Konkani*	Panaji	■ Punjab *Punjabi*	Chandigarh
■ Gujarat *Gujarati*	GandhiNagar	■ Rajasthan *Hindi, Rajasthani*	Jaipur
■ Haryana *Hindi*	Chandigarh	■ Sikkim *Sikkimese and Gorkhali*	Gangtok
■ Himachal Pradesh *Hindi and Pahari*	Shimla	■ Tamil Nadu *Tamil*	Chennai
■ Jammu & Kashmir *Kashmiri, Dongri, Urdu, Ladakhi, Dardi and Pahari*	Srinagar	■ Tripura *Bengali, Tripuri and Manipuri*	Agartala
■ Jharkhand *Hindi*	Ranchi	■ Uttar Pradesh *Hindi*	Lucknow
■ Kerala *Malyalam*	Thiruvananthpuram	■ Uttarakhand *Hindi*	Dehradun
■ Karnataka *Kannada*	Bengluru	■ West Bengal *Bengali*	Kolkata
■ Madhya Pradesh *Hindi*	Bhopal	■ Telangana *Telgu and Urdu*	Hyderabad
■ Maharashtra *Marathi*	Mumbai		

Union Territories / Principal Languages	Capitals	Union Territories / Principal Languages	Capitals
■ Andaman and Nicobar Islands *Hindi, Nicobarese, Bengali, Malayalam, Tamil, Telugu*	Port Blair	■ Daman and Diu *Gujarati*	Daman
■ Chandigarh *Hindi, Punjabi, English*	Chandigarh	■ Delhi *(Hindi, Punjabi)*	Delhi
■ Dadar and Nagar Haveli *Gujarati, Hindi*	Silvasa	■ Lakshadweep *Malayalam*	Kavaratti
		■ Puducherry *Tamil, Telugu, Malayalam, English and French*	Puducherry

HIGH COURTS IN INDIA

Name	Year	Territorial Jurisdiction	Seat
Allahabad	1866	Uttar Pradesh	Allahabad (Bench at Lucknow)
Andhra Pradesh	1954	Andhra Pradesh / Telangana	Hyderabad
Bombay	1862	Maharashtra, Goa, Dadar & Nagar Haveli and Daman & Diu	Mumbai (Benches at Nagpur, Panaji and Aurangabad)
Calcutta	1862	West Bengal and Andaman & Nicobar	Kolkata (Circuit Bench at Port Blair)
Chhattisgarh	2000	Chhattisgarh	Bilaspur
Delhi	1966	Delhi	Delhi
Guwahati	1948	Assam, Nagaland, Mizoram and Arunachal Pradesh	Guwahati (Benches at Kohima, Aizawl and Itanagar)
Gujarat	1960	Gujarat	Ahmedabad
Himachal Pradesh	1971	Himachal Pradesh	Shimla
Jammu & Kashmir	1928	Jammu & Kashmir	Srinagar and Jammu
Jharkhand	2000	Jharkhand	Ranchi
Karnataka	1884	Karnataka	Bengaluru (Circuit Benches at Dharwar and Gulbarga)
Kerala	1958	Kerala & Lakshadweep	Ernakulam
Madhya Pradesh	1956	Madhya Pradesh	Jabalpur (Benches at Gwalior and Indore)
Madras	1862	Tamil Nadu & Puducherry	Chennai (Bench at Madurai)
Orissa	1948	Odisha	Cuttack
Patna	1916	Bihar	Patna
Punjab and Haryana	1966	Punjab, Haryana and Chandigarh	Chandigarh
Rajasthan	1949	Rajasthan	Jodhpur (Bench at Jaipur)
Sikkim	1975	Sikkim	Gangtok
Uttarakhand	2000	Uttarakhand	Nainital
Tripura	2013	Tripura	Agartala
Meghalaya	2013	Meghalaya	Shillong
Manipur	2013	Manipur	Imphal

HILL STATION

Station	State
1. Almora, Mussoorie Nainital	: Uttarakhand
2. Cherrapunji (Shillong), Khasi Hills (Shillong)	: Meghalaya
3. Ooty, Kodaikanal Yereaud	: Tamil Nadu
4. Dalhousie, Kassauli	: Himachal Pradesh
5. Darjeeling	: West Bengal
6. Gulmarg, Srinagar	: Kashmir
7. Mahabaleshwar	: Maharashtra
8. Mt. Abu	: Rajasthan
9. Panchmarhi	: Madhya Pradesh
10. Ranchi	: Jharkhand

NATIONAL PARKS

1. Corbett National Park	:	Nainital, Uttarakhand
2. Dudhwa National Park	:	Lakhimpur Kheri, Uttar Pradesh
3. Kaziranga National Park	:	Jorhat, Assam
4. Kanha National Park	:	Jabalpur, Bhedaghat
5. Gir National Park	:	Rajkot, Junagarh, Gujarat
6. Guindy National Park	:	Guindy, Chennai, Tamil Nadu
7. Nagairhole National Park	:	Coorg, Karnataka
8. Bandipur National Park	:	Mysore, Karnataka

NATIONAL WILDLIFE SANCTUARIES

1. Dachigam Wildlife Sanctuary	:	Srinagar, Jammu and Kashmir
2. Sariska	:	Alwar, Rajasthan
3. Hazaribagh Wildlife Sanctuary	:	Hazaribagh, Jharkhand
4. Tiger Project	:	Sawai Madhopur, Rajasthan
5. Mudhumali Wildlife Sanctuary	:	Mudhumalia, Nilgiri, Tamil Nadu
6. Periyar Wildlife Sanctuary	:	Idukki, Kottayam, Kerala

HOLY PLACES IN INDIA

1.	Amarnath	Kashmir
2.	Ayodhya	Uttar Pradesh
3.	Badrinath	Uttarakhand
4.	Dwarka	Gujarat
5.	Haridwar	Uttarakhand
6.	Kancheepuram	Tamil Nadu
7.	Kedarnath	Uttarakhand
8.	Mathura	Uttar Pradesh
9.	Puri	Odisha
10.	Rameswaram	Tamil Nadu
11.	Tirupati	Andhra Pradesh
12.	Ujjain	Madhya Pradesh
13.	Varanasi	Uttar Pradesh
14.	Bodh Gaya	Bihar

SPORTS

Terms Associated With Sports :

Cricket : Ashes, Bye, Bodyline, Bowling, Break, Cover-point, Creases, Chinaman, Chucker, Drive, Duck, Follow on, Googly, Hit-Wicket, Hat-trick, Leg-before-wicket, Leg break, Leg-bye, Maiden over, No ball, Night-watchman, Runner, Run-out, Stumped, Silly-point, Slip.

Football : Handball, Corner kick, Dribble, Free Kick, Hat-trick, Off-side, Penalty Kick, Try, Throw in, Wembley.

Hockey : Bully, Carry, Corner kick, Corner, Penalty stroke, Off-side, Penalty, Roll in scoop, Sticks, Sudden death, Striking circle, Short Corner, Scoop, Tie-breaker, Under-cutting, Hat-trick.

Tennis : Backhand drive, Deuce, Fault, Half-volley, Net, Let, Volley, Smash, Service.

Billiards : Break, Cannons, Cue, Pot, Jigger, Scratch, In Bauk, In, Off.

Bridge : Dummy, Finesse, Grand-slam, Little Slam, Revoke, Ruff slam, Trump, Tricks, Vulnerable.

Volley Ball : Booster, Love, Service, Volley, Smasher.

Badminton : Smash, Drop, Let.

Chess : Check, Checkmate, Gambit, State-mate.

Golf : Bogy, Caddie, Hole, Links, Stymie, Tee, Put.

Polo : Chukker, Mallet, Bunder.

Baseball : Bunting, Diamond, Pitcher, Put-out, Strike, Home.

Boxing : Knockout, Punch, Upper-cut, Jab, Hook.

FAMOUS TROPHIES

Agha Khan Cup	Hockey
Beighton Cup	Hockey
Corbillion Cup	World Table Tennis (Women)
Davis Cup	Lawn Tennis
Duleep Trophy	Cricket
Durand Cup	Football
Ezra Cup	Polo
I.F.A. Shield	Football
Irani Cup	Cricket (India)
Jayalaxmi Cup	Table Tennis (Women)
Lady Rattan Tata Trophy	Hockey (Women)
Nehru Cup	Hockey (India)
Obaidullah Cup	Hockey
Ranji Trophy	Cricket (India)
Rangaswamy Cup	Hockey (India)
Rovers Cup	Football (India)
Santosh Trophy	Football (India)
Subroto Cup	Football
Thomas Cup	Badminton
Uber Cup	Badminton (Women)
Wellington Trophy	Rowing (India)

BIGGEST, LARGEST, TALLEST OF THE WORLD

Airport, *Largest*—King Fahd International Airport, Dammon (Saudi Arabia)

Animal, *Tallest*—Giraffe (Average height 6.09 m); *Largest and Heaviest*—Blue Whale (190 tonnes)

Longest recorded Animal—Boot lace Worm (55 m); *Fastest*—Cheetah (Approximately 100 km/hr)

Bay, *With max. shore line*—Hudson Bay (Canada: 12268 km); *With maximum area*—Bay of Bengal (India: 217 million hc)

Bridge, *Highest*—Sidu River Bridge (China 1627 ft); *Railway (longest)*—Danyang—Kunshan Grand Bridge (China)

Continent, *biggest*—Asia (31,845,872 km^2); *Smallest*—Australia Mainland (Area 76,17,930 km^2)

Dam, *Largest (concrete)*—Grand Coulee Dam (1272 m on Columbia River (Washington State, USA); *Highest*—Jinping-I (305 m)

Desert, *Largest*—Sahara (N. Africa; maximum length 5,150 km EW; maximum width 3,200 km NS)

Dome, *Largest*—Singapore National Stadium (310 m)

Fish, *Largest fresh water*—Plabeuk (China, Laos and Thailand); *Most abundant*—Bristle mouth; *Most venomous*—Stone Fish (Indo-Pacific Waters)

Fountain, *Tallest*—King Fahd's Fountain (Jeddah, Saudi Arabia)

Gulf, *Largest*—Gulf of Mexico (1,544,000 sq. km)

Island, *Biggest*—Greenland (now known as Kalaatdlit Nunaat---2,175,000 sq km)

Lake, *Largest*—Caspian Sea (Azerbaijan, Russia, Iran border: 37.18 lakh km^2); *Deepest*—Baikal (Siberia); *Largest (fresh water)*—Superior Lake (USA---Canada border: 82,350 km^2)

Mountain, *Highest peak*—Mt. Everest (8848 m; Nepal); *Highest range*—Himalayas, Asia (upto 4200 m); *Greatest mountain range*—Himalaya-Karakoram (96 out of 109 peaks over 7315 m are here)

Museum, *Largest*—American Museum of Natural History, New York

Ocean, *Largest and Deepest*—The Pacific (Area: 166,240,000 km^2; Depth: 10,924 m)

Platform, *Longest (rail)*—Gorakhpur (Uttar Pradesh; India, 1355.4 m. long)

Port, *Largest*—Port of New York and New Jersey (USA); *Busiest*—Rotterdam (Netherlands)

Railway Station, *Largest*—Grand Central Terminal (New York City; 19 hc); *Highest*—Condor (Bolivia; 4786 m)

Rivers, *Longest*—(i) Nile (6650 km) (ii) Amazon (6437 km)

Sea, *Largest*—South China Sea (2,974,600 sq. km); *Largest (inland)*—Mediterranean

Star, *Brightest*—Sirius A (also called Dog Star)

Telescope, *Largest (radio)*—Five Hundred meter Apertune Spherical Telescope (FAST), China.; *Largest (solar)*—Kitt Peak National Observatory, (Arizona; USA); *Largest refractor*—At Yerkes observatory (Wisconsin; USA; 18.9 m)

Temple, *Largest*—Angkor Vat (Cambodia: 402 acres)

Train, *Fastest*—Japan's magnetically levitated (magler) train (Speed over 500 km/hr)

Tunnel, *Longest (railway)*—Gotthard Base Rail Tunnel (Switzerland; 57.1 km); *Largest (road)*—Laerdal, Norway (24.51 km)

Volcano, *Greatest concentration in*—Indonesia; *Highest (extinct)*—Cerro Aconcagua (6960 m; Andes);

Zoo, *Largest*—Etosha Reserve (Namibia; area 10 million hc approx.).

FIRST IN INDIA

Governor General of Independent India — Lord Mountbatten

Commander-in-chief of free India — General Roy Bucher

Cosmonaut — Sq. Ldr. Rakesh Sharma

Field Marshal — S.H.F.J. Manekshaw

Indian Governor General of Indian Union — C. Rajagopalachari

Indian I.C.S. Officer — Satyendra Nath Tagore

Indian to swim across English Channel — Mihir Sen

Indian Women to swim across English Channel — Miss Arti Saha

Man to climb Mount Everest — Tenzing Norgay

Man to climb Mount Everest without Oxygen — Phu Dorjee

Man to climb Mount Everest twice — Nwang Gombu

Nobel Prize Winner — Rabindra Nath Tagore

President of Indian National Congress — W.C. Banerjee

President of Indian Republic — Dr. Rajendra Prasad

Talkie Film — Alam Ara (1931)

Test Tube Baby (Documented) — Indira

Viceroy of India — Lord Canning

Woman Minister of Indian Union — Rajkumari Amrit Kaur

Woman Governor — Mrs. Sarojini Naidu

Woman President of Indian National Congress — Dr. Annie Besant

Woman Prime Minister — Mrs. Indira Gandhi

Woman Speaker of a State Assembly — Mrs. Shanno Devi

Prime Minister of India — Pt. Jawaharlal Nehru

Muslim President of Indian Union — Dr. Zakir Hussain

Speaker of Lok Sabha — G.V. Mavlankar

Women to Climb Mount Everest — Bachhendri Pal

Woman Judge in Supreme Court — Mrs. Meera Sahib Fatima Biwi

Women Chief Justice of a High Court — Smt. Leela Seth

The First Indian Weightlifter to Win bronze medal in Olympics — Karnam Malleshwari (Sydney, in 2000)

World Chess Champion — Vishwanathan Anand

India's First Woman Merchant Navy Officer
— Sonali Banerjee

The First Woman Air Vice-Marshal
— P. Bandopadhyaya

The First Indian to be appointed as
United Nations Civilian Police Advisor
— Ms. Kiran Bedi

The First Women to be appointed Deputy
Governor of Reserve Bank of India — K.J. Udeshi

The First Indian Lady to win a medal in
World Athletic Championship
— Anju Bobby George

The First Sikh Prime Minister of India
— Dr. Manmohan Singh

IMPORTANT DAYS

15th January	—	Army Day
26th January	—	Republic Day
30th January	—	Leprosy Eradication Day/ Martyr's Day
28th February	—	National Science Day
8th march	—	International Women's Day
15th March	—	World Consumer's Day
21st March	—	World Disabled Day
5th April	—	National Marine Day
7th April	—	World Health Day
18th April	—	World Heritage Day
22nd April	—	International Earth Day
Ist May	—	Worker's Day
3rd May	—	International Sun Day
21st May	—	Anti-Terrorism Day
24th May	—	Commonwealth Day
31st May	—	World No Tobacco Day
5th June	—	World Environment Day
21st June	—	World Yoga Day
26th June	—	International Day against Drug Abuse
11th July	—	World Population Day
27th July	—	World Diabetes Day
15th August	—	Independence Day
24th August	—	Sanskrit Day
5th September	—	Teacher's Day
8th September	—	World Literacy Day
29th September	—	World Tourism Day
1st October	—	World Elder's Day
6th October	—	World Animal Day
8th October	—	Air Force Day
10th October	—	National Solidarity Day
16th October	—	World Food Day
24th October	—	U.N. Day
14th November	—	Children's Day
19th November	—	National Integration Day
26th November	—	Law Day
1st December	—	World AIDS Day
4th December	—	Navy Day
7th December	—	Flag Day
10th December	—	Human Rights Day

PARLIAMENTS OF IMPORTANT COUNTRIES

Afghanistan	—	Shora
Britain	—	Parliament House of Commons, House of Lords
Denmark	—	Folketing
The Netherlands	—	States General
India	—	Sansad
Israel	—	Knesset
Iran	—	Majlis
Ireland	—	Airetann
Iceland	—	Althing
Japan	—	Diet
Norway	—	Storting
Russia	—	Supreme Soviet
Spain	—	Cortes
Sweden	—	Riksdag
U.S.A.	—	Congress Senate
Germany	—	Bundestag

MINERAL RESOURCES OF THE WORLD

Mineral	Largest Producers
Iron Ore	China, Japan, Russia
Tin	China, Indonesia, Peru
Lead	China, Australia, U.S.A.
Zinc	China, Australia, Peru
Manganese	South Africa, Brazil, Australia
Aluminium	China, Russia, Canada
Petroleum	Saudi Arabia, Russia, USA
Silver	Peru, Mexico, China
Coal	China, USA, India

WORLD'S LARGEST PRODUCERS

Articles	Producers	Articles	Producers
Carpets	Iran	Cheese	USA
Cocoa	Cote d'Ivoire	Coffee	Brazil
Copper	Chile	Cotton	China
Diamonds	Russia	Jute	India
Rice	China	Rubber	Thailand
Silk	China	Steel	China
Sugar	Brazil	Tea	China
Tin	China	Wheat	China
Wool	Australia		

TEN LARGEST COUNTRIES BY AREAS

Rank by Area	Country	Area (sq. km.)
1.	Russia	17,075,400
2.	Canada	9,976,139
3.	China	9,561,000
4.	U.S.A.	9,363,123
5.	Brazil	8,511,965
6.	Australia	7,686,848
7.	India	3,287,263
8.	Argentina	2,776,889
9.	Kazakhstan	2,724,900
10.	Algeria	2,381,741

PRESIDENT OF INDIA

He is the constitutional head of the Republic but not the real executive.

Qualifications: (1) Indian citizen; (2) age not less than 35 years; (3) should have qualifications for election to Lok Sabha; (4) should not hold any office of profit; (5) should not be a Member of Parliament or State Legislature.

Election: He is elected by the elected Members of Parliament and State Legislative Assemblies in accordance with the system of proportional representation by means of single transferable vote.

Powers: He makes appointment to all the Constitutional posts. He can address either House of Parliament and send message to them. He can summon and prorogue either House of Parliament and dissolve Lok Sabha. All Bills passed by Parliament must receive his assent to become an Act. He issues Ordinance when Parliament is not in session. No money Bill can be introduced in Lok Sabha without his recommendation. He can grant pardon, reprieve or remit punishment and he can commute death sentences. He can declare national emergency, state emergency and financial emergency.

VICE-PRESIDENT OF INDIA

The Vice-President acts as the ex-officio Chairman of Rajya Sabha and acts as the President when the latter is unable to discharge his functions due to illness, absence or any other reason, or till the election of a new President when a vacancy is caused by the death, resignation or removal of the President.

The Vice-President is elected by an electoral college consisting of the members of both Houses of Parliament in accordance with the system of proportional representation by means of the single transferable vote. He must be a citizen of India, not less than 35 years of age, and should be eligible for election as a member of the Council of States.

PRIME MINISTER OF INDIA

The Prime Minister is the leader of the majority party in the Parliament and the President cannot exercise his discretion in the appointment of the Prime Minister. He stays in office till the majority of the members of Lok Sabha has confidence in him. He occupies an important posi-tion in relation to the council of Ministers. He recommends the names of the persons to be included in the Council of Ministers. He allocates portfolios among them and can ask any minister to tender resignation. He can drop a minister while reshuffling the ministry. He coordinates the administration of various departments. He is the chief link between the President and the Council. He is the leader of the majority party and so, he has a great influence on the Parliament and the party. The Prime Minister enjoys such extensive powers as have been described as the virtual ruler of the country.

THE SOLAR SYSTEM: SOME FACTS

Number of Planets: 8—Mercury, Venus, Earth, Mars, Jupiter, Saturn, Uranus and Neptune.

Largest most

Massive planet .... Jupiter
Brightest planet .... Venus
Brightest star .... Sirius
Fastest orbiting planet .... Mercury
Longest (Synodic)
day .... Mercury
Most moons Jupiter-69
Planet with largest
moon .... Jupiter
Greatest average density .... Jupiter
Tallest mountain .... Earth

Strongest magnetic fields .... Jupiter
Most circular orbit .... Venus
Shortest (synodic) day .... Jupiter
Hottest planet .... Venus
No moons .... Mercury, Venus
Planet with moon with
most eccentric orbit .... Neptune
Lowest average density .... Saturn
Deepest Oceans .... Jupiter
Greatest amount of
liquid on the surface .... Earth

THE EARTH: FACTS AND DATA

Composition of the Earth: Aluminium (0.4%), Sulphur (2.7%), Silicon (13%), Oxygen (28%), Calcium (1.2%), Nickel (2.7%), Magnesium (17%), Iron (35%)

Surface area	: 510100500 sq km	Polar Circumference	: 39992 km
Land Surface (29.1%)	: 148950800 sq km	Polar diameter	: 12710 km
Ocean Surface (70.9%)	: 361149700 sq km	Equatorial radius	: 6376 km
Type of water	: 97% salt, 3% fresh	Polar radius	: 6335 km
Total area of water	: 382672000 sq km	Mass (estimated weight)	: 594×10^{19} metric tons
Equatorial diameter	: 12753 km		
Equatorial Circumference	: 40066 km	Mean distance from the Sun	: 149407000 km

Earth's orbit speed (around sun) : 107320 kmph
Period of Revolution
(round the sun) : 365 days 5 hrs 48 min. 45.51 seconds

Time of Rotation (on its axis) : 23 hrs 56 min 4.09 seconds
Inclination of the axis
(to the plane of the ecliptic) : 23°27'

PRINCIPAL MOUNTAIN PEAKS OF THE WORLD

	Mountains	Height in Metres	Range	Date of First Ascent
1.	Mount Everest	8,848	Himalayas	May 29, 1953
2.	K-2 (Godwin Austen)	8,611	Karakoram	July 31, 1954
3.	Kanchenjunga	8,597	Himalayas	May 25, 1955
4.	Lhotse	8,511	Himalayas	May 18, 1956
5.	Makalu I	8,481	Himalayas	May 15, 1955
6.	Dhaulagiri I	8,167	Himalayas	May 13, 1960
7.	Mansalu I	8,156	Himalayas	May 9, 1956
8.	Chollyo	8,153	Himalayas	Oct. 19, 1954
9.	Nanga Parbat	8,124	Himalayas	July 3, 1953
10.	Annapurna I	8,091	Himalayas	June 3, 1950
11.	Gasherbrum I	8,068	Karakoram	July 5, 1958
12.	Broad Peak I	8,047	Karakoram	June 9, 1957
13.	Gasherbrum II	8,034	Karakoram	July 7, 1956
14.	Shisha Pangma (Gosainthan)	8,014	Himalayas	May 2, 1964
15.	Gasherbrum III	7,952	Karakoram	Aug. 11, 1975

POPULAR NICK NAMES OF SOME FAMOUS PERSONALITIES

Andhra Kesari	T. Prakasam	Lal, Bal, Pal	Lala Lajpat Rai, Bal Gangadhar Tilak, Bipin Chandra Pal
Anna	C.N. Anna Durai		
Bang Bandhu	Sheikh Mujibur Rehman	Little Corporal	Napoleon Bonaparte
Bapu	Mahatma Gandhi	Lokmanya	Bal Gangadhar Tilak
Bard of Avon	William Shakespeare	Mahamana	Pt. Madan Mohan Malaviya
Chachaji	Jawaharlal Nehru	Maid of Orleans	Joan of Arc
Desh Bandhu	C.R. Das	Maiden Queen	Queen Elizabeth I
Frontier Gandhi	Khan Abdul Gaffar Khan	Missile Man	A.P.J. Abdul Kalam
Fuhrer	Adolf Hitler	Man of Destiny	Napoleon Bonaparte
G.B.S.	George Bernard Shaw	Netaji	Subhash Chandra Bose
Grand Old Man of India	Dadabhai Naoroji	Nightingale of India	Sarojini Naidu
Grand Old Man of Britain	Gladstone	Panditji	Jawaharlal Nehru
Guru Dev	Rabindra Nath Tagore	Punjab Kesari	Lala Lajpat Rai
Guruji	M.S. Golwalkar	Shastriji	Lal Bahadur Shastri
Iron Man of India	Sardar Patel	Uncle Ho	Ho Chi Minh
Lok Nayak	Jayaprakash Narayan	Wizard of the North	Walter Scott
Lady with the Lamp	Florence Nightingale		

FAMOUS INTERNATIONAL ORGANISATIONS, HEADQUARTERS AND YEAR OF ESTABLISHMENT

International Organisations	Headquarters	Year of Establishment
United Nations Organisations (U.N.O.)	New York	1945
International Monetary Fund (I.M.F.)	Washington	1945
World Health Organisation (W.H.O.)	Geneva	1948
Food & Agricultural Organisation (FAO)	Rome	1943
International Labour Organisation (ILO)	Geneva	1919
UNESCO	Paris	1946
International Court of Justice	The Hague	—
Universal Postal Union (UPU)	Berne	1874
International Civil Aviation Organisation (ICAO)	Montreal	1947
UNIDO	Vienna	1967
International Atomic Energy Agency (IAEA)	Vienna	1957
International Finance Corporation (IFC)	Washington	1956
United Nations Development Programme (UNDP)	New York	—
UNICEF	New York	1946
International Maritime Organisation (IMO)	London	1948
World Meteorological Organisation (WMO)	Geneva	1951
International Telecommunication Union (ITU)	Geneva	1947
Arab League	Tunis	1945
Commonwealth of Nations	London	1931
World Trade Organisation (WTO)	Geneva	1995
International Development Association (IDA)	Washington D.C.	1960
International Bank for Reconstruction and Development (IBRD)	Washington D.C.	1946
World Intellectual Property Organisation (WIPO)	Geneva	1967
Organisation of Islamic Conference (OIC)	Mecca (Saudi Arabia)	1971
European Economic Community (EEC)	Geneva	1957
Red Cross	Geneva	1863
Interpol	Lyons (France)	1923
Asian Development Bank (ADB)	Manila	1966
North Atlantic Treaty Organisation (NATO)	Brussels	1949
Association of South East Asian Nations (ASEAN)	Jakarta	1967

BHARAT RATNA AWARD WINNERS

#	Name	Year	#	Name	Year	#	Name	Year
1.	Dr. S. Radhakrishnan	1954	17.	K. Kamraj*	1976	33.	M.S. Subbalakshmi	1998
2.	C. Rajagopalachari	1954	18.	Mother Teresa	1980	34.	C. Subramaniam	1998
3.	Dr. C.V. Raman	1954	19.	Acharya Vinoba Bhave*	1983	35.	Jaya Prakash Narayan*	1999
4.	Dr. Bhagwan Das	1955	20.	Khan Abdul Ghaffar Khan	1987	36.	Prof. Amartya Sen	1999
5.	Dr. M. Visvesvaraya	1955	21.	M.G. Ramachandran*	1988	37.	Pt. Ravi Shankar	1999
6.	Jawaharlal Nehru	1955	22.	Dr. B.R. Ambedkar*	1990	38.	Gopinath Bardoloi	1999
7.	Govind Ballabh Pant	1957	23.	Dr. Nelson R. Mandela	1990	39.	Lata Mangeshkar	2001
8.	Dr. D.K. Karve	1958	24.	Rajiv Gandhi*	1991	40.	Bismillah Khan	2001
9.	Dr. Bidhan Chandra Roy	1961	25.	Sardar Vallabhbhai Patel*	1991	41.	Bhimsen Joshi	2008
10.	Purushottam Das Tandon	1961	26.	Morarji R. Desai	1991	**		
11.	Dr. Rajendra Prasad	1962	27.	Maulana Abdul Kalam Azad*	1992	42.	C.N.R. Rao	2014
12.	Dr. Zakir Hussain	1963	28.	Jehangir Ratanji Dadabhai Tata	1992	43.	Sachin Tendulkar	2014
13.	Dr. Pandurang Vaman Kane	1963	29.	Satyajit Roy	1992	44.	Madan Mohan Malaviya*	2015
14.	Lal Bahadur Shastri*	1966	30.	Gulzari Lal Nanda	1997	45.	Atal Bihari Vajpayee	2015
15.	Indira Gandhi	1971	31.	Mrs. Aruna Asaf Ali*	1997			
16.	V.V. Giri	1975	32.	Dr. A.P.J. Abdul Kalam	1998			

* Posthumous   ** The award has not been given from 2002 to 2007 and 2009 to 2012.

ART AND CULTURE

☞ Classical Dances

Dance	State	Famous Artists
Bharat Natyam	Tamil Nadu	Yamini Krishnamurthy, Rukmini Devi Arundale, Swapna Sundari, Sonal Mansingh, Vaijanti Mala, Mrinalini Sarabhai, Chandralekha, Indrani, Ram Gopal, Bal Saraswati
Kathakali	Kerala	Gopinath, K.K. Nayar, Kunju-Kurup, T.K. Chandu
Kuchipudi	Andhra Pradesh/ Telangana	Sapna Sundari, Raja Reddy, Shobha Nayar, Radha Reddy, Vedantam Satyanarayan, Vimpanti Chinna Satyam.
Kathak	North India	Birju Maharaj, Gopi Krishna, Shambhu Maharaj, Sitara Devi, Vishnu Sharma, Durga Lal, Shobhana Narayan
Odissi	Odisha	Kelucharan Mahapatra, Indrani Rehman, Madhavi Mudgal, Pratima Bedi, Samyukta Panigrahi, Sonal Mansingh, Debudas
Manipuri	Manipur	Uday Shankar, Bipin Singh, Suryamukhi, Darohra Jhaveri

☞ Famous Folk Dances

State	Folk Dance	State	Folk Dance
Andhra Pradesh/ Telangana	Dandari, Banjara	Kerala	Mohini Attam, Padayuni
Assam	Bihu, Keli Gopal, Sataria	Madhya Pradesh	Lota Nritya, Jawara
Bihar	Chhau, Magahi, Durga dance	Maharashtra	Tamasha, Dahi Handi, Gof, Deepak Dindi
W. Bengal	Kirtan, Kalatri, Asweabadh, Brita, Kalidance	Manipur	Dhol Cholam
Chhattisgarh	Saila, Karama, Bhagoria	Meghalaya	Nongakarem
Gujarat	Garba, Rasalila, Tippani, Dandia,	Nagaland	Bamboo dance
		Odisha	Chhau, Maya Shabari, Dalachai
Haryana	Damyal, Lahoor	Punjab	Gidda, Bhangra, Panihari
Himachal Pradesh	Dussehra dance, Hikat, Notio	Rajasthan	Thumar, Kathaputali, Tera Tali
Jammu & Kashmir	Dumhal	Tamil Nadu	Terukalathu, Kabalatam, Kargam, Pulivesham
Jharkhand	Jhau, Ghumakudia, Jadur, Sarhul, Soharai, Karama, Vaima, Loojhari, Jat-Jatin, Vidayat	Tripura	Hazagiri
		Uttar Pradesh	Rasalila, Nautanki, Thali, Dhurang, Jhumela, Huraka, Bol.
		Uttarakhand	Kajari, Karan
Karnataka	Yakshagan, Dolu Kunitha	Goa	Dhode Modini

MUSIC

Main Schools of Classical Music

- There are two main schools of classical music, namely, the Hindustani and the Carnatic. The Hindustani school of classical music is in vogue in north-western India, eastern India and northern parts of the South India.

Musical Instruments

- *They are:* Tabla, Mridangam, Pakhawaj, Chandai, Dholak, Veena, Sitar, Sarod, Gootuvadhyam, Sarangi, Flute, Nadaswaram, Shehnai, Shringi and Turahi.

FAMOUS INTERNATIONAL AIR SERVICES

Air Service	Name of Country	Air Service	Name of Country
Air India	India	Lufthansa Airlines	Germany
British Overseas Airways Corporation	Britain	Iraqi Airways	Iraq
Trans World Airlines	America	National Airlines	Iran
Russian Airlines	Russia	Quantas Airlines	Australia
Japan Airlines	Japan	Hong-Kong Airlines	Hong-Kong
Pakistan International Airlines	Pakistan	Egypt Airlines	Egypt
Malaysia Airlines	Malaysia	Slovak Airlines	Slovakia
Royal Nepal Airlines	Nepal	S.I.A.	Singapore
Swiss Airways	Switzerland	Garuda Airways	Indonesia
Air France	France	Bangladesh Viman Sewa	Bangladesh
Kuwait Airways	Kuwait	Air Lanka	Sri Lanka
Pan American World Airways	America	Elitalia Airlines	Italy
K.L.M. Royal Airlines	The Netherlands (Holland)	Air Canada	Canada

FAMOUS RELIGIONS, FOUNDERS, HOLY BOOKS & PLACES OF WORSHIP

Religion	Founder	Holy Books	Place of Worship
Hinduism	Hinduism has no one Founder. (This religion is based upon the religion of original Aryan Settlers)	Ramayan, Vedas, Puranas and Geeta	Temple
Sikh	Guru Nanak Dev	Guru Grantha Sahib	Gurdwara
Christianity	Jesus Christ	Bible	Church
Islam	Prophet Mohammed	Koran (Quran)	Mosque
Parsi	Zoroaster	Zend Avesta	Fire Temple
Jainism	Adinath Rishavdev	Jain Granth	Jain Temple
Buddhism	Gautam Buddha	Tripitaka	Buddha Temple
Jew	Moosa	Torah	Synagogue

INTELLIGENCE AGENCIES OF SOME PROMINENT COUNTRIES

Country	Intelligence Agency	Country	Intelligence Agency
India	Research & Analysis Wing (RAW), Intelligence Bureau (I.B.), Central Bureau of Investigation (C.B.I.)	Russia	K.G.B. (Komitel Gosudarstvennoy Bezopasnosty) (Committee for State Security)
Pakistan	Inter Service Intelligence (I.S.I.)	Canada	Security Intelligence Service
U.S.A.	Central Intelligence Agency, Federal Bureau of Investigation	S. Africa	Bureau of State Security
		Iran	Sabak
Britain	Military Intelligence (M.I.)-5 and 6, Special Branch, Ultra, Joint Intelligence Organisation	Iraq	Al-Mukhabarat
		Australia	Australian Security and Intelligence Organisation
Israel	Mosad	France	S.D.E.C.E.
Egypt	Mukhabarat	Spain	C.E.S.I.D.
Japan	Nicho	Cuba	D.G.I.

SOME PROMINENT RACES OF THE WORLD

Races	Country	Races	Country	Races	Country	Races	Country
Veddas	Sri Lanka	Pygmy	Congo Basin	Eskimo	Canada, Tundra Region	Bushman	Kalahari Desert
Somaid	West Siberia	Bantu	Central and South Africa	Lapps	European Tundra	Red Indian	North America
Masai	East Africa						
Muree	New Zealand	Tartars	Siberia				
Yakoot	Russian Tundra	Baddu	Arab's Desert	Hausa	Nigeria		
Papuans	New Guyana	Semang	Malaysia	Kirghiz	Steppes (Russia)		

FAMOUS STRAITS OF THE WORLD

Strait	Between	Country
Malacca Strait	Andaman Sea and South China Sea	Indonesia
Palk Strait	Mannar and Bay of Bengal	India-Sri Lanka
Magellan Strait	Pacific and South Atlantic Ocean	Chile
Dover Strait	English Channel and North Sea	England-France
Berring Strait	Berring Sea and Chukasi Sea	Alaska-Russia
Sugaroo Strait	Japan Sea and Pacific Ocean	Japan
Sunda Strait	Java and Indian Ocean	Indonesia
Gibralter Strait	Mediterranean Sea and Atlantic Ocean	Spain
Harmuj Strait	Persia and Bay of Oman	Oman-Iran
Hudson Strait	Bay of Hudson and Atlantic Ocean	Canada

FAMOUS NEWSPAPERS OF THE WORLD

Newspaper	Place of Publishing	Language	Newspaper	Place of Publishing	Language
Daily News	New York (America)	English	Hindu, Hindustan,		
Guardian	London (Britain)	English	Times of India,		
Pravada	Moscow (Russia)	Russian	Tribune, Statesman,		
Al-Ahram	Cairo (Egypt)	Arabic	Indian Express,		
Merdeca	Jakarta (Indonesia)	Indonesian	Economic Times	India	English
Times	London (Britain)	English	Hindustan,		
People's Daily	Beijing (China)	Chinese	Nav Bharat Times,		
New Statesman	Britain	English	Dainik Bhaskar,		
Daily Mirror	Britain	English	Dainik Jagaran,		
			Punjab Kesari	India	Hindi

IMPORTANT BOUNDARY LINES

Boundary Line	Countries	Boundary Line	Countries
Durand Line	Pakistan and Afghanistan	17th Parallel	The line which defined the boundary between North Vietnam and South Vietnam before the two were united.
Hindenberg Line	Germany-Poland		
Maginot Line	France and Germany		
Mannerhein Line	Russia-Finland		
Mc Mahon Line	India-China		
Order Niesse Line	Germany-Poland		
Radcliff Line	India-Pakistan	38th Parallel	North Korea and South Korea
Seigfrid Line	Germany-France		
24th Parallel	India-Pakistan	49th Parallel	U.S.A. and Canada

SIGNALS/SIGNS AND MEANING

Signal/Sign	Meaning	Signal/Sign	Meaning
Red Triangle	Family Planning	White Flag	Treaty or Surrender
Red Cross	Medical Help	Yellow Flag	Vehicles with patients
Red Light	Danger, 'Stop' for the		of contagious diseases
	movement of vehicles	Two Bones across	Danger of electricity
Green Light	Go	with a Skull	
Olive Branch	Peace	Half mast flown Flag	National mourning
White Pigeon or Dove	Peace	Lotus and culture	Sign of civilization
Black Strip on Arm	(i) Opposition	Wheel (Chakra)	Sign of Progress
	(ii) Sorrow	A blind folded	
Black Flag	Opposition	woman with	
Red Flag	(i) Danger	scale in hand	Sign of Justice
	(ii) Revolution	Reversed flown	National calamity flag

NATIONAL EMBLEMS OF IMPORTANT COUNTRIES

Country	National Emblem	Country	National Emblem
America	Golden Rod	New Zealand	Kiwi, Fern Southern Cross
Australia	Kangaroo	Norway	Lion
Ireland	Shamrock	Nepal	Kukri
Italy	White Lily	Pakistan	Crescent
Israel	Candelabrum	Poland	Eagle
Iran	Rose	France	Lily
Canada	White Lily	Belgium	Lion
Great Britain	Rose	Bangladesh	Water Lily
Chile	Candor and Huemul	Mongolia	The Soyombo
Germany	Corn Flower	Russia	Double headed eagle
Japan	Chrysanthemum	Lebanon	Cedar Tree
Zimbabwe	Zimbabwe Bird	Sudan	Secretary Bird
Denmark	Beach	Syria	Eagle
Turkey	Crescent and Star	India	Lioned Capital
The Netherlands	Lion		

THE CONTINENTS OF THE WORLD

Name	Area (In sq. km.)	Population (2017) (In million)	Per cent of the world's population
Asia	4,40,30,000	4,504	59.66
Africa	2,97,85,000	1,256	16.64
Europe	1,04,98,000	742	9.83
North America	2,42,55,000	582	7.71
South America	1,77,98,000	424	5.62
Australia	76,87,120	40.69	0.54
Antarctica	1,33,38,500	NA	NA

COMPUTER

The computer is the system of that electronic device through which various informations are processed on the basis of a definite set of instructions called program and mathematical (numerical) and non-mathematical both types of informations are processed.

The first mechanical computer was composed or fabricated by Blaise Pascal in 1642 and it is called Pascalene. But in 1833, Charles Babbage first time conceived an automatic calculator or computer. Charles Babbage is called the father of modern computer. Herman made an electronic tabulating machine based on punch cards which operates automatically.

In 1937, first mechanical computer mark-I was fabricated by Howard Akeen. The most outstanding contribution in the development of modern computer goes to John Wan Newmaan who brought the 2nd revolution in the area of computer in 1951. He discovered EDVAC (Electronic Discrete Variable Automatic Computer) and utilised the stored program and the binary number system in the computer.

FUNCTIONS OF COMPUTER

1. Collection and composition (input) of datas;
2. Storage of datas.
3. Processing of datas.
4. Retrieval or output of the proccessed informations and datas.

UNITS OF COMPUTER

1. Input unit.
2. Central processing unit–CPU.
3. External Memory unit.
4. Output unit.

The CPU of the computer is called brain of the computer and sometimes CPU is also called Micro Processor of the computer. The data is entered through the input unit in the computer and through the central processing unit with the help of External Memory Unit datas are arranged and processed. Ultimately by the output unit these datas or informations are issued or released.

PARTS OF COMPUTER

- **Monitor :** The monitor of the computer is like a television in which the picture appears in the form of doted points on the screen and these are called pixcels.
- **Hard Disc and Floppy Disc :** The Hard Disc is the permanent disc in the computers while the Floppy Disc is the disc utilised when datas or informations are to be transferred from one computer to another.
- **Mouse :** The mouse of the computer is like the remote control of TV through which computer is directly regulated or controlled without utilising the key-board.
- **Printer :** The printer is a device which prints any documents or processed informations of the computer.

SOME HIGH LEVEL LANGUAGES

1. **FORTRAN :** This language was developed for solving the mathematical formulae very quickly and conveniently.
2. **COBOL :** This language was developed for the commerical purposes. For the processing of this language a group of sentences is selected called paragraph and all paragraphs composed are called a section, while all sections composed are called a division.
3. **BASIC :** In basic a definite part of the prescribed instruction is only inserted in the computer.
4. **ALGOL :** This was basically fabricated and designed for the complex algebraic calculations.
5. **PASCAL :** It is an amplified and modified form of ALGOL.
6. **COMAL :** This computer language is used for the students of secondary level.
7. **LOGO :** This language is used for children and kids for drawing Graphic line diagrams.
8. **PROLOG :** This language is developed in 1973 in France and this language is used for Artificial Intelligence which is capable and equivalent to the logical program.

9. FORTH : This language was invented by Charles Mure which is frequently used in all types of the works in the computer.

COMPUTER VIRUS

The computer virus is an electronic code which is used to abolish or erradicate the inclusive informations or programs of the computer. Some important computer viruses are Micheleanjalo, Dork Avangor, kilo, filip, Macmug, Scores, Casecade, Jeruslem, Date crime, Coloumbs crime, Internet virus, Pachcom, Pach EXE, COM-EXE, Marizuana, C-brain, bloody, Chenge Mungu and Desi etc.

COMPUTER NETWORKING

There are two types of networkings which are usually occur—Local Area Networking (LAN) and Wide Area Networking (WAN). By LAN all the computers of the same buildings are connected like the computers of university premises, computers of offices etc.

By WAN all the comptuers of a large area are connected like the computers of all the offices of a city or town etc. In India a very large computer network namely INDONET has been installing through which all the main towns and cities has to be interlinked.

COMPUTER TERMINOLOGY

- **Bit :** The bit is a unit of measurement of the electronic data. One bit is either 0 or 1 but not both. On composing 8 bits, 1 byte is formed.
- **Bug :** The Bug is the error in the computer program or system and its eradication is called Debug.
- **Byte :** Total eight bits compose a byte. Thus 8 bits = 1 byte.
- **CD-ROM :** A CD like of music CD in which data can be stored substantially called CD-ROM. In a CD with comparison to floppy extremely more datas can be stored but one problem in it is that one time recorded data can not be deleted or modified.
- **Chip :** It is a thin slice on which by a special mechanism a circuit is designed which is normally made from Silicon.
- **Memory System :** The place where computer data and program are temporarily kept is called Memory system. Usually memory is implied from RAM.
- **Modem :** The device which converts digital signals into analogue signals and vice-versa is called Modem.

- **RAM :** It is Random Access Memory (a place) where datas to be processed are kept temporarily and it is unstable memory.
- **ROM :** It is Read Only Memory and it is stable or Non-valatile memory which doesn't ended after power off.
- **Scanner :** It is a device through which graphic image is transformed to digital image and the scanners are of usually two types one desktop and another hand operating.

PROGRAMING

Computers perform phenomenal feats of calculation, but they do not do so in a complicated way. They actually carry out very simple operations, such as addition and subtraction. They achieve their fantastic computing power by carrying out these operations at incredible speed.

The programme, or set of instructions for operating the computer, is therefore written as a sequence of very simple steps. (See box below) Several computer languages have been developed for different applications, including BASIC, COBOL, FORTRAN and PASCAL. Writing programmes is very skilled and time-consuming work. But for most typical computer applications ready-written programmes are available, called "packages".

☞ **How A Programme Works**

Without a programme to tell it what to do and how to do it, a computer is unable to function. If, for example, you wanted to know how many times the word 'the' appears in this paragraph, or in the whole book, it would not be enough merely to put the text into a computer and then ask it how many times the word appears. For the computer to accomplish the calculations it has to be told what to do in simple steps. The instructions might be:

1. Scan the text until a space followed by 'T' or 't' is found.
2. If the next letter is not 'h', go back to step 1.
3. If the letter is 'h', is the next letter 'e'?
4. If not, go back to step 1. If it is, go to step 5.
5. If 'e' is followed by a space, add 1 to the total.
6. Go back to step 1.

A full computer programme for this operation would need to be broken down into even more simple steps, but a series of such programmes could enable a computer to analyse any amount of text in great detail.

DEFENCE

The Supreme Command of the Armed Forces is vested in the hands of the President of the Country. The responsibility for national defence, however, rests with the Cabinet. All important questions having a bearing on defence are decided by the Cabinet Committee on Political Affairs, which is presided over by the Prime Minister. The Defence Minister is responsible to Parliament for all matters concerning the Defence Services. All the administrative and operational control of Armed Forces are exercised by the Ministry of Defence. The three services – Army, Navy and Air Force function through their respective service headquarters headed by the chief of Staff.

COMMISSIONED RANKS IN DEFENCE SERVICES

Army	Navy	Air Force
General	Admiral	Air Chief Marshal
Lieutenant-General	Vice-Admiral	Air Marshal
Major-General	Rear-Admiral	Air Vice-Marshal
Brigadier	Commodor	Air Commodor
Colonel	Captain	Group Captain
Lieutenant-Colonel	Commander	Wing Commander
Major	Lt.Commander	Squadron Leader
Captain	Lieutenant	Flight Lieutenant
Lieutenant	Sub-Lieutenant	Flying Officer

INTERNAL SECURITY ORGANISATIONS OF INDIA

S. No.	Name of Organisation	Year of Creation	Headquarters
1.	Assam Rifles (A.R.)	1835	Shillong
2.	Central Reserve Police Force (C.R.P.F.)	1939	New Delhi
3.	National Cadet Corps (N.C.C.)	1948	New Delhi
4.	Territorial Army	1948	In different States
5.	Indo-Tibetan Border Police	1962	New Delhi
6.	Home Guard	1962	In different States
7.	Coast Guard	1978	New Delhi
8.	Border Security Force (B.S.F.)	1965	New Delhi
9.	Central Industrial Security Force (C.I.S.F.)	1969	New Delhi
10.	National Security Guard	1984	New Delhi
11.	Police	—	In different States

COMMANDER-IN-CHIEFS OF INDIA

1.	General Roy Bucher	Jan. 1, 1948 — Jan. 14, 1949
2.	General K. M. Kariappa	Jan. 15, 1949 — Jan. 14, 1953
3.	General Maharaj Rajendra Sinhji	Jan. 15, 1953 — March 31, 1955
4.	First Marshal of the Indian Air Force Arjan Singh	

FIRST CHIEFS OF STAFF OF INDIAN FORCES

1.	General Maharaj Rajendra Sinhji (Army Staff)	April 1, 1955 — May 14, 1955
2.	Vice Admiral R.D. Katari (Naval Staff)	April 22, 1958 — June 4, 1962
3.	Air Marshal Sri Thomas Elmherst (Air Staff)	Aug. 15, 1947 — Feb. 21, 1950

ARMY INSTITUTES

1.	Sainik Schools upto +2 Level	18 places in India
2.	Rashtriya Indian Military College (prepare for entrance to N.D.A)	Dehradun
3.	National Defence Academy (three services)	Khadakwasla, Pune
4.	Indian Military Academy (Army)	Dehradun
5.	Officers Training Academy (3 services) Short Courses	Chennai
6.	National Defence College	New Delhi
7.	The College of Combat	Mhow
8.	The College of Military Engineering	Kirkee
9.	Military College of Telecommunication Engineering	Mhow
10.	The armoured Corps Centre and School	Ahmed Nagar
11.	The School Artillery	Deolali
12.	The Infantry School	Mhow and Belgaum
13.	College of Material Management	Jabalpur

AIR FORCE INSTITUTIONS

Air Force Academy	Hyderabad
Helicopter Training School	Hakimpet
Flying Instructors School	Tambaram, Chennai
The College of Air Warfare	Secunderabad
Air Force Administrative College	Coimbatore
Air Force Technical College	Jalahalli

DEFENCE PRODUCTION UNITS

1.	Bharat Dynamites Ltd.	Hyderabad
2.	Praga Tools	Hyderabad
3.	Mishra Dattu Nigam	Hyderabad
4.	Bharat Electronics Ltd.	Bangalore
5.	Bharath Earthmovers Ltd.	Bangalore
6.	Heavy Vehicles Ltd.	Avadi, Chennai
7.	Garden Reach Ship Builders and Engineers Ltd.	Kolkata
8.	Mazagaon Dock	Mumbai
9.	Goa Shipyard	Marmugao
10.	Hindustan Shipyard Ltd.	Vishakhapatnam
11.	Hindustan Aeronautics Ltd.	Bangalore, Hyderabad, Nasik, Koraput, Kanpur, Lucknow

☞ Indian Army Commands

Command	HQ Location	Command	HQ Location
Eastern Command	Kolkata	Western Command	Chandigarh
Northern Command	Udhampur	Southern Command	Pune
Central Command	Lucknow	Training Command	Shimla
South-Western Command	Jaipur		

☞ Indian Air Force Commands

Command	HQ Location	Command	HQ Location
Western Air Command	New Delhi	South-Western Air Command	Gandhinagar
Central Air Command	Allahabad	Eastern Air Command	Shillong
Southern Air Command	Thiruvananthapuram	Training Command	Bengaluru

☞ Indian Navy Commands

Command	HQ Location	Command	HQ Location
Eastern Naval Command	Vishakhapatnam	Western Naval Command	Mumbai
Southern Naval Command	Cochin		

☞ Missile and Other Weapons

Name	Class	Range
✳ Agni I	SRBM	850 km
✳ Agni II	MRBM	2500 km
✳ Agni III	IRBM	3500 km-5500 km
✳ Agni IV *or* Agni II Prime	IRBM	4000 km
✳ Agni V	ICBM	5000 km-6000 km
✳ Agni VI	ICBM	8000 km-10000 km
✳ Agni 3SL	ICBM	5200 km-11600 km
✳ Dhanush	SRBM	350 km
✳ Nirbhay	Subsonic Cruise Missile	1000 km

Name	Class	Range
✳ Brahmos	Supersonic Cruise Missile	290 km
✳ Brahmos 2	Hypersonic Cruise Missile	290 km
✳ Prithvi I	SRBM	150 km
✳ Prithvi III	SRBM	350 km
✳ Sagarika	SLBM	700 km-2200 km
✳ Shaurya	TBM	700 km-2200 km
✳ Astra	Air to Air Missile	80 km-100 km
✳ Barak-I	SRSAM	12 km
✳ Barak-8	SRSAM	90 km

MULTIPLE CHOICE QUESTIONS

1. Match List-I with List-II and select the correct answer from the codes given below the lists:
   List-I
   (*a*) Napoleon Bonaparte
   (*b*) Jean Jacques Rousseau
   (*c*) Croce
   (*d*) Madame Roland
   List-II
   1. 'A history is contemporary history'
   2. 'Liberty what crimes are committed in thy name'
   3. 'Man is born free but everywhere he is in chains.'
   4. 'I am the Child of Revolution'
   Codes :

	(*a*)	(*b*)	(*c*)	(*d*)
A.	1	2	3	4
B.	4	3	1	2
C.	3	4	2	1
D.	3	4	1	2

2. Abraham Lincon was elected the President of United States in:
   A. 1862   B. 1860
   C. 1875   D. 1855

3. Who was known as the 'Prince of Humanists'?
   A. Francisco Petrarch   B. Dante
   C. Boccacio   D. Erasmus

4. D-Day is the day when:
   A. Germany declared war on Britain
   B. US dropped the atom bomb on Hiroshima.
   C. Allied Troops landed in Normandy
   D. Germany surrendered to the allies

5. Whose teachings inspired the French Revolution?
   A. Locke
   B. Rousseau
   C. Hegel
   D. Plato

6. At a time when empires in Europe were crumbling before the might of Napoleon which one of the following Governor-Generals kept the British flag flying high in India?
   A. Warren Hastings   B. Lord Cornwallis
   C. Lord Wellesley   D. Lord Hastings

7. Which one of the following statements regarding Fascism in Italy is *not* true?
   A. The Fascists came to power as a result of popular uprising
   B. In 1926, all political parties except Mussolini's party were banned
   C. The Fascists suppressed the Socialist movement
   D. The Fascists were hostile to the Communists

8. The fall of Czar Nicholas-II is known as:
   A. Bloody Sunday
   B. Bolshevik Revolution
   C. February Revolution
   D. October Revolution

9. Industrial Revolution took place first in:
   A. France   B. Germany
   C. United Kingdom D. Japan

10. The British Prime Minister at the outbreak of World War II was :
    A. Churchill   B. Baldwin
    C. Attlee   D. Chemberlain

11. The 'Great Depression' (1929) economic crisis was met by adopting the policy of
    A. Stimulus   B. Marshall Plan
    C. New Deal   D. Open Door

12. The slogan "No taxation without representation" was raised during the:
    A. American War of Independence
    B. Russian Revolution
    C. French Revolution
    D. Indian Freedom struggle

13. In the nineteenth century the people of Europe started moving from the villages to the cities due to the impact of :
A. Epidemics
B. War
C. Industrialisation
D. Population explosion in villages

14. The important cause of the Civil War in America was:
A. Abolition of slavery
B. Quest for freedom
C. Industrialisation
D. Rebellion by the native Americans

15. Industrial Revolution could not have come about without:
A. Merchant capitalism
B. The Enclosure Movement
C. The services of the proletariat class
D. An agricultural revolution

16. Consider the following statements :
The French Revolution came about mainly due to the :
1. Extreme poverty of the people
2. Impact of the works of great writers
3. Cruelty of the rulers
4. Impact of impulsive reaction
Which of the above statements are correct?
A. 1, 2 and 4   B. 2 and 3
C. 1, 3 and 4   D. 1, 2, 3 and 4

17. Asia's oldest and largest Buddhist monastery is situated in :
A. Tawang (Arunachal Pardesh)
B. Lhasa (Tibet)
C. Trincomallee (Sri Lanka)
D. Ulan Bator (Mongolia)

18. Who was the main architect of the Russian Revolution?
A. Karl Marx   B. Lenin
C. Stalin   D. Tolstoy

19. V.I. Lenin is associated with :
A. Russian Revolution of 1917
B. Chinese Revolution of 1949
C. German Revolution
D. French Revolution of 1789

20. Which one of the following statements is *not* correct?
A. Voltaire believed in Natural Religion
B. Rousseau wrote *Social Contract*
C. Montesquieu authored *The Spirit of Laws*
D. Necker believed in 'General Will'

21. 6th April, 1930 is well known in the history of India because this date is associated with...........
A. Dandi March by Mahatma Gandhi
B. Quit India Movement
C. Partition of Bengal
D. Partition of India

22. Which ruler enforced the system of 'Price Control' in India?
A. Mohammad Tughlak
B. Razia Begum
C. Alauddin Khilji
D. Sher Shah Suri

23. The concept of 'Din-e-Elahi' was founded by which king?
A. Dara Shikoh   B. Akbar
C. Sher Shah Suri   D. Shahjahan

24. Who are supposed to be the earliest inhabitants of India? Where did they come from?
A. Aryans from Central Asia
B. Dravidians from Mediterranean
C. Negroids from Africa
D. Bhils and the Santhals from West Asia

25. The one chief characteristic of temple architecture of the Gupta Age was :
A. Absence of dome
B. Huge size
C. Beautiful carvings
D. absence of a covered courtyard for the gathering of worshippers

26. The Rigveda consists of :
A. 1000 hymns   B. 2028 hymns
C. 1028 hymns   D. 1038 hymns

27. The central point in Ashoka's dharma was :
A. royalty to kings
B. peace and non-violence
C. respect to elders
D. religious tolerance

28. The social evil which was conspicuously absent during ancient India was :
A. *Sati*-System   B. *Devadasi*-System
C. Polygamy   D. *Purdah*-System

29. Which, among the following, can be accepted as a novelty introduced by Mughal emperors to their buildings?
A. Domes   B. Minarets
C. Arches   D. Attached gardens

30. The first ruler of India who defeated Muhammud of Ghur was :
A. Mularaja II of Gujarat
B. Prithviraja Chauhan of Delhi
C. Jayachand of Kannauj
D. Parmaldeva of Bundelkhand

31. What important event happened in India in 1911?
A. Bengal was partitioned
B. Non-Cooperation movement was launched
C. India's capital was shifted from Calcutta to Delhi
D. Mahatma Gandhi presided over the Congress session

32. The first phase of the Congress Party (1885-1905) was characterized by its efforts to secure:
A. limited independence
B. complete freedom
C. Indianization of services
D. constitutional reforms

33. The Muslim League demanded a separate homeland for the Indian Muslims openly for the first time at its annual session held in Lahore in the year :
A. 1931 A.D.   B. 1936 A.D.
C. 1940 A.D.   D. 1941 A.D.

34. Under whose governorship did the East India Company secure the Diwani Rights in Bengal, Bihar and Odisha from Emperor Shah Alam?
A. Lord Cornwallis
B. Lord William Bentinck
C. Lord Clive
D. Lord Wellesley

35. The Simon Commission was generally boycotted by the Indian political parties. What was the reason for this general non-cooperation?
A. the Commission aimed at dividing the people
B. it was an 'all white' Commission
C. it came after the Jallianwala Bagh carnage
D. it was an eye wash

36. Aligarh Muslim University was founded by :
A. Dr. Saifuddin Kitchlu
B. Mohammad Ali Jinnah
C. Sir Syed Ahmed Khan
D. Maulana Mohammad Ali

37. Ibn Batutah was an African traveller visiting India during the time of :
A. Alivardi Khan
B. Ala-ud-din Khalji
C. Iltutmish
D. Mohammad-bin-Tughlaq

38. The battle of Wandiawash was fought in :
A. 1726   B. 1760
C. 1818   D. 1857

39. The abolition of *Sati* by government regulation was at the time of :
A. Warren Hastings   B. Lord Wellesley
C. Lord Bentinck   D. Lord Ahmerst

40. Pick out the wrong combination :
A. Dilwara Temple : Mt. Abu
B. Pashupati Temple : Kathmandu
C. Padmanabh Temple : Bangalore
D. Minakshi Temple : Madurai

41. Match the following:
(a) Chanhudaro   *(b)* Kalibangan
(c) Lothal   *(d)* Surkotada
1. Alleged discovery of the skeleton of horse.
2. Bead making.
3. Traces of a dock and ship on seal.
4. Evidence of ploughing the fields.
The Correct code is :

	(a)	*(b)*	*(c)*	*(d)*
A.	2	4	3	1
B.	2	1	3	4
C.	1	2	3	4
D.	2	1	4	3

42. Match the Harappan settlements with the banks of rivers on which they were located :

(*a*) Harappa   1. Ravi
(*b*) Mohenjodaro   2. Indus
(*c*) Ropar   3. Sutlej
(*d*) Kalibangan   4. Ghaggar
(*e*) Lothal   5. Bhogava

Codes :

	(*a*)	(*b*)	(*c*)	(*d*)	(*e*)
A.	1	2	3	4	5
B.	1	2	3	5	4
C.	2	1	3	5	4
D.	2	1	4	3	5

43. The Goddess 'Kannagi' whose many temples were erected during the 'Sangam Age' was the goddess of :

A. Chastity   B. Love
C. Prowess   D. Wisdom

44. The Jain goal of life is to attain deliverance from the fetters of mudane existence, the way to which lies through three jewels. Which one of the following was not included among the 'three jewels' of Jainism?

A. Right faith   B. Right action
C. Right knowledge   D. Right conduct

45. The most striking feature of the Ashokan pillar is polish. Name the Ashokan pillar which is considered to be the most graceful of all Ashokan pillars.

A. Sarnath
B. Rampurva
C. Laurya-Nandangarh
D. Rummindei

46. Which are the correct statements?

1. The land grants, started in Satavahana period, paved the way for feudal developments in India.
2. Silk and spices were the Chief Indian export articles of Indo-Roman trade.
3. The Guptas issued the largest number of gold coins in ancient India.
4. The first memorial of a 'SATI' dated 510 A.D. is found at Eran in Madhya Pradesh.

A. 1 and 2   B. 1, 3, and 4
C. 1 and 4   D. 1, 2, 3 and 4

47. Who among the following patronised the 'Gandhara' (Indo-Greek style) School of Art?

A. Ashoka, the Great
B. Harsha Vardhana
C. Kanishka
D. Chandragupta Vikramaditya

48. The Sultanate of Delhi had five ruling dynasties. The dynasty having longest and shortest period were :

A. Ilbari and Khalji
B. Tughlaq and Khalji
C. Tughlaq and Sayyid
D. Ilbari and Lodis

49. Which one of the following events took place at the last during reign of Muhammad-bin-Tughlaq?

A. Introduction of token currency
B. Increase of land-revenue in Doab
C. Transfer of Capital from Delhi to Devagiri.
D. Conquest of Khurasan and Iraq

50. The most learned medieval Muslim ruler who was well versed in various branches of learning including astronomy, mathematics and medicine was :

A. Jalaluddin Khilji
B. Sikander Lodi
C. Ghiyasuddin Tughlaq
D. Muhammad-bin-Tughlaq

51. The 'Sufis' had 12 silsilas. They propounded the idea of Union with God through:

A. Love   B. Rituals
C. Fasts   D. Prayers

52. Match the following:

(*a*) Peshwa   1. Foreign affairs
(*b*) Panditrao   2. Audit and accounts
(*c*) Amatya   3. Providing grants to scholars
(*d*) Sumant   4. General supervision
               5. Military affairs

Select the correct code :

	(*a*)	(*b*)	(*c*)	(*d*)
A.	2	3	4	5
B.	4	1	2	3
C.	4	3	2	1
D.	3	1	4	2

53. The Regulating Act of 1773 can be regarded as the first measure to :
A. assert the right of British Parliament to legislate for India
B. separate the legislature from the executive
C. separate the judiciary from the executive
D. centralise law-making

54. What was the exact constitutional status of the Indian Republic on 26th January, 1950?
A. A Democratic Republic
B. A Sovereign, Democratic Republic
C. A Sovereign, Secular, Democratic Republic
D. A Sovereign, Socialist, Secular, Democratic Republic

55. When the British obtained the grant of Diwani of Bengal, Bihar and Odisha they acquired the right to :
A. maintain law and order in these territories
B. administer civil justice and collect revenue in these territories
C. collect revenue and establish revenue administration in these territories
D. militarily defend these territories

56. Which of the following were responsible for the growth of nationalism in India during the British rule?
1. Economic exploitation of India.
2. Impact of western education.
3. Role of the Press.
Select the correct answer using the codes given below :
Codes:
A. 1, 2 and 3   B. 1 and 2
C. 2 and 3   D. 1 and 3

57. Which one of the following nationalist leaders has been described as being radical in politics but conservative on social issues?
A. G.K. Gokhale
B. B.G. Tilak
C. Lala Lajpat Rai
D. Madan Mohan Malviya

58. Provincial Autonomy in British India was envisaged by the :
A. Act of 1909   B. Act of 1919
C. Act of 1935   D. Act of 1947

59. Dyarchy means :
A. double government
B. a government in which the centre is very powerful
C. a government based on division of power between centre and provinces
D. None of the above

60. The Indian National Congress observed 'Independence Day' for the first time on 26th January in :
A. 1920   B. 1925
C. 1930   D. 1947

61. ....is situated near the banks of Sabarmati River
A. Bhavnagar   B. Aurangabad
C. Ahmedabad   D. Rajkot

62. Sericulture is:
A. science of the various kinds of serum
B. artificial rearing of fish
C. art of silkworm breeding
D. study of various cultures of a community

63. The most abundant constituents of earth's crust are:
A. Igneous rocks
B. Sedimentary rocks
C. Metamorphic rocks
D. Granite

64. Indian Standard Time is based on:
A. 80°E longitude   B. 82½°E longitude
C. 110°E longitude   D. 25°E longitude

65. Tides in the oceans are caused by :
A. Gravitational pull of the moon on the earth's surface including sea water
B. Gravitational pull of the sun on the earth's surface only and not on the sea water
C. Gravitational pull of the moon and the sun on the earth's surface including the sea water
D. None of these

66. Nagarjunasagar Project is situated on the river:
A. Tungabhadra
B. Cauvery
C. Krishna
D. Godavari

67. The difference between the Indian Standard Time and the Greenwich Mean Time is:
A. – 3½ hours
B. + 3½ hours
C. – 5½ hours
D. + 5½ hours

68. Which of the following dams is not on Narmada river?
A. Indira-Sagar Project
B. Maheshwar Hydel Power Project
C. Jobat Project
D. Koyna Power Project

69. Which of the following statements is **not true** about the availability of water on the earth, the crisis for which is going to increase in the years to come?
A. About 97.5 per cent of the total volume of water available on the earth is salty
B. 80 per cent of the water available to us for use comes in bursts as monsoons
C. About 2.5 per cent of the total water available on the earth is polluted water and cannot be used for human activities
D. Possibility is that some big glaciers will melt in the coming ten-fifteen years and sea level will rise by 3-4 metres all over the earth

70. Which of the following is **not** a cash crop?
A. Jute
B. Paddy
C. Cashewnut
D. Sugarcane

71. Through which States does Cauvery River flow?
A. Gujarat, M.P., Tamil Nadu
B. Karnataka, Kerala, Tamil Nadu
C. Karnataka, Kerala, Andhra Pradesh
D. M.P., Maharashtra, Tamil Nadu

72. Indian Standard Time is the local time of 82½°E which passes through :
A. Guntur
B. Delhi
C. Allahabad
D. Kolkata

73. The 17th parallel defines the boundary between:
A. North and South Korea
B. USA and Canada
C. North and South Vietnam
D. China and Russia

74. During the period of south-west monsoon, Tamil Nadu remains dry because:
A. the winds do not reach this area
B. there are no mountains in this area
C. it lies in the rain shadow area
D. the temperature is too high to let the winds cool down

75. Which country does top in producing cocoa?
A. Cote d'Ivoire
B. Brazil
C. Ivory Coast
D. Nigeria

76. The biggest reserves of thorium are in :
A. India
B. China
C. The Soviet Union
D. U.S.A.

77. The Girnar Hills are situated in which of the following states?
A. Gujarat
B. Karnataka
C. Madhya Pradesh
D. Maharashtra

78. During December 22nd the sun is vertically over:
A. Tropic of Cancer
B. Tropic of Capricorn
C. The Equator
D. None of the above

79. Photosphere is described as the :
A. Lower layer of atmosphere
B. Visible surface of the sun from which radiation emanates
C. Wavelength of solar spectrum
D. None of the above

80. Broadly, there are three layers of the earth of the crust, the mantle and the core. The crust forms what percentage of the volume of the earth?
A. 0.5%
B. 2.5%
C. 7.5%
D. 12.5%

81. The grassland of Argentina is known as :
A. Pampas
B. Campos
C. Savanna
D. None of the above

82. Different seasons are formed because :
A. Sun is moving around the earth
B. of revolution of the earth around the Sun on its orbit
C. of rotation of the earth around its axis
D. All of the above

83. Eskers and Drumlins are features formed by:
A. underground water
B. running water
C. the action of wind
D. glacial action

84. Match List-I and List-II and select the correct answer using the codes given below the Lists :

List-I	**List-II**
(Rivers)	*(Towns)*
(a) Ghaghara	1. Lucknow
(b) Brahmaputra	2. Hoshangabad
(c) Narmada	3. Ahmedabad
(d) Sabarmati	4. Guwahati
	5. Ayodhya

	(a)	(b)	(c)	(d)
A.	4	5	1	2
B.	5	4	2	3
C.	5	4	3	1
D.	3	5	2	1

85. Which of the statements as regards the consequences of the movement of the earth is not correct?
A. Revolution of the earth is the cause of the change of seasons.
B. Rotation of the earth is the cause of days and nights.
C. Rotation of the earth causes variation in the duration of days and nights.
D. Rotation of the earth effects the movement of winds and ocean currents.

86. The world is divided into :
A. 12 time zones
B. 20 time zones
C. 24 time zones
D. 36 time zones

87. The 'Kiel' canal links the :
A. Pacific and Atlantic Oceans
B. Mediterranean Sea and Red Sea
C. Mediterranean Sea and Black Sea
D. North Sea and Baltic Sea

88. Match the following :

List-I	**List-II**
(a) Himadri	1. Outer Himalayas
(b) Shivalik	2. Inner Himalayas
(c) Himanchal	3. Middle Himalayas
(d) Sahyadri	4. Western Ghats

Codes:

	(a)	(b)	(c)	(d)
A.	1	2	3	4
B.	4	2	3	1
C.	2	1	3	4
D.	1	2	3	4

89. The term 'Regur' refers to:
A. Laterite soils
B. Black Cotton soils
C. Red Soils
D. Deltaic Alluvial Soils

90. Location of sugar industry in India is shifting from north to south because of:
A. cheap labour
B. expanding regional market
C. cheap and abundant supply of power
D. high yield and high sugar content in sugarcane

91. Consider the following statements :
1. Ozone is found mostly in the Stratosphere.
2. Ozone layer lies 55-75 km above the surface of the earth.
3. Ozone absorbs ultraviolet radiation from the Sun.
4. Ozone layer has no significance for life on the earth.
Which of the above statements are correct?
A. 1 and 3
B. 2 and 4
C. 2 and 3
D. 1 and 4

92. Match List-I with List-II and select the correct answer using the codes given below the Lists :

List-I	**List-II**
(Crops)	*(Producer)*
(a) Banana	1. Brazil
(b) Cocoa	2. Cote d'Ivoire
(c) Coffee	3. India
(d) Tea	4. China

Codes :

	(a)	(b)	(c)	(d)
A.	2	3	1	4
B.	3	2	1	4
C.	3	2	4	1
D.	2	3	4	1

93. Darjeeling and Dharamsala would be the right places to visit if one wanted to get a clear view respectively of :
A. Kanchanjunga and Dhauladhar ranges
B. Nandadevi and Dhauladhar ranges
C. Kanchanjunga and Nandadevi ranges
D. Nandadevi and Nanga Parvat

94. Atmosphere exists because:
A. The Gravitational force of the Earth
B. Revolution of the Earth
C. Rotation of the Earth
D. Weight of the gases of atmosphere

95. Victoria lake is located in the continent:
A. Africa
B. Asia
C. North America
D. South America

96. The famous Lagoon Lake of India is :
A. Dal Lake   B. Chilka Lake
C. Pulicat Lake   D. Mansarover

97. Where are most of the earth's active volcanoes concentrated?
A. Indian Ocean   B. Pacific Ocean
C. Aral Sea   D. Atlantic Ocean

98. Through which of the following states does the river Chambal flow?
A. U.P., M.P., Rajasthan
B. M.P., Gujarat, U.P.
C. Rajasthan, M.P., Bihar
D. Gujarat, M.P., U.P.

99. Which country is called the sugar bowl of the world?
A. Cuba   B. India
C. Argentina   D. USA

100. The area covered by forest in India is about:
A. 46%   B. 33%
C. 23%   D. 21.54%

101. A closed economy is the one which :
A. does not permit emigration or immigration
B. permits emigration but no immigration
C. engages in no foreign trade
D. engages in no foreign and domestic trade or transit

102. In a developed economy the major share of employment originates in the :
A. primary sector   B. tertiary sector
C. secondary sector   D. any of the above

103. The Economic and Social Commission for Asia and Pacific (ESCAP) is located at :
A. Bangkok   B. Kuala Lumpur
C. Manila   D. Singapore

104. Commercial vehicles are not produced by which of the following companies in India?
A. TELCO   B. Ashok Leyland
C. DCM Daewoo   D. Birla Yamaha

105. In India, the Public Sector is most dominant in:
A. transport
B. steel production
C. commercial banking
D. organised term-lending financial institutions

106. The main argument advanced in favour of small scale and cottage industries in India is that:
A. cost of production is low
B. they require small capital investment
C. they advance the goal of equitable distribution of wealth
D. they generate a large volume of employment

107. The most serious economic problems of India are:
A. Poverty and unemployment
B. Stagnation, not poverty
C. Unemployment, not poverty
D. Underdevelopment, not poverty

108. Which of the following is not one of the three central problems of an economy?
A. What to produce
B. How to produce
C. When to produce
D. For whom to produce

109. If saving exceeds investment, the national income will:
A. fall   B. rise
C. fluctuate   D. remain constant

110. In which of the following industries in India are the maximum number of workers employed?
A. Sugar
B. Jute
C. Textiles
D. Iron and Steel

111. Terrace Cultivation is practiced mostly:
A. in urban areas
B. on slopes of mountains
C. on tops of hills
D. in undulating tracts

112. Which of the following is a Selective Credit Control method?
A. Bank Rate
B. RBI directives
C. Cash Reserve Ratio
D. Open market operations

113. Which of the following taxes is not shared by the Central Government with the States?
A. Union excise duties
B. Customs duty
C. Income tax
D. Estate duty

114. ICICI is the name of a:
A. Financial Institution
B. Chemical Industry
C. Cotton Industry
D. Chamber of Commerce and Industry

115. Structural Unemployment arises due to
A. Deflationary conditions
B. Heavy industry bias
C. Shortage of raw material
D. Inadequate productive capacity

116. Which of the following is the largest single source of the government's earning from tax revenue?
A. Excise duties
B. Customs duties
C. Corporation tax
D. Income tax

117. The largest public sector bank in India is:
A. Central Bank of India
B. Punjab National Bank
C. State Bank of India
D. Indian Overseas Bank

118. Which of the following statements best explains the term contraband goods?
A. Goods produced only for exports
B. Goods produced in joint sector only
C. Goods for the trading of which licence is not required
D. Goods that are forbidden, from export, import or even possession, by law

119. Price in the market is fixed by:
A. Stock exchange rates
B. The demand and supply ruling in the market at a particular time
C. The Finance Minister
D. None of the above

120. Devaluation of currency helps to promote:
A. National Income
B. Savings
C. Imports at lower cost
D. Exports

121. Balanced economic growth can be achieved only if:
A. All the sectors of economy grow at the same rate
B. Population growth is arrested
C. All the inter dependent sectors grow in harmony
D. Basic and heavy industries are assigned highest priority

122. Which one of the following contributes most to the National Income in India?
A. Agricultural Sector
B. Industrial Sector
C. Foreign Trade Sector
D. Tertiary Sector

123. 'MODVAT' stands for:
A. Ad Valorem tax on output
B. Deduction of cost of inputs from the value of output
C. Reduction in import duties
D. Imposition of tax on professions

124. Largest revenue in India is obtained from:
A. Excise duties
B. Corporation tax
C. Income tax
D. None of the above

125. The term 'devaluation' means:
A. Reducing the value of a currency in terms of another currency
B. Increasing the value of a currency
C. Revising the value of a currency
D. None of the above

126. Per capita net availability of pulses has shown a tendency of:
A. Increase over time
B. Decrease over time
C. Constant over time
D. First increase then decrease

127. National Income is the same as:
A. Net national product at market price
B. Net domestic product at market price
C. Net national product at factor cost
D. Net domestic product at factor cost

128. Which one of the following is not an example of indirect tax?
A. Sales tax   B. Excise duty
C. Customs duty   D. Expenditure tax

129. The major aim of devaluation is to:
A. encourage imports
B. encourage exports
C. encourage both exports and imports
D. discourage both exports and imports

130. Structural unemployment arises due to:
A. deflationary conditions
B. heavy industry bias
C. shortage of raw materials
D. inadequate productive capacity

131. When was the Family Planning Programme officially started in India?
A. 1950   B. 1952
C. 1956   D. 1962

132. When was the Reserve Bank of India nationalised?
A. 1947   B. 1949
C. 1950   D. 1951

133. Which of the following is *not* a feature of the Indian economy?
A. High rate of population growth
B. Disguised unemployment
C. Lowest rate of adult literacy
D. High rate of exports

134. The 'Relative Deprivation' approach for measuring poverty has been adopted by:
A. developing countries
B. developed countries
C. under-developed countries
D. None of the above

135. One of the main factors that led to rapid expansion of Indian exports is:
A. Imposition of import duties
B. Liberalisation of the economy
C. Recession in other countries
D. Diversification of exports

136. Sustainable economic development means an increase in the rate of growth of real:
A. total and per capita product
B. total and per capita product and level of literacy rate
C. total and per capita product and life expectancy at birth
D. total and per capita product, taking into account the cost of degradation of the quality of environment in this process

137. Functional unemployment occurs when:
A. unemployed have no qualification for job
B. people frequently change their job
C. people were thrown out from job due to recession
D. None of these

138. Which among the following does **not** have a 'free trade zone'?
A. Kandla   B. Mumbai
C. Visakhapatnam   D. Thiruvanantpuram

139. Sun Belt of USA is important for which one of the following industries?
A. Cotton textile
B. Petrochemicals
C. Hi-tech electronics
D. Food Processing

140. Commercial banking system in India is
A. unit banking   B. branch banking
C. mixed banking   D. None of the above

141. Who gives recognition to political parties in India?
A. Parliament

B. President
C. Supreme Court
D. Election Commission

142. The Quorum of the Legislative Council is :
A. one-fourth of its total membership
B. one-third of its membership
C. one-tenth of its membership
D. 25

143. The Indian Constitution is:
A. federal
B. unitary
C. a happy mixture of the federal and unitary
D. federal in normal times and unitary in times of emergency

144. Universal adult franchise implies a right to vote to all:
A. adult residents of the State
B. adult male citizens of the State
C. residents of the State
D. adult citizens of the State

145. When a resolution prefering a charge against the President has been passed by a specified majority in the House, it is sent to the other House for investigation. If, as a result of such an investigation, a resolution is passed through a specified majority by the other House, declaring that the charge has been sustained, the President shall leave his office. The specified special majority must not be less than :
A. two-third of the members present and voting
B. one-third of the members present and voting
C. three-fourth of the members present and voting and two-third of the total membership
D. two-third of the total membership

146. Which one of the following judicial powers of the President of India has been *wrongly* listed?
A. he appoints the Chief Justice and other judges of the Supreme Court
B. he can remove the judges of the Supreme Court on grounds of misconduct

C. he can consult the Supreme Court on any question of law or fact which is of public importance
D. he can grant pardon, reprieves and respites to persons punished under Union Law

147. The Vice-president of India can be removed from his office before the expiry of his term if :
A. the Rajya Sabha passes a resolution by a majority of its members and the Lok Sabha agrees with the resolution
B. if the Supreme Court of India recommends his removal
C. the President so desires
D. None of the above

148. The Chief Justice of a High Court in India is appointed by the :
A. Governor of the State
B. Prime Minister of India
C. Chief Justice of the Supreme Court
D. President of India

149. Which of the following statements is constitutionally not true about the passing of the Union Budgets, Railway Budgets and Finance Bill in India?
1. Under the law, Finance Bill should be adopted by both the Houses of the Parliament within 45 days of its introduction.
2. If the Finance Bill is not adopted within specified period, the government loses its authority to levy the taxes proposed in the budgets.
3. In the absence of full budget, a vote-on-account gives the power to the government to spend.
4. Government cannot raise revenues without a proper approval of the Finance Bill
A. Only 2   B. Only 3
C. Only 4   D. Only 1, 2 and 3

150. Normally, on whose advice the President's Rule is imposed in a State?
A. Chief Minister
B. Legislative Assembly
C. Governor
D. Chief Justice of High Court

151. Which Article of the Indian Constitution deals with Amendment procedure?
A. Article 368   B. Article 358
C. Article 367   D. All of these

152. Government is the agency through which the will of :
A. the state is expressed
B. the people is expressed
C. the head of the state is expressed
D. the majority is expressed

153. In a unitary system of government :
A. The centre is all powerful
B. The centre is weaker than the states
C. The centre and states stand at par
D. The states and centre are supreme in their respective spheres

154. In Cabinet System of Government the real executive authority rests with :
A. The Council of Ministers
B. The Prime Minister
C. The Constitution
D. The Parliament

155. The Head of the State under a parliamentary government:
A. is an elected representative
B. is a hereditary person
C. is a nominated person
D. may be any one of the above

156. In the event of a ministerial proposal being defeated on the floor of the legislature, under the parliamentary system :
A. the government waits for a general no-confidence motion
B. the minister concerned is taken to task by the Prime Minister
C. the minister is forced to resign
D. the whole Council of Ministers resign

157. The "due process of law" is an essential characteristic of the judicial system of:
A. UK   B. France
C. USA   D. India

158. Under the Constitution it is :
A. obligatory for the President to accept the advice of the Council of Ministers but is not obliged to follow it
B. obligatory for the President to accept the advice of the Council of Ministers
C. not obligatory for the President to seek or accept the advice of the Council of Ministers
D. obligatory for the President to seek the advice of the Council of Ministers if his own party is in power

159. Which one of the following statements is correct?
A. the Presiding Officer of Rajya Sabha is elected every year
B. the Presiding Officer of Rajya Sabha is elected for a term of two years at a time
C. the Presiding Officer of Rajya Sabha is elected for a term of six years
D. the Vice-President of India is the ex-officio Presiding Officer of Rajya Sabha

160. The introduction of "no confidence" motion in the Lok Sabha requires the support of at least:
A. 50 members   B. 70 members
C. 60 members   D. 80 members

161. The High Court comes under :
A. State List   B. Union List
C. Concurrent List   D. None of the above

162. Which one of the following has been wrongly listed as a Fundamental Duty of the Indian citizens?
A. to develop scientific temper, humanism and spirit of inquiry and reform
B. to work for raising the prestige of the country in the international sphere
C. to protect and improve the natural environment
D. to strive towards excellence in all spheres of individual and collective activity

163. Which one of the following is not a Fundamental Duty as outlined in Article 51A of the Constitution?
A. to abide by the Constitution and respect its ideals
B. to defend the country and render national service when called upon to do so

C. to work for the moral upliftment of the weaker sections of society

D. to preserve the rich heritage

164. The main characteristics of the Directive Principles of State Policy given in the Indian Constitution are :
A. not enforceable by any court
B. fundamental in the governance of the country
C. 'Like instruments, instructions, political manifesto and a code of moral precepts which have to guide governors of the country'
D. no law can be passed, which is opposed to these principles

165. Of the following which are true?
A. In a State, the Legislative Council is dominant with regard to non-financial bills and the Legislative Assembly with regard to financial (money) bills
B. Vidhan Parishad can virtually block legisla-tion even if the same is passed by the Vidhan Sabha
C. In case of a tie between the two Houses, the Governor is duty-bound to call a joint session of the two Houses to have the issue settled on a majority verdict
D. If a Bill is twice approved by the Vidhan Sabha, it becomes law even if rejected by the Vidhan Parishad

166. Which one of the following types of emergency can be declared by the President?
A. Emergency due to threat of war and external aggresion
B. Emergency due to break-down of constitu-tional machinery in a State
C. Financial emergency on account of threat to the financial credit of India
D. all the three emergencies

167. The chairman of which of the following parliamentary committees is invariably from the members of ruling party?
A. Committee on public undertakings
B. Public accounts committee
C. Estimates committee
D. Committee on delegated legislation

168. Which of the following is not a formally prescribed device available to the members of parliament?
A. Question hour
B. Zero hour
C. Half-an-hour discussion
D. Short duration discussion

169. Which of the following is not a tool of executive control over public administration?
A. Power of appointment and removal
B. Line agencies
C. Appeal to public opinion
D. Civil services code

170. If the Speaker of the State Legislative Assembly decides to resign, he should submit his resignation to the:
A. Judges of the High Court
B. Deputy Speaker
C. Chief Minister
D. Finance Minister

171. The Constitution of India provides for the nomination of two members of Lok Sabha by the President to represent:
A. the Parsis
B. men of eminence
C. the business community
D. the Anglo-Indian community

172. India is a Federal State because of:
A. dual judiciary
B. dual citizenship prevalent here
C. share of power between the Centre and the States
D. rigid Constitution

173. Residuary Subjects are those subjects which are:
A. contained in the State list
B. contained in the Union list
C. contained in the Concurrent list
D. not covered by any of the three lists

174. Which of the following writs can be issued, by the Supreme Court, to enforce Fundamental Rights?
A. Writ of Habeas Corpus
B. Writ of Mandamus
C. Writ of Quo Warranto
D. All of these

175. When the offices of both the President and the Vice-President of India are vacant, who will discharge their functions?
A. Prime Minister
B. Home Minister
C. Chief Justice of India
D. The Speaker

176. The Supreme Court tenders advice to the President of India on a matter of law or fact:
A. on its own
B. only when such advice is sought
C. only if the matter relates to some basic issue
D. only if the issue poses a threat to the unity and integrity of the country

177. Six months shall **not** intervene between two sessions of the Indian Parliament because :
A. it is the customary practice
B. it is the British convention followed in India
C. it is an obligation under the Constitution of India
D. None of the above

178. The States of the Indian Union can be recognised or their boundaries altered by:
A. the Union Parliament by a simple majority in the ordinary process of legislation
B. two-thirds majority of both the Houses of Parliament
C. two-thirds majority of both the Houses of Parliament and the consent of the legislatures of concerned States
D. an executive order of the Union government with the consent of the concerned State governments

179. The Basic Feature theory of the Constitution of India was propounded by the Supreme Court in the case of :
A. Minerva Mills Vs. Union of India
B. Golaknath Vs. State of Punjab
C. Maneka Gandhi Vs. Union of India
D. Keshavananda Vs. State of Kerala

180. Which one of the following writs is issued by a court in case of illegal detention of a person?
A. Habeas corpus
B. Mandamus
C. Certiorari
D. Quo-warranto

181. Name the instrument with the help of which a sailor in a submarine can see the objects on the surface of the sea.
A. Telescope
B. Periscope
C. Gycroscope
D. Stereoscope

182. 'HEMOPHILLIA' is the disease of ....
A. liver
B. blood
C. brain
D. bones

183. Vitamin A is abundantly found in ....
A. Brinjal
B. Tomato
C. Carrot
D. Cabbage

184. .... is not soluble in water.
A. Vitamin A
B. Vitamin B
C. Vitamin C
D. None of these

185. The blood vessels with the smallest diameter are called ....
A. capillaries
B. arterioles
C. venules
D. lymphatics

186. Out of the following .... has the greatest elasticity.
A. steel
B. rubber
C. aluminium
D. annealed copper

187. Cooking gas is a mixture of which of the following two gases?
A. Carbon Dioxide and Oxygen
B. Butane and Propane
C. Carbon Monoxide and Carbon Dioxide
D. Methane and Ethylene

188. The substance most commonly used as a food preservative is:
A. sodium carbonate
B. tartaric acid
C. acetic acid
D. benzoic acid

189. Normally, the substances that fight against diseases in human systems are known as:
A. dioxyribonucleic acids
B. carbohydrates
C. enzymes
D. antibodies

190. The SI unit of temperature is ....
A. Kelvin
B. Celsius
C. Fahrenheit
D. None of the above

191. One of the common fungal diseases of man is :
A. plague
B. ringworm
C. cholera
D. typhoid

192. A clear sky is blue because:
A. red light is scattered more than blue
B. ultraviolet light has been absorbed
C. blue light is scattered more than red
D. blue light has been absorbed

193. Jenner introduced the method of making people immune to :
A. small pox   B. rabies
C. cholera   D. polio

194. The largest cell in the human body is :
A. Nerve cell   B. Live cell
C. Muscle cell   D. Kidney cell

195. What is the device that steps up or steps down the voltage?
A. Dynamo   B. Conductor
C. Inductor   D. Transformer

196. The protein deficiency disease is known as :
A. Kwashiorker   B. Cirrhosis
C. Eczema   D. Clycoses

197. Iron deficiency causes :
A. rickets   B. anaemia
C. cirrhosis   D. goitre

198. Blood group of an individual is controlled by :
A. Haemoglobin   B. Shape of RBC
C. Shape of WBC   D. Genes

199. In a normal man the amount of blood pumped out by the heart per minute is about :
A. 1 litre   B. 3 litres
C. 4 litres   D. 5 litres

200. Red/green colour blindness in man is known as :
A. Protanopia
B. Deutetanopia
C. Both A and B above
D. Marfan's syndrome

201. The blue colour of the water in the sea is due to :
A. Reflection of the blue light by the impurities in sea water
B. Reflection of the blue sky by sea water and scattering of blue light by water molecules
C. Absorption of other colours by water molecules
D. None of the above

202. The image formed on the retina of the eye is:
A. upright and real
B. larger than the object
C. small and inverted
D. enlarged and real

203. Unit of loudness of sound is:
A. bel   B. decibel
C. phon   D. none of these

204. Oil rises up the wick in a lamp :
A. because oil is volatile
B. due to the capillary action phenomenon
C. due to the surface tension phenomenon
D. because oil is very light

205. The 'stones' formed in human kidney consist mostly of :
A. calcium oxalate
B. sodium acetate
C. magnesium sulphate
D. calcium

206. We hear the sound later, while the light is seen earlier:
A. because light's speed is more than that of sound
B. because lights travel in a straight direction while sound in a zigzag direction
C. because sound's frequency is lower than light
D. All of the above

207. Which part of an eye is transplanted?
A. Cornea   B. Retina
C. Iris   D. Sciera

208. The Universal donor group of blood is:
A. O   B. A
C. B   D. AB

209. The green colour of the leaf is due to :
A. Presence of Chloroplast
B. Presence of Chromium
C. Presence of Nicoplast
D. Presence of excess of oxygen

210. Voice of a child is more shrill than that of an elderly person because:
A. the pitch of the child's voice is higher than that of the person
B. the pitch is lower
C. the child is more energetic
D. None of the above

ANSWERS

1	2	3	4	5	6	7	8	9	10
B	C	D	C	B	C	A	C	C	D

11	12	13	14	15	16	17	18	19	20
C	A	C	A	A	D	A	B	A	D

21	22	23	24	25	26	27	28	29	30
A	C	B	C	D	C	B	D	D	B

31	32	33	34	35	36	37	38	39	40
C	D	C	C	B	C	D	B	C	C

41	42	43	44	45	46	47	48	49	50
A	A	A	B	C	D	C	B	B	D

51	52	53	54	55	56	57	58	59	60
A	C	A	B	B	A	B	C	A	C

61	62	63	64	65	66	67	68	69	70
C	C	B	B	C	C	D	D	D	B

71	72	73	74	75	76	77	78	79	80
B	C	C	C	A	A	A	B	B	A

81	82	83	84	85	86	87	88	89	90
A	B	D	B	C	C	D	C	B	D

91	92	93	94	95	96	97	98	99	100
A	B	A	A	A	B	B	A	A	D

101	102	103	104	105	106	107	108	109	110
C	B	A	D	D	D	A	C	D	C

111	112	113	114	115	116	117	118	119	120
B	B	B	A	D	A	C	D	B	D

121	122	123	124	125	126	127	128	129	130
C	A	A	B	A	D	C	D	B	D

131	132	133	134	135	136	137	138	139	140
B	B	D	A	B	D	B	D	D	C

141	142	143	144	145	146	147	148	149	150
D	C	D	D	D	B	A	D	C	C

151	152	153	154	155	156	157	158	159	160
A	B	A	A	A	D	C	B	D	A

161	162	163	164	165	166	167	168	169	170
B	B	C	B	D	D	C	B	B	B

171	172	173	174	175	176	177	178	179	180
D	C	D	D	C	B	C	A	D	A

181	182	183	184	185	186	187	188	189	190
B	B	C	A	A	A	B	D	D	A

191	192	193	194	195	196	197	198	199	200
B	C	A	A	D	A	B	D	D	A

201	202	203	204	205	206	207	208	209	210
B	B	B	B	A	A	A	A	A	A

1808

KNOWLEDGE OF COMPUTER

A BRIEF HISTORY OF COMPUTERS

INTRODUCTION OF COMPUTER

Computer is the most amazing machine man has ever created. Today computers are used in almost all walks of life: bank, hospitals, schools, publishing, manufacturing, entertainment, shops, libraries, factories, games, elections, security services etc. A computer is basically a programmable computing machine. In this chapter we will discuss the various parts of the computer which make the fast and better computation. We will provide a better solution to the problems related to the organization of computer.

GENERATIONS OF COMPUTERS

The first Generation: Vacuum Tubes

ENIAC

The ENIAC (Electronic Numerical Integrator And Computer), designed by and constructed under the supervision of John Mauchly and John Presper Eckert at the University of Pennsylvania, was the world's first general-purpose electronic digital computer. The project was a response to U.S. wartime needs. Mauchly, a professor of electrical engineering at the University of Pennsylvania and Eckert, one of his graduate students, proposed to build a general-purpose computer using vacuum tubes. In 1943, this proposal was accepted by the Army, and work began on the ENIAC. The resulting machine was enormous, weighing 30 tons, occupying 15,000 square feet of floor space, and containing more than 18,000 vacuum tubes. When operating, it consumed 140 kilowatts of power. It was also substantially faster than any electronic-mechanical computer, being capable of 5000 additions per second.

The ENIAC was decimal rather than a binary machine. That is, numbers were represented in decimal form and arithmetic was performed in the decimal system. Its memory consisted of 20 "accumulators", each capable of holding a 10-digit decimal number. Each digit was represented by a ring of 10 vacuum tubes. At any time, only one vacuum tube was in the ON state, representing one of the 10 digits. The major drawback of the ENIAC was that it had to be programmed manually by setting switches and plugging and unplugging cables.

The ENIAC was completed in 1946, too late to be used in the war effort. Instead, its first task was to perform a series of complex calculations that were used to help determine the feasibility of the H-bomb. The ENIAC continued to be used until 1955.

The Von Neumann Machine

The programming process could be facilitated if the program could be represented in a form suitable for storing in memory alongside the data. Then, a computer could get its instructions by reading them from memory, and a program could be set of altered by setting the values of a portion of memory.

This idea, known as the Stored-program concept, is usually attributed to the ENIAC designers, most notably the mathematician John Von Neumann, who was a consultant on the ENIAC project. The idea was also developed at about the same time by Turing. The first publication of the idea was in a 1945 proposal by Von Neumann for a new computer, the EDVAC (Electronic Discrete Variable Computer).

In 1946, von Neumann and his colleagues began the design of a new stored-program computer, referred to as the IAS computer, at the Princeton

Institute for Advanced Studies. The IAS computer, although not completed until 1952, is the prototype of all subsequent general-purpose computers. Figure below shows the general structure of the IAS computer. It consists of:

- A main memory, which stores both data and instructions.
- An arithmetic-logical unit (ALU) capable of operating on binary data.
- A control unit, which interprets the instructions in memory and causes them to be executed.
- Input and output (I/O) equipment operated by the control unit.

Commercial Computers

The 1950's saw the birth of the computer industry with two companies, Sperry and IBM, dominating the marketplace.

In 1947, Eckert and Mauchly formed the Eckert-Mauchly Computer Corporation to manufacture computers commercially. Their first successful machine was the UNIVAC I (Universal Automatic Computer), which was commissioned by the Bureau of the Census for the 1950 calculations. The Eckert-Mauchly Computer Corporation became part of the UNIVAC division of Sperry-Rand Corporation, which went on to build a series of successor machines.

The UNIVAC II, which had greater memory capacity and higher performance than the UNIVAC I, was delivered in the late 1950's and illustrates several trends that have remained characteristic of the computer industry. First, advances in technology allow companies to continue to build larger, more powerful computers. Second, each company tries to make its new machines upward compatible with the older machines. This means that the programs written for the older machines can be executed on the new machine. This strategy is adopted in the hopes of retaining the customer base; that is, when a customer decides to buy a newer machine, he is likely to get it from the same company to avoid losing the investment in programs.

The UNIVAC division also began development of the 1100 series of computers, which was to be its bread and butter. This series illustrates a distinction that existed at one time. The first model, the UNIVAC 1103, and its successors for many years were primarily intended for scientific applications, involving long and complex calculations. Other companies concentrated on business applications, which involved processing large amounts of text data. This split has largely disappeared but it was evident for a number of years.

IBM, which was then the major manufacturer of punched-card processing equipment, delivered its first electronic stored-program computer, the 701, in 1953. The 701 was intended primarily for scientific applications. In 1955, IBM introduced the companion 702 product, which had a number of hardware features that suited it to business applications. These were the first of a long series of 700/7000 computers that established IBM as the overwhelmingly dominant computer manufacturer.

The Second Generation: Transistors

The first major change in the electronic computer came with the replacement of the vacuum tube by the transistor. The transistor is smaller, cheaper, and dissipates less heal than a vacuum tube but can be used in the same way as a vacuum tube to construct computers. Unlike the vacuum tube, which requires wires, metal plates, a glass capsule, and a vacuum, the transistor is a solid-state device, made from silicon. The transistor was invented at Bell Labs in 1947 and by the 1950's had launched an electronic revolution. It was not until the late 1950s, however, that fully transistorized computers were commercially available. IBM again was not the first company to deliver the new technology. NCR and more successfully RCA were the front-runners with some small transistor machines. IBM followed shortly with the 7000 series.

The use of the transistor defines the second generation of computers. It has become widely accepted to classify computers into generations based on the fundamental hardware technology employed. Each new generation is characterized by greater processing performance, larger memory capacity, and smaller size than the previous one.

The Third Generation: Integrated Circuits

A single, self-contained transistor is called a discrete component. Throughout the 1950s and early 1960s, electronic equipment was composed largely of discrete components—transistors, resistors, capacitors, and so on. Discrete components were manufactured separately, packaged in their own containers, and soldered or wired together onto circuit boards, which were then installed in computers, oscilloscopes, and other electronic equipment. Whenever an electronic device called for a transistor, a little tube of metal containing a pinhead-sized piece of silicon had to be soldered to a circuit board. The entire manufacturing process, from transistor to circuit board, was expensive and cumbersome.

These facts of life were beginning to create problems in the computer industry. Early second-generation computers contained about 10,000 transistors. This figure grew to the hundreds of thousands, making the manufacture of newer, more powerful machines increasingly difficult. In 1958 came the achievement that revolutionized electronics and started the era of microelectronics: the invention of the integrated circuit. It is the integrated circuit that defines the third generation of computers. Perhaps the two most important members of the third generation are the IBM System/360 and the DEC PDP-8.

Later Generations

Beyond the third generation there is less general agreement on defining generations of computers. There have been a fourth and a fifth generation, based on advances in integrated circuit technology. With the introduction of large-scale integration (LSI), more than 1000,000 components can be placed on a single integrated circuit chip.

The Summary of Generations of Computer

- Vacuum tube - 1946-1957
- Transistor - 1958-1964
- Small scale integration: 1965

Up to 100 devices on a chip
- **Medium scale integration: -1971**
100-3,000 devices on a chip
- **Large scale integration :1971-1977**
3,000 - 100,000 devices on a chip
- **Very large scale integration: 1978 -1991**
100,000 - 100,000,000 devices on a chip
- **Ultra large scale integration : 1991**
Over 100,000,000 devices on a chip

FUNCTIONAL UNITS OF COMPUTER

Computer allocates the task between its various functional units. The computer system is divided into three separate functional units for its operation. They are:
- Central Processing Unit (CPU)
- Arithmetic Logical Unit (ALU)
- Control Unit (CU)

Central Processing Unit (CPU)

The ALU and the CU of a computer system are jointly known as the Central Processing Unit. You may call CPU as the brain of any computer system. It is just like brain that takes all major decisions, makes all sorts of calculations and directs different parts of the computer functions by activating and controlling the operations.

Arithmetic Logical Unit (ALU)

After you enter data through the input device it is stored in the Primary storage unit. The actual processing of the data and instruction are performed by Arithmetic Logical Unit. The major operations performed by the ALU are addition, subtraction, multiplication, division, logic and comparison. Data is transferred to ALU from storage unit when required. After processing the output is returned back to storage unit for further processing or getting stored.

Control Unit (CU)

The next component of computer is the Control Unit, which acts like the supervisor seeing that things are done in proper fashion. The control unit determines the sequence in which computer programs and instructions are executed. Things like processing of programs stored in the main memory, interpretation of the instructions and issuing of signals for other units of the computer to execute them. It also acts as a switch board operator when several users access the computer simultaneously. Thereby it coordinates the activities of computer's peripheral as they perform the input and output.

PARTS OF THE COMPUTER

There is basically two parts of the computer:
  (a) Hardware
  (b) Software

(a) Hardware

Hardware is best described as a device that is physically connected to your computer or something that can be physically touched. A CD-ROM, Monitor, Printer, and video card are all examples of computer hardware. Without any hardware your computer would not exist and software would have nothing to run on. The image to the right is of a web cam, an example of an external hardware peripheral that allows users to make basic videos, transmit videos of themselves over the Internet, and take pictures.

Computer hardwares are:
- **Central Processing Unit (CPU):** The "microprocessor" brain of the computer system is called the central processing unit. Everything that a computer does is overseen by the CPU.
- **Memory:** This is very fast storage used to hold data. It has to be fast because it connects directly to the microprocessor. There are several specific types of memory in a computer.
- **RAM (Random Access Memory):**It is used to temporarily store information that the computer is currently working with.
- **ROM (Read Only Memory):** A permanent type of memory storage used by the computer for important data that does not change.

- **Keyboard:** Generally used to type or select an option on the screen. It is an input device.
- **Mouse:** It is an input device which is used to point and select some option on VDU.
- **VDU (Visual Display Unit):** It is an output device where the output of any command is displayed *i.e.,* The screen.
- **Printer:** It is the output device. Different types of printer are:
  1. Dot matrix printer
  2. Inkjet Printer
  3. Laser Printer etc.
- **Floppy Disk Drives:** It is a common form of removable storage. Floppy disk are extremely inexpensive and easy to save information.
- **Scanner:** It is an input device. A scanner scans an image and transform the image to ASCII Graphics. These codes can be edited, manipulated & then printed.
- **CD-ROM Drive:** It is an input device. To read a CD-ROM disk a CD-ROM drive is required. One can only read from it and cannot write on it.
- **DVD-ROM:** DVD-ROM is similar to Cd-Rom but is capable of holding much more information.
- **CD-Writer:** It is input device. To write from other CD to your CD, writer is used.

(b) Software

Software is a collection of commands that help users to communicate with the computer or help the computer perform specific tasks for them. Without any type of software the computer would be of no use.

Examples of software **programs** or **applications** would be the **Operating System** (DOS, Windows, UNIX, MacOS and various others), **Wordprocessor** (typing letters), **Spreadsheet** (financial info), **Database** (inventory control and address book), **Graphics program, Internet Browser, Email** and many others.

Software is capable of performing specific tasks, as opposed to hardware which only perform mechanical tasks that they are mechanically designed for. Practical computer systems divide software systems into three major groups:

System Software

System software is a program that manages and supports the computer resources and operations of a computer system while it executes various tasks such as processing data and information, controlling hardware components, and allowing users to use application software. That is, systems software functions as a *bridge* between computer system hardware and the application software. System software is made up of many control programs, including the operating system, communications software and database manager. Computer software includes operating systems, device drivers, diagnostic tools and more.

Systems software consists of three kinds of programs. The system management programs, system support programs, and system development programs. These are explained briefly.

System Management Programs

These are programs that manage the application software, computer hardware, and data resources of the computer system. These programs include operating systems, operating environment programs, database management programs, and telecommunications monitor programs. Among these, the most important system management programs are operating systems. The operating systems are needed to study more details. There are two reasons. First, users need to know their functions first. For the second, there are many kinds of operating systems available today.

Telecommunications monitor programs are additions of the operating systems of microcomputers. These programs provide the extra logic for the computer system to control a class of communications devices.

System Support Programs

These are the programs that help the operations and management of a computer system. They provide a variety of support services to let the computer hardware and other system programs run efficiently. The major system support programs are system utility programs, system performance monitor programs, and system security monitor programs (virus checking programs).

System Development Programs

These are programs that help users develop information system programs and prepare user programs for computer processing. These programs may analyze and design systems and program itself. The main system development programs are programming language translators, programming environment programs, computer-aided software engineering packages.

Programming Software

Software that assists a programmer in writing computer programs.

Application Software

Allows users to accomplish one or more tasks. Application software utilizes the capacities of a computer directly for a dedicated task. Application software is able to manipulate text, numbers and graphics. It can be in the form of software focused on a certain single task like word processing, spreadsheet or playing of audio and video files. Here, we look at the application software types along with some examples of application software of each type.

Different Types of Application Software

- **Word Processing Software:** This software enables users to create and edit documents. The most popular examples of this type of software are MS-Word, WordPad and Notepad among other text editors.
- **Database Software:** Database is a structured collection of data. A computer database relies on database software to organize data and enable database users to perform database operations. Database software allows users to store and retrieve data from databases. Examples are Oracle, MSAccess, etc.

- **Spreadsheet Software:** Excel, Lotus 1-2-3 and Apple Numbers are some examples of spreadsheet software. Spreadsheet software allows users to perform calculations using spreadsheets. They simulate paper worksheets by displaying multiple cells that make up a grid.
- **Multimedia Software:** They allow users to create and play audio and video files. They are capable of playing media files. Audio converters, audio players, burners, video encoders and decoders are some forms of multimedia software. Examples of this type of software include Real Player and Media Player.
- **Presentation Software:** The software that is used to display information in the form of a slide show is known as presentation software. This type of software includes three functions, namely, editing that allows insertion and formatting of text, methods to include graphics in the text and a functionality of executing slide shows. Microsoft PowerPoint is the best example of presentation software.
- **Enterprise Software:** It deals with the needs of organization processes and data flow. Customer relationship management or the financial processes in an organization are carried out with the help of enterprise software.
- **Information Worker Software:** Individual projects within a department and individual needs of creation and management of information are handled by information worker software. Documentation tools, resource management tools and personal management systems fall under the category of this type of application software.
- **Educational Software:** It has the capabilities of running tests and tracking progress. It also has the capabilities of a collaborative software. It is often used in teaching and self-learning. Dictionaries like Britannica and Encarta, mathematical software like Matlab and others like Google Earth and NASA World Wind are some of the well-known names in this category.
- **Simulation Software:** It is used to simulate physical or abstract systems. Simulation software finds applications in both, research and entertainment. Flight simulators and scientific simulators are examples of simulation software.
- **Content Access Software:** It is used to access content without editing. Common examples of content access software are web browsers and media players.
- **Application Suites:** An application suite is an important type of application software. It consists of a group of applications combined to perform related functions. OpenOffice.org and Microsoft Office are the best examples of this type of application software. These application suites, as you know, come as bundles of applications like word processors, spreadsheets, presentation software, etc. Applications in the suite can work together or operate on each other's files.

Utility Software

Utility software is system software designed to help analyze, configure, optimize or maintain a computer. A single piece of utility software is usually called a utility or tool.

Utility software usually focuses on how the computer infrastructure (including the computer hardware, operating system, application software and data storage) operates. Due to this focus, utilities are often rather technical and targeted at people with an advanced level of computer knowledge - in contrast to application software, which allows users to do things like creating text documents, playing games, listening to music or viewing websites.

Utility Software Examples

- **Anti-virus** utilities scan for computer viruses.
- **Backup** utilities can make a copy of all information stored on a disk, and restore either the entire disk (e.g. in an event of disk failure) or selected files (e.g. in an event

of accidental deletion).

- **Data compression** utilities output a shorter stream or a smaller file when provided with a stream or file.
- **Disk cleaners** can find files that are unnecessary to computer operation, or take up considerable amounts of space. Disk cleaner helps the user to decide what to delete when their hard disk is full.
- **Disk compression** utilities can transparently compress/uncompress the contents of a disk, increasing the capacity of the disk.
- **Disk defragmenters** can detect computer files whose contents are broken across several locations on the hard disk, and move the fragments to one location to increase efficiency.
- **Disk partitions** can divide an individual drive into multiple logical drives, each with its own file system which can be mounted by the operating system and treated as an individual drive.
- **Disk space analyzers** for the visualization of disk space usage by getting the size for each folder (including sub folders) & files in folder or drive, showing the distribution of the used space.
- **Archive** utilities output a stream or a single file when provided with a directory or a set of files. Archive utilities, unlike archive suites, usually do not include compression or encryption capabilities. Some archive utilities may even have a separate un-archive utility for the reverse operation.

- **File managers** provide a convenient method of performing routine data management tasks, such as deleting, renaming, cataloging, uncataloging, moving, copying, merging, generating and modifying data sets.
- **Memory testers** check for memory failures.
- **Network utilities** analyze the computer's network connectivity, configure network settings, check data transfer or log events.
- **Registry cleaners** clean and optimize the Windows registry by removing old registry keys that are no longer in use.
- **Screensavers** were desired to prevent phosphor burn-in on CRT and plasma computer monitors by blanking the screen or filling it with moving images or patterns when the computer is not in use. Contemporary screensavers are used primarily for entertainment or security.

Firmware

Firmware is a program for the hardware. It is an embedded coded (program) for the hardware. So, it can perform its function specifically for which device is made. Every device has inbuilt firmware that gives the device ability to perform its work. There are lots of devices that use a screen and buttons. The device consists of firmware that instruct the device to perform certain functions on given command. Examples are a video card and sound card.

COMPUTER FUNDAMENTAL

COMPUTER

Computer is an advanced electronic device that takes raw data as input from the user and processes these data under the control of set of instructions (called program) and gives the result (output) and saves output for the future use. It can process both numerical and non-numerical (arithmetic and logical) calculations.

A computer has four functions:

(*a*) accepts data **Input**
(*b*) processes data **Processing**
(*c*) produces output **Output**
(*d*) stores results **Storage**

Input (Data)

Input is the raw information entered into a computer from the input devices. It is the collection of letters, numbers, images etc.

Process

Process is the operation of data as per given instruction. It is totally internal process of the computer system.

Output

Output is the processed data given by computer after data processing. Output is also called as Result. We can save these results in the storage devices for the future use.

COMPUTER SYSTEM

All of the components of a computer system can be summarized with the simple equations.

COMPUTER SYSTEM = HARDWARE + SOFTWARE + USER

Hardware = Internal Devices + Peripheral Devices

All physical parts of the computer (or everything that we can touch) are known as Hardware.

Software = Programs

Software gives "intelligence" to the computer.

USER = Person, who operates computer.

PROCESSOR

The main unit inside the computer is the CPU. This unit is responsible for all events inside the computer. It controls all internal and external devices, performs arithmetic and logic operations. The CPU (Central Processing Unit) is the device that interprets and executes instructions.

SOFTWARE

Software, simply are the computer programs. The instructions given to the computer in the form of a program is called Software. Software is the set of programs, which are used for different purposes.

All the programs used in computer to perform specific task is called Software.

Types of Software

1. System software

(a) Operating System Software: Operating system is an example of system software, which provide the platform to the application softwares.

DOS, Windows XP, Windows Vista, Unix/Linux, MAC/OS X etc.

(b) Utility Software: Windows Explorer (File/Folder Management), Windows Media Player, Anti-Virus Utilities, Disk Defragmentation, Disk Clean, BackUp, WinZip, WinRAR etc...

2. Application software

(a) Package Software: MS Office 2003, MS Office 2007, Macromedia (Dreamweaver, Flash, Freehand), Adobe (PageMaker, PhotoShop)

(b) Tailored or Custom Software: SAGE (Accounting), Galileo/Worldspan (Travel) etc.

COMPUTER LANGUAGES & SCRIPTING

Low Level Language

(*i*) Machine Level Language
(*ii*) Assembly Language

Machine language

These language instructions are directly executed by CPU. It is in the form of '0' and '1' means in binary language.

Assembly language

The endeavor of giving machine language instructions a name structure that means bit strings of instructions of machine language are given name here.

- **High Level Language:** The user friendly language ...more natural language than assembly language. Like C++, Java etc.
- **Assembler:** It is a program written in a computer language which convert assembly language into machine language.
- **Compiler:** It is also a program written in a computer language, which convert high level language to machine language.

High Level Language

COBOL (Common Business Oriented Language), FORTRAN (Formula Translation), BASIC (Beginner's All-purpose Symbolic Instruction Code), C, C++ etc. are the examples of High Level Language.

TYPES OF COMPUTER

On the Basis of Working Principle

(a) **Analog Computer:** An analog computer (spelt analogue in British English) is a form of computer that uses *continuous* physical phenomena such as electrical, mechanical, or hydraulic quantities to model the problem being solved.

(b) **Digital Computer:** A computer that performs calculations and logical operations with quantities represented as digits, usually in the binary number system.

(c) **Hybrid Computer (Analog + Digital):** A combination of computers those are capable of inputting and outputting in both digital and analog signals. A hybrid computer system setup offers a cost effective method of performing complex simulations.

COMPUTER TYPES ON THE BASIS OF SIZE

(a) Super Computer

The fastest type of computer. Supercomputers are very expensive and are employed for specialized applications that require immense amounts of mathematical calculations. For example, weather forecasting requires a supercomputer. Other uses of supercomputers include animated graphics, fluid dynamic calculations, nuclear energy research, and petroleum exploration.

The chief difference between a supercomputer and a mainframe is that a supercomputer channels all its power into executing a few programs as fast as possible, whereas a mainframe uses its power to execute many programs concurrently.

(b) Mainframe Computer

A very large and expensive computer capable of supporting hundreds, or even thousands, of users simultaneously. In the hierarchy that starts with a simple microprocessor (in watches, for example) at the bottom and moves to supercomputers at the top, mainframes are just below supercomputers. In some ways, mainframes are more powerful than supercomputers because they support more simultaneous programs. But supercomputers can execute a single program faster than a mainframe.

(c) Mini Computer

A midsized computer. In size and power, minicomputers lie between *workstations* and *mainframes*. In the past decade, the distinction between large minicomputers and small mainframes has blurred, however, as has the distinction between small minicomputers and workstations. But in general, a minicomputer is a multiprocessing system capable of supporting from 4 to about 200 users simultaneously.

(d) Micro Computer

(i) **Desktop Computer:** A personal or micro-mini computer sufficient to fit on a desk.

(ii) **Laptop Computer:** A portable computer complete with an integrated screen and keyboard. It is generally smaller in size than a desktop computer and larger than a notebook computer.

(iii) **Palmtop Computer/Digital Diary/ Notebook/PDAs:** A hand-sized computer. Palmtops have no keyboard but the screen serves both as an input and output device.

(e) Workstations

A terminal or desktop computer in a network. In this context, workstation is just a generic term for a user's machine (client machine) in contrast to a "server" or "mainframe."

BOOTING

The process of loading the system files of the operating system from the disk into the computer memory to complete the circuitry requirement of the computer system is called booting.

Types of Booting

There are two types of booting:

- **Cold Booting:** If the computer is in off state and we boot the computer by pressing the power switch 'ON' from the CPU box then it is called as cold booting.
- **Warm Booting:** If the computer is already 'ON' and we restart it by pressing the 'RESET' button from the CPU box or CTRL, ALT and DEL key simultaneously from the keyboard then it is called warm booting.

COMPUTER HARDWARE

HARDWARE

The **hardware** are the parts of the computer itself including the Central Processing Unit (CPU) and related **microchips** and **micro-circuitry**, keyboards, monitors, case and drives (hard, CD, DVD, floppy, optical, tape, etc...). Other extra parts called **peripheral components** or **devices** include mouse, printers, modems, scanners, digital cameras and cards (sound, colour, video) etc... Together they are often referred to as a **personal computer**.

Central Processing Unit

Though the term relates to a specific chip or the **processor** a CPU's performance is determined by the rest of the computer's **circuitry** and **chips**.

Currently the Pentium chip or processor, made by Intel, is the most common CPU though there are many other companies that produce processors for personal computers. Examples are the CPU made by Motorola and AMD.

With faster processors the **clock speed** becomes more important. Compared to some of the first computers which operated at below 30 **megahertz** (MHz) the Pentium chips began at 75 MHz in the late 1990's. Speeds now exceed 3000+ MHz or 3 **gigahertz** (GHz) and different chip manufacturers use different measuring standards (check your local computer store for the latest speed). It depends on the **circuit board** that the chip is housed in, or the **motherboard**, as to whether you are able to upgrade to a faster chip. The motherboard contains the circuitry and connections that allow the various components to communicate with each other.

Though there were many computers using many different processors previous to this I call the 80286 processor the advent of home computers as these were the processors that made computers available for the average person. Using a processor before the 286 involved learning a proprietary system and software. Most new software are being developed for the newest and fastest processors so it can be difficult to use an older computer system.

Keyboard

The keyboard is used to type information into the computer or **input** information. There are many different keyboard layouts and sizes with the most common for Latin based languages being the QWERTY layout (named for the first 6 keys). The standard keyboard has 101 keys. Notebooks have embedded keys accessible by special keys or by pressing key combinations (CTRL or Command and P for example). **Ergonomically** designed keyboards are designed to make typing easier. Hand held devices have various and different keyboard configurations and **touch screens**.

Some of the keys have a special use. They are referred to as command keys. The 3 most common are the Control (CTRL), Alternate (Alt) and the Shift keys though there can be more (the Windows key for example or the Command key). Each key on a standard keyboard has one or two characters. Press the key to get the lower character and hold Shift to get the upper.

Removable Storage and/or Disk Drives

All disks need a **drive** to get information off - or **read** - and put information on the disk - or **write**. Each drive is designed for a specific type of disk whether it is a CD, DVD, hard disk or floppy. Often the term 'disk' and 'drive' are used to describe the same thing but it helps to understand that the disk is the **storage device** which contains computer files - or software - and the drive is the mechanism that runs the disk.

Digital flash drives work slightly differently as they use **memory cards** to store information so there are no moving parts. Digital cameras also use Flash memory cards to store information, in this case photographs. **Hand held devices** use digital drives and many also use removable or built in memory cards.

Mouse

Most modern computers today are run using a mouse controlled pointer. Generally if the mouse has two buttons the left one is used to **select** objects and text and the right one is used to **access menus**. If the mouse has one button (Mac for instance) it controls all the activity and a mouse with a third button can be used by specific software programs.

One type of mouse has a round ball under the bottom of the mouse that rolls and turns two wheels which control the direction of the pointer on the screen. Another type of mouse uses an optical system to track the movement of the mouse. **Laptop** computers use touch pads, buttons and other devices to control the pointer. Hand helds use a combination of devices to control the pointer, including touch screens.

Note: It is important to clean the mouse periodically, particularly if it becomes sluggish. A ball type mouse has a small circular panel that can be opened, allowing you to remove the ball. Lint can be removed carefully with a tooth pick or tweezers and the ball can be washed with mild detergent. A build up will accumulate on the small wheels in the mouse. Use a small instrument or finger nail to scrape it off taking care not to scratch the wheels. Track balls can be cleaned much like a mouse and touch-pad can be wiped with a clean, damp cloth. An optical mouse can accumulate material from the surface that it is in contact with which can be removed with a finger nail or small instrument.

Monitors

The monitor shows information on the screen when you type. This is called **outputting** information. When the computer needs more information it will display a message on the screen, usually through a **dialog box**. Monitors come in many types and sizes. The resolution of the monitor determines the sharpness of the screen. The resolution can be adjusted to control the screen's display..

Most desktop computers use a monitor with a **cathode tube** or **liquid crystal display**. Most notebooks use a liquid crystal display monitor.

To get the full benefit of today's software with full colour graphics and animation, computers need a colour monitor with a display or **graphics** card.

Printers

The printer takes the information on your screen and transfers it to paper or a **hard copy**. There are many different types of printers with various levels of quality. The three basic types of printer are; **dot matrix**, **inkjet**, and **laser**.

- Dot matrix printers work like a typewriter transferring ink from a ribbon to paper with a series or 'matrix' of tiny pins.
- Ink jet printers work like dot matrix printers but fire a stream of ink from a cartridge directly onto the paper.

- Laser printers use the same technology as a photocopier using heat to transfer toner onto paper.

Modem

A modem is used to translate information transferred through telephone lines, cable, satellite or line-of-sight wireless.

The term stands for **modulate and demodulate** which changes the signal from **digital**, which computers use, to **analog**, which telephones use and then back again. **Digital modems** transfer digital information directly without changing to analog.

Modems are measured by the speed that the information is transferred. The measuring tool is called the **baud rate**. Originally modems worked at speeds below 2400 baud but today analog speeds of 56,000 baud are standard. Cable, wireless or digital subscriber lines can transfer information much faster with rates of 300,000 baud and up.

Modems also use **Error Correction** which corrects for transmission errors by constantly checking whether the information was received properly or not and Compression which allows for faster data transfer rates. Information is transferred in **packets**. Each packet is checked for errors and is re-sent if there is an error.

Anyone who has used the Internet has noticed that at times the information travels at different speeds. Depending on the amount of information that is being transferred, the information will arrive at it's destination at different times. The amount of information that can travel through a line is limited. This limit is called **bandwidth**.

There are many more variables involved in communication technology using computers, much of which is covered in the section on the Internet.

Scanners

Scanners allow you to transfer pictures and photographs to your computer. A scanner 'scans' the image from the top to the bottom, one line at a time and transfers it to the computer as a series of bits or a bitmap. You can then take that image and use it in a paint program, send it out as a fax or print it. With optional **Optical Character Recognition** (OCR) software you can convert printed documents such as newspaper articles to text that can be used in your word processor. Most scanners use **TWAIN** software that makes the scanner accessable by other software applications.

Digital cameras allow you to take digital photographs. The images are stored on a memory chip or disk that can be transferred to your computer. Some cameras can also capture sound and video.

Case

The case houses the microchips and circuitry that run the computer. Desktop models usually sit under the monitor and tower models beside. They come in many sizes, including desktop, mini, midi, and full tower. There is usually room inside to expand or add components at a later time. By removing the cover off the case you may find plate covered, empty slots that allow you to add cards. There are various types of slots including IDE, ASI, USB, PCI and Firewire slots.

Depending on the type notebook computers may have room to expand. Most Notebooks also have connections or ports that allows expansion or connection to exterior, peripheral devices such as monitor, portable hard-drives or other devices.

Cards

Cards are components added to computers to increase their capability. When adding a peripheral device make sure that your computer has a slot of the type needed by the device.

Sound cards allow computers to produce sound like music and voice. The older sound cards were 8 bit then 16 bit then 32 bit. Though the human ear can't distinguish the fine difference between sounds produced by the more powerful sound card they allow for more complex music and music production.

Colour cards allow computers to produce colour (with a colour monitor of course). The first colour cards were 2 bit which produced 4 colours [CGA]. It was amazing what could be done with those 4 colours. Next came 4 bit allowing for 16

[EGA and VGA] colours. Then came 16 bit allowing for 1064 colours and then 24 bit which allows for almost 17 million colours and now 32 bit and higher allow monitors to display almost a billion separate colours.

Video cards allow computers to display video and animation. Some video cards allow computers to display television as well as capture frames from video. A video card with a digital video camera allows computers users to produce live video. A high speed connection is required for effective video transmission.

Network cards allow computers to connect together to communicate with each other. Network cards have connections for cable, thin wire or wireless networks for more information.

Cables connect internal components to the **Motherboard**, which is a board with series of electronic path ways and connections allowing the CPU to communicate with the other components of the computer.

Memory

Memory can be very confusing but is usually one of the easiest pieces of hardware to add to your computer. It is common to confuse **chip memory** with disk storage. An example of the difference between memory and storage would be the difference between a table where the actual work is done (memory) and a filing cabinet where the finished product is stored (disk). To add a bit more confusion, the computer's hard disk can be used as **temporary memory** when the program needs more than the chips can provide.

Random Access Memory or **RAM** is the memory that the computer uses to temporarily store the information as it is being processed. The more information being processed the more RAM the computer needs.

One of the first home computers used 64 kilobytes of RAM memory (Commodore 64). Today's modern computers need a minimum of 64 Mb (recommended 128 Mb or more) to run Windows or OS 10 with modern software. RAM memory chips come in many different sizes and speeds and can usually be **expanded**. Older computers came with 512 Kb of memory which could be expanded to a maximum of 640 Kb. In most modern computers the memory can be expanded by adding or replacing the memory chips depending on the processor you have and the type of memory your computer uses. Memory chips range in size from 1 Mb to 4 Gb. As computer technology changes the type of memory changes as well making old memory chips obsolete. Check your computer manual to find out what kind of memory your computer uses before purchasing new memory chips

MULTIPLE CHOICE QUESTIONS

1. Android is a mobile operating system designed primarily for touchscreen mobile devices such as smartphones and tablets. Which among the following was the first Android Operating System?
   - A. Cupcake
   - B. Alpha
   - C. Gingerbread
   - D. Doughnut
   - E. Eclair

2. Which among the following key combinations can be used to search in Windows Explorer?
   - A. Ctrl + F
   - B. Ctrl + S
   - C. Ctrl + G
   - D. Alt + S
   - E. None of the above

3. A router is a networking device that forwards data packets and is connected to two or more data lines from different networks. Which among the following was the earliest device which had almost the same functionality as that of a router?
   - A. Interface Delay Device
   - B. Interface Traffic Manager
   - C. Interface Routing Processor
   - D. Interface Message Processor
   - E. Interface Data Manager

4. A vacuum tube (also called a VT, electron tube or, in the UK, a valve) is a device sometimes used to amplify electronic signals. Vacuum Tubes were used in which generation of Computers?
A. 1st Generation   B. 2nd Generation
C. 3rd Generation   D. 4th Generation
D. 5th Generation

5. In Computer programming API is a set of subroutine definitions, protocols, and tools for building software and applications. Which among the following is an application programming interface for the programm-ing language Java, which defines how a client may access a database?
A. J2EE   B. JDK
C. JAVA SE   D. JDBC
E. JSX

6. Which of the following errors occurs when software tries to access protected memory?
A. Segmentation Fault
B. Displaytime Error
C. IO Error
D. Runtime Error
E. Zero Division Error

7. Which among the following is a term representing unit of data storage in computer memory?
A. Pixel   B. Decimal
C. Octet   D. Point
E. Fragment

8. Microsoft PowerPoint is a slide show presentation program for use on both Microsoft and Apple Macintosh operating systems. In MS PowerPoint Broadcast is a feature available in which tab?
A. File   B. View
C. Slide Show   D. Transitions
E. Review

9. Which among the following carries signals that control the actions of the computer?
A. Control Bus   B. Data Bus
C. Memory Unit   D. NIC
E. Address Bus

10. Which among the following is not a secondary memory?
A. Cache   B. Pen Drive
C. Hard Disk   D. Memory Card
E. Memory Stick

11. Which among the following is a cloud computing platform and infrastructure created by Microsoft?
A. Simple Storage Service
B. Atmos
C. Openstack Swift
D. OceanStore
E. Azure

12. After a credit card transaction has been authorized by the issuing bank by sending an authorization code to the merchant, the settlement stage of the process begins. Which of the following is a system type used to process such statements?
A. Multi-tasking   B. Memory Processing
C. Level Processing   D. Batch Processing
E. Online Processing

13. Assembly is a ________ based low-level language replacing binary machine-code instructions, which are very hard to remember, it is the classic and uncontroversial example of a low level language.
A. Memory   B. High Level
C. Key   D. Mnemonic
E. FORTRAN

14. China now has more of the world's fastest supercomputers than other countries. Which among the following is a Chinese super-computer?
A. BlueGene/Q system
B. Cray XC30
C. Shaheen II
D. Fujitsu's K
E. Tianhe-2

15. Which among the following is an important circuitry in a computer system that does the arithmetic and logical processing?
A. Memory   B. ALU
C. Flag Register   D. CU
E. Calculator

16. Which among the following is not a mobile Operating System?
A. Bada
B. Safari
C. Symbian
D. MeeGo
E. WebOS

17. Which among the following key can be used as a shortcut to rename a folder in Microsoft Windows 8 and higher versions?
A. F2
B. F4
C. F6
D. F9
E. F11

18. AT & T designed its first commercial modem, specifically for converting digital computer data to analog for transmission across its long distance network. What is the name of the modem?
A. Telex
B. Memex
C. CompuServe
D. Bell 103 dataset
E. Dataphone

19. Integrated Chips or IC's were started to be in use from which generation of computers?
A. 1st Generation
B. 2nd Generation
C. 3rd Generation
D. 4th Generation
E. 5th Generation

20. In Computer programming there is a set of subroutine definitions, protocols, and tools for building software and applications. Which among the following is a term for sets of requirements that govern how one application can talk to another?
A. UPS
B. API
C. CGI
D. J2EE
E. OLE

21. When you first turn on a computer, the COU is preset to execute instructions stored in ....
A. RAM
B. Flash memory
C. ROM
D. The CD-ROM
E. The ALU

22. Which of the following is **not** a function of the control unit?
A. Read instructions
B. Interpret instructions
C. Execute instructions
D. Direct operations
E. Provide control signals

23. What are .bas, .doc, .htm examples of in computing?
A. Extensions
B. Protocols
C. Databases
D. Other than those given as options
E. Domains

24. Documents converted to .... can be published to the web.
A. a doc file
B. http
C. Other than those given as options
D. machine language
E. HTML

25. What kind of software would you most likely use to keep track of a billing account?
A. Web authoring
B. electronic publishing
C. spreadsheet
D. word processing
E. Power point

26. A computer virus normally attaches itself to another computer program known as a ....
A. host program
B. target program
C. backdoor program
D. Bluetooth
E. Trojan horse

27. When a file contains instructions that can be carried out by the computer. It is often called a(n) .... file.
A. Other than those given as options
B. information
C. application
D. executable
E. data

28. Data duplication wastes the space, but also promotes a more serious problem called ....
A. Isolated data
B. Data inconsistency
C. Other than those given as options
D. Program dependency
E. Separated data

29. Which of the following is **not** a version of the Windows operating system software for the PC?
- A. ME
- B. 98
- C. XP
- D. 10
- E. 95

30. The main directory of a disk is called the .... directory.
- A. network
- B. folder
- C. root
- D. File
- E. Other than those given as options

31. Which of the following is **not** an example of application software?
- A. Word processing software
- B. Spreadsheet software
- C. Operating system software
- D. Database software
- E. Graphics software

32. Which of the following is **not** true about RAM?
- A. RAM is the same as hard disk storage
- B. RAM is a temporary storage area
- C. RAM is volatile
- D. RAM is a primary memory
- E. All are true

33. The data storage hierarchy consists of ....
- A. Bits, Bytes, Records, Fields, files and databases
- B. Characters, fields, records, files and databases
- C. Bytes, bits, fields, records, files and databases
- D. Bits, bytes, fields, records, files and databases
- E. Other than those given as options

34. = Sum (B1 B0) is an example of a ....
- A. function
- B. cell address
- C. formula
- D. value
- E. Other than those given as options

35. .... are often delivered to a PC through an email attachment and are often designed to do harm.
- A. Portals
- B. Spam
- C. Viruses
- D. Other than those given as options
- E. E-mail messages

36. Decreasing the amount of space required to store data and programs is accomplished by ....
- A. Crashing
- B. Disk caching
- C. RAID
- D. file compression
- E. Other than those given as options

37. What is the difference between a CD-ROM and CD-RW?
- A. They are the same —just two different terms used by different manufacturers
- B. A CD-Rom can be written to and a CD-RW cannot
- C. Other than those given as options
- D. A CD-ROM holds more information than a CD-RW
- E. A CD-RW can be written to but a CD-ROM can only be read from

38. Computer program are written in a high-level programming language, however, the human readable version of a program is called ....
- A. word size
- B. source code
- C. instruction set
- D. Read & Write code
- E. None of these

39. The clock rate of a processor is measured in ....
- A. megabytes or gigabytes
- B. milliseconds
- C. megahertz or gigahertz
- D. nanoseconds
- E. micro hertz

40. When cutting and pasting, the item cut is temporarily stored in the ....
- A. dashboard
- B. ROM
- C. hard drive
- D. Diskette
- E. clipboard

41. Copying the Excel 2007 formula = SUM (A1:A5) from cell A6 to cell B6 will result in what formula for cell B6?
- A. = SUM (B6:A6)
- B. < SUM (A1:B6)
- C. = SUM (B1:A5)

D. > SUM (B1:B5)
E. Other than those given as options

42. RAM is used as a short memory because it—
A. has small capacity B. is very expensive
C. is programmable D. volatile
E. not very useful

43. The Num Lock Key and Caps Lock Key are considered .... because their function changes each time you press them.
A. toggle   B. dual
C. function   D. cursor control
E. control

44. OLE stands for—
A. Offline Linking and Embedding
B. Online Link Emulation
C. Object Link Export
D. Object Linking and Embedding
E. Online Link Embedding

45. Microsoft Word is an example of—
A. Application software
B. An input device
C. System software
D. A processing system
E. An operating system

46. Which of the following is not an example of an output device?
A. Speaker   B. Plotter
C. Microphone   D. Printer
E. Monitor

47. The digital telecommunications, termed as ISDN is an abbreviation for—
A. Interactive Standard Dynamic Networks
B. Integrated Standard Digital Networks
C. Internet Services Data Network
D. International Services Data Network
E. Integrated Services Digital Network

48. Which of the following places the common data elements in order to the smallest from the largest?
A. Character, file, field, record, database
B. Character, field, record, file, database
C. Character, record, field, database, file
D. Character, file, record, field, database
E. Character, field, record, database, file

49. Software made freely available to the public by the publisher is called—
A. Fair use
B. Compact disc
C. Freeware
D. Process ware
E. Copyright

50. A web site's own unique Internet address that no other web site can use is its—
A. Search Engine   B. FTP
C. URL   D. WWW
E. IP v 6

51. The windows shortcut to delete an item permanently is—
A. Shift + Delete   B. Shift + F1
C. Ctrl + F1   D. Ctrl + F2
E. Shift + F2

52. WAN is a type of computer network. It stands for—
A. Wireless Array Network
B. Wild Area Network
C. Wide Access Network
D. Wide Area Network
E. Wireless Area Network

53. Which of the following is a type for intercepting computer communications?
A. Hacking   B. Sniffing
C. Pretexting   D. Spoofing
E. Phishing

54. Which key allows movement from one cell of a table to the next?
A. Shift   B. CTRL
C. Esc   D. Tab
E. ALT

55. Pressing the .... key will make the number pad act as directional arrows.
A. Caps lock   B. Arrow lock
C. Shift   D. Esc
E. Num lock

56. The most widely used device in communication is a —
A. Coprocessor   B. Channel
C. Bus   D. Modem
E. Scanner

57. Codes consisting of light and dark marks which may be optically read is known as—
A. Mnemonics   B. Stripe-code
C. Decoder   D. Special-code
E. Bar code

58. Which of the following is not a type of data storage media?
A. Magnetic Tape   B. A Database
C. Hard Disc   D. Optical Disc
E. Magnetic Disc

59. Compiler means—
A. A program which translates source code into object program
B. Keypunch Operator
C. A person who compiles source programs
D. The same thing as a programmer
E. Computer data operator

60. Which of the following is operating system software?
A. Microsoft Access
B. Microsoft Windows
C. Microsoft Power Point
D. Microsoft Excel
E. Microsoft Word

61. Reusable optical storage will typically have the acronym ....
A. CD   B. DVD
C. ROM   D. RW
E. None of these

62. .... is processed by the computer into information.
A. Data   B. Numbers
C. Alphabets   D. Pictures
E. None of these

63. A .... is an electronic device that process data, converting it into information.
A. computer   B. processor
C. case   D. stylus
E. None of these

64. File extensions are used in order to
A. name the file
B. ensure the filename is not lost
C. identify the file
D. identify the file type
E. None of these

65. The most common type of storage devices are ....
A. persistent   B. optical
C. magnetic   D. flash
E. None of these

66. "GUI" stands for ....
A. Gnutella Universal Interface
B. Graphical User Interface
C. Graphic Uninstall/Install
D. General Utility Interface
E. None of these

67. A .... is a design tool that graphically shows the logic in a solution algorithm.
A. flowchart   B. hierarchy chart
C. structure chart   D. context diagram
E. None of these

68. A file that contains definitions of the paragraph and character styles for your document and all things you customised toolbars and menus is called a ....
A. guide   B. pattern
C. base document   D. template
E. None of these

69. Programs designed specifically to address general-purpose applications and special-purpose applications are called ....
A. operating system
B. system software
C. application software
D. Management information systems
E. None of these

70. A .... contains buttons and menus that provide quick access to commonly used commands.
A. toolbar   B. menu bar
C. window   D. find
E. None of these

71. .... has invented the mechanical calculator for adding numbers
A. Charles Babbage   B. Newton
C. Pascal   D. Peano
E. E.F. Codd

72. A unit of hardware used to monitor the computer processing
A. Terminal   B. Console

C. CPU   D. Server
E. Client

73. Which of these is not a feature of a reentrant procedure
    A. multiple users can share a single copy of a program during the same period
    B. The program code can modify itself
    C. The local data for each user process must be stored separately
    D. the permanent part is the code
    E. the temporary part is the pointer back to the calling program and local variables used by that program

74. What is the split-MAC architecture
    A. The split-MAC architecture uses MAC addresses to create a forward/filter table and break up broadcast domains
    B. The split-MAC architecture uses MAC addresses on the wireless network and IP addresses on the wired network
    C. The split-MAC architecture allows the splitting of 802.11 protocol packets between the AP and the controller to allow processing by both devices
    D. The split-MAC architecture uses MAC addresses to create a forward/filter table and break up collision domains
    E. All of these

75. In .... normal form, all non-key fields of data structure are dependent on the whole key
    A. First   B. Second
    C. Third   D. Fourth
    E. Fifth

76. For selecting or highlighting, which of the following is generally used?
    A. Icon   B. Keyboard
    C. Mouse   D. Floppy Disk
    E. None of these

77. What does storage unit provide?
    A. Place for typing data
    B. Storage for information and instruction
    C. Place for printing information
    D. All of the above
    E. None of these

78. Which type of memory is closely related to processor?
    A. Main Memory
    B. Secondary Memory
    C. Disk Memory
    D. Tape Memory
    E. None of these

79. Which device is used to access your computer by other computer or for talk over phone?
    A. RAM   B. CD ROM Drive
    C. Modem   D. Hard Drive
    E. None of these

80. Permanent Memory in computer is called
    A. RAM   B. ROM
    C. CPU   D. CD ROM
    E. None of these

81. .... allows users to upload files to an online site so they can be viewed and edited from another location.
    A. General-purpose application
    B. Microsoft Outlook
    C. Web-hosted technology
    D. Office Live
    E. None of these

82. What feature adjusts the top and bottom margins so that the text is centered vertically on the printed page?
    A. Vertical justifying
    B. Vertical adjusting
    C. Dual centering
    D. Horizontal centering
    E. Vertical centering

83. Which of these is **not** a means of personal communication on the internet?
    A. chat   B. instant messaging
    C. instanotes   D. electronic mail
    E. None of these

84. What is the overall term for creating, editing, formating, storing, retrieving, and printing a text document?
    A. Word processing
    B. Spreadsheet design
    C. Web design
    D. Database management
    E. Presentation generation

85. Fourth-generation mobile technology provides enhanced capabilities allowing the transfer of both .... data, including full-motion video, high-speed internet access, and video-conferencing.
 A. video data and information
 B. voice and nonvoice
 C. music and video
 D. video and audio
 E. None of these

86. .... is a form of denial of service attack in which a hostile client repeatedly sends SYN packets to every port on the server using fake IP addresses.
 A. Cybergaming crime
 B. Memory shaving
 C. Syn flooding
 D. Software piracy
 E. None of these

87. Which of these is a point-and-draw device?
 A. mouse   B. scanner
 C. printer   D. CD-ROM
 E. keyboard

88. The letter and number of the intersecting column and row is the—
 A. cell location
 B. cell position
 C. cell address
 D. cell coordinates
 E. cell contents

89. A set of rules for telling the computer what operations to perform is called a—
 A. procedural language
 B. structures
 C. natural language
 D. command language
 E. programming language

90. A detailed written description of the programming cycle and the program, along with the test results and a printout of the program is called—
 A. documentation   B. output
 C. reporting   D. spec sheets
 E. Directory

91. Forms that are used to organize business data into rows and columns are called—
 A. transaction sheets B. registers
 C. business forms   D. sheet-spreads
 E. spreadsheets

92. In Power Point, the Header & Footer button can be found on the Insert tab in what group?
 A. Illustrations group B. Object group
 C. Text group   D. Tables group
 E. None of these

93. A(n) .... is a set of programs designed to manage the resources of a computer, including starting the computer, managing programs, managing memory and coordinating tasks between input and output devices.
 A. application suite
 B. compiler
 C. input/output system
 D. interface
 E. operating system (OS)

94. A typical slide in a slide presentation would **not** include—
 A. photo images charts and graphs
 B. graphs and clip art
 C. clip art and audio clips
 D. full-motion video
 E. content templates

95. The PC productivity tool that manipulates data organized in rows and columns is called a—
 A. spreadsheet
 B. word processing document
 C. presentation mechanism
 D. database record manager
 E. EDI creator

96. In the absence of parentheses, the order of operation is —
 A. Exponentiation, addition or subtraction, multiplication or division
 B. Addition or subtraction, multiplication or division, exponentiation
 C. Multiplication or division, exponentiation, addition or subtraction
 D. Exponentiation, multiplication or division, addition or subtraction
 E. Addition or subtraction, exponentiation, Multiplication or division

97. To find the Paste Special option, you use the Clipboard group on the ...... tab of PowerPoint.
A. Design B. Slide Show
C. Page Layout D. Insert
E. Home

98. Which view display miniature images of photographs within a folder?
A. Tiles view and Icons view
B. Thumbnails view and Filmstrip view
C. Details view and List view
D. All views display a miniature image
E. None of these

99. Usually downloaded into folders that hold temporary internet files, ... are written to your computer's hard disk by some of the Web sites you visit.
A. anonymous files B. behaviour files
C. banner ads D. large files
E. cookies

100. What is the easiest way to change the phrase, revenues, profits, gross margin, to read revenues, profit and gross margin?
A. Use the insert mode, position the cursor before the g in gross, then type the word and followed by a space
B. Use the insert mode, position the cursor after the g in gross, then type the word and followed by a space
C. Use the overtype mode, position the cursor before the g in gross, then type the word and followed by a space
D. Use the overtype mode, position the cursor after the g in gross, then type the word and followed by a space
E. None of these

101. A program, either talk or music, that is made available in digital format for automatic download over the internet is called a —
A. wiki B. broadcast
C. vodcast D. blog
E. podcast

102. Which PowerPoint view displays each slide of the presentation as a thumbnail and is useful for rearranging slides?
A. Slide Sorter B. Slide Show

C. Slide Master D. Notes Page
E. Slide Design

103. Different components on the motherboard of a PC unit are linked together by sets of parallel electrical conducting lines. What are these lines called?
A. Conductors B. Buses
C. Connectors D. Consecutives
E. None of these

104. What is the name given to those applications that combine text, sound, graphics, motion video, and/or animation?
A. motionware B. anigraphics
C. videoscapes D. multimedia
E. maxomedia

105. A USB communication device that supports data encryption for secure wireless communication for notebook users is called a—
A. USB wireless network adapter
B. wireless switch
C. wireless hub
D. router
E. None of these

106. A(n) .... language reflects the way people think mathematically.
A. cross-platform programming
B. 3GL business programming
C. event-driven programming
D. functional
E. None of these

107. When entering text within a document, the Enter key is normally pressed at the end of every—
A. Line B. Sentence
C. Paragraph D. Word
E. File

108. When a real-time telephone call between people is made over the Internet using computers, it is called—
A. a chat session
B. an e-mail
C. an instant message
D. Internet telephony
E. None of these

109. Which of the following is the first step in sizing a window?
A. Point to the title bar
B. Pull down the View menu to display the toolbar
C. Point to any corner or border
D. Pull down the View menu and change to large icons
E. None of these

110. Which of the following software could assist someone who **cannot** use their hands for computer input?
A. Video conferencing
B. Speech recognition
C. Audio digitizer
D. Synthesizer
E. None of these

111. .... a document means the file is transferred from another computer to your computer.
A. Uploading
B. Really Simple Syndication (RSS)
C. Accessing
D. Downloading
E. Upgrading

112. Which computer memory is used for storing programs and data currently being processed by the CPU?
A. Mass memory
B. Internal memory
C. Non-volatile memory
D. PROM
E. None of these

113. Computers that control processes accept data in a continuous—
A. data traffic pattern
B. data highway
C. infinite loop
D. feedback loop
E. slot

114. What refers to a set of characters of a particular design?
A. keyface　　　　B. formation
C. calligraph　　　D. stencil
E. typeface

115. .... is used by public and private enterprises to publish and share financial information with each other and industry analysts across all computer platforms and the Internet.
A. Extensible Markup Language (EML)
B. Extensible Business Reporting Language (XBRL)
C. Enterprise Application Integration (EAI)
D. Sales Force Automation (SFA) software
E. None of these

116. Which part of the computer is used for calculating and comparing?
A. ALU　　　　　B. Control unit
C. Disk unit　　　D. Modem
E. None of these

117. The method of Internet access that requires a phone line, but offers faster access speeds than dial-up is the .... connection.
A. cable access
B. satellite access
C. fibre-optic service
D. Digital Subscriber Line (DSL)
E. modem

118. .... software creats a mirror image of the entire hard disk, including the operating system, application, files and data.
A. Operating system　B. Backup software
C. Utility programs　　D. Driver imaging
E. None of these

119. What is a URL?
A. a computer software program
B. a type of programming object
C. the address of a document or "page" on the World Wide Web
D. an acronym for Unlimited Resources for Learning
E. a piece of hardware

120. What is the significance of a faded (dimmed) command in a pull-down menu?
A. The command is not currently accessible
B. A dialog box appears if the command is selected
C. A Help window appears if the command is selected

D. There are no equivalent keystrokes for the particular command
E. None of these

121. Your business has contracted with another company to have them host and run an application for your company over the Internet. The company providing this service to your business is called an —
A. Internet service provider
B. Internet access provider
C. Application service provider
D. Application access provider
E. Outsource agency

122. A(n) .... allows you to access you e-mail from anywhere.
A. Forum
B. Webmail interface
C. Message Board
D. Weblog
E. None of these

123. Which of the following would you find on LinkedIn?
A. Games
B. Connections
C. Chat
D. Applications
E. None of these

124. .... is a technique that is used to send more than one call over a single line.
A. Digital transmission
B. Infrared transmission
C. Digitizing
D. Streaming
E. Multiplexing

125. The Search Companion can —
A. Locate all files containing a specified phrase
B. Restrict its search to a specified set of folders
C. Locate all files containing a specified phrase and restrict its search to a specified set of folders
D. Cannot locate all files containing a specified phrase or restrict its search to a specified set of folders
E. None of these

126. Which of the following **cannot** be part of an e-mail address?
A. Period (.)
B. At sign (@)
C. Space ( )
D. Underscore (_)
E. None of these

127. Which of the following must be contained in a URL?
A. a protocol identifier
B. the letters, www.
C. the unique registered domain name
D. www. and the unique registered domain name
E. a protocol identifier, www. and the unique registered domain name

128. Which of the following information systems focuses on making manufacturing processes more efficient and of higher quality?
A. Computer-aided manufacturing
B. Computer-integrated manufacturing
C. Computer-aided software engineering
D. Computer-aided system engineering
E. None of these

129. A mistake in an algorithm that causes **incorrect** results is called a—
A. logical error
B. syntax error
C. procedural error
D. compiler error
E. machine error

130. Unsolicited e-mail is known as—
A. spam
B. bologna
C. RAMJAM
D. ham
E. None of these

131. To change selected text to all capital letters, click the change case button, then click ....
A. UPPERCASE
B. UPPER ALL
C. CAPS LOCK
D. Lock Upper
E. Large Size

132. A person who used his or her expertise to gain access to other people's computers to get information illegally or do damage is a ....
A. hacker
B. analyst
C. instant messenger
D. programmer
E. spammer

133. A device that connects to a network without the use of cables is said to be ....
A. distributed   B. free
C. centralized   D. open source
E. None of these

134. Reusable optical storage will typically have the acronym ....
A. CD   B. DVD
C. ROM   D. RW
E. ROS

135. The most common type of storage devices are ....
A. persistent   B. optical
C. magnetic   D. flash
E. steel

136. Codes consisting of lines of varying widths or lengths that are computer-readable are known as–
A. an ASCII code
B. a magnetic tape
C. an OCR scanner
D. a bar code
E. None of these

137. A Web site's main page is called its–
A. Home Page
B. Browser Page
C. Search Page
D. Bookmark
E. None of these

138. Part number, part description, and number of parts ordered are examples of–
A. control   B. output
C. processing   D. feedback
E. input

139. To access properties of an object, the mouse technique to use is–
A. dragging   B. dropping
C. right-clicking D. shift-clicking
E. None of these

140. Computers use the .... number system to store data and perform calculations.
A. binary   B. octal
C. decimal   D. hexadecimal
E. None of these

141. .... are attempts by individuals to obtain confidential information from you by falsifying their identity.
A. Phishing trips   B. Computer viruses
C. Spyware scams D. Viruses
E. Phishing scams

142. Why is it unethical to share copyrighted files with your friends?
A. It is not unethical, because it is legal.
B. It is unethical because the files are being given for free.
C. Sharing copyrighted files without permission breaks copyright laws.
D. It is not unethical because the files are being given for free.
E. It is not unethical—anyone can access a computer.

143. Which of the following can be used to select the entire document?
A. CTRL + A   B. ALT + F5
C. SHIFT + A   D. CTRL + K
E. CTRL + H

144. To instruct Word to fit the width of a column to the contents of a table automatically, click the .... button and then point to AutoFit Contents.
A. Fit to Form   B. Format
C. Autosize   D. Contents
E. AutoFit

145. The simultaneous processing of two or more programs by multiple processors is–
A. multiprogramming B. multitasking
C. time-sharing   D. multiprocessing
E. None of these

146. A disk's content that is recorded at the time of manufacture and that cannot be changed or erased by the user is–
A. memory-only   B. write-only
C. once-only   D. run-only
E. read-only

147. What is the permanent memory built into your computer called?
A. RAM   B. Floppy
C. CPU   D. CD-ROM
E. ROM

148. The default view in Excel is .... view.
- A. Work
- B. Auto
- C. Normal
- D. Roman
- E. None of these

149. What displays the contents of the active cell in Excel?
- A. Namebox
- B. RowHeadings
- C. Formulabar
- D. Taskpane
- E. None of these

150. In Word you can force a page break–
- A. By positioning your cursor at the appropriate place and pressing the F1 key
- B. By positioning your cursor at the appropriate place and pressing Ctrl+Enter
- C. By using the Insert/Section Break
- D. By changing the font size of your document
- E. None of these

151. Grouping and processing all of a firm's transactions at one time is called–
- A. a database management system
- B. batch processing
- C. a real-time system
- D. an on-line system
- E. None of these

152. Help Menu is available at which button?
- A. End
- B. Start
- C. Turn off
- D. Restart
- E. Reboot

153. You can keep your personal files/folders in–
- A. My Folder
- B. My Documents
- C. My Files
- D. My Text
- E. None of these

154. A central computer that holds collections of data and programs for many PCs, work-stations, and other computers is a(n) –
- A. supercomputer
- B. minicomputer
- C. laptop
- D. server
- E. None of these

155. When you save to this, your data will remain intact even when the computer is turned off–
- A. RAM
- B. motherboard
- C. secondary storage device
- D. primary storage device
- E. None of these

156. The .... folder retains copies of messages that you have started but are not yet ready to send.
- A. Drafts
- B. Outbox
- C. Address Book
- D. Sent Items
- E. Inbox

157. You can..........a search by providing more information the search engine can use to select a smaller, more useful set of results.
- A. refine
- B. expand
- C. load
- D. query
- E. slowdown

158. The contents of .... are lost when the computer turns off.
- A. storage
- B. input
- C. output
- D. memory
- E. None of these

159. The .... enables you to simultaneously keep multiple Web pages open in one browser window.
- A. tab box
- B. pop-up helper
- C. tab row
- D. address bar
- E. Esc key

160. A DVD is an example of a(n) –
- A. hard disk
- B. optical disc
- C. output device
- D. solid-state storage device
- E. None of these

161. The basic unit of a worksheet into which you enter data in Excel is called a ....
- A. tab
- B. cell
- C. box
- D. range
- E. None of these

162. .... is the process of dividing the disk into tracks and sectors.
- A. Tracking
- B. Formatting
- C. Crashing
- D. Allotting
- E. None of these

163. Which ports connect special types of music instruments to sound cards?
A. BUS   B. CPU
C. USB   D. MIDI
E. MINI

164. The process of transferring files from a computer on the Internet to your computer is called ....
A. downloading   B. uploading
C. FTP   D. JPEG
E. downsizing

165. In Excel, ... allows users to bring together copies of work books that other users have worked on independently.
A. Copying   B. Merging
C. Pasting   D. Compiling
E. None of these

166. If you want to connect to your own computer through the Internet from another location, you can use–
A. e-mail   B. FTP
C. instant message   D. Telnet
E. None of these

167. To reload a Web page, press the .... button.
A. Redo   B. Reload
C. Restore   D. Ctrl
E. Refresh

168. Mobile Commerce is best described as–
A. The use of Kiosks in marketing
B. Transporting products
C. Buying and selling goods/services through wireless handheld devices
D. Using notebook PC's in marketing
E. None of the above

169. Video processors consist of .... and .... , which store and process images.
A. CPU and VGA   B. CPU and memory
C. VGA and memory D. VGI and DVI
E. None of these

170. .... are words that a programming language has set aside for its own use.
A. Control words   B. Control structures
C. Reserved words   D. Reserved keys
E. None of these

171. What is the process of copying software programs from secondary storage media to the hard disk called?
A. configuration   B. download
C. storage   D. upload
E. installation

172. This first step in the transaction processing cycle captures business data through various modes such as optical scanning or at an electronic commerce website–
A. Document and report generation
B. Database maintenance
C. Transaction processing start-up
D. Data Entry
E. None of these

173. When the pointer is positioned on a ...., it is shaped like a hand.
A. Grammar error   B. Formatting error
C. ScreenTip   D. Spelling error
E. Hyperlink

174. The computer abbreviation KB usually means–
A. Key Block   B. Kernel Boot
C. Key Byte   D. Kit Bit
E. Kilo Byte

175. Which of the following are advantages of CD-ROM as a storage media?
A. CD-ROM is an inexpensive way to store large amount of data and information
B. CD-ROM disks retrieve data and information more quickly than magnetic disks do
C. CD-ROMs make less errors than magnetic media
D. All of the above
E. None of the above

176. A(n) ....is a special visual and audio effect applied in PowerPoint to text or content.
A. animation   B. flash
C. wipe   D. dissolve
E. None of these

177. Which of the following is a storage device that uses rigid, permanently installed magnetic disks to store data/information–
A. floppy diskette   B. hard disk

C. permanent disk   D. optical disk
E. None of these

178. The piece of hardware that converts your computer's digital signal to an analog signal that can travel over telephone lines is called a–
A. red wire   B. blue cord
C. tower   D. modem
E. None of these

179. Personal computers can be connected together to form a–
A. server   B. supercomputer
C. network   D. enterprise
E. None of these

180. A .... is the term used when a search engine returns a Web page that matches the search criteria.
A. blog   B. hit
C. link   D. view
E. success

181. What type of resource is most likely to be a shared common resource in a computer network?
A. Printers
B. Speakers
C. Floppy disk drives
D. Keyboards
E. None of these

182. Example of non-numeric data is ....
A. Employee address B. Examination score
C. Bank balance   D. All of these
E. None of these

183. ....represents raw facts, whereas .... is data made meaningful.
A. Information, reporting
B. Data, information
C. Information, bits
D. Records, bytes
E. Bits, bytes

184. A word in a web page that, when clicked, opens another document ....
A. Anchor   B. URL
C. Hyperlink   D. Reference
E. None of these

185. A computer cannot "boot" if it does not have the ....
A. Compiler   B. Loader
C. Operating System D. Assembler
E. None of these

186. What characteristic of read-only memory (ROM) makes it useful?
A. ROM information can be easily updated
B. Data in ROM is nonvolatile, that is, it remains there even without electrical power
C. ROM provides very large amounts of inexpensive data storage
D. ROM chips are easily swapped between different brands of computers
E. None of these

187. Which of the following refers to a small, single-site network?
A. LAN   B. DSL
C. RAM   D. USB
E. CPU

188. Which keystroke will take you at the beginning or the end of a long document?
A. Ctrl + PageUp and Ctrl + PageDown
B. Shift + Home and Shift + End
C. Ctrl + Home and Ctrl + End
D. The only way is by using the right scroll bar
E. None of these

189. Coded entries which are used to gain access to a computer system are called ....
A. Entry codes   B. Passwords
C. Security commands   D. Code words
E. None of these

190. In Word you can force a page break ....
A. By positioning your cursor at the appropriate place and pressing the F1 key
B. By using the Insert/Section Break
C. By positioning your cursor at the appropriate place and pressing Ctrl+Enter
D. By changing the font size of your document
E. None of these

ANSWERS

1 B	**2** A	**3** D	**4** A	**5** D	**6** A	**7** C	**8** C	**9** A	**10** A
11 E	**12** D	**13** D	**14** E	**15** B	**16** B	**17** A	**18** E	**19** C	**20** B
21 C	**22** D	**23** A	**24** E	**25** C	**26** E	**27** D	**28** B	**29** A	**30** C
31 C	**32** A	**33** D	**34** C	**35** C	**36** D	**37** E	**38** B	**39** C	**40** E
41 A	**42** D	**43** A	**44** D	**45** A	**46** C	**47** E	**48** B	**49** C	**50** C
51 A	**52** D	**53** B	**54** D	**55** B	**56** D	**57** E	**58** B	**59** A	**60** B
61 D	**62** A	**63** A	**64** D	**65** B	**66** B	**67** A	**68** D	**69** C	**70** A
71 C	**72** B	**73** B	**74** D	**75** D	**76** C	**77** B	**78** A	**79** C	**80** B
81 C	**82** E	**83** C	**84** A	**85** B	**86** C	**87** A	**88** C	**89** E	**90** A
91 E	**92** C	**93** E	**94** E	**95** A	**96** D	**97** E	**98** B	**99** E	**100** A
101 E	**102** A	**103** B	**104** D	**105** A	**106** D	**107** C	**108** D	**109** C	**110** B
111 D	**112** B	**113** D	**114** E	**115** B	**116** A	**117** D	**118** B	**119** C	**120** A
121 E	**122** B	**123** B	**124** E	**125** C	**126** C	**127** C	**128** B	**129** A	**130** A
131 A	**132** A	**133** E	**134** B	**135** C	**136** D	**137** A	**138** E	**139** C	**140** A
141 A	**142** C	**143** A	**144** A	**145** D	**146** E	**147** E	**148** C	**149** C	**150** B
151 C	**152** B	**153** B	**154** D	**155** D	**156** A	**157** A	**158** B	**159** C	**160** B
161 B	**162** B	**163** C	**164** A	**165** B	**166** D	**167** E	**168** C	**169** C	**170** C
171 E	**172** D	**173** C	**174** E	**175** D	**176** A	**177** B	**178** D	**179** C	**180** C
181 A	**182** A	**183** B	**184** C	**185** C	**186** B	**187** A	**188** A	**189** B	**190** C

● ● ●

TRADE TEST

- *Electrician*
- *Electronics*
- *Pump Mechanic*
- *Diesel Mechanic*
- *Refrigeration & Airconditioning*
- *Fitter*
- *Welding*
- *Plumbing*
- *Forger/Heat Treatment/Blacksmith*

1

ELECTRICIAN/ELECTRONICS

Coulomb's law : According to this law, the force of attraction or repulsion between two points charges is directly proportional to the product of the two charges and inversely proportional to the square of the distance between them.

$$F = \frac{1}{4\pi\varepsilon_0} \cdot \frac{q_1 q_2}{r^2}$$

where

$$\frac{1}{4\pi\varepsilon_0} = 9 \times 10^9 \text{ Nm}^2/\text{C}^2.$$

One Coulomb : One coulomb is that charge which when placed at a distance of 1m from an identical charge, in free space, repels it with a force of 9×10^9 N.

Electric field : It is the region or space around a charged body within which it exerts a force on another charged body.

$$E(r) = \frac{F}{q}$$

Electric lines of force : It may be defined as the path along which a small positive charge would tend to move when free to do so in an electric field and the tangent to which at any point gives the direction of the electric field at that point.

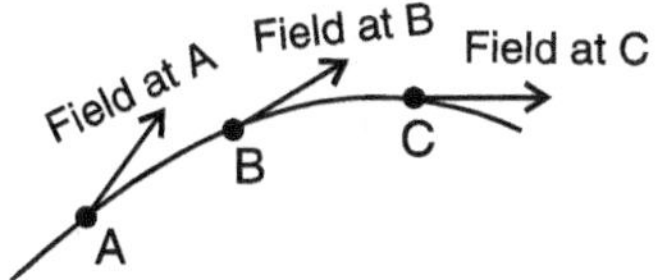

Electric dipole : It is a pair of equal and opposite point charges separated by a small distance. The strength of an electric dipole is called its dipole moment.

Electrostatic potential : The electric potential at any point in an electric field is defined as the amount of work done in bringing a unit positive charge from infinity to that point against the electric field.

Potential difference : The potential difference between two points in an electric field is defined as the amount of work done in bringing a unit positive charge from one point to the other against the electric field.

$$\phi(r_B) - \phi(r_A) = -\int_A^B E(r).dl$$

Volt : The potential difference between two points in an electric field is said to be one volt if one joule of work has to be done in bringing a positive charge of one coulomb from one point to another against the electric field.

Relation between electric field and electric potential : If E be the electric field and V be the electric potential then

$$E = -\frac{dV}{dr}$$

Equipotential Surface : The surface which has same electric potential at every point is called an equipotential surface. It can be drawn throughout the region in which an electric field exists.

Capacitance (C) : It may be defined as the charge required to raise the potential of the conductor by unit amount.

$$C = \frac{Q}{V} = \frac{\text{Charge}}{\text{Voltage}}$$

Symbol of capacitor :

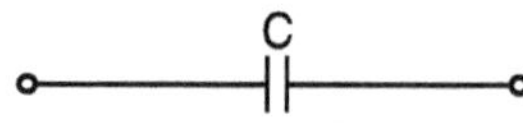

Symbol of variable capacitor:

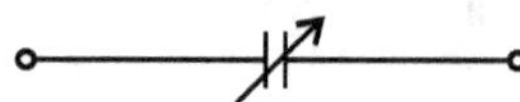

Its S.I. unit is Farad (F).

Dimensions of capacitance $= [M^{-1}L^{-2}T^4A^2]$

Farad : The capacitance of a conductor is one farad (F) if on the addition of a charge of 1 coulomb to it, its potential difference increases by 1 volt.

Static electricity : It deals with the electric charges at rest.

Current electricity : It deals with the charges in motion.

Electric current : It is defined as the flow of electric charges through a conductor.

$$I = \frac{q}{t}$$

S.I. unit of current is ampere (A).

Ohm's law : It states that the current flowing through a conductor is directly proportional to the potential difference across its ends, provided the temperature and the other physical conditions remain unchanged.

$$I \propto V$$
$$\Rightarrow V = IR$$

where R is the constant of proportionality called the resistance of the conductor.

Ohmic conductors : These are the conductors which obey ohm's law.

V–I graph is a straight line passing through the origin.

Ex : A pure metal, an electrolyte like $CuSO_4$ sol. etc.

Non-ohmic conductors : These are the conductors which do not obey ohm's law.

V–I graph is a straight line not passing through the origin.

Ex : P-N-junction, Thermistor, water voltameter etc.

Resistance (R) : It is the property of a conductor by virtue of which it opposes the flow of current

through it.

Numerically, it is equal to the ratio of the potential difference applied across the conductor to the current flowing through it, *i.e.*

$$R = \frac{V}{I}$$

Symbol of resistor :

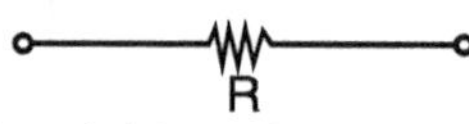

Symbol of variable resistor :

S.I. unit of resistance is ohm (Ω).

Ohm (Ω) : The resistance of a conductor is said to be 1 ohm, if a current of 1 ampere flows through it on applying a potential difference of 1 volt.

Series connection of resistance : If a number of resistances are connected end to end so that the same current flows through each of them in succession, then they are said to connected in series.

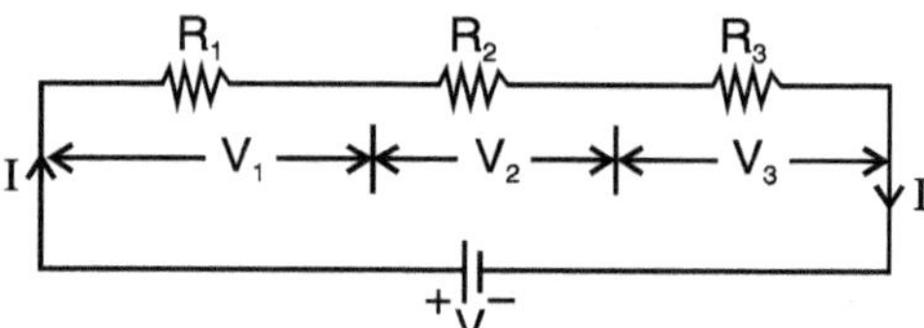

$$R_s = R_1 + R_2 + R_3$$
$$I = I_1 + I_2 + I_3 \text{ (same)}$$
$$V_s = V_1 + V_2 + V_3$$
(Different in each resistor)

Parallel connection of resistance : If a number of resistances are connected in between two common points so that each of them provides a separate path for current, then they are said to be connected in parallel.

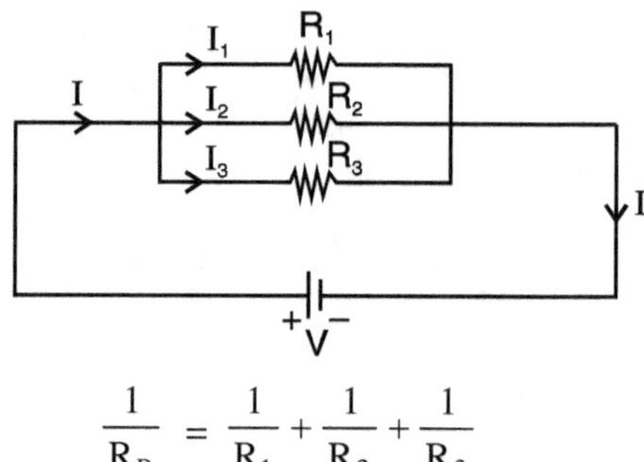

$$\frac{1}{R_P} = \frac{1}{R_1} + \frac{1}{R_2} + \frac{1}{R_3}$$

$$V = V_1 = V_2 = V_3 \text{ (same)}$$
$$I_1 = I_1 + I_2 + I_3$$

(Different in each resistor)

Factors affecting the resistance of a conductor: At a constant temperature, the resistance of a conductor depends on the following factors :

(a) length of the conductor

$$R \propto l \qquad \qquad ...(i)$$

(b) cross-sectional area of the conductor

$$R \propto \frac{1}{A} \qquad \qquad ...(ii)$$

From equations *(i)* & *(ii)*

$$R \propto \frac{l}{A}$$

$$\Rightarrow R = \rho\frac{l}{A} \qquad \qquad ...(iii)$$

where ρ be the constant of proportionality called as specific resistance or resistivity of a conductor.

Specific resistance or resistivity of a conductor (ρ) : It is numerically equal to the resistance offered by a unit cube of the material.

S.I. unit of specific resistance is ohm-metre. Resistivity increases with rise of temperature, for conductor. Mathematically,

$$\sigma = \sigma_0 (1 + \alpha\theta)$$

where σ and σ_0 indicates resistivity at $\theta°C$ and $0°C$ respectively.

Kirchhoff's laws for an electric network :

(i) **Law of current :** At any branch point in a network, the algebric sum of currents is zero.

In other words, the sum of currents flowing towards the junction is equal to the sum of currents moving away from the junction.

$$I_1 + I_2 + I_3 = I_4 + I_5.$$

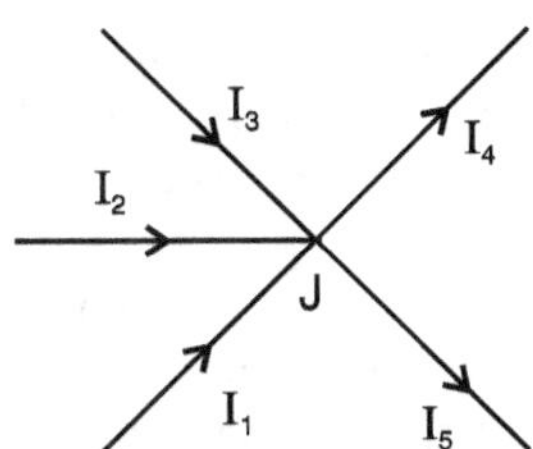

The currents flowing towards the junction are taken as positive and currents flowing away from the

junction are taken as negative, *i.e.*

$$I_1 + I_2 + I_3 - I_4 - I_5 = 0.$$

(ii) **Law of voltages :** The algebric sum of the e.m.f.'s in any closed loop in a network is equal to algebric sum of IR products in the closed loop. The plus and minus sign before product IR and e.m.f. E is put according to the following rules.

- The product IR is positive if current is in same direction as the direction of traversal of loop.
- The e.m.f. E is positive if it would, on its own send current is same direction as the direction of traversal.

In loop ABEFA,

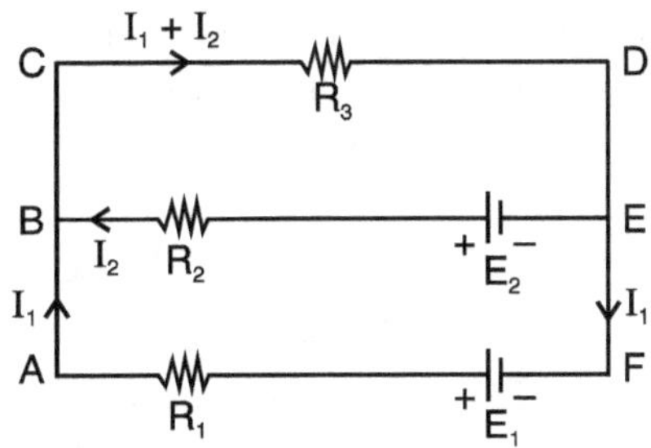

$$E_1 - E_2 = I_1R_1 - I_2R_2 \qquad ...(i)$$

In loop BCDEB,

$$E_2 = I_2R_1 + (I_1 + I_2)\, R_3 \qquad ...(ii)$$

In loop ACDFA,

$$E_1 = I_1R_1 + (I_1 + I_2)R_3 \qquad ...(iii)$$

from equations *(ii)* and *(iii)*, we conclude that equ. *(i)* is also true.

Electric power (P) : It is defined as the product of voltage and current, *i.e.*,

$$P = VI$$
$$= I^2R \qquad \qquad [\because V = IR]$$

S.I. unit of power is watt (W).

The bigger unit of power is Horse Power (H.P.).

$$1 \text{ H.P.} = 746 \text{ Watts}$$
$$1 \text{ kWh} = 3.34 \text{ H.P.}$$
$$1 \text{ Metric H.P.} = 735.5 \text{ Watts.}$$

B.H.P. : B.H.P. is that power which is in machine output to run the load.

Electric energy (E) : It is defined as the rate of doing work.

$$\text{Energy} = \text{Power} \times \text{Time}$$
$$E = P \times t$$
$$= VIt$$

$$= I^2 R t$$

$$= \frac{V^2}{R} t \text{ Joule} = \frac{V^2 t}{4.18 \, R} \text{ Calorie}$$

S.I. unit of energy is Joule (J).

The commercial unit of energy is Board of Trade (B.O.T.) or kWh.

$$1 \text{ kWh} = 3.6 \times 10^6 \text{ Joules}.$$

Earthing : We know that the voltage value of earth is zero. If the body of machine is connected to earth then its voltage is reduced to zero. This process is called earthing.

The maximum resistance of earth line in wiring must be nearly equal to 1Ω.

Joule's law of heating : According to this law, heat H is produced in a conductor having resistance R and carrying a current I is

$$H = I^2 R t$$

where 't' is the time for which current passes.

Faraday's law of electrolysis :

(a) **Ist law :** The mass of an element or radical deposited or liberated at an electrode is directly proportional to the quantity of charge passing through the electrolyte.

Mathematically,

$$m = ZIt,$$

where m is the mass deposited or liberated when a current I passes for time t second. Z is a constant for an element or radical and is known as the electrochemical equivalent.

(b) **IInd law :** When same quantity of charge passes through solutions of different electrolytes, the mass of elements or radicals liberated at electrodes are in the ratio of their chemical weights.

Mathematically,

$$\frac{m_1}{m_2} = \frac{E_1}{E_2}$$

where m_1 and m_2 indicate the mass liberated of three different elements. E_1 and E_2 indicates their respective equivalent weights.

Cell : A device which converts chemical energy into electrical energy is called an electrochemical cell.

Difference between a primary cell and a secondary cell : In a primary cell, when all its constituents are put together an e.m.f. is produced. In a secondary cell, there is no e.m.f. produced when all its constituents are put together. A secondary cell has to be charged first. It produces an e.m.f. during discharge. The internal resistance of secondary cell is quite small as compared to that of a primary cell.

Primary cells → Voltaic cell, Dry cell, Leclanche cell, Daniel cell, Mercury cell etc.

Secondary cells → Lead acid storage cell, Edison cell, Ni-Cd cell etc.

Fuel cells → Hydrogen-Oxygen fuel cell.

Ampere's Swimming Rule : This rule predicts the direction of deflection of the magnetic needle in the Oersted's experiment and can be stated as follows:

Imagine a man swimming along the wire in the direction of the flow of the current with his face always turned towards the magnetic needle, then the north pole of the needle will get deflected towards his left hand.

Magnetic field : The space around a magnet within which its influence can be experienced is called its magnetic field.

Uniform magnetic field : A uniform magnetic field is that in which the strength of the magnetic field is the same at all points of the field.

In this field, all the lines of force are parallel to one another.

Direction of magnetic field :

(A) Right Hand/Grip Rule : Grasp the conductor in the right hand so that the thumb points in the direction of the current, then the magnetic field will be in the direction of the curl of the fingers.

(B) Maxwell's Cork Screw Rule : If a right handed screw be rotated along the wire so that it advances in the direction of current, then the direction in which the thumb rotates gives the direction of the magnetic field.

Tesla : It is the S.I. unit of magnetic field. One Tesla is 10^7 times the magnetic field produced by a conducting wire of length one metre and carrying current of one ampere at a distance of one metre from it and perpendicular to it.

Comparison between magnetic and electric fields :

(A) Similar Points :

(i) Both the fields are of long range.

(ii) Both the fields obey inverse square law.

(B) Dissimilar Points :

(i) The two fields have quite different directions. The electric field of a point charge is radial, while the magnetic field due to a current element is perpendicular to both the current element and the position vector of the observation point.

(ii) The source of magnetic field is not a magnetic charge, whereas the source of electric field is an electric charge which is a scalar.

Fleming's Left Hand Rule : Stretch the thumb and the first two fingers of the left hand so that they are at right angles to each other. If the forefinger points in the direction of the field, central finger in the direction of the current, then the thumb gives the direction of the thrust/force on the charged particle.

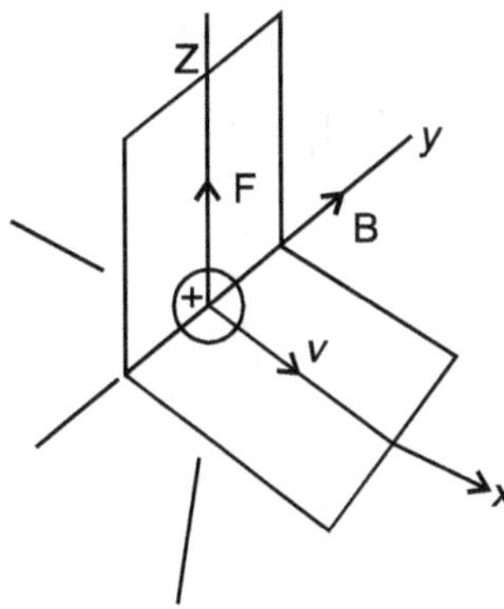

Right Hand Palm Rule : Open the right hand and place it so that tips of the fingers point in the direction of the magnetic field and thumb in the direction of the velocity of the charge, then the palm faces towards the force F.

Lorentz Force : It is defined as the total force experienced by a charged particle moving in a region where both electric and magnetic fields are present.

Mathematically,

$$\vec{F} = q\left[\vec{E} + \left(v \times \vec{B}\right)\right]$$

where electric force, $\vec{F}_E = q\vec{E}$ and

magnetic force, $\vec{F}_M = q\left(v \times \vec{B}\right)$.

Ampere's Circuital Law : It states that the line integral of the magnetic field B around any closed circuit is equal to the μ_o (permeability constant) times the net current I threading (or passing through) this closed circuit.

Mathematically,

$$\oint B.dl = \mu_o I$$

Toroid : A toroid (or toroidal solenoid) is a torus (anchor ring) around which a large number of turns of a current carrying wire are wrapped.

M.F. for toroid, $B = \mu_o nI$

where n is the number of turns per unit length of the solenoid.

Solenoid : If we imagine the radius of a toroid becoming larger and larger, then any small portion of it can be considered a straight solenoid. In other words, it is a long wire closely wound in the form of a helix. Its length is very large as compared to its diameter.

Galvanometer : It is device used to measure electric current. It is a sensitive current detector. The commonly used moving coil galvanometer has been named so because it uses a current loop (or coil) that rotates (moves) in a magnetic field, as a result of the torque on it.

Voltmeter : It is a device for measuring potential difference across any two points in a circuit.

It is a high resistance galvanometer.

- Conversion of a galvanometer into a voltmeter:

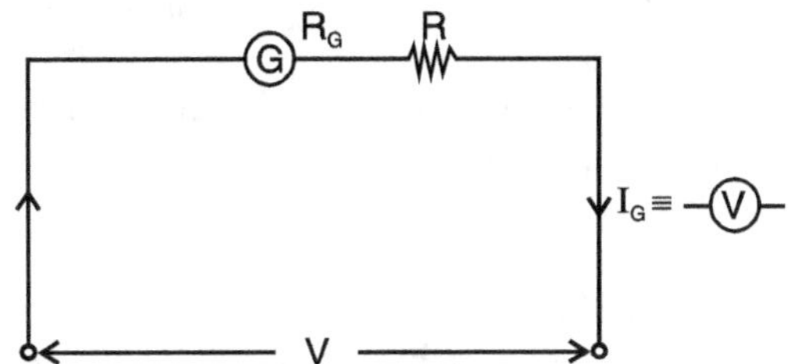

A galvanometer can be converted into a voltmeter of given range by connecting a high resistance in series with the galvanometer.

$$R = \frac{V}{I_G} - R_G$$

- An ideal voltmeter should have infinite resistance.

Ammeter : It is a device for measuring current in a circuit. It is a low resistance galvanometer.

- Conversion of a galvanometer into an ammeter: A galvanometer can be converted into an ammeter of given range by connecting a small resistance (called shunt) in parallel with the galvanometer.

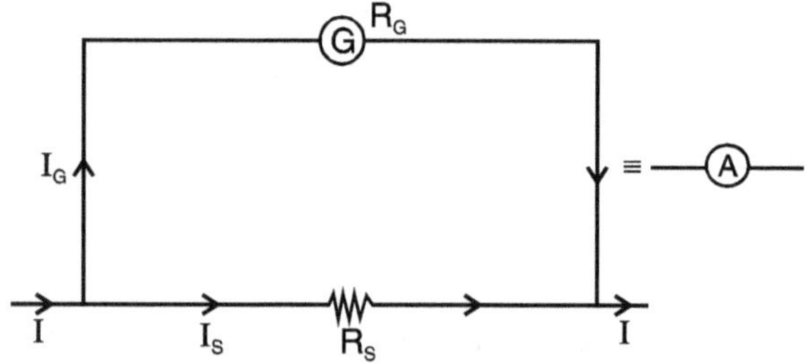

- An ideal ammeter should have zero resistance.

Magnets and magnetism : Magnets are the substances which have the property of attracting small pieces of iron, nickel, cobalt etc. and this property of attraction is called magnetism. Natural magnets (called loadstones) were found as early as the sixth century B.C. in the province of Magnesia in ancient Greece, from which the word magnetism derives its name.

Properties of magnets :

(i) A magnet attracts small pieces of iron, nickel, cobalt, etc.

(ii) A freely suspended magnet aligns itself nearly in the geographical north-south direction.

(iii) Like magnetic poles repel, and unlike magnetic poles attract.

(iv) Isolated magnetic poles do not exist. If we break a magnet into two pieces, we get two smaller dipole magnets.

Artificial Magnets : Pieces of iron and other magnetic materials can be made to acquire the properties of natural magnets. Such magnets are called artificial magnets. Their different forms are bar magnet : magnetic needle, ball ended magnet and horseshoe magnet.

Conditions for permanent magnets : The material used should have —

(i) high residual magnetism so that they may exert high forces of attraction.

(ii) high coercivity so that the residual magnetism may last long and is not destroyed by stray magnetic fields.

Conditions for electromagnets : The material used should have —

(i) large magnetisation even for small magnetising field, *i.e.*, high permeability.

(ii) low hysteresis loss as the material is to be subjected continuously to cycles of magnetisation.

Magnetic flux (ϕ_B) : The magnetic flux through a given area may be defined as the total number of magnetic lines of force passing normally through this area.

It is equal to the product of the normal components of the magnetic field $\vec{B}$ and the area over which it is uniform.

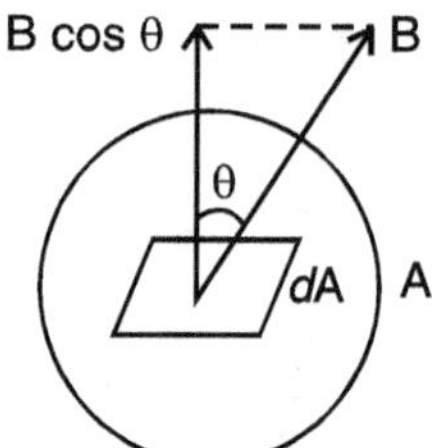

$$d\phi_B = B\cos.\theta\,dA$$

$$= \vec{B}.dA$$

The net flux through the entire area A is the sum of the contributions from all such area elements and is given as

$$\phi_B = \int_A B.dA$$

Weber : It is the unit of magnetic flux. If a magnetic field of 1 tesla passes normally through a surface of area 1 square metre, then the magnetic flux linked with this surface is said to be 1 weber.

Gauss's theorem (in magnetism) : It states that "The surface integral of a magnetic field over a closed surface is always zero."

$$\oint_s \vec{B}.\vec{ds} = 0.$$

Classification of magnetic materials : On the basis of their behaviour in external magnetic fields, Faraday classified the various materials into three categories:

(i) **Diamagnetic substances** → These are the substances which are feebly repelled by magnets and tend to move from stronger to weaker parts of a magnetic field.

Examples : Gold, water, tin, lead, copper, zinc, bismith and sodium chloride.

(ii) **Paramagnetic substaces** → These are the substances which are feebly attracted by magnets and tend to move from weaker to stronger parts of a magnetic field.

Examples : Oxygen, manganese, sodium, copper chloride, aluminuim, chromium and platinum.

(iii) **Ferromagnetic substances** → These are the substances which are strongly attracted by magnets and tend to move from weaker to stronger parts of a magnetic field.

Examples : Iron, nickel, cobalt, godolinium and alloys like alnico.

Hysteresis : The phenomenon of lagging of intensity of magnetisation (I) or magnetic induction (B) behind magnetic intensity (H) when a specimen of a magnetic material is subjected to a cycle of magnetisation is called hysteresis.

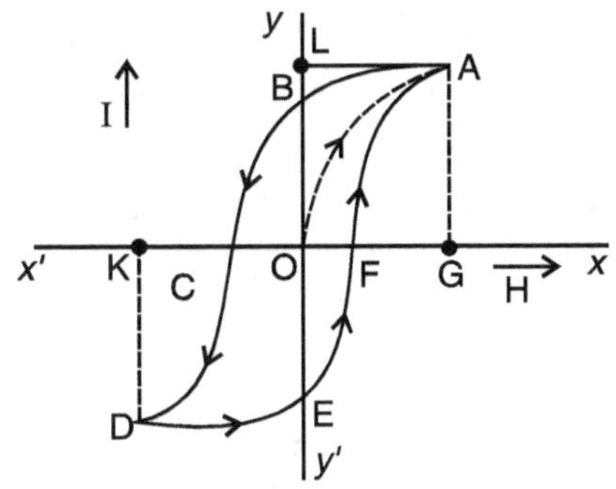

(i) **Residual magnetism :** The value of the intensity of magnetisation of a material, when the magnetising field is reduced to zero is called Retentivity or residual magnetism.

In figure, OB indicates the retentivity.

(ii) **Coercivity :** The value of the reverse magnetising field intensity required for the residual magnetism of a sample to become zero is called coercivity of the sample.

Electromagnetic Induction : It is the phenomenon of generating current or e.m.f. by changing the number of magnetic lines of force associated with the conductor. The e.m.f. so developed is called an induced e.m.f. of the conductor is in the form of a closed circuit, a current flows in the circuit which is known as induced current.

Laws of electromagnetic induction :

1. Faraday's laws (gives the magnitude of the induced e.m.f.) : Faraday's first law : Whenever the amount of magnetic flux linked with a circuit changes, an e.m.f. is induced in the circuit. This induced e.m.f. lasts so long as the change in magnetic flux continues.

Faraday's second law : The magnitude of e.m.f. induced in a circuit is directly proportional to the rate of change of magnetic flux linked with the circuit, *i.e.,*

$$\varepsilon = \frac{\phi_2 - \phi_1}{t}$$

$$\Rightarrow \quad \varepsilon = \frac{d\phi}{dt}$$

2. Lenz's Law (gives the direction of the induced e.m.f.) : This law states that "the direction of induced e.m.f. in a circuit is always such as to oppose the change in magnetic flux responsible for it."

Eddy currents : These are the currents induced in the body of a conductor when the amount of magnetic flux linked with the conductor changes. These currents are also called Focault currents.

The magnitude of eddy current is given as

$$i = -\frac{\varepsilon}{R} = \frac{(d\phi/dt)}{R}$$

where R is the resistance of the conductor. The direction of eddy currents is given by Fleming's right hand rule or Lenz's law.

Laminated cores are used to minimise these currents.

Important applications of eddy currents are electromagnetic damping, electromagnetic brakes, speedometers, induction motor and induction furnace etc.

Self Induction : It is the property of an electrical circuit by virtue of which the circuit opposes any change in the strength of current flowing through it by inducing an e.m.f. in itself.

$$L = \frac{\phi_B}{I}$$

where L is the self-inductance of the coil, ϕ_B is the amount of magnetic flux linked with the coil and I, the current flows through the coil.

Self-inductance of a long solenoid is given as

$$L = \frac{\mu_o N^2 A}{l}$$

where l is the length of the solenoid, N is the total number of turns of solenoid and A is the cross-sectional area of the solenoid.

S.I. unit of self-inductance is Henry (H).

Mutual Induction : It is the property of two coils by virtue of which each opposes any change in the strength of current flowing through the other by developing an induced e.m.f.

$$M = \frac{\phi_B}{I}$$

where M is the mutual inductance of two coils, ϕ_B is the amount of magnetic flux linked with one coil when a current I flows through the other coil. Mutual inductance of two long co-axial solenoids, each of length l, cross-sectional area A, wound on an air core is given as

$$M = \frac{\mu_o N_1 N_2 A}{l}$$

where N_1 and N_2 are total number of turns of the two solenoids.

Transformer : It is a device used for converting a low alternating voltage at high current into a high alternating voltage at low current and vice-versa.

It works on the principle of mutual induction between the coils, *i.e.*, when a changing current is passed in one coil, an induced e.m.f. is set up in the another coil.

Classification of transformer :

1. On the basis of voltage :

(a) Step-up transformer

(b) Step-down transformer

2. On the basis of core :

(a) Transformers having rectangular core

(b) Transformers having shell core

(c) Transformers having berry core

3. On the basis of phase :

(a) Single-phase transformer

(b) Three-phase transformer

4. On the basis of output :

(a) Auto transformer

(b) Instrument transformer

1. Step-up transformer : If transformer increases the input voltage, it is called step-up transformer.

In this transformer, number of turns in secondary coil is greater than as compared to that in primary coils.

$$\therefore \quad N_S > N_P$$
$$\Rightarrow \quad \varepsilon_S > \varepsilon_P$$
$$\text{or} \quad K > 1$$
$$\therefore \quad I_P > I_S$$

$$\left[\because \frac{E_S}{E_P} = \frac{\varepsilon_S}{\varepsilon_P} = \frac{N_S}{N_P} = K \right.$$
$$\left. \text{where K is the turns ratio of transformer.} \right]$$

2. Step-down transformer : If transformer decreases the input voltage, it is called step-down transformer. In this transformer, number of turns in secondary coil is smaller than as compared to that in primary coils.

$$\therefore \quad N_S < N_P$$
$$\Rightarrow \quad \varepsilon_S < \varepsilon_P$$
$$\text{or} \quad K < 1$$
$$\therefore \quad I_P < I_S$$

$$\left[\because \frac{E_S}{E_P} = \frac{\varepsilon_S}{\varepsilon_P} = \frac{N_S}{N_P} = K \right.$$
$$\left. \text{where K is the rurns ratio of transformer.} \right]$$

Efficiency of tranformer is defined as

$$\eta = \frac{\text{Output power}}{\text{Input power}} \times 100$$

Energy losses in transformers : In ideal transformer,

Output power = Input power

But in actual transformer,

Output power < Input power, because of unavoidable energy losses. These losses are

(i) Copper loss

(ii) Iron loss

(iii) Magnetic flux leakage

(iv) Humming loss

(v) Hysteresis loss

Uses of transformers :

(i) Transformers are used in voltage regulators for refrigerator, computer, television etc.

(ii) A step-down transformer is used for welding purposes.

(iii) In long distance transmission of electrical power.

Alternating current : Alternating current is that current which varies in magnitude continuously and reverses its direction periodically.

$$I = I_0 \sin \omega t$$

where I is the instantaneous value of current at any instant t and I_o is the maximum value (or peak value) of current.

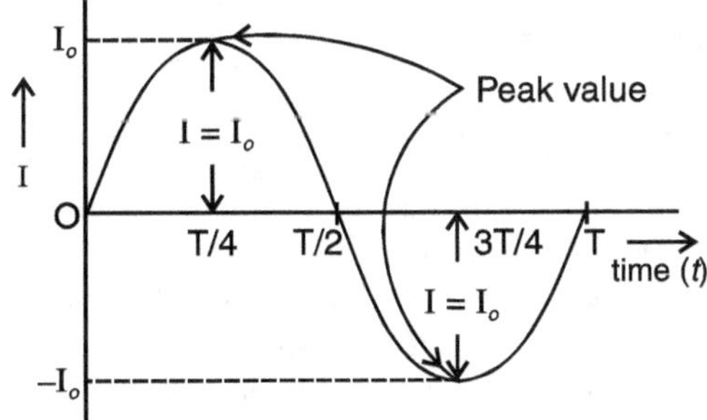

Advantages of alternating current over direct current :

(i) A.C. can be transmitted over long distances using step-up transformer and loss of energy in process is negligible.

(ii) A.C. can be easily converted into *d.c.* by means of rectifier.

(iii) The generation of *a.c.* is less expensive.

Disadvantages of alternating current over direct current :

(i) It cannot be used in a number of electrolytic processes (like electro-typing, electro-plating etc.)

(ii) The peak value of *a.c.* is much higher ($\sqrt{2}$ times the r.m.s. value) and so it is more dangerous to use and needs better insulation.

Time period (T) : It is defined as the time taken to complete one cycle.

Frequency (*f*) : It is defined as the number of cycles completed per second.

$$f = 1/T \text{ Hertz}$$

Average value of *a.c.* : It is that steady current which sends the same charge in a circuit in the same time as is sent by the *a.c.* in the same circuit in its half-time period.

$$I_{ave} = \frac{2I_o}{\pi} = 63.7\% \text{ of } I_o$$

where I_o is the peak value of current.

Virtual value of *a.c.* : The virtual value of current is that value of *d.c.* current which will produce same heat in a resistance in a given time as is being done by the actual *a.c.*

$$I_{vir} = \frac{I_o}{\sqrt{2}} = 70.7\% \text{ of } I_o$$

where, I_o is the peak value of current.

Energy associated with

(a) a pure inductor $\quad = \quad 0$

(b) a pure capacitor $\quad = \quad 0$

(c) a pure resistor $\quad = \quad E_{rms} I_{rms}$

LR – Circuit :

(a) Impedance, $\quad Z = \sqrt{R^2 + X_L^2}$

$$= \sqrt{R^2 + \omega^2 L^2}$$

(b) Phase angle, $\quad \phi = \tan^{-1}\left(\frac{\omega L}{R}\right)$

(c) Power, $\quad P = \dfrac{E^2_{rms} . R}{\left(R^2 + \omega^2 L^2\right)}$

CR - Circuit :

(a) Impendance, $\quad Z = \sqrt{R^2 + X_C^2}$

$$= \sqrt{R^2 + \frac{1}{\omega^2 C^2}}$$

(b) Phase angle, $\quad \phi = \tan^{-1}\left(\frac{1}{\omega CR}\right)$

(c) Power, $\quad P = \dfrac{E^2_{rms} . R}{\left(R^2 + \dfrac{1}{\omega^2 C^2}\right)}$

LCR-circuit :

(a) Impedance, $\quad Z = \sqrt{R^2 + (X_L - X_C)^2}$

$$= \sqrt{R^2 + \left(\omega L - \dfrac{1}{\omega C}\right)^2}$$

(b) Phase angle, $\quad \phi = \tan^{-1}\left(\dfrac{\omega L - \dfrac{1}{\omega C}}{R}\right)$

(i) When $\omega L > \dfrac{1}{\omega C}$, ϕ is positive so that current lags behind the applied voltage.

(ii) When $\omega L < \dfrac{1}{\omega C}$, ϕ is negative so that current leads the applied voltage.

(iii) When $\omega L = \dfrac{1}{\omega C}$, ϕ is zero, and the current is in phase with the applied voltage.

Thus, $\qquad \omega L = \dfrac{1}{\omega C}$

$\Rightarrow \qquad \omega = \dfrac{1}{\sqrt{LC}}$

or $\qquad f = \dfrac{1}{2\pi\sqrt{LC}}$

Thus, at resonance,

$Z_{min} = R$, $\quad I_{max} = \dfrac{E_{rms}}{R}$ and power dissipation is maximum.

(c) $\qquad$ Power, $P = \dfrac{E^2_{rms}.R}{\left[R^2 + \left(\omega L - \dfrac{1}{\omega C}\right)^2\right]}$

Reactance : It is defined as the non-resistive opposition to the flow of current. It may be inductive or capacitive.

Inductive Reactance (X_L)	Capacitive Reactance (X_C)
It is defined as the effective resistance offered by the inductor to the flow of current.	It is defined as the effective resistance offered by the capacitor to the flow of current.
$X_L \propto f$	$X_C \propto \dfrac{1}{f}$
where f is the frequency of the a.c. supply	where f is the frequency of the a.c. supply.
For d.c., $X_L = 0$	For d.c. $X_C = \infty$

A.C. Generator : It is the generator which produces a current that changes its direction regularly after a fixed internal of time.

It is based on the principle of the electromagnetic induction, *i.e.*, when a closed coil is rotated in a uniform magnetic field with its plane perpendicular to the field, the magnetic flux linked with the coil changes and an induced e.m.f. and hence a current is set up in the closed coil.

Instantaneous induced e.m.f. is given by
$$\varepsilon = \varepsilon_0 \sin \omega t$$
where ε_0 is called as peak value/maximum value of current.

Types of *d.c.* motor :

   (i) Series motor

   (ii) Shunt motor

   (iii) Compound motor

D.C. Generator : It is a device which is used for producing direct current energy from mechanical energy.

The only essential difference between *d.c.* generator and *a.c.* generator is that slip ring arrangement of *a.c.* generator is replaced by split ring arrangement of commutator arrangement in *d.c.* generator.

D.C. Motor : A *d.c.* motor converts direct current energy from a battery into mechanical energy of rotation.

It is based on the fact that when a coil carrying current is held in a magnetic field, it experiences a torque, which rotates the coil.

It consists of the following five parts as—

(i)   Armature
(ii) Field magnet
(iii) Split-rings or commutator
(iv) Brushes
(v)   Battery

Efficiency of the *d.c.* motor :

$$\eta = \frac{\text{Output mechanical power}}{\text{Input mechanical power}}$$

or

$$\eta = \frac{\text{back e.m.f.}}{\text{applied e.m.f.}}$$

A *d.c.* motor delivering maximum output has an efficiency of only 50%.

Uses of *d.c.* motor :

(i)   For pumping water
(ii) For running tram-cars and even trains
(iii) In *d.c.* fans (exhaust, ceiling or table) for cooling and ventilation.

Calculation of load for electric wiring :

(i)   Lamp (60 watt)
(ii) Fluorescent tube (40 watt)
(iii) Fan (60 watt)
(iv) Socket (100 watt)
(v)   Mercury vapour lamp (80 watt)
(vi) Power circuit (1000 watt)

Alternator : It is an electrical device used to create alternating current from the mechanical energy.

It can be classified on the following three basis—

1. On the basis of prime-mover :

(a) Water-turbine alternator
(b) Vapour-turbine alternator
(c) Deisel engine type alternator

2. On the basis of phases :

(a) Single phase alternator (upto 250 volts)
(b) 3-phase alternator (From 650 to 6600 volts)

3. On the basis of moving part :

(a) Types of moving armature
(b) Types of moving field

4. On the basis of excited method :

(a) Auto-excited alternator

(b) Manual-excited alternator

It consists of the following four parts :

(i)   Stator
(ii) Rotor
(iii) Slip rings brushes and rockers
(iv) Exciter

Semiconductors : If there is a small energy gap or forbidden gap in the energy band diagram, the solid behaves as a semiconductor.

The forbidden gap in pure germanium is 0.72 eV and for silicon, it is 1.1 eV.

The number of electrons or holes in a semiconductor at temperature TK is given by

$$\eta_e = \eta_h = \eta_i = AT^{3/2} e^{-EG/kT}$$

It means on increasing temperature, the number of current carriers increases. This increases the conductivity of the semiconductor with increase in temperature.

Types of semiconductors :

S. No.	Intrinsic Semi-conductor	Extrinsic Semi-conductor
1.	It is pure semiconducting material and no impurity atoms are added to it.	It is prepared by doping a small quantity of impurity atoms to the pure semiconducting material.
2.	Examples are crystalline forms of pure silicon and germanium.	Examples are silicon and germanium crystals with impurity atoms of arsenic, antimony, phosphorous etc or indium, boron, aluminium etc.
3.	Its electrical conductivity is a function of temperature alone.	Its electrical conductivity depends upon the temperature as well as on the quantity of impurity atoms doped in the structure.
4.	Its electrical conductivity is low.	Its electrical conductivity is high.
5.	The number of free electrons in conduction band and the number of holes in valence band is exactly equal and very small indeed.	The number of free electrons and holes is never equal. There is excess of electrons in *n*-type semiconductors and excess of holes in *p*-type semiconductors.

Types of extrinsic semiconductors

S. No	*n-type semi-conductor*	*p-type semi-conductor*
1.	It is an extrinsic semiconductor which is obtained by doping the impurity atoms of Vth group of periodic table to the pure germanium or silicon semiconductor.	It is an extrinsic semiconductor which is obtained by doping the impurity atoms of III group of periodic table of the pure germanium or silicon semi-conductor.
2.	The impurity atoms added, provide extra electrons in the structure, and are called donor atoms.	The impurity atoms added, create vacancies of electrons (*i.e.* holes) in the structure and are called acceptor atoms.
3.	The electron density is much greater than the hole density.	The hole density is much greater than the electron density.
4.	The electrons are the majority carriers.	The electrons are the minority carriers.
5.	The holes are the minority	The holes are the majority carriers.
6.	The fermi energy level lies in between the donor energy level and conduction band.	The fermi energy level lies in between the acceptor energy level and valence band.

p-n-junction : When a *p*-type semiconductor is brought into a close contact with *n*-type semiconductor crystal, the resulting arrangement is called a *p-n* junction or junction diode.

Symbolic representation of *p-n* junction : In this, the direction of the arrow is from the *p* to *n*-side. The *p*-side is known as anode and *n*-side is known as cathode.

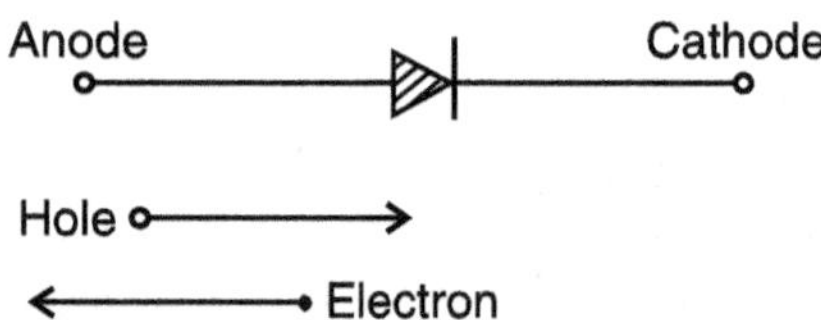

Biasing and characteristics of the *p-n* junction :

1. Forward biasing and forward characteristics : A *p-n* junction is said to be forward biased if the positive terminal of the external battery B is connected to *p*-side and the negative terminal to the *n*-side of the *p-n*-junction. The circuit diagram for forward biasing of *p-n* junction is shown in figure *(i)*

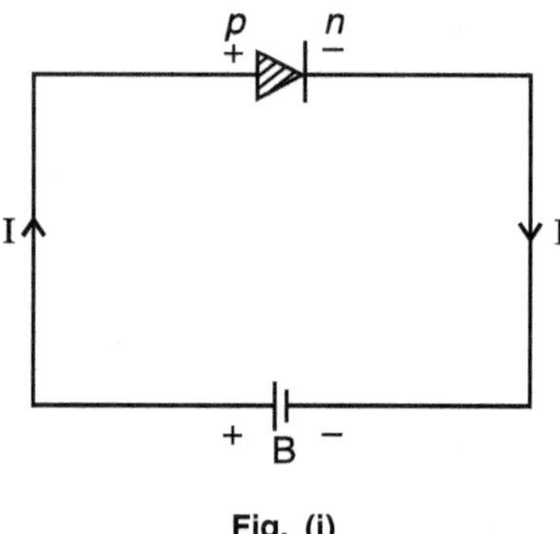

Fig. (i)

Forward characteristics are the graphical relations between forward bias voltage applied to the *p-n* junction and the forward current flowing through the *p-n* junction. In this figure *(ii)*, **Knee voltage (V_K)** is the forward voltage beyond which the current through the junction starts increasing rapidly with voltage, showing the linear variation. But below the knee voltage the variation is non-linear.

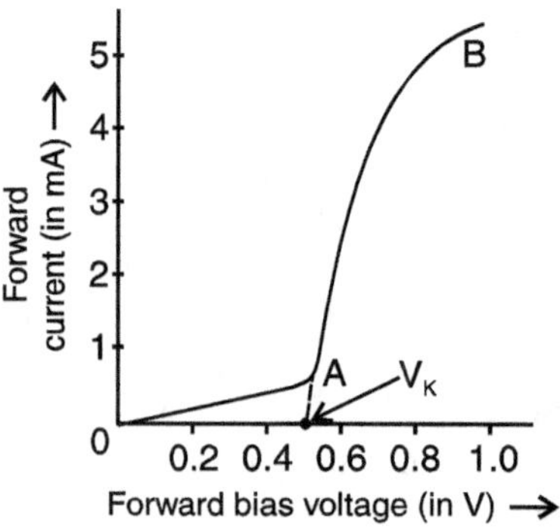

Fig. (ii)

Forward baising

(ii) **Reverse biasing and reverse characteristics :** A *p-n* junction is said to be reverse biased if the positive terminal of the external battery B is connected to *n*-side and the negative terminal to the *p*-side of the *p-n* junction. The circuit diagram for reverse biasing of *p-n* junction is shown in figure *(i)*.

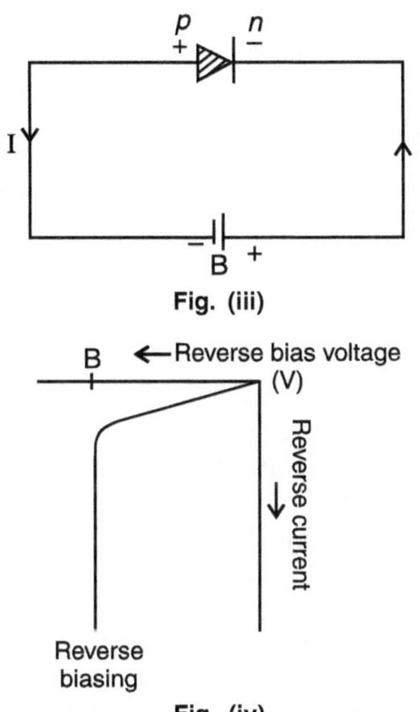

Reverse Characteristics are the graphical relations between reverse bias voltage applied to the *p-n* junction and the reverse current flowing through the *p-n* junction.

Dynamic resistance (or *a.c.* resistance of junction diode) : It is defined as the ratio of a small change in voltage ΔV applied across the *p-n* junction to a small change in junction current ΔI, *i.e.*

$$R_D \text{ or } R_{a.c.} = \frac{\Delta V}{\Delta I}$$

Uses of *p-n* junction diode : *p-n* junction diodes are used for detection and rectification.

Rectifier : It is a device which is used for converting alternating current (or alternating voltage) into direct current (or direct voltage).

A *p-n* junction diode can be used as rectifier in three ways :

   (i) Vacuum tube rectifier
   (ii) Metal rectifier
   (iii) Solid state rectifier

Half-wave rectifier : Its working is based on the fact that the resistance of *p-n* junction becomes low when forward biased and becomes high when reverse biased. In this rectifier, only one diode is used. This rectifier converts *a.c.* into *d.c.* only in positive half cycles.

Full-wave rectifier : In this rectifier, two diodes are used. Two diodes are connected in such a way that the *a.c.* is converted into *d.c.* in both negative half cycles and positive half-cycles.

Bridge rectifier : This rectifier includes four diodes and used for full wave rectification without the use of transformer.

Voltage doubler rectifier : This rectifier gives the twice of *d.c.* output voltage.

Ripple factor of a rectifier : It is defined as the ratio of the value of *a.c.* component to the value of *d.c.* component, *i.e.*,

$$\text{Ripple factor, } \gamma = \frac{I_{a.c.}}{I_{d.c.}} = \frac{E_{a.c.}}{E_{d.c.}} = \sqrt{\left(\frac{I_{rms.}}{I_{d.c.}}\right)^2 - 1}$$

Efficiency of a rectifier : It is defined as

$$\eta = \frac{\text{Output d.c power}}{\text{Input a.c. power}} \times 100\%$$

Power supply : It is a device used to generate that maximum voltage or electric current which is particularly used to operate any electric or electronic instrument.

Types of power supply :
   (i) A.C. mains
   (ii) Voltage regulator
   (iii) Voltage stabilizer
   (iv) Converter
   (v) Inverter
   (vi) Uninterrupted power supply (U.P.S.)
   (vii) Switch mode power supply (S.M.P.S.)

Silicon controlled Rectifier (SCR) or Thyristor: This rectifier act as diode. It is used to rectify the alternating currents from 30 to 100 amperes. On this basis, it is used in battery-charger.

Types of SCR or thyristor
   (i) SCR
   (ii) GCS (or GTO)
   (iii) SCS
   (iv) TRIAC
   (v) DIAC

Types of junction diodes :

   1. Zener Diode : It is a specially designed junction diode which can operate continuously, without being damaged in the region of reverse breakdown voltage.

2. Light Emitting Diode (LED) : It is a *p-n* junction diode made of gallium-arsenide or indium phosphide, as the semiconductor, and, its working is based on the production of light from electric current.

3. Photo-diode : It is a junction diode made from photosensitive semiconductor material and, its working is based on electric conduction from light.

4. Solar cell : It is a junction diode that can convert light energy into electrical energy and, its working is based on the production of potential difference by sun light.

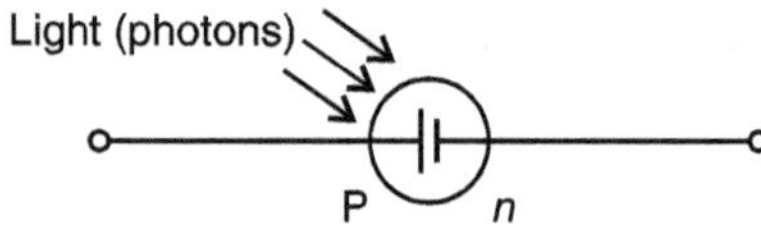

Transistor : A junction transistor is obtained by growing a thin layer of one type semiconductor in between two thick layers of other similar type semiconductor.

Thus, a junction transistor is a semiconductor device having two junctions and three terminals.

There are two types of junction transistors namely *n-p-n* transistor and *p-n-p* transistor.

n-p-n transistor	*p-n-p transistor*
It is obtained by growing a thin layer of *p*-type semiconductor in between two relatively thick layers of *n*-type semiconductors.	It is obtained by growing a thin layer of *n*-type semiconductor in between two relatively thick layers of *p*-type semiconductor.

Amplifier : It is a device which is used to increase the amplitude of variation of alternating current or voltage or power.

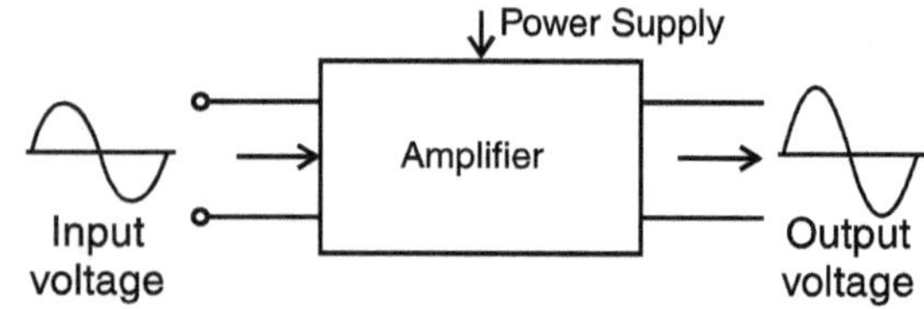

Current gains of a transistor :

1. a.c. current gain/common base current amplification factor (α): It is defined as the ratio of the small change in the collector current to the small change in the emitter current when the collector-base voltage is kept constant.

$$\alpha = \left[\frac{\Delta I_C}{\Delta I_E}\right]_{V_{CB} = constant}$$

2. a.c. current gain/common emitter current amplification factor (β) : It is defined as the ratio of the small change in the collector current to the small change in the base current when the collector-emitter voltage is kept constant.

$$\beta = \left[\frac{\Delta I_C}{\Delta I_B}\right]_{V_{CE} = constant}$$

It can be shown that

$$\alpha = \frac{\beta}{1+\beta} \text{ or } \beta = \frac{\alpha}{1-\alpha}$$

The maximum value of α and β is upto 0.999 and 99 respectively.

Voltage gain : Voltage gain of an amplifier is defined as the ratio of a small change in output voltage and the small change in input voltage.

$$A_u = \frac{V_{out}}{V_{in}} = \frac{\Delta V_{CE}}{\Delta V_{BE}} = \beta_{ac}.\frac{R_{out}}{R_{in}}$$

$$\Rightarrow A_v = A_i . A_R$$

$\Rightarrow$ voltage gain = current gain × resistance gain.

Power gain : Power gain of an amplifier is defined as the ratio of output power and the input power.

$$A_P = A_i . A_v = \beta_{ac}^2 . \frac{R_{out}}{R_{in}}$$

= current gain × voltage gain

Three configurations of a transistor :
1. Common-base circuit :

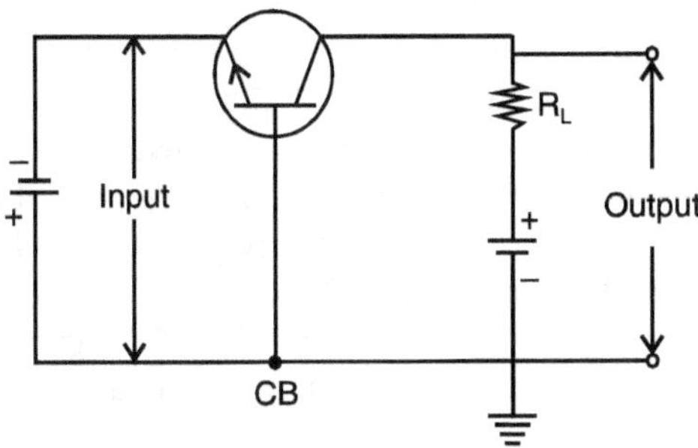

2. Common-emitter circuit :

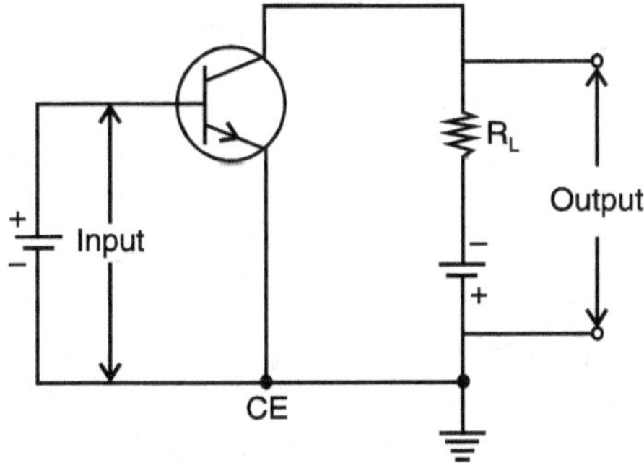

3. Common-collector circuit :

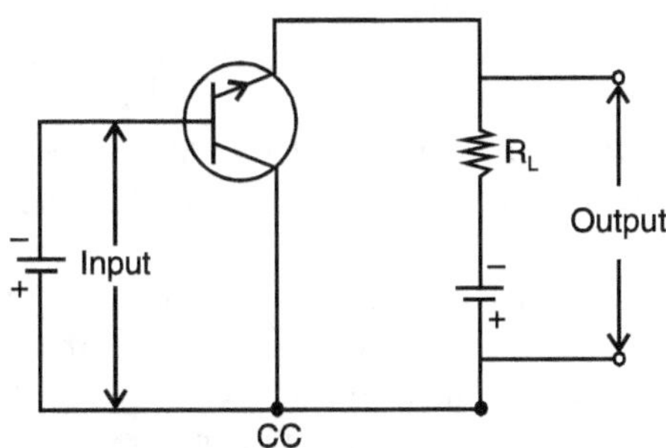

All above figures shows circuit arrangement for an *n-p-n* transistor. In each case, the emitter-base junction is forward biased while the collector-base junction is reverse biased.

Classification of amplifier :

1. On the basis of frequency :

(a) A.F. Amplifier   (20 Hz – 20 kHz)

(b) R.F. Amplifier   (> 20 kHz)

(c) I.F. Amplifier   (450 kHz – 460 kHz)

(d) Video Amplifier   (50 Hz – 7 MHz)

2. On the basis of ability :

(a) Class-A Amplifier (In Audio Amplifiers)

(b) Class-B Amplifier (In stages of Push-Pull Amplifier)

(c) Class-AB Amplifier (In the operation of general Amplification)

(d) Class-C Amplifier (In transmitters)

3. On the basis of power :

(a) Voltage Amplifier

(b) Power Amplifier

Distortion in the amplifiers : One of the main objectives of an amplifier is to reproduce an exact replica of the input signal. However, the output wave-form is not an exact replica. This is due to many factors, inherent non-linearity in the characteristics, or from the influence of the associated circuits.

The distortions are of three types, non-linear distortion, frequency distortion and phase or delay distortion. These may be present either seperately or simultaneously.

1. Non-linear distortion : A distortion is said to be non-linear distortion when in the output new frequencies are produced which are not present in the input signal.

The new frequencies appear in the output due to the operation of the tube over non-linear characteristic curve.

2. Frequency distortion : A signal is composed of many frequencies. Ideally each frequency should be amplified by the same amount. The frequency distortion is said to exist when various frequencies are amplified by different amounts.

This distortion is caused by the internal capacitances or may arises due to the circuit associated with the tubes.

3. Phase/delay distortion : This distortion results from unequal phase shifts of signals of different frequencies.

This distortion is not important in A.F. amplifiers because ear cannot distinguish small delay between different frequency components.

This kind of distortion arises because phase becomes function of frequency.

Integrated circuits : A single semiconductor crystal which contains a number of passive and active circuit elements like resistance, transistor, diode, capacitor etc. together with interconnections is known as integrated circuit (IC).

There are four type of techniques used for manufacturing of integrated circuits:

(i) mono-lithic,

(ii) thin film,

(iii) thick film and

(iv) hybrid.

Classification of ICs :

Name of IC	No. of logic gates
(i) Small Scale Integration (SSI)	≤ 10
(ii) Medium Scale Integration (MSI)	≤ 100
(iii) Large Scale Integration (LSI)	≤ 1000
(iv) Very Large Scale Integration (VLSI)	>1000

Advantages of an integrated circuit :

(i) The size of a chip is extremely small.

(ii) A close matching of components is possible.

(iii) The cost of a chip is low because number of similar chips are grown on a single layer.

(iv) Since there are no soldered points, the circuit reliability is high.

Disadvantages of an integrated circuit :

(i) It is not possible to produce high power integrated circuits.

(ii) A capacitor greater than so pico farad cannot be formed. Larger capacitors must be joined from outside.

(iii) The noise production is higher than the discrete component circuits.

(iv) An inductor cannot be formed.

Uses of integrated circuits : The integrated circuits are widely used in making the television, radio, video cassette recorders and computers.

Antenna : It is a vital component of any communication system, that is used both at the transmitting end and the receiving end.

The length of the antenna is always so chosen that it acts as a resonant circuit at the frequency of operation. If λ is the wavelength of the radio frequency signal applied, then the length of antenna is $\lambda/2$.

The design of an antenna depends on the frequency of carrier wave and the directivity of the beam etc.

Types of antenna :

(i) Dipole antenna

(ii) Dish type antenna

Telephone links : Telephone is probably the most important and also the most common means of communication. Now a days, telephones are used not only for conversing from one corner of earth to any other corner, but also for conversation from earth to other heavenly bodies like mars and moon.

A telephone link can be established using ground waves, sky waves, microwaves, co-axial cables and latest the optical fiber cables.

A point to point telephone link is shown in figure.

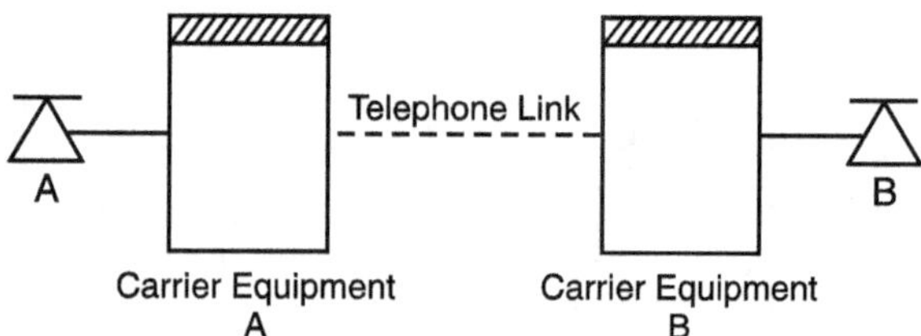

Fax (Facsimile) : It is defined as the electronic reproduction of a document at a distant place. A fax machine is the most popular example of a digital communication system.

A fax machine digitizes pointed images and transmits the corresponding data over the telephone lines.

Automatic Gain Control (AGC) : AGC is used in a receiver so that the strength of received signal is almost constant.

Remote Control : It is an electronic device which helps the observer to operate the television from a distance without leaving his or her seat.

In a remote control, there are main units :

(i) A transmitting unit—which transmits the command signal,

(ii) A frequency controller—which selects the suitable frequency for a particular function to be performed and

(iii) A mechanical drive (or electronic colour unit)—Which changes the volume (or colour) according to the signal.

Types of remote control receivers :

(i) Electromechanical system

(ii) Electronic system

OBJECTIVE TYPE QUESTIONS

1. A body can be negatively charged by
   (a) giving electrons to it
   (b) removing some electrons from it
   (c) giving some protons to it
   (d) removing some neutrons from it

2. The electric lines of force
   (a) never intersect each other
   (b) always intersect each other
   (c) sometimes intersect and sometimes do not intersect
   (d) are always parallel to each others

3. The unit of charge is
   (a) Volt   (b) Coulomb
   (c) Farad   (d) Ampere

4. A charged body at rest produces
   (a) electric field only
   (b) magnetic field only
   (c) neither electric field nor magnetic field
   (d) both electric and magnetic fields

5. Electricity .... on the moist day.
   (a) increases   (b) decreases
   (c) leaks   (d) spreads

6. Two conductors identical in shape and size but one of copper and the other of aluminium (which is less conducting) are both placed in an identical electric field. The magnitude of the induced charges in aluminium will be
   (a) less than in copper
   (b) greater than in copper
   (c) equal to that in copper
   (d) having no definite relationship with that of copper

7. The magnitude of an electric field E is such that an electron placed in it would experience an electrical force equal to its weight is given by
   (a) mge   (b) e/mg
   (c) mg/e   (d) $e^2 g/m^2$

8. The smallest charge that occur in nature is of—
   (a) 1.6×10^{19} C   (b) 1.6×10^{-19} C
   (c) 3.2×10^{19} C   (d) 3.2×10^{-19} C

9. S.I. unit of dipole moment is
   (a) Coulomb   (b) Coulomb-metre
   (c) Tesla   (d) Tesla-metre

10. Check the correct relation :
    (a) Charge = $\dfrac{\text{Potential}}{\text{Capacity}}$
    (b) Capacity = Potential × Charge
    (c) Potential = $\dfrac{\text{Charge}}{\text{Capacity}}$
    (d) Potential = Capacity + Charge

11. A condenser is charged through a potential difference of 200 volts and possesses charge of 0.1 coulomb. When discharged it would release an energy of
    (a) 1 J   (b) 2 J
    (c) 10 J   (d) 20 J

12. The equivalent capacitance between points P and Q in figure is

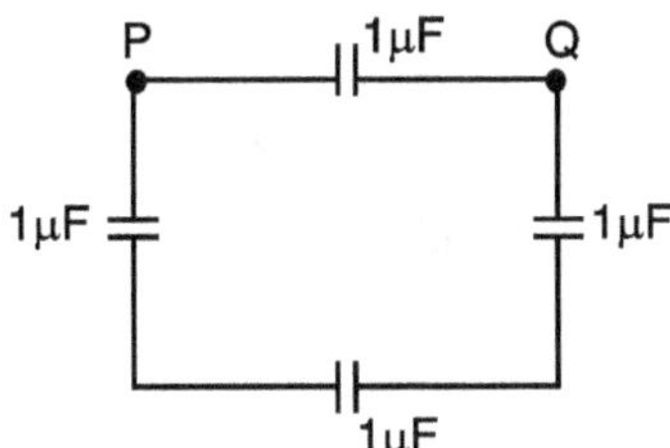

    (a) 4 µF   (b) $\dfrac{1}{4}$ µF
    (c) $\dfrac{3}{4}$ µF   (d) $\dfrac{4}{3}$ µF

13. If α is the dielectric constant of medium and ε_0 permittivity of free-space, then the energy stored per unit volume of the medium is
    (a) $\dfrac{1}{2} \alpha \varepsilon_0 E$ (b) $\dfrac{1}{2} \alpha \varepsilon_0 E^2$
    (c) $\dfrac{1}{2} \alpha \varepsilon_0^2 E$ (d) $\dfrac{1}{2} \alpha^2 \varepsilon_0^2 E$

14. Figure below shows electric lines of force due

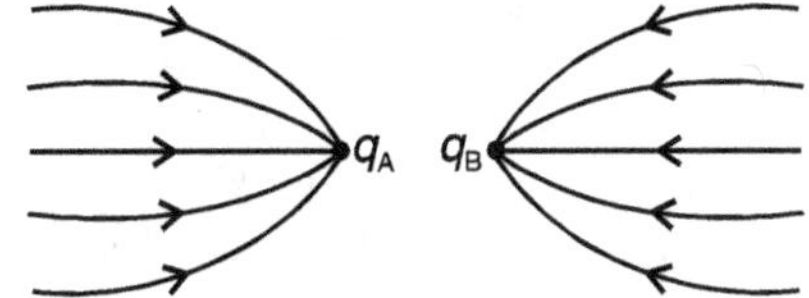

to two charges q_A and q_B. What are signs of two charges?
(a) q_A is positive and q_B is negative
(b) q_A is negative and q_B is positive
(c) Both q_A and q_B are positive
(d) Both q_A and q_B are negative

15. An electron and a proton are placed in a uniform electric field, then
(a) electric forces acting on them will be equal
(b) their accelerations will be equal
(c) both acceleration and electric force will be equal
(d) magnitude of forces acting on them will be equal

16. Eight dipoles of charge of magnitude q are placed inside a cube, total electric flux coming out of cube is
(a) Zero
(b) $\dfrac{q}{\varepsilon_0}$
(c) $\dfrac{8q}{\varepsilon_0}$
(d) $\dfrac{16q}{\varepsilon_0}$

17. For which of the following dependences of drift velocity v_d on electric field E, is ohm's law valid—
(a) $v_d \propto E$
(b) $v_d \propto \sqrt{E}$
(c) $v_d \propto E^2$
(d) $v_d = $ constant

18. If an electric current is passed through a nerve, the man
(a) begins to laugh
(b) is excited
(c) begins to weep
(d) becomes insensitive to pain

19. The resistance between points P and Q of the circuit shown below is

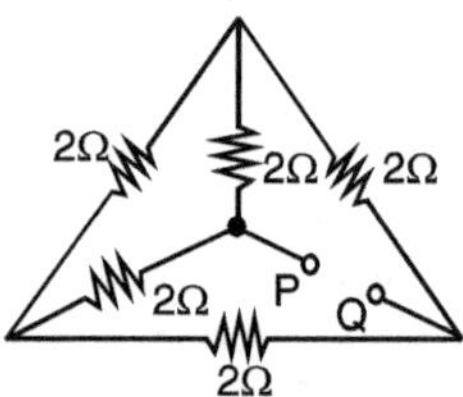

(a) $4\ \Omega$
(b) $3\ \Omega$
(c) $2\ \Omega$
(d) $0.5\ \Omega$

20. By what per cent will the incandescent of a lamp decrease if the current drops by 2%.
(a) 4%
(b) 2%
(c) 1%
(d) 0.01%

21. Fuse wire is a wire of
(a) low resistance and low melting point
(b) low resistance and high melting point
(c) high resistance and high melting point
(d) high resistance and low melting point

22. One kilo watt hour is equal to
(a) 3.6×10^6 J
(b) 3.6×10^3 J
(c) 3.6×10^{-6} J
(d) 3.6×10^{-3} J

23. An increase in the resonance frequency can be brought about by
(a) decreasing R
(b) increasing L
(c) decreasing L
(d) increasing R

24. The symbol of LED is as
(a) 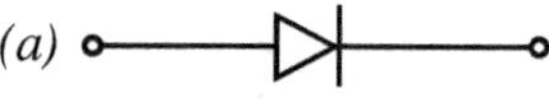
(b) 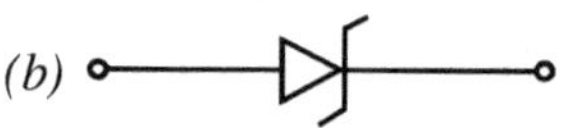
(c) 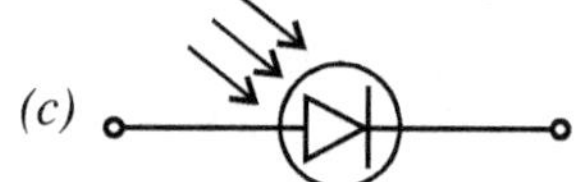
(d) 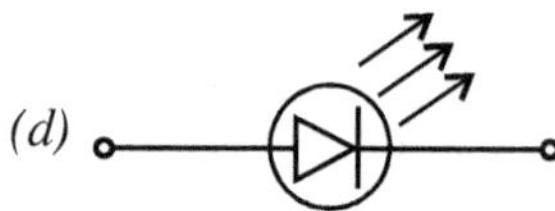

25. Which of the following quantities remains constant in a step-down transformer?
(a) Current
(b) Voltage
(c) Power
(d) None of the above

26. The torque developed by d.c. motor is
(a) directly proportional to field current
(b) directly proportional to flux and armature current
(c) inversely proportional to armature current
(d) inversely proportional to flux and armature current

27. In an a.c. circuit, the r.m.s. value of current, I_{rms} is related to the peak current, I_o by the relation
(a) $I_{rms} = \dfrac{I_o}{\sqrt{2}}$
(b) $I_{rms} = \dfrac{I_o}{\pi}$
(c) $I_{rms} = I_o \sqrt{2}$
(d) $I_{rms} = \pi I_o$

27. Match the following :
 A. Extra High Tension Cable I. upto 66 kV
 B. High Tension Cable   II. upto 11 kV
 C. Low Tension Cable   III. upto 1 kV
 D. Super Tension Cable   IV. upto 33 kV

	A	B	C	D
(a)	I	II	III	IV
(b)	I	III	II	IV
(c)	III	I	II	IV
(d)	III	II	I	IV

29. The relation between magnetic susceptibility and relative permeability is
 (a) $\chi = 1 - \mu_r$ *(b)* $\chi = 1 + \mu_r$
 (c) $\mu_r = 1 + \chi$ *(d)* $\chi = \mu_r$

30. Assuming that junction diode is ideal, the current in arrangement shown in figure is

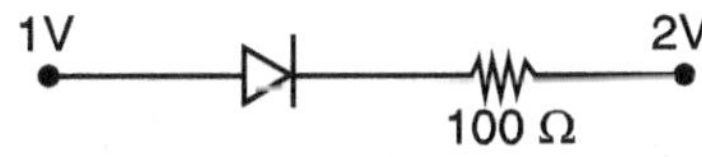

 (a) 2 mA   *(b)* 10 mA
 (c) 20 mA   *(d)* 30 mA

31. At resonance, is a series LCR circuit, which relation does not hold
 (a) $\omega = \dfrac{1}{LC}$ *(b)* $\omega = \dfrac{1}{\sqrt{LC}}$
 (c) $L\omega = \dfrac{1}{C\omega}$ *(d)* $C\omega = \dfrac{1}{L\omega}$

32. The use of coupling capacitor in transistor amplifier is
 (a) to safe the transistor
 (b) to pass a.c. and block d.c.
 (c) to develope bias
 (d) to increase the output impedance of transistor

33. On the basis of structure, number of a.c. windings are
 (a) 2   *(b)* 4
 (c) 6   *(d)* 8

34. Tesla is the S.I. unit of
 (a) magnetic flux
 (b) magnetic flux density
 (c) magnetic susceptibility
 (d) None of the above

35. A *p-n* junction has a depletion layer of thickness of the order of
 (a) 10^{-10} m   *(b)* 10^{-8} m

(c) 10^{-6} m   *(d)* 10^{-4} m

36. Energy dissipates in LCR circuit in
 (a) L only   *(b)* C only
 (c) R only   *(d)* all of the above

37. Collector circuit of a transistor in the stage of amplification, is
 (a) of low resistance
 (b) full time reverse biased
 (c) full time forward biased
 (d) none of the above

38. In 3-phase winding, coil group is equal to
 (a) $\dfrac{\text{No. of phases}}{\text{No. of poles}}$
 (b) $\dfrac{(\text{No. of phases})^2}{\text{No. of poles}}$
 (c) No. of phases $\times$ No. of poles
 (d) (No. of phases)^2 $\times$ No. of poles

39. For high frequency, capacity offers
 (a) more resistance *(b)* less resistance
 (c) zero resistance *(d)* None of the above

40. The number of depletion layers in transistor—
 (a) 1   *(b)* 2
 (c) 3   *(d)* zero

41. Temperature coefficient =
 (a) $\dfrac{R_T - R_0}{R_0 \cdot T}$ *(b)* $\dfrac{R_T - R_0}{R_0 \cdot T^2}$
 (c) $\dfrac{R_T - R_0}{R_0^{\,2} \cdot T}$ *(d)* $\dfrac{R_T - R_0}{R_0^{\,2} \cdot T^2}$

42. In a.c., peak factor is
 (a) 0   *(b)* 1
 (c) 1.11   *(d)* 1.414

43. Henry is the unit of
 (a) Inductance   *(b)* Impedance
 (c) Capacitance   *(d)* Admittance

44. The binary for 14 is
 (a) 1110   *(b)* 1010
 (c) 0101   *(d)* 1100

45. When we apply reverse bias to a junction diode, it
 (a) lowers the potential barrier
 (b) raises the potential barrier
 (c) increases the majority carrier current
 (d) increases the minority carrier current

46. Energy needed to establish an a.c.I in a coil of self inductance L is

(a) $L\dfrac{dI}{dt}$

(b) $\dfrac{LI^2}{2}$

(c) $\dfrac{L^2I}{2}$

(d) zero

47. A P-N junction act as
(a) unidirectional switch
(b) bi-directional switch
(c) controlled switch
(d) none of the above

48. Which relation is correct for the coefficient of coupling:

(a) $K = \dfrac{M}{L_1 L_2} \times 100$

(b) $K = \dfrac{M}{\left(L_1 L_2\right)^2} \times 100$

(c) $K = \dfrac{M}{\sqrt{L_1 . L_2}} \times 100$

(d) $K = \sqrt{\dfrac{M}{L_1 L_2}} \times 100$

49. How many types of MOSFET?
(a) 2   (b) 4
(c) 5   (d) 6

50. When an impurity is dopped into an intrinsic semiconductor, the conductivity of the semi-conductor
(a) decreases
(b) increases
(c) remains the same
(d) becomes zero

51. The working of a dynamo is based on the principle of
(a) chemical effect of current
(b) thermal effect of current
(c) magnetic effect of current
(d) electromagnetic induction

52. The circuit used in timer is—
(a) Astable   (b) Monostable
(c) Bistable   (d) Unstable

53. How many types of single phase motors?
(a) 4   (b) 6
(c) 8   (d) 10

54. The unit of inductance is
(a) Henry   (b) Lux
(c) Candela   (d) ohm

55. Figure shows currents in a part of an electric circuit, then current is

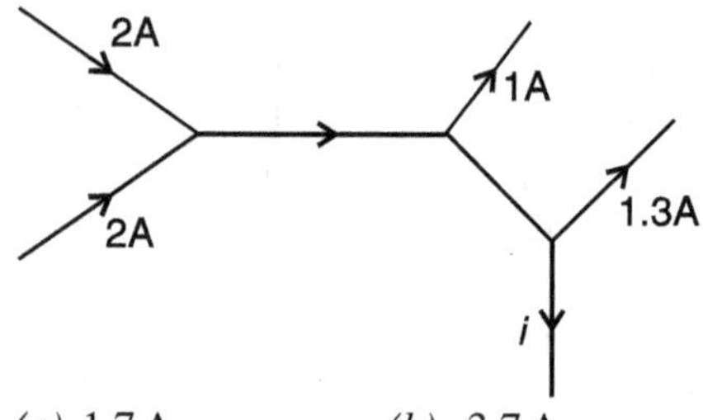

(a) 1.7 A   (b) 3.7 A
(c) 1.3 A   (d) 1 A

56. For television broadcasting, the frequency employed is normally
(a) 30-300 Hz   (b) 30-300 kHz
(c) 30-300 GHz   (d) 30-300 MHz

57. In general, in an a.c. circuit,
(a) the average value of current is zero
(b) the average value of square of current is zero
(c) the average power dissipation is zero
(d) the phase difference between voltage and current is zero

58. The bandwidth in colour television transmission in comparison with black and white television transmission is
(a) Same   (b) Small
(c) Double   (d) Thrice

59. Which relation is correct :
(a) $f = \lambda/v$ (b) $f = v/\lambda$
(c) $f = v^2\lambda$ (d) $f = v\lambda$

60. An electric field is applied to a semiconductor. Let the number of charge carriers be n and the average drift speed v. If the temperature is increased,
(a) both n and v will decrease
(b) both n and v will increase
(c) n will increase but v will decrease
(d) n will decrease but v will increase

61. The permeability of air is
(a) 0.5   (b) 1
(c) 1.5   (d) 2

62. The characteristic impedance of a lossless transmission line is given by
(a) $Z_0 = \sqrt{LC}$
(b) $Z_0 = \sqrt{L/C}$
(c) $Z_0 = LC$
(d) $Z_0 = \sqrt{C/L}$

63. In Cathode Ray Oscilloscope, x-axis represent
(a) voltage
(b) current
(c) time
(d) gain

64. The motors used in drill machine, blower, funs and washing machine are
(a) split-phase motors
(b) capacitor induction motors
(c) shaded phase motor
(d) universal motor

65. Ohm is the unit of
(a) Resistance
(b) Reactance
(c) Impedance
(d) All of these

66. The power factor of a series LCR circuit when at resonance is
(a) zero
(b) 0.5
(c) 1.0
(d) depends on the values of L,C and R

67. The value of α in transistor is
(a) 1
(b) <1
(c) >1
(d) None of the above

68. Repulsion motors are made
(a) from $\dfrac{1}{5}$ Horse power to $\dfrac{1}{10}$ Horse power
(b) from $\dfrac{1}{10}$ Horse power to 5 Horse power
(c) from $\dfrac{1}{10}$ Horse power to 20 Horse power
(d) None of the above

69. In LCR-circuit, resonance condition is
(a) $X_L < X_C$
(b) $X_L = X_C$
(c) $X_L > X_C$
(d) $X_L = \dfrac{1}{X_C}$

70. In an electrolytic solution, current is carried by
(a) electrons only
(b) positive ions only
(c) negative ions only
(d) both positive and negative ions

71. Radio waves of constant amplitude can be generated with
(a) Filter
(b) Rectifier
(c) Oscillator
(d) FET

72. A pair of slip rings is used in
(a) a.c. generator
(b) a.c. motor
(c) d.c. generator
(d) d.c. motor

73. The work under the weekly inspection of d.c. motor are—
(a) overhauling of switch and starter
(b) check the 'earth' resistance
(c) check the foundation bolts
(d) change the damaged carbon bush and bush holders

74. The cell which can be rechaged is
(a) Lead-acid cell
(b) Fuel cell
(c) Daniel cell
(d) Leclanche cell

75. The self-inductance of a straight conductor is
(a) zero
(b) infinity
(c) very large
(d) very small

76. The colour sequence in three-phase line is
(a) Red, Black (for neutral), Green, Yellow
(b) Red, Yellow, Blue, Black
(c) Black, Red, Blue, Green
(d) Yellow, Blue, Red, Green

77. The motor used in mixer grinder is
(a) Universal a.c. motor
(b) Repulsion induction motor
(c) Synchronous motor
(d) Single phase slipring induction

78. The simple and famous motor synchronising method is
(a) Dark lamp method
(b) Bright lamp method
(c) Dark and bright lamp method
(d) Synchroscope method

79. The imedance of CR circuit is
(a) $Z = \sqrt{R^2 + \left(X_L - X_C\right)^2}$
(b) $Z = \sqrt{R^2 + X_L^{\,2}}$
(c) $Z = \sqrt{R^2 + X_C^{\,2}}$
(d) $Z = \sqrt{R^2 - X_C^{\,2}}$

80. In the following circuit, the bulb B will

become suddenly bright if

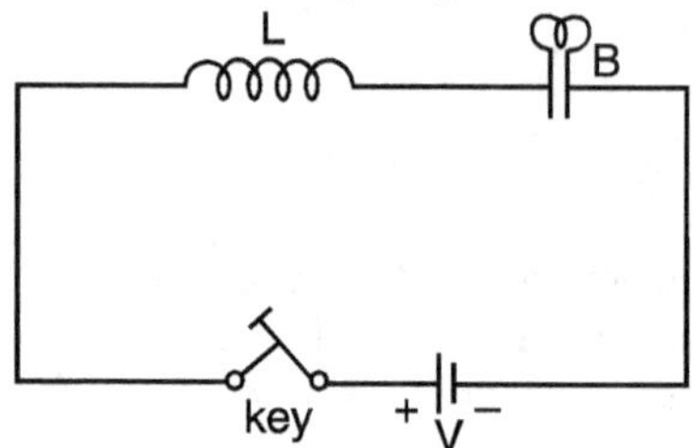

(a) contact is made or broken
(b) contact is made
(c) contact is broken
(d) won't become bright at all

81. Lenz's law is a consequence of the law of conservation of
(a) charge   (b) momentum
(c) energy   (d) mass

82. It is used to start d.c. shunt and compound motor
(a) 2-point starter   (b) 3-point starter
(c) 4-point starter   (d) None of the above

83. The capacitors used in electric fans are of
(a) $0.5 - 1.5$ µF   (b) $1.5 - 2.5$ µF
(c) $2.5 - 3.5$ µF   (d) None of the above

84. Number of alternators on the basis of phase are
(a) 9   (b) 7
(c) 5   (d) 2

85. Kirchhoff's first law is merely the law of conservation of
(a) charge
(b) momentum
(c) angular momentum
(d) energy

86. Kirchhoff's second law is related to the law of conservation of
(a) charge
(b) momentum
(c) angular momentum
(d) energy

87. An inductor may store energy in
(a) its coils
(b) its electric field
(c) its magnetic field
(d) both in electric and magnetic field

88. In d.c. motor, shaft-torque =

(a) $\dfrac{\phi.Z.N}{60} \times \dfrac{P}{A}$ (b) $\dfrac{B.H.P.}{2\pi N}$

(c) $\dfrac{735.5 \times B.H.P.}{2\pi N}$ (d) $\dfrac{735.5 \times N}{2\pi \times B.H.P.}$

89. The direction of electronic current is always opposite to
(a) the direction of conventional current in metallic conductors
(b) one ohm
(c) the electrical work done
(d) none of these

90. Sound produced by a tuning fork is a sort of
(a) digital signal   (b) analog signal
(c) both (a) & (b)   (d) neither (a) nor (b)

91. No force is exerted by magnetic field on a stationary
(a) electric dipole
(b) magnetic dipole
(c) current loop
(d) current carrying conductor

92. The angular frequency of a.c. at which a coil of inductance 1 mH has a reactance of 1Ω is
(a) 10^{-3} (b) 1
(c) 10   (d) 10^3

93. In insulation tester, d.c. generator or a.c. generator is used to produce
(a) 50 volt   (b) 500 volt
(c) 5000 volt   (d) 50,000 volt

94. Lines of force due to earth's horizontal magnetic field are
(a) straight and parallel
(b) concentric circles
(c) elliptical
(d) curved lines

95. The process of superimposing signal frequency on the carrier wave is known as
(a) transmission   (b) reception
(c) detection   (d) modulation

96. In an ideal capacitor, current
(a) leads the e.m.f. by $180°$
(b) lags the e.m.f. by $180°$
(c) leads the e.m.f. by $90°$
(d) is in phase with e.m.f.

97. In generator, sparking is reduced by using
(a) interpoles
(b) brushes having large resistance
(c) short-pitched windings
(d) all of the above

98. FM broadcast band is—
(a) 80 MHz – 150 MHz
(b) 88 MHz – 108 MHz
(c) 100 MHz – 200 MHz
(d) 140 MHz – 220 MHz

99. A magnetic needle is kept in a non-uniform magnetic field. It experiences
(a) a force and a torque
(b) a force but not a torque
(c) a torque but not a force
(d) neither a force nor a torque

100. A.C. is converted into D.C. by
(a) dynamo   (b) motor
(c) rectifier   (d) transformer

101. What is the immaterial for an electric fuse?
(a) its specific resistance
(b) its length
(c) its radius
(d) current flowing through it

102. The angle of dip is 90° at the
(a) magnetic poles   (b) magnetic equator
(c) mountains   (d) none of the above

103. The e.m.f. relation for d.c. generator is

(a) $\varepsilon = \dfrac{\phi.N.Z}{60} \times \dfrac{P}{A}$ (b) $\varepsilon = \dfrac{\phi.N.A}{60} \times \dfrac{Z}{P}$

(c) $\varepsilon = \dfrac{\phi.P.A}{60} \times \dfrac{N}{Z}$ (d) $\varepsilon = \dfrac{\phi.N.P}{60} \times \dfrac{A^2}{Z}$

104. Match the following

A. Capacitance	I. Coulomb
B. Charge	II. Henry
C. Inductance	III. Ohm
D. Impedance	IV. Farad

	A	B	C	D
(a)	I	II	III	IV
(b)	I	II	IV	III
(c)	IV	II	I	III
(d)	IV	I	II	III

105. The maximum value of a.c. in a circuit is 707 V. Its virtual value is
(a) 70.7 V   (b) 500 V
(c) 707 V   (d) 900 V

106. Number of logic gates used in LSI are
(a) ≤ 10 (b) ≤ 100
(c) ≤ 1000 (d) > 1000

107. A.F. Amplifier is used in
(a) 20 Hz – 20 kHz   (b) 20 kHz and above
(c) 450 - 460 kHz   (d) 50 Hz - 7 MHz

108. A transformer is employed to
(a) Obtain a suitable AC voltage
(b) Obtain a suitable DC voltage
(c) Convert AC into DC
(d) Convert DC into AC

109. Thermoelectric effects was discovered by
(a) Ampere   (b) Thomson
(c) Seebeck   (d) Peltier

110. In figure, the input is across the terminals P and R and the output is across Q and S. Then the output is

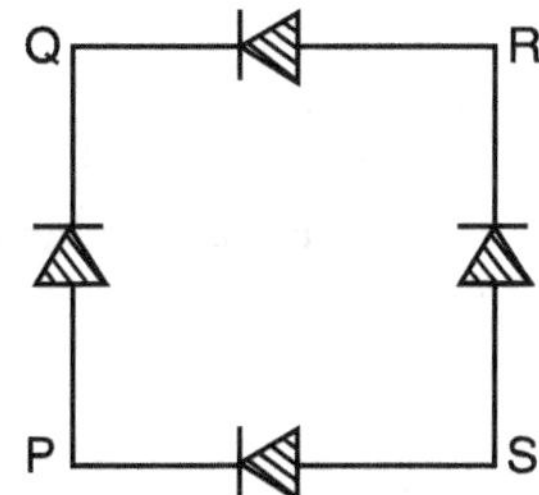

(a) half-wave rectified
(b) full-wave rectified
(c) zero
(d) same as the input

111. To convert mechanical energy into electrical energy, one can use
(a) a.c. dynamo   (b) d.c. dynamo
(c) a and b   (d) Neither (a) nor (b)

112. Which one is currect
(a) 1 H.P. = 1.34 kWh
(b) 1 kWh = 1.34 H.P.
(c) 1 H.P. = 75 kWh
(d) 1 kWh = 75 H.P.

113. In the distribution line of electricity, the maximum distance between two poles must be equal to—
(a) 40 Foot   (b) 80 Foot
(c) 160 Foot   (d) 220 Foot

114. Which relation is correct for transformation ratio—

(a) $K = \dfrac{V_s}{V_p} = \dfrac{I_s}{I_p}$ (b) $K = N_s N_p = V_s V_p$

(c) $K = \dfrac{N_p}{N_s} = \dfrac{V_s}{V_p}$ (d) $K = \dfrac{V_s}{V_p} = \dfrac{N_s}{N_p}$

115. The instrument used to measure power consumption in electricity is called
(a) Wattmeter   (b) Ammeter
(c) Voltmeter   (d) None of the above

116. Which of the following curves may represent the reactance of a series LC combination

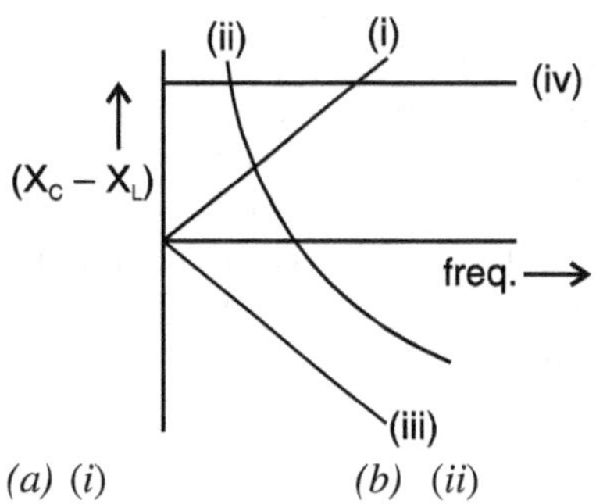

(a) (i)   (b) (ii)
(c) (iii)   (d) (iv)

117. The core of a transformer is laminated to reduce energy losses due to
(a) hysteresis
(b) eddy currcuts
(c) resistance in windings
(d) none of these

118. This modulation technique is used in remote control system and cordless telephone receiver—
(a) Amplitude modulation
(b) Frequency modulation
(c) Pulse modulation
(d) None of the above

119. The minimum distance of the 11 kV line from the wall and roof of the building is
(a) 9 foot and 14 foot respectively
(b) 7 foot and 12 foot respectively
(c) 4 foot and 12 foot respectively
(d) 2 foot and 6 foot respectively

120. The device adverse and opposite to dynamo in function is
(a) electric motor   (b) electric fun
(c) both of these   (d) none of these

121. The electric power is provided to the consumer by
(a) the overhead lines
(b) the underground lines
(c) overhead or underground lines
(d) none of the above

122. The unit of capacitive reactance is
(a) coulomb   (b) lux
(c) henry   (d) ohm

123. On what principle, moving coil instrument based—
(a) a.c. motor   (b) d.c. motor
(c) Pony-motor   (d) Synchronous motor

124. Reactance of a capacitor of $\dfrac{1}{\pi}$ farad at 50 Hz is
(a) $10^{-2}\ \Omega$ (b) $10\ \Omega$
(c) $50\ \Omega$ (d) $100\ \Omega$

125. The cable used for earth line in wiring is
(a) 7 SWG single core cable
(b) 14 SWG single core cable
(c) 7 SWG double core cable
(d) 14 SWG double core cable

126. Match the following :

A. Multiple winding — I. In this winding, 4 to 6 windings are placed in a single slot

B. Duplex wave winding — II. It is the parallel connection of two simplex wave windings

C. Quadruplex wave winding — III. It is the parallel connection of four simplex windings

D. Triplex lap winding — IV. It is the parallel connection of two simplex wave windings

	A	B	C	D
(a)	I	II	III	IV
(b)	I	III	II	IV
(c)	III	I	II	IV
(d)	III	II	I	IV

127. In transformer, H.T. is
(a) 1–200 volts supply
(b) 200–15,000 volts supply
(c) greater than 15,000 volts supply
(d) none of the above

128. The value of pitch factor is
(a) less than unit
(b) equal to unit
(c) greater than unit
(d) reciprocal of unit

129. The amplitude of current oscillations in LCR-circuit will be maximum when ω is

(a) as large as possible

(b) $\sqrt{LC}$

(c) $\sqrt{1/LC}$

(d) equal to natural frequency of LCR system

130. In a P-N junction,

(a) high potential at N-side and low potential at P-side

(b) high potential at P-side and low potential at N-side

(c) P and N both are at the same potential

(d) undetermined

131. The meniscus of a liquid contained in one of the limbs of a narrow U-tube is held in an electro-magnetic with the meniscus in line with the field. The liquid is seen to rise. This indicates the liquid is

(a) diamagnetic   (b) paramagnetic

(c) ferromagnetic   (d) non-magnetic

132. An a.c.ammeter connected in series in an a.c. circuit reads 5 ampere. The peak value of current is

(a) 5 A   (b) $\dfrac{5}{\sqrt{2}}$ A

(c) $5\sqrt{2}$ A   (d) $\dfrac{10}{\pi}$ A

133. The relation between metric-Horse-power and watts is

(a) 1 Metric Horse Power = 746 watts

(b) 1 Metric Horse Power = 735.5 watts

(c) 1 Metric Horse Power = 500 watts

(d) None of the above

134. Eddy current loss is equal to

(a) $B_{max} \times f$ (b) $(B_{max})^2 \times f$

(c) $(B_{max})^2 \times f^2$ (d) $\dfrac{B_{max}}{f}$

135. If 5 resistances each of 5 ohms are connected in parallel, the resultant resistance will be

(a) 1 ohm   (b) 5 ohm

(c) 15 ohm   (d) 25 ohm

136. Match the following :

A.	Recording Instrument	I.	Energy meter
B.	Absolute Instrument	II.	Power factor recorder
C.	Integrated Instrument	III.	Galvanometer
D.	Indicating Instrument	IV.	Ammeter, ohm metre, voltmeter (Avo meter)

	A	B	C	D
(a)	I	II	III	IV
(b)	I	III	II	IV
(c)	II	III	I	IV
(d)	II	I	III	IV

137. If the length of wire is doubled, the resistance will be

(a) halved   (b) doubled

(c) tripled   (d) none of these

138. The semiconductor A is made by doping a germanium crystal with arsenic (Z = 33). A second semiconductor B is made by doping germanium with indium (Z = 49). The two are joined end to end and connected to a battery as shown, which of the following statements is correct?

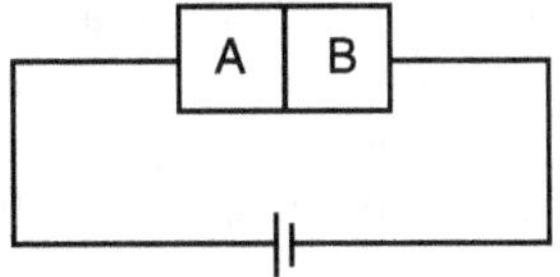

(a) A is P-type, B is N-type and the junction is forward biased.

(b) A is N-type, B is P-type and the junction is forward biased.

(c) A is P-type, B is N-type and the junction is reverse biased.

(d) A is N-type, B is P-type and the junction is reverse biased.

139. If a charged particle kept at rest experiences an electromagnetic force

(a) the electric field may or may not be zero

(b) the magnetic field may or may not be zero

(c) the electric field must not be zero

(d) the magnetic field must not be zero

140. A bar magnet is dropped through a copper ring. Acceleration of magnet is

(a) = g

(b) < g
(c) > g
(d) depends on diameter of ring

141. 1 Horse Power = ... kg/m sec
    (a) 50   (b) 75
    (c) 100   (d) 175

142. In Coulomb's law, the force of attraction or repulsion between two charged bodies is
    (a) directly proportional to the product of their charges distance
    (b) directly proportional to the square of the distance between
    (c) inversely proportional to the square of the distance between them
    (d) (a) and (c)

143. Two streams of electrons moving parallel to each other in the same direction
    (a) attract each other
    (b) repel each other
    (c) cancel the magnetic field of each other
    (d) cancel the electric field of each other

144. The transistor provide good power amplification when they are used in
    (a) common-emitter configuration
    (b) common-base configuration
    (c) common-collector configuration
    (d) None of these

145. Electromagnets are made of soft-iron because it has
    (a) large susceptibility and large retentivity
    (b) small susceptibility and large retentivity
    (c) small susceptibility and small retentivity
    (d) large susceptibility and small retentivity

146. A choke is used as a resistance in
    (a) a.c. circuits
    (b) d.c. circuits
    (c) both a.c. and d.c. circuits
    (d) neither of the two

147. Resistance law is—
    (a) $R = \dfrac{l}{\rho A}$ (b) $\rho = RA\,l$
    (c) $R = \rho\dfrac{l}{A}$ (d) $\rho = A\dfrac{l}{R}$

148. The connection used in 3-phase transformer is
    (a) Star connection
    (b) Delta connection
    (c) Inter-Star connection
    (d) All of the above

149. Dark lamp method, Bright lamp method, Dark and bright lamp method, and Synchroscope method are the methods of
    (a) Running machine
    (b) Synchronising
    (c) Alternator
    (d) None of the above

150. Permittivity of vacuum is
    (a) 1.6×10^{19} C/m   (b) 9.31×10^{-34} C/m
    (c) 8.854 C/m   (d) 1.6×10^{-19} C/m

ANSWERS

1	2	3	4	5	6	7	8	9	10
(b)	(a)	(b)	(a)	(c)	(a)	(c)	(b)	(b)	(c)
11	12	13	14	15	16	17	18	19	20
(c)	(d)	(b)	(d)	(d)	(a)	(a)	(b)	(c)	(a)
21	22	23	24	25	26	27	28	29	30
(d)	(a)	(c)	(d)	(c)	(b)	(a)	(a)	(c)	(c)
31	32	33	34	35	36	37	38	39	40
(a)	(b)	(d)	(b)	(b)	(c)	(b)	(c)	(b)	(a)
41	42	43	44	45	46	47	48	49	50
(a)	(d)	(a)	(a)	(b)	(b)	(a)	(c)	(a)	(b)
51	52	53	54	55	56	57	58	59	60
(d)	(a)	(b)	(a)	(a)	(d)	(a)	(a)	(b)	(c)

61	62	63	64	65	66	67	68	69	70
(b)	(b)	(c)	(a)	(d)	(a)	(b)	(c)	(b)	(d)
71	72	73	74	75	76	77	78	79	80
(c)	(a)	(c)	(a)	(a)	(b)	(a)	(c)	(c)	(a)
81	82	83	84	85	86	87	88	89	90
(c)	(b)	(b)	(d)	(a)	(d)	(c)	(c)	(a)	(b)
91	92	93	94	95	96	97	98	99	100
(c)	(d)	(c)	(a)	(d)	(c)	(d)	(b)	(a)	(c)
101	102	103	104	105	106	107	108	109	110
(b)	(a)	(a)	(d)	(b)	(c)	(a)	(a)	(c)	(b)
111	112	113	114	115	116	117	118	119	120
(c)	(b)	(d)	(d)	(a)	(b)	(b)	(c)	(c)	(c)
121	122	123	124	125	126	127	128	129	130
(c)	(d)	(b)	(a)	(b)	(a)	(c)	(a)	(c)	(a)
131	132	133	134	135	136	137	138	139	140
(c)	(c)	(b)	(c)	(a)	(c)	(b)	(d)	(a)	(b)
141	142	143	144	145	146	147	148	149	150
(b)	(d)	(a)	(a)	(a)	(a)	(c)	(d)	(c)	(c)

———

2

PUMP MECHANIC AND DIESEL MECHANIC

Pump : It is an instrument used to create air. Through water pump, water or other liquid substances can be sent to high up places with more pressure. Motor or engine pumps draw water in more quantity.

Pumps are used for the following works –

1. to increase pressure in pipe lines
2. to carry water to high up storeys
3. to draw out wasted water
4. to fill in elevated tanks
5. to draw out water from underground sources.

Different types of pump :

(i) **Centrifugal Pump :** This pump is used to carry water and other liquid to high up places. It works on the principle of centrifugal force. Centrifugal pumps are of two kinds—

(a) **Turbine pump :** In this pump, after drawing out water through impeller, the part in which it flows, its cross-section is equal at every place. It throws out water with maximum speed.

(b) **Volute pump :** The impeller used in this pump is in the form of volute. In this type of pump, the motion of water remains constant at every time this impeller is driven through electric motor.

(ii) **Air Lift Pump :** These pumps are used where acid, alkali like substances are mixed with water which harm the other pumps. It is also called as compressor pump.

(iii) **Reciprocating Pump :** This type of pump can pump water in definite quantity at different pressure.

Reciprocating pumps are of two kinds :

(a) **Hand pump :** This pump is used in public places, road sides and to draw out water from underground sources.

It has following parts :

1. Clamp
2. Handle
3. G.I. cylinder pipe
4. Check valve
5. Strainer Filter
6. G.I. Suction pipe
7. Gun metal cylinder
8. Piston rod
9. Plunger/piston
10. Piston valve

(b) **Power pump :** This pump is just like hand pump but it is driven by engine or motor and its piston is kept upto water level. It has no suction pipe.

(iv) **Rotary Pump :** This pump is used to pump liquid substances like water, oil etc. in large quantity. There is no valve in this type of pump.

The cost of this pump is high but its capacity to do work is about 60 to 80%.

Reciprocating pump moves upwards and downwards while in case of rotary pump, gears or cam revolves.

(v) **Hydraulic Pump/Impulse Pump :** This pump is used at that place where water is stored and the water needs small falls before storing. It has following parts'.

1. Inlet pipe
2. Outlet pipe
3. Waste valve
4. Oulet valve
5. Air chamber

(vi) **Mono Block Pump :** In this type of pump, impeller are fitted with electric motor shaft. It is fitted with spiral casing and packing gland. These pumps have lower weight, hence these pump can be fitted anywhere easily

Power for pumping :

1. Electric motor
2. Diesel engine
3. Steam engine

Selection of pumps : The selection of pump is very important so select the pump according to work.

(i) Use deep well vertical turbine pump for deep well.
(ii) Centrifugal pumps are used for increasing pressure or boosting.
(iii) Centrifugal pumps are also used for low height (For low lift).
(iv) Reciprocating pump (driven by hand pump and motor) are used in houses for water supply.
(v) Pump should not have greater effect of load.
(vi) Pump should occupy lesser space.
(vii) Pump maintenance should be easy.
(viii) Pump operating method should also be easy.
(ix) Low pump cost
(x) Maximum pump efficiency.

Four stroke cycle of diesel engine :

(i) **Section stroke :** In this stroke, piston moves from T.D.C. to B.D.C. Inlet valve remains open. Because of moving downward the piston, as a result of zero created in the cyliner, only fresh air from air cleaner, passing through inlet manifold comes in the cylinder from the way of inlet valve.

(ii) **Compression stroke :** In this stroke, piston moves from B.D.C. to T.D.C. Opening inlet valve is closed, when piston moves upwards, the air of cylinder is pressurised. There is no way to draw out air from cylinder, and finally it goes underground in combustion chamber.

(iii) **Power/Firing Stroke :** In this stroke in underground hot air, diesel is made fine spray by injector. The diesel starts burning with the contact of hot air and there is increase in the volume of air. As a result of this, the piston is pushed and the piston starts

moving from T.D.C. to B.D.C. This force of piston moves to flywheel by way of connecting rod or crank shaft where, this power is used for other works.

(iv) **Exhaust stroke :** In this stroke, the piston moves from B.D.C. to T.D.C. Exhaust valve remains open. Because of moving piston, burned gases are pressed. These gases through exhaust valve and manifold silencer come out from cylinder from the way of silencer or pipe

Points to be ponder : In diesel engine,

1. Compression ratio : 1 : 12 – 1 : 22
2. Compression ratio : 350 – 550 Pound per square inch
3. Temperature of combustion chamber after compression : 600°C – 800°C
4. Injection pressure for diesel spray after compression : 1500 – 2500 pound per square inch
5. Pressure of gases after combustion : 750 – 950 pound per square inch

Ceitane Number : It shows the burning capacity of diesel fuel. Its rate is measured by a scale. It is compared with a standard fuel ceitane ($C_{16}H_{31}$).

Diesel Knock : At the burning of diesel knock, a sharp sound is created. By this knock, unequel and heavy load is put on the piston and hammering like sound comes and the engine gets hot very soon.

Following remedies to prevent diesel knock:

1. Keep more compression ratio.
2. Increase the temperature of combustion chamber.
3. Create turbulance in the combustion chamber air.
4. Increase the inlet pressure.
5. Increase the injection pressure.
6. Mix 1% of ethyl nitrate in diesel.

Delay Period : The time which is consumed in diesel spray and its burning by injector is called diesel spray. The motion of engine remains equal because of lower delay period.

Factors affecting delay period :

1. Temperature
2. Pressure
3. Fuel Automisation
4. Engine load
5. Ceitane Number of Fuel

6. Air Turbulance
7. Engine speed
8. Injection Timing

Liquefied Petroleum Gas (LPG) : In this gas, propane and butane gases are used. Propane and butane burns at 44°F and 32°F respectively. These gases can be used in any atmosphere. Both the gases are acquired by digging walls in the earth.

Advantages of L.P.G. :

1. Early inflammation
2. Lesser knocking
3. Early mixed with air
4. Completely vaporisation
5. Mixture (Fixed quantity) reaches in all the cylinders.
6. Mixture makes in the air at all temperature

Carburettor : It transforms liquid petrol after dividing it into micro particles and mixing it with air. It is applied on inlet manifold.

Principle of Carburettor : If air outlet is made narrower at any place, velocity of air is increased on emitting the air from that way.

Types of Carburettor :

(*i*) **Up-draft Carburettor :** These carburettors are fitted reversely. In these type of carburettors, air moves from down to up. But the mouth of main nozzle remains upward. There is no acceleration pump with it. Hence it is safe only for small engines.

(*ii*) **Down-draft Carburettor :** These carburettors are fitted straightly on manifold. Air comes upward to downward direction in them. Mostly these are used in engines.

(*iii*) **Horizontal Carburettor :** This carburettor remains fitted on the side of inlet manifold. Its air horn is made in laid condition and main nozzle is fitted upwardly in ventury.

Classification of Carburettor :

(*i*) **according to barrel number –**
   (*a*) Single barrel carburettor
   (*b*) Double barrel carburettor
   (*c*) Four barrel carburettor

(*ii*) **according to Venturi –**
   (*a*) Plain venturi type carburettor
   (*b*) Double venturi type carburettor
   (*c*) Wein venturi type carburettor
   (*d*) Nozzle venturi type carburettor
   (*e*) Triple Venturi type carburettor

(*iii*) **According to Float chamber –**
   (*a*) Excentric floor chamber type carburettor
   (*b*) Concentric floor chamber type carburettor

(*iv*) **According to metering system –**
   (*a*) Air bleat jet type carburettor
   (*b*) Metering rod type carburettor

(*v*) **According to power system –**
   (*a*) Manually operated carburettor
   (*b*) Vacuum operated carburettor

(*vi*) **According to changing mixture power –**
   (*a*) Constant choke type carburettor
   (*b*) Constant vacuum type carburettor

Main parts of Carburettor

   (*i*)   Float chamber
   (*ii*) Air horn and venturi
   (*iii*) Throatal valve
   (*iv*) Chock valve
   (*v*)   Needle valve and sheet
   (*vi*) Main jet and other jets
   (*vii*) Accelerating pump

Circuits in Carburettor

   (*i*)   Float circuit
   (*ii*) Ideal and low speed circuit
   (*iii*) High speed partload circuit
   (*iv*) High speed full power circuit
   (*v*)   Accelerating pump circuit

Essential works for the Carburettor maintenance:

1. Keep the carburettor clean from outside.
2. Keep the carburettor clean from inside.
3. Rightly adjusted the float level.
4. Tight the carburettor foundation.
5. Change the old throatal after friction

Fuel Injection Systems :

(*i*) **Master Fuel Injection system :** In this system, only one master pump is used. This pump supply the diesel to injectors with the pressure of pump. Its injectors are of special quality which look like plunger from top. Helix are made in this type of system, by which quantity of diesel is made more or less. Its downward portion is just like normal injector.

(ii) **Distributor Fuel Injection System :** From its single pumping element, diesel in equal quantity is supplied to the injectors of multi cylinder engines. For this, distributor is supplied diesel with sufficient pressure from master pump. From these, all the injectors get enough diesel according to firing order.

(iii) **Individual Fuel Injection system :** This system has pump of plunger type or Jak type, which has the following parts – barrel, plunger, control switch, sleeve, tuthed quadrant, delivery valve, delivery valve spring, camshaft, plunger spring and governer.

Lubrication : When two parts moves with friction, then the temperature of them increases and hence volume increases. Due to this, there is hurdle in their operation. To avoid this type of fault, in the middle of two parts, a thin layer of oil etc. is made by lubrication.

Essential qualities of any lubricant :

   (i)   Viscosity
  (ii)   Oilness
 (iii)   Flash point
 (iv)   Fire point
  (v)   Adhesiveness
 (vi)   Chemical stability
 (vii)   Physical stability
(viii)   Specific gravity
 (ix)   Acidity
  (x)   Emulsification

S.A.E. Number of Lubricants : Society of Automobile Engineers (S.A.E.) indicates the viscosity number of all lubricants. The lesser numbered the lubricant, the thinner it is. The lubricant is viscous with increasing numbers.

Air Cooling System : In this system, engine is cooled due to the atmospheric air. In this type of engine, taper fins are made on four sides of cylinder. Due to this fins, the area covered by air increases around the cylinder. In few engines, air fans are used to cool the engine.

Advantages of air cooling system :

1. Engines come at working temperature soon.
2. It does not need maintenance.
3. Lighter engines are made by this system.
4. This system can be used at cold places also

Disadvantages of air cooling system :

1. Maximum sound from engine.
2. Opposite effect on the capacity of engine.

OBJECTIVE TYPE QUESTIONS

1. Centigrade in 110° Fahrenheit is –
   (a) 89.6°C   *(b)* 273.3°C
   (c) 43.33°C   *(d)* 40.51°C

2. It is two lagged pointed tool like caliper, by which we sketch arc, circle etc.
   (a) Center punch   *(b)* Divider
   (c) Trai square   *(d)* Vernier calliper

3. Normally, the length of file is
   (a) 1" – 2.5"   *(b)* 2.5" – 4"
   (c) 4" – 16"   *(d)* 16" – 20"

4. According to grade, the number of file is –
   (a) three   *(b)* four
   (c) five   *(d)* six

5. It is a tool for opening and binding –
   (a) cheisel   *(b)* hacksaw
   (c) spanner   *(d)* scraper

6. Match the following :

A. Drill Machine	I.	Used to cut the rod, pipe and metal sheets (and flat)
B. Reemer	II.	Used to cut/sharp the metal
C. Cheisel	III.	Used to hole in the metallic jobs.
D. Hacksaw	IV.	Used to set right the wrong whole and increase the size of small hole.

	A	B	C	D
(a)	IV	III	II	I
(b)	I	II	III	IV
(c)	IV	III	I	II
(d)	III	IV	II	I

7. Of which measure are the spanner in the spanner set of circular inch –

(a) $\dfrac{13''}{16} \times \dfrac{8''}{7}$ (b) $\dfrac{16''}{17} \times \dfrac{15''}{7}$

(c) $1'' \times \dfrac{15''}{16}$ (d) $\dfrac{1''}{2} \times \dfrac{19''}{16}$

8. The types of jacks in number –
(a) 1   (b) 2
(c) 4   (d) 8

9. It is used for greasing in various essential parts of motor vehicle –
(a) Grease gun   (b) Oil gun
(c) Oil spray gun   (d) Pipe vice

10. The work of spark cleaner is –
(a) to make setting when the fuel injection of diesel engine is at fault.
(b) to clean the dirty spark plug of petrol engine
(c) to open or fit the lock washers after spreadings
(d) none of the above.

11. Which statement is false regarding combustion engine –
(a) These fuels can be made of lesser power
(b) Engines are with more capacity
(c) Fuel burns at larger space
(d) These engines have lower cost

12. Which statements are true regarding external combustion engine –
I. In these type of engines, after burning fuel outside the cylinder, water vapour is made of that heat. With the pressure of vapour power is attained which is used in other instrumental works.
II. Fuels are of lesser capacity.
III. Engines are made of increasing power
IV. It takes more time in starting engine.
(a) I, II and III   (b) I, II, and IV
(c) I, III and IV   (d) I, II, III and IV

13. When were invented automobiles vehicles
(a) 1968   (b) 1978
(c) 1988   (d) 1990

14. Valve opening is called before time –
(a) Valve timing   (b) Valve leg
(c) Valve lead   (d) Valve overlap

15. Do inlet and exhaust valves remain opening for some time :
(a) Yes

(b) No
(c) Sometimes Yes, never
(d) Never

16. Compression ignition engine was invented by–
(a) Farady   (b) Auto
(c) Dr. Rudolf diesel   (d) None of the above

17. Tally

A. Compression ratio in petrol engine   I. 1 : 4 to 1.10

B. Compression ratio in diesel engine   II. 1 : 12 to 1.22

C. Compression pressure in diesel engine   III. 350 to 55 pound per square inch

D. Pressure of gases in diesel engine after combustion   IV. 750 to 950 pound per square inch

	A	B	C	D
(a)	I	II	III	IV
(b)	II	III	IV	I
(c)	III	IV	I	II
(d)	IV	I	II	III

18. Of which metal are cylinders made?
(a) Iron   (b) Cast iron
(c) Copper   (d) Zinc

19. In liner with cast cylinder iron, which metal is used –
(a) Copper   (b) Maganese
(c) Tin   (d) Brass

20. The formula of cylinder reboring–
(a) Complete friction = taper friction + (avality)^2
(b) Taper friction = complete friction/(avality)^2
(c) Complete friction = Taper friction + avality
(d) Taper friction = complets friction/avality

21. Which statements are true in the following
I. Width of wet liner is 1.5 to 6 mm
II. Packing is not made with Flenge of dried liner
III. At the time of reboring, the cylinders which have thinner walls or bigger measurement piston is not available, in such type of cylinders, cylinders liners or sleeves are fited.
IV. Cylinders heads are of five types –
(a) I, II And III   (b) I, II and IV
(c) II, III and IV   (d) I, II, III and IV

22. Of which metal are pistons made –
 (a) Aluminium Alloy
 (b) Semi-steel
 (c) Cast iron
 (d) All of the above

23. How many types are the joints of piston ring–
 (a) 2   *(b)* 3
 (c) 8   *(d)* 10

24. If the friction of ring is more in piston, the reason of it is –
 (a) Rings are worn out
 (b) Lesser ring gap
 (c) Ring and gap is lesser
 (d) Compression is weak

25. Four cylinder firing order is –
 (a) 1 – 2 – 3 – 4   *(b)* 4 – 3 – 2 – 1
 (c) 1 – 2 – 4 – 3   *(d)* 1 – 3 – 4 – 2

26. The method of fixing valve in engines –
 (a) 'A' type valve arrangement
 (b) Side valve arrangement
 (c) 'T' type valve arrangement
 (d) *(b)* and *(c)*

27. Tally the following properly

Name of Indian Vehicle		*Exhaust*
(a) Tata		I. 0.22"
(b) Fiat		II. 0.18"
(c) Ambassador		III. 0.028"
(d) Mahindra and Mahindra Jeep		IV. 0.027"

	A	B	C	D
(a)	I	II	III	IV
(b)	IV	III	II	I
(c)	I	III	IV	II
(d)	I	III	II	IV

28. How many types are silencers –
 (a) Two   *(b)* Three
 (c) Eight   *(d)* Twelve

29. Which are the following qualities in gasoline are true –
 I. No knocking by the use of gasoline
 II. To make gasoline without gum
 III. On 90°C, 0.5 to 1.0 (Centimetre)^2 fly by means of vapour pressure
 IV. Not existing of dust particles and water etc. in gasoline
 (a) I, III and IV   *(b)* II, III and IV

(c) I, II and III   *(d)* I, II, III and IV

30. Remedies to prevent diesel noke—
 (a) To keep lesser compression ratio
 (b) to reduce injection pressure
 (c) to inrease the temperature of combustion chamber
 (d) to reduce inlent pressure of air

31. In LPG, automobiles, propane and Butane gases are used which start burning on the following temperature –
 (a) 44° F and 32°F   *(b)* 32°F and 44°F
 (c) 32°F and 24°F   *(d)* 24°F and 32°F

32. Supply terminal, diaform, C.B. pointer are the parts of ——
 (a) Petrol engine
 (b) Mechanical Fuel Pump
 (c) S.U. Electrical fuel Pmp
 (d) Paper air cleaner

33. Main parts are in diesel engine fuel supply is –
 (a) Diesel Tank   *(b)* Injector
 (c) Fuel Filter   *(d)* Fuel injection Pump

34. When showed be cleaned Diesel Filter?
 (a) After 1000 km   *(b)* After 1500 km
 (c) After 3000 km   *(d)* None of the above

35. Whose second name is throttle –
 (a) choke valve   *(b)* water supply
 (c) carburettor jet   *(d)* air cleaner

36. In carburettor, engine does not run with fast speed because :
 (a) Plazer shaft is curved
 (b) Petrol leaks from carburettor union
 (c) Air bleed hole is closed
 (d) Pipes of Float are contracted or stagnated

37. Which carburettor is used in Indian Vehicle 'Fiat' –
 (a) Ford Carburettor
 (b) Solics Carburettor
 (c) Zenith Carburettor
 (d) None of the above

38. It is a fixed type carburettor and its Float chamber surface is regulated/controlled by Togil lever
 (a) S.U. Carburettor
 (b) Zenith Carburettor
 (c) Carter Carburettor
 (d) Solux Carburettor

39. How many carburettors are on the basis of ventury

(a) 2   (b) 3
(c) 5   (d) 7

40. How many carburettors are according to metering system

(a) 2   (b) 3
(c) 5   (d) 7

41. What is the capacity of diesel tank in heavy vehicles?

(a) 40 litre   (b) 60 litre
(c) 90 litre   (d) 110 litre

42. How fuel transfer pump is operated

(a) Roller Pin
(b) Guide Pin
(c) Engine camp shaft
(d) Handle

43. How much pressure is needed for diesal spray by injector?

(a) From 500 to 1000 pound per square inch
(b) from 1000 to 1500 pound per square inch
(c) From 1500 to 2000 pound per square inch
(d) From 2000 to 2500 pound per square inch

44. Concave type piston is used in this type of chamber. By this injection is made straightly in combustion chamber

(a) Pre-ignition chamber
(b) Centre sphere chamber
(c) Sviral chamber
(d) Solid chamber

45. Diesel drips in drops in injector because –

(a) Broken spring
(b) Jam Nozzle valve
(c) Losse cape net
(d) Cut/blocking Nozzle valve

46. After driving how many kms engine oil should be replaced?

(a) 1000 km   (b) 2000 km
(c) 5000 km   (d) 6000 km

47. After how many kilometers, the oil of transmission and differential should be changed?

(a) 1000 km   (b) 2000 km
(c) 5000 km   (d) 6000 km

48. In water cooling system, how is water made cold?

(a) Radiator
(b) Thermostat valve
(c) Anti Fridge Lotion
(d) No any out of above

49. The distance of both front tyres of a vehicle is called –

(a) chassis   (b) wheel base
(c) wheel track   (d) None of the above

50. From the middle of front tyre of a vehicle, the distance of the middle of back/rear tyre is called–

(a) chassis   (b) wheel base
(c) whool track   (d) No any out of above

51. In this type of suspension, two control arms are fitted up and down. Its outer sides are joined with stub excel by rubber bush. Besides this, coil spring and shalls, observer are also used with arm.

(a) Swinging arm independent suspension
(b) Vertical guide independent suspension
(c) Parallel Link type independent suspension
(d) None of the above

52. Tally :

A. Closed circuit — I. When in some circuit, electricity, control switch and there is a medium of current flowing and to consume elecricity, there is a lamp or other ingredients and the switch is made ON, the lamp will start lighting

B. Open circuit — II. When a wire of the switch of closed circuit is taken out or broken the lamp will not light on switching ON.

C. Leakage circuit — III When a wire of a circuit completes circuits with a body of ingredient etc.

D. Short circuit — IV When in some circuit, orbit is not complete with lamp etc. and starts straightly flowing in some wire etc.

	A	B	C	D
(a)	I	II	III	IV
(b)	I	II	IV	III
(c)	III	II	I	IV
(d)	III	II	IV	I

53. Which substance of the following is conductor–
(*a*) Chinese mud   (*b*) mica
(*c*) Platinum   (*d*) Fiber

54. Which type of battery is used in motor vehicle–
(*a*) Lead Acid battery
(*b*) Alkaline battery
(*c*) Any out of the above
(*d*) None of the above

55. In ignition system, how much volt current reaches on spark plugs?
(*a*) 5,000 volt   (*b*) 10,000 volt
(*c*) 15,000 volt   (*d*) 20,000 volt

56. Magneto does not function on heating the engine becaue –
(*a*) condenser is burst
(*b*) magnet coil gets short circuit
(*c*) C.B. point gap is lesser
(*d*) None of the above

57. Spark plug is fitted –
(*a*) In head or cylinder block
(*b*) In ignition coil
(*c*) In copper washer
(*d*) In insulator

58. One good spark plug has characteristics –
(*a*) plug is able to work at more temperature also
(*b*) Able to wear highest voltage
(*c*) Lesser blockage of carbon
(*d*) All out of above

59. When mixture burns with a jerk, explosion is caused. By this, piston is jerked suddenly and its temperature is increased. As a result of this, there is fear of the breaking of crank shaft. It is called a fault
(*a*) Detonation   (*b*) Pre-ignition
(*c*) Short reach   (*d*) Long reach

60. These magnet rods are used in the shape of horse shoe and magnet niddle –
(*a*) Temporary magnet
(*b*) Permanent magnet
(*c*) Any out of above
(*d*) None of the above

61. By which method electricity is generated by dynamo–
(*a*) Lenz's law of Electromagnetic Induction
(*b*) Faraday's law of Electromagnetic Induction

(*c*) Fleming's Right Hand Rule
(*d*) None of the above

62. Which following remedy is right in regulating dynamo–
(*a*) Third Bush control system
(*b*) Cut-out system
(*c*) Current and voltage current system
(*d*) All of the above

63. The main part of alternator is –
(*a*) Diode Rectifier   (*b*) Core
(*c*) Hinge   (*d*) Side plate

64. Alternator makes more current because –
(*a*) Points of Regulator are sticky/greasy
(*b*) Regulator is not in order
(*c*) Regulator is wrongly adjusted
(*d*) All of the above

65. Act of self starting, in one time, maximum how many seconds should not be done
(*a*) 30 seconds   (*b*) 60 seconds
(*c*) 90 seconds   (*d*) 120 seconds

66. Match the following :
Electric instruments Requirement of current of motor vehicle
A. Head Light   I. 13 to 15 ampere
B. Self starter   II 18 to 20 ampere
C. Electric Horn   III 150 to 300 ampere
D. Other all lights   IV 8 to 12 ampere

	A	B	C	D
(*a*)	I	II	III	IV
(*b*)	II	IV	I	III
(*c*)	I	III	II	IV
(*d*)	IV	III	II	I

67. The measurement of wires using in motor vehicles –
(*a*) 1 mm to 3 mm   (*b*) 2 mm to 4 mm
(*c*) 4 mm to 8 mm   (*d*) 8 mm to 12 mm

68. Blue coloured wire is used :
(*a*) Any instrument for earth
(*b*) For fuel gauge
(*c*) For electric horn
(*d*) For tale light

69. Brown coloured wire is used –
(*a*) Any instrument for earth
(*b*) For fuel gauge
(*c*) For electric horn
(*d*) For Tale light

70. Advantages of water coolness system –
    (a) Life of engine is more
    (b) working capacity of engine increases
    (c) Engine can be made cold soon
    (d) All of the above

71. On ideal speed, in spark ignition engine, the ratio of air and petrol remains in mixture –
    (a) 4 : 1   *(b)* 1 : 4
    (c) 16 : 1   *(d)* 1 : 16

72. Which statement is true in the following –
    (a) S.A.E. 90 No. oil is lighter than 40 No. oil
    (b) S.A.E 90 No. oil is stronger than 40 No. oil
    (c) There are four types of valves in internal combustion engine
    (d) A.C. current is generated by Dynamo.

73. C.B. point is a gap –
    (a) 0.5 mm to 0.3 mm
    (b) 0.17 mm to 0.12 mm
    (c) 0.22 mm to 0.9 mm
    (d) 0.36 mm to 0.5 mm

74. Work of oil ring is –
    (a) burning oil
    (b) Preventing oil pumping
    (c) Oil pumping
    (d) None of the above

75. Work of fly wheel is –
    (a) To light weight
    (b) to complete disadvantageous stroke
    (c) to drive engine
    (d) None of the above

76. Engine oil is called filling in part –
    (a) Oil storage   *(b)* Oil Gun
    (c) Oil Tank   *(d)* Oil Pump

77. By the impact of air, in hydroelectric brake
    (a) Brakes are applied nicely
    (b) Brakes are fixed
    (c) Brakes do not apply
    (d) None of the above

78. The vehicles which have differential in the front are called –
    (a) Four wheel drive *(b)* Two wheel drive
    (c) Reverse drive   *(d)* Salooncar

79. Universal joints are made–
    (a) On the basis of machine joints
    (b) On the basis of animal joints
    (c) On the basis of human joints
    (d) None of the above

80. To keep cool the lubrication oil some engines are fitted with –
    (a) Oil cooler   *(b)* Air Filter
    (c) Air cooler   *(d)* No any out of above

81. Battery water Contains
    (a) 40% sulphuric acid
    (b) 80% sulphuric acid
    (c) 100% sulphuric acid
    (d) 120% sulphuric acid

82. Outside sheets of air cooled engine cylinder are called –
    (a) Fins
    (b) Plate
    (c) Cam
    (d) Non one out of above

83. Most important lubricating parts are –
    (a) In engine   *(b)* In universal joint
    (c) In stearing   *(d)* In differential

84. Diesel filter is used –
    (a) Before diesel Tank
    (b) In diesel pipe line
    (c) With injector
    (d) No where used

85. Fuel injection pump is used –
    (a) in petrol engine
    (b) in diesel engine
    (c) in both engines
    (d) None of the above

86. Lubrication oil is mixed in two stroke engine–
    (a) in petrol   *(b)* in water
    (c) in grease   *(d)* None of the above

87. At the time of section stroke in diesel engine
    (a) Petrol comes
    (b) Diesel and air comes
    (c) Only clean/fresh air comes
    (d) None of the above

88. In petrol engine, to generate spark is applied –
    (a) spark lighter   *(b)* Injector
    (c) Sparker   *(d)* Spark plug

89. In cold weather, it is essential in engine –
    (a) Thermostat valve *(b)* Heater valve
    (c) Radiator valve   *(d)* None of the above

90. Which is the engine in which piston and crank shaft is not used –
    (a) spark ignition engine

(b) compression engine
(c) Vencal Rotary engine
(d) V 8 engine

91. In fuel pump, both non-returned valves are fitted
    (a) Inlet   *(b)* Outlet
    (c) same type   *(d)* Different type

92. The reason of engine nock is
    (a) Dirty oil
    (b) Over flow
    (c) Tight run of engine
    (d) More compression ratio

93. The distance between T.D.C. and B.D.C. is
    (a) 90°   *(b)* 180°
    (c) 360°   *(d)* None of the above

94. Diesel engine contains battery or magnet –
    (a) More essential
    (b) Not essential
    (c) Both are essential
    (d) No any

95. Diesel burns in diesel engine –
    (a) By injector   *(b)* By compression
    (c) By spark plug   *(d)* None of the above

96. Piston has main function–
    (a) Preventing gases
    (b) to increase power
    (c) to make the engine revolve
    (d) to complete the strokes of engine

97. How much volt has a battery cell?
    (a) 2 volt   *(b)* 3 volt
    (c) 6 volt   *(d)* 12 volt

98. Pump means –
    (a) to make water   *(b)* to make mud
    (c) to make air   *(d)* All above

99. In this type of pump, motion of water remains the same all the time –
    (a) Centrifugal Pump
    (b) Volute Pump
    (c) Turbine Pump
    (d) Air lift Pump

100. How many binds are reciprocating pumps –
    (a) 2   *(b)* 4
    (c) 11   *(d)* 13

101. The use of this type of pump is made to pump out water or oil etc. in large quqntity –
    (a) Air lift pump   *(b)* Hydraulic Ram

(c) Rotary Pump   *(d)* None of the above

102. Which is also called implus pump in the following–
    (a) Air lift pump   *(b)* Hydraulic pump
    (c) Rotary pump   *(d)* None of the above

103. What means are used to drive Mono Block Pump?
    (a) Electric motor   *(b)* Diesel engine
    (c) Steam engine   *(d)* All above

104. Tally –
    A. For water at home   I. Centrifugal Pump
    B. For deep well   II. Reciprocating Pump
    C. For low lift   III. Deep well Vertical Turbine Pump
    D. to increase pressure

	A	B	C	D
(a)	I	II	III	I
(b)	II	III	I	I
(c)	III	II	II	I
(d)	III	I	III	II

105. For irrigation in villages, which one is used –
    (a) Steam engines   *(b)* Diesel engines
    (c) Both above   *(d)* None of the above

106. Gears or cam of which the following pump revolve–
    (a) Reciprocating Pump
    (b) Hydraulic Pump
    (c) Rotary Pump
    (d) Power Pump

107. Which Pump runs up and down of the following –
    (a) Reciprocating Pump
    (b) Hydraulic Pump
    (c) Rotary Pump
    (d) Power Pump

108. This pump is used to draw out water from public places and houses –
    (a) Power Pump   *(b)* Hand Pump
    (c) Rotary Pump   *(d)* None of the above

109. This pump functions on the principle of centrifugal face
    (a) Air lift Pump   *(b)* Centrifugal pump
    (c) Hand pump   *(d)* Power pump

110. How many types of pumps –
    (a) 4   *(b)* 6

(c) 10   (d) 12

111. Ideal water is that water which contains –
(a) One part of hydrogen and two parts of oxygen in volume
(b) One part of hydrogen and one part of oxygen in volume
(c) Two part of hydrogen and one part of oxygen in volume
(d) Two part of hydrogen and two part of oxgen in volume

112. How many types of hardness is in water –
(a) 2   (b) 4
(c) 5   (d) 6

113. Permanent hardness is created in water –
(a) By mixing calcium and magnesium carbonates
(b) By remaining calcium and magnesium bicarbonates
(c) By mixing calcium and magnesium sulphates
(d) None of the above

114. Temporary hardness is created in water –
(a) By mixing calcium and magnesium carbonates
(b) By remaining calcium and magnesium bicarbonates
(c) By mixing calcium and magnesium sulphates
(d) None of the above

115. In how many main parts of water supply is divided –
(a) 2   (b) 3
(c) 5   (d) 7

116. For heating up water, like fuel is used –
(a) wood   (b) solar energy
(c) steam coal   (d) All above

117. Gear change liver is applied on or on .... in gear box –
(a) Clutch   (b) Stearing Gear box
(c) Stearing Column (d) None of the above

118. Main function in mechanical brake is of–
(a) Shoe adjuster   (b) Spring
(c) Cam   (d) Clutch

119. Which oil is used in Hydrolic oil system –
(a) Gear oil   (b) Brake oil
(c) Engine oil   (d) None of the above

120. At what degree universal joints do not work properly –
(a) 15°   (b) 30°
(c) 45°   (d) 90°

121. In oil bath type air cleaner which one is filled
(a) water   (b) kerosene oil
(c) mustard oil   (d) mobil oil

122. Delivery valve is fitted in fuel injection pump–
(a) middle   (b) above
(c) Down/below   (d) Corner

123. Performs diesel supply work to injector –
(a) Feed Pump   (b) Fuel injection
(c) Air Pump   (d) No any

124. In carburettor Float chamber, pump comes first and foremost –
(a) water   (b) oil
(c) petrol   (d) current

125. Used for knowing Brake horse power –
(a) Dynamometer   (b) Voltmeter
(c) Techometer   (d) None of the given

ANSWERS

1	2	3	4	5	6	7	8	9	10
(c)	(b)	(c)	(d)	(c)	(d)	(c)	(b)	(a)	(b)

11	12	13	14	15	16	17	18	19	20
(c)	(d)	(b)	(c)	(a)	(c)	(a)	(b)	(b)	(a)

21	22	23	24	25	26	27	28	29	30
(a)	(d)	(b)	(c)	(d)	(d)	(c)	(b)	(d)	(c)

31	32	33	34	35	36	37	38	39	40
(a)	(c)	(d)	(c)	(b)	(d)	(b)	(b)	(c)	(a)

41	42	43	44	45	46	47	48	49	50
(c)	(c)	(c)	(d)	(d)	(d)	(c)	(a)	(c)	(b)

51	52	53	54	55	56	57	58	59	60
(c)	(a)	(c)	(a)	(d)	(b)	(a)	(d)	(a)	(b)
61	62	63	64	65	66	67	68	69	70
(b)	(d)	(a)	(d)	(a)	(c)	(c)	(d)	(c)	(d)
71	72	73	74	75	76	77	78	79	80
(c)	(b)	(d)	(b)	(b)	(d)	(c)	(a)	(c)	(c)
81	82	83	84	85	86	87	88	89	90
(a)	(a)	(a)	(b)	(b)	(a)	(c)	(d)	(a)	(c)
91	92	93	94	95	96	97	98	99	100
(c)	(d)	(b)	(b)	(b)	(c)	(a)	(c)	(b)	(a)
101	102	103	104	105	106	107	108	109	110
(c)	(b)	(d)	(b)	(b)	(c)	(a)	(b)	(b)	(b)
111	112	113	114	115	116	117	118	119	120
(c)	(a)	(c)	(b)	(b)	(d)	(c)	(c)	(b)	(c)
121	122	123	124	125					
(d)	(b)	(b)	(c)	(c)					

———

3

REFRIGERATION AND AIR CONDITIONING

Refrigerator : It is a device used for cooling things. It is also called a heat pump.

In refrigeration system, the temperature of some place is made smaller than the temperature of atmosphere.

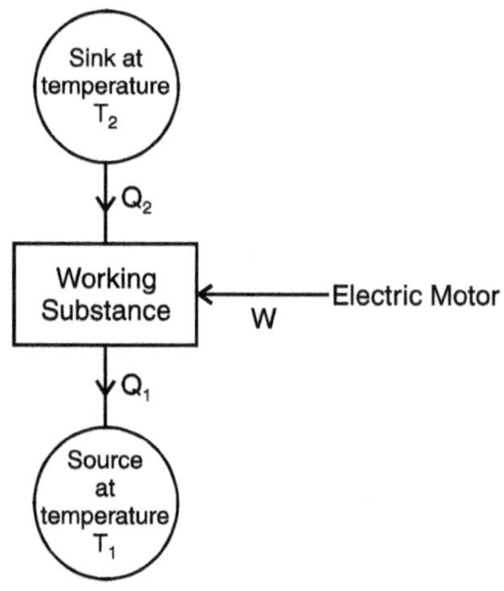

Work done on the system is given by
$$W = Q_1 - Q_2$$

Coefficient of performance (β) of a refrigerator: It is defined as the ratio of quantity of heat removed per cycle from the contents of the refrigerator (Q_2) to the energy spent per cycle (W) to remove this heat, *i.e.,*

$$\beta = \frac{Q_2}{W} = \frac{Q_2}{Q_1 - Q_2}$$

β stands for efficiency of the refrigerator. Thus, higher the value of β, more efficient is the refrigerator.

Uses of refrigerator : It is used for making ice, cold storage, diary, bakeries, and for cooling the drinking water in buildings and restaurants.

Heat : We know that when a piece of red hot iron is dropped into a beaker containing water, the water becomes hot and the red hot iron piece cools down till the temperatures of the two become equal. It appears that 'something' has flown from red hot iron piece to water. This 'something' which flows from a body at higher temperature to another body at lower temperature, when the two are in contact, is called 'heat'.

Unit of heat : The practical unit of heat is a calorie. One calorie is defined as the amount of heat energy required to raise the temperature of one gram of water through 1°C.

1 calorie = 4.186 joules

Different kinds of heat:
 (i) Specific heat
 (ii) Sensible heat
 (iii) Latent heat

Transfer of heat : Heat can be transmitted from one place to the other by three modes:
 (i) **Conduction :** It is the phenomenon of transfer of heat through one part of the body to another, from particle to particle in the direction of fall of temperature without any actual movement of the particles.
 (ii) **Convection :** It is the phenomenon of transfer of heat with the actual movement of the

particles of the body.

(iii) **Radiation :** It is the phenomenon of transfer of heat from the source to the receiver without any actual movement of source or receiver and also without heating the intervening medium.

Radiation is the fastest mode of heat transfer, having velocity in vacuum is given by
$$C = 3 \times 10^8 \text{ m/s}.$$

Temperature : Temperature of a body as the degree of hotness or coldness of the body. It is now regarded as one of the seven fundamental quantities like length, mass and time.

Thermometer : It is a device, which uses any property of matter that changes with temperature, to measure the unknown temperature.

Several kinds of thermometers have been developed *e.g.* mercury thermometer, electrical resistance thermometers, ideal gas thermometers, thermoelectric thermometers and radiation thermometers (called as pyrometers).

Mercury freezes at –40°C and starts boiling at 357°C. Thus alcohol freezes at –115°C and starts boiling at 78°C.

Various scales of temperatures:

(i) **Celsius scale (formerly called centigrade scale) :** It was designed by Celsius in 1710. Here, the melting point of ice is regarded as 0°C and the boiling point of water as 100°C. The space between these two fixed points is divisible into 100 equal parts. Each part represent 1°C.

(ii) **Fahrenheit scale :** It was designed by Fahrenheit in the year 1717. The lower fixed point on the scale is chosen as 32° F, which is the melting point of ice at standard atmospheric pressure. The upper fixed point on the scale is 212°F, which is the boiling point of water at standard atmospheric pressure. The space between the two fixed points is divided into 180 equal parts. Each part represents 1°F.

(iii) **Reaumer Scale :** It was designed by Reaumer in the year 1730. The lower fixed point is 0°R representing melting point of ice. The upper fixed point is 80°R, which

represents boiling point of water. The space between the two fixed points is divided into 80 equal parts. Each part represens 1°R.

If θ_C, θ_F and θ_R are temperature values of a body on Celsius scale, Fahrenheit scale and Reaumer scale respectively, then

$$\frac{\theta_C - 0}{100} = \frac{\theta_F - 32}{180} = \frac{\theta_R - 0}{80}$$

Specific heat : Specific heat of a substance may be defined as the amount of heat required to raise the temperature of unit mass of the substance through unit degree. It is represented by (small) c.

Molar specific heat : Molar specific heat of a substance is defined as the amount of heat required to raise the temperature of one gram mole of the substance through a unit degree. It is represented by (capital) C.

Dulong and Petit law : This law states that, "the average molar specific heat of all metals at room temperature is constant, being nearly equal to $3R = 6$ cal. mole^{-1} K^{-1} = 25 J mole^{-1}K^{-1}, where R is gas contant for one mole of the gas."

Heat capacity : Heat capacity (or thermal capacity) of a body is defined as the amount of heat required to raise the temperature of the (whole) body through 1°C or 1K.

Water equivalent : Water equivalent of a body is defined as the mass of water which would absorb or evolve the same amount of heat as is done by the body in rising (or falling) through the same range of temperature. It is represented by w.

Latent heat : Latent heat of a substance is the amount of heat energy required to change the state of unit mass of the substance from solid to liquid or from liquid to gas/vapour without any change in temperature.

Gas Laws :

(i) **Boyle's Law :** This gas law was discovered by Robert Boyle in 1662.

This law states that the temperature remaining constant, the volume V of given mass of a gas is inversely proportional to its pressure P, *i.e.*

$$V \propto \frac{1}{P}$$

$$= \frac{K}{P}$$

$$\Rightarrow PV = K$$

Where K is a constant, which depends upon nature and temperature of the gas.

Boyle's law is perfectly obeyed at high temperature and low pressure of a gas.

(ii) **Charle's Law :** It states that the pressure remaining constant, the volume of a given mass of a gas increases or decreases by $\dfrac{1}{273.15}$ of its volume at $0°C$, for each $1°C$ rise or fall in temperature.

$$\frac{V}{T} = K$$

where K is a constant, which depends upon nature and pressure of the gas.

(iii) **Gay Lussac's Law or Regnault's Law :** It states that the volume remaining constant, the pressure of a given mass of a gas increases or decreases by $\dfrac{1}{273.15}$ of its pressure at $0°C$ for each $1°C$ rise or fall in temperature.

$$\frac{P}{T} = \text{constant (K)}$$

Perfect gas equation : It is an equation which relates to the pressure, volume and temperature of the given state of an ideal gas. It can be obtained by combining Boyle's law and Charle's law.

It is given by

$$PV = nRT$$

where *n* is the number of moles contained in the given gas of volume V, pressure P and temperature TK.

R is a universal gas constant,

$$R = \frac{PV}{nT}$$

$$= \frac{\text{pressure} \times \text{volume}}{\text{number of moles} \times \text{temperature}}$$

$$= \frac{\text{work done}}{\text{number of moles} \times \text{temperature}}$$

Thus universal gas constant signifies the work done by (or on) a gas per mole per Kelvin.

S.I. unit of R is J/mole/K.

Ideal gas : It is that gas which strictly obeys the gas laws, (such as Boyle's law, Charle's law and Gay Lussac's law).

Characteristics of an ideal gas are given below:

(i) The size of the molecule of a gas is zero *i.e.* each molecule of a gas is a point mass with no dimensions.

(ii) There is no force of attraction or repulsion amongst the molecules of the gas.

Avogadro Number : It is defined as the number of atoms in 12 grams of C-12. In general, Avogadro number is the number of molecules in one gram mole of a substance. It is represented by N.

Its accepted numerical value is 6.023×10^{23} per gram mole.

Avogadro number helps us

(i) to calculate the number of molecules in given volume of a gas.

(ii) to calculate number of atoms in the given amount of an element.

(iii) to calculate the actual weight of molecule of a substance.

(iv) to calculate actual weight of one atom of an element.

Enthalpy : It is defined as the fragment of energy present in some flowing substance.

$$\text{Enthalpy} = \frac{\text{Internal energy} \times \text{specific volume} \times \text{extreme pressure}}{\text{Joule}}$$

Condensation : In this method, after drawing out heat, vapour is transformed into matter.

Joule's law : Internal energy of given quantity of gas only depends upon temperature.

Joule's equivalent : The quantity of heat is always created by definite quantity of the doing of mechanical work.

$$J = \frac{W}{H}$$

where W is the work done, H is the heat and J the mechanical energy produced by Joule.

Instruments used in refrigeration and air conditioning :

(i) Screw driver

(ii) Flat file
(iii) Knife
(iv) Hacksaw
(v) Insulated plier
(vi) Steel rule
(vii) Poker
(viii) Ballpen hammer
(ix) Hand drill machine
(x) Spaner set

Relay : It is an automatic switch used for ON or OFF supply.

Snip : It is used to cut light sheet of a metal.

Taps : This tool is used to make bangles in the hole.

Dye : This tool is used to make bangle on iron rod. It is made up of steel.

Flairing tool : It is used for making copper tubes flairs of different things.

Gas cylinder : It is made up of cast iron and it contains various gases.

Valve : This method is used to control the charging or discharging of gas.

Vacuum pump : It is used in refrigeration system to draw out air completely before charging of gas.

Vapour compression refrigerator : In this system, vapours of refrigerant from compression of compressor are transformed into liquid. The liquid after taking heat of whose place, it makes vapour, the place gets cold.

Its main factors are given below:

(i) **Vaporization :** Transformation of refrigerant liquid from purified heat into vapour.

(ii) **Condensation :** Removing heat from refrigerant vapours, again transforming into liquid.

The parts of vapour compression refrigeration system are given below:

(i) Discharge line
(ii) Receiver tank
(iii) Section line
(iv) Liquid line
(v) Expansion valve
(vi) Compressor
(vii) Condenser
(viii) Evaporator

Absorption refrigeration system : In this system, heat energy is used and the heat of place, which is to be made cold is purified. The invention of this system was made by French scientist, Ferdind care.

In exploitation method, mostly ammonia refrigerant is used. This method has following main parts:

(i) **Generator :** It is a kind of appliance in which aqua-ammonia (solution of ammonia and water) is heated by outer means burner, heater etc.

(ii) **Condenser :** It is an appliance with two shells. In one shell, refrigerant vapours flow and in other shell, cold liquid is existed. It makes liquid ammonia after reducing temperature and making cold ammonia vapoure. Three kinds of condenser are used :
- Air Cooled Condenser
- Water Cooled Condenser
- Air and water cooled Condenser

(iii) **Receiver :** This appliance is filled with liquid refrigerant and, refrigerant is used in it according to necessity. It is fitted between condenser and expansion valve.

(iv) **Expansion valve :** It is used to control the flow of refrigerant and, is fitted between receiver and evaporator.

(v) **Evaporator :** In this part, ammonia and hydrogen gas go into the exchanger. When hydrogen gas passes through heat exchanger, it gives coolness.

(vi) **Absorber :** There is an arrangement of cooling in this appliance, hence tubes are fitted. It cools the refrigerant at low pressure.

Types of refrigerant :

(i) **Primary Refrigerant :** These refrigerants are used directly in refrigerant system and also starts working at low temperature.

Examples :

Halocarbon compound (CCl_2F_2, CCl_3F, $CClF_2$, $CClF_2$) Aceotropes (Mixture of 25% of freeon-12 and 15% of freeon-22)

Hydrocarbon (CH_4, CH_3CH_3, $CH(CH_3)_3$).

Inorganic compounds (NH_3, CO_2, H_2O, SO_2).

(ii) **Secondary Refrigerant :** These refrigerants first get cold by primary refrigerants, then they work at colder place. This type of refrigerants are used in

air conditioning installations and ice factories. These are mainly of two kinds—water and brian.

Compressor : It is that part of refrigerant system in which refrigerants vapours are acquired at lesser pressure and are compressed at higher pressure in lower volume. It pulls refrigerant to condensor from evaporator.

Types of Compressor :

(i) **Reciprocating compressor :** In this type of compressor, piston runs forward and backward. It has following main parts:
- *(a)* Cylinder,
- *(b)* Connecting rod,
- *(c)* Valve,
- *(d)* Gasket,
- *(e)* Crank,
- *(f)* Crank shaft, and
- *(g)* Piston

(ii) **Rotary compressor :** In this type of compressor, in four sides closed cylinder, gas is compressed by the motion of the roller of rotary. These compressor are of two types :
- *(a)* Rotary blade type and
- *(b)* Stationary blade type.

(iii) **Centrifugal compressor :** In this type of compressor, centrifugal force is used for compression. On its main body, inlet and outlet are fixed. In the middle of main body, impellers are fitted with electric motor.

These compressors are mainly used in air-conditioning plant. These are used in the refrigeration plants having capacity 50 tons to 5,000 tons.

Regulatory equipments : The necessary means which are used for the running of refrigeration system, safely and properly, are called regulatory equipments.

These equipments regulate refrigerant flow, capacity of compressor, pressure and temperature.

Capacity regulator : Capacity is unable to be controlled by fluctuation of load. For this, another equipment is used, which is called as capacity regulator.

Pressure regulation : In this regulation, the pressure of refrigerating machine is regulated to a specific limit. It is regulated in four ways—
- *(i)* by liquid pressure valve,
- *(ii)* by pressure regulating valve,
- *(iii)* by section pressure hold valve, and
- *(iv)* by high and low pressure cut out.

Temperature regulation : This regulation is just like thermostat type. This is of two kinds—
- *(i)* Bi-metallic thermostat and
- *(ii)* Thermal valve thermostat.

Atmosphere : The gaseous envelope surrounding the earth is called earth's atmosphere. The earth's atmosphere mainly consists of nitrogen 78% and oxygen 21% along with a little portion of argon, carbon-dioxide, water vapour, hydrocarbons, sulphur compound and dust particles.

The density of the atmospheric air goes on decreasing gradually as we go up. It has been divided into various regions as given below:
- *(i)* Troposphere
- *(ii)* Stratosphere
- *(iii)* Mesosphere
- *(iv)* Ionosphere/thermosphere

Smoke : It is to be present in small particles of dust (CO_2). The radius of smoke particles is approximately from 0.002 mm to 0.001 mm.

Dew : Having saturated, water vapours in the air start freezing on things but heat of a thing look in the shape of water vapour drops.

Fog : It is a moisture present on that temperature which is a saturated temperature of the air.

Duct : It is defined as the path for emitting air. These are made of thin tinned sheet of iron, galvanised steel, aluminium, copper or brass. Fibre board is fixed on the upper surface of duct. Duct has three types :
- *(i)* Rigid type,
- *(ii)* Flexible round type, and
- *(iii)* Pre-fabricated duct.

Grill : It is used to cover the sides of duct and, it regulates the direction of air flowing in a room. It is of two types :
- *(i)* stable grill, and
- *(ii)* adjustable grill.

Registor : This grill which is fitted with damper for regulating the quantity of passing air is called registor.

There are two types of registors :
- *(i)* stable registor, and
- *(ii)* adjustable registor.

Humidity : Water vapours or moisture in the air of some area is called humidity.

The instrument used to measure humidity is called as 'Sling Psychrometer'. In this instrument, a set of dried bulb and wet bulb is kept.

Humidity can be drived in two ways—

(i) Absolute humidity and

(ii) Relative humidity

Ice : The solid state of any liquid (just like water) is called as ice.

Snow : On the peaks of mountains, the ice creating with the contact of cold air is called snow.

Frost : The ice freezing on the plants, trees etc., in contact with the cold air is called frost.

Raw water ice : The ice made from freezing ordinary water is called raw water ice.

Crystal ice : The ice made from distilled water is called crystal ice.

Ice plant : It is that machine by which ice is frozen.

Cold storage : It is that airconditioned room in which food stuffs is kept safe on low temperatrue for a long time.

Types of cold storage :

(i) Temporary storage,

(ii) Permanent storage and

(iii) Frozen storage

Electric charges and electricity : Thales, a Greek philospher (640–556BC) observed that a piece of amber, on being rubbed with fur or cat skin, developed the property of attracting small bits of paper, straw or feathers towards it.

Now it is known that any two substances on being rubbed acquire this attractive property. The bodies are then considered to become electrified or to have acquired electricity or charged with electricity.

The charge that developes on glass rod on being rubbed with silk is known as positive charge and the silk used for rubbing also acquires an equal negative charge.

Types of electricity :

(i) **Static electricity :** This electricity deals with the electric charges at rest.

(ii) **Current electricity :** This electricity deals with the electric charges in motion.

Electronic principle of electricity : In every substance, electrons moves around protons and neutrons. When by some means, the number of protons is to be greater than the number of electrons and that positive side be more lesser then negative side is made.

Electric potential (V) : Electric potential at a point is defined as the amount of work done in moving a unit positive charge from infinity to that point without acceleration against electric forces.

The electric potential at a point near an isolated positive charge will be positive. In this case, work has to be done.

The electric potential at a point near an isolated negative charge will be negative. It is a scalar quantity.

S.I. unit of electric potential is volt (V).

Voltmeter : It is an instrument is used to measure the potential difference between two points.

Resistance (R) : It is the property of a conductor that opposes the flow of electron. The component used for this purpose is called resistor.

S.I. unit of resistance is ohm (Ω).

Electric current (I) : It is defined as the rate of flow of charge through any section of a conductor. If 'Q' be the charge flowing in the conductor for 't' seconds, then current is given by

$$I = \frac{Q}{t}$$

S.I. unit of electric current is ampere.

Ammeter : It is an instrument used for measuring electric current in a circuit.

Earth : It is a safe method in which the voltage of earth is zero. Equipments fitted with earth make safely for human being inspite of coming electricity.

Wire : It is used to pass electricity from one place to another.

Colours of wire :

(i) Live wire → Reddish colour,

(ii) Neutral wire → Black colour, and

(iii) Earth wire → Green colour.

Types of wire :

(i) Fuse wire

(ii) Winding wire

(iii) Flexible wire

(iv) P.V.C. wire

(v) C.T.S. wire

(vi) V.I.R. wire

Electric Power : The electric power of an electric circuit or an appliance is the rate at which it converts electric energy into heat energy.

$$\text{Power} = \frac{\text{work}}{\text{time}} = \text{voltage} \times \text{current}$$

$$= (\text{current})^2 \times \text{Resistance}$$

$$= \frac{(\text{Voltage})^2}{\text{Resistance}}$$

S.I. unit of electric power is watt.

1 Horse power = 746 watt.

Energy : It is the capacity to do work. It is of three types :

(i) **Kinetic energy :** The kinetic energy of a moving body is defined as its ability to do work by virtue of its motion.

$$\text{K.E.} = \frac{(\text{mass}) \times (\text{velocity})^2}{2}$$

(ii) **Potential energy :** A body is said to have potential energy if by virtue of its position or state it is able to do work.

P.E. = (mass) × (acceleration due to gravity) × (height reached).

(iii) **Mechanical energy :** It is defined as the sum of the kinetic and the potential energy of an object.

M.E. = K.E. + P.E.

Other types of energy are as given below :

(i) Heat/thermal energy

(ii) Light energy

(iii) Electrical energy

(iv) Sound energy

(v) Atomic energy

(vi) Nuclear energy

(vii) Wind energy

Alternating current (a.c.) : It is that current which changes continuously in magnitude and periodically in direction. It can be represented by a sine curve or a cosine curve, *i.e.,*

$$I = I_o \sin \omega t$$

or $\qquad I = I_o \cos \omega t$

where I_o is the peak value of current and I is the instantaneous value of current.

$\omega = 2\pi f = \dfrac{2\pi}{T}$, where T is the period of a.c. and f is the frequency of a.c.

The alternating e.m.f. can similarly be represented as

$$E = E_o \sin \omega t$$

or $\qquad E = E_o \cos \omega t.$

Direct current (d.c.) : The direction of the current in d.c. always remains the same. Its magnitude also remains the same. This current is generated by battery, d.c. generator or dynamo.

D.C. motor : A d.c. motor converts direct current energy from a battery into mechanical energy of rotation. It is based on the fact that when a coil carrying current is held in a magnetic field, it experiences a torque, which rotates one coil.

Efficiency of d.c. motor :

$$\eta = \frac{\text{back e.m.f.}}{\text{e.m.f. of battery}}$$

The efficiency (η) becomes maximum when back

$$\text{e.m.f.} = \frac{\text{e.m.f. of battery}}{2}$$

Requirements of d.c. motor :

(i) Magnetic field

(ii) Armature

(iii) Commutator and brush etc.

(iv) Electrical energy

Loss in d.c. motor :

(i) Copper loss

(ii) Iron loss

(iii) Stray loss

Types of d.c. motor :

(i) Series motor

(ii) Shunt motor

(iii) Compound motor

Starter : A motor starter is a variable resistance, which protects the motor from damage, when it is switched on.

D.C. generator : It produces direct current energy from mechanical energy of rotation of a coil.

A.C. motor : It is a motor which runs by a.c. electricity. Two types of a.c. motor are used—

(i) Synchronous motor

(ii) Induction motor

A.C. generator : It produces alternating current energy from mechanical energy of rotation of a coil.

Air conditioner : It is a machine which regulates the temperature, humidity, air revolution and the purity and cleanness of air.

Air outdoor is the outer door of air conditioner where air comes in a room in such a way that the air may not move from backward.

Types of air coditioner :

(i) **Room Air Conditioner :** The equipment creating comfortableness in a room for human being is called air conditioner.

Normally for rest, temperature necessity is 21°C–27°C. The cooling capacity of room air conditioner is 4,000 to 36,000 British Thermal Unit (B.T.U.) per hour.

(ii) **Central Air Conditioner :** These conditioners are used to air conditioned two or more rooms simultaneously. The cooling capacity of central air conditioner is 24,000 to 1,00,000 British Thermal Unit (B.T.U.) per Hour. These are of four types :

(i) Package unit
(ii) Remote system
(iii) Heating and cooling system
(iv) Heat pump unit

Air conditioning Installation: The process of installing air conditioner at proper place with proper method is called air conditioning installation.

Air conditioners are installed in the following ways.

(i) **Window Installation :** Having fitted iron frame on four sides of a window, unit is fitted.
(ii) **Transam Installation :** After fitting metal frame on the door, unit is fitted.
(iii) **Through-the-wall Installation :** After cutting wall on the necessary spot and fitting metal frame, unit is fitted.

Cooler : It is a refrigeration machine creating cold, in which drinking substances are cooled.

Types of cooler :

(i) **Water cooler :** This cooler is used to cool the water. Water gets cooled from 10°C to 12.5°C.

A. On the basis of work, water coolers are of two types:

(a) Bottle cooler and
(b) Pressure cooler

B. On the basis of capacity, water coolers arc of three types,

(a) 40 litre per hour,
(b) 60 litre per hour and
(c) 160 litre per hour.

(ii) **Milk cooler :** This cooler is used to cool the milk. For storing milk, milk is made cold at temperature of 4°C. Milk coolers are of three types:

(a) Airater type,
(b) Vet type and
(c) Tube type

(iii) **Bottled Beverage cooler :** It is a cooler cabinet in which things (which are to be made cold) are kept. This rectangular tank is made up of steel. Opening door is an airtight.

OBJECTIVE TYPE QUESTIONS

1. Primary refrigerant in cold storage is
   (a) Water (b) Ethene
   (c) Methane (d) Ammonia
2. The suitable temperature difference for eggs is
   (a) 10°C (b) 8°C
   (c) 5°C (d) 2°C
3. In the cooling chamber of coolers, shells are—
   (a) circular (b) rectangular
   (c) U-type (d) V-type
4. The capacity of package type central air conditioner is—
   (a) 10 ton (b) 50 ton
   (c) 100 ton (d) 1000 ton
5. Which relation is true for the coefficient of performance (β) of a refrigerator—

(a) $\beta = \dfrac{Q_1}{Q_1 - Q_2}$ (b) $\beta = \dfrac{Q_2}{Q_1 - Q_2}$

(c) $\beta = \dfrac{Q_1 - Q_2}{Q_1}$ (d) $\beta = \dfrac{Q_1 - Q_2}{Q_2}$

6. S.I. unit of universal gas constant is
(a) J/cal./K (b) Jcal./K
(c) J/mole/K (d) Jmole/K

7. The instrument used to measure current, voltage and resistance is called as
(a) Voltmeter (b) Ammeter
(c) Galvanometer (d) Multimeter

8. The primary refrigerant of brian is—
(a) NaCl (b) NH_3
(c) CO_2 (d) SO_2

9. The temperature of cold storage for fig is
(a) 42°C (b) 34°C
(c) 45°C (d) 31°C

10. Gas cylinder is used in
(a) gas charging
(b) drawing out gas
(c) completely air free
(d) none of the above

11. The test done before filling the gas is—
(a) Closed test (b) Short test
(c) Open test (d) Leakage test

12. Which method is wrong for transferring the heat from one place to another—
(a) Refraction (b) Convection
(c) Conduction (d) Radiation

13. The temperature of cold milk is—
(a) 0°C (b) 4°C
(c) 6°C (d) 10°C

14. Unit of heat is
(a) Ohm (b) Calorie
(c) Ampere (d) Volt

15. The working of a dynamo is based on the principle of
(a) thermal effect of current
(b) magnetic effect of current
(c) chemical effect of current
(d) electromagnetic induction

16. Unit of work is
(a) Farad (b) Second
(c) Joule (d) Watt

17. 1 C.H.U. equals
(a) 453.6 calorie (b) 361.6 calorie
(c) 301.7 calorie (d) 153.6 calorie

18. A lot of germs of substance are killed at—
(a) normal temperature
(b) freezing point
(c) boiling point
(d) none of the above

19. It is used to measure temperature—
(a) Thermometer (b) Gauge meter
(c) Barometer (d) Lactometer

20. At absolute scale, zero gauge pressure relevant to—
(a) 1.03 kg/cm^2 (b) 100 litre water
(c) 50 cm of Hg (d) None of the above

21. Evaporator exploits—
(a) Sensible heat (b) Latent heat
(c) Kinetic energy (d) Potential energy

22. The normal temperature of frozen storage is
(a) –17.8°C (b) –15.4°C
(c) –11.2°C (d) 0°C

23. The heat of a substance which transforms its temperature is called—
(a) Sensible heat (b) Specific heat
(c) Latent heat (d) None of the above

24. Which one is not the unit of heat—
(a) Ampere (b) Calorie
(c) C.H.U. (d) Kilo calorie

25. For keeping safe of food stuffs for long time, which one is used—
(a) Refrigerator (b) Air conditioner
(c) Cold storage (d) Cooler

26. Refrigeration machine started in—
(a) 1909 (b) 1911
(c) 1920 (d) 1941

27. Fruits are kept in storage—
(a) Keeping in hot water
(b) Keeping in squash (solution)
(c) Wrapping in waxy paper
(d) Taking out from oil

28. .... is constant in the conversion of state of a substance.
(a) Volume (b) Force
(c) Temperature (d) Pressure

29. It is used to block the unneccessary water vapours from ammonia vapours—
(a) Analyser (b) Heat exchanger
(c) Rectifier (d) Absorber

30. In exploitation method, refrigerant is—
(a) CO_2 (b) NH_3
(c) Freeon (d) C_4H_{10}

31. Water cooler are of—
(a) 40 Watts (b) 150 Watts
(c) 200 Watts (d) 250 Watts

32. To convert mechanical energy into electrical energy one can use
   (a) a.c. dynamo   *(b)* d.c. dynamo
   (c) electric motor   *(d)* *(a)* and *(b)*

33. In cold storage, the form of refrigerant used is
   (a) Brian   *(b)* NH_3
   (c) SO_2 *(d)* CO_2

34. 'Fast running train' is an example of—
   (a) Light energy   *(b)* Kinetic energy
   (c) Potential energy   *(d)* Atomic energy

35. The upper fixed point in Reaumer Scale is
   (a) $0°$ R   *(b)* $32°R$
   (c) $80°R$ *(d)* $212°R$

36. Vaporisation is used to
   (a) cool the heat
   (b) reduce power expenditure
   (c) increase compression work
   (d) to exploit heat quantity

37. The part to make dry ammonia vapour is called
   (a) Rectifier
   (b) Evaporator
   (c) Heat exchanger
   (d) Pressure reducing valve

38. Out of the following, which one is also named as water separator—
   (a) Evaporator
   (b) Pressure reducing valve
   (c) Heat exchanger
   (d) Rectifier

39. It is used to give heat in electrolax system.
   (a) stove   *(b)* electric heater
   (c) electric spark   *(d)* kerosene oil burner

40. Condenser pressure gets more because
   (a) Water supply is not proper
   (b) air enters
   (c) cooling surface gets dirty
   (d) all of the above

41. 1 Calorie equals
   (a) 2.186 Joules   *(b)* 2.093 Joules
   (c) 4.186 Joules   *(d)* 4.093 Joules

42. The famous system of wiring is
   (a) Looping system
   (b) Connector system
   (c) Tree system
   (d) All of these

43. Match the following:
   A. Halocarbon   I. CH_4
      compound
   B. Azeotrope   II. NH_3
   C. Hydrocarbon   III. Mixture of 25% of freeon-12 and 75% of freeon-22
   D. Inorganic   IV. $CClF_2\ CClF_2$
      compound

	A	B	C	D
(a)	I	II	III	IV
(b)	I	III	II	IV
(c)	IV	III	I	II
(d)	IV	I	III	II

44. Ozone layer absorbs
   (a) Ultra-violet radiations
   (b) X-rays
   (c) γ-rays
   (d) All of the above

45. Multi temperature system are of .... type.
   (a) three   *(b)* five
   (c) seven   *(d)* nine

46. Heat energy is used—
   (a) Low grade   *(b)* Medium grade
   (c) High grade   *(d)* Without grade

47. The temperature of pressure type water cooler is
   (a) $0°C – 4°C$ *(b)* $4°C – 9°C$
   (c) $10°C – 15°C$ *(d)* $15°C – 20°C$

48. A motor starter is
   (a) a fixed resistance
   (b) a fixed capacitor
   (c) a variable capacitor
   (d) a variable resistance

49. Which formula is incorrect—
   (a) Power = Voltage × Current
   (b) Absolute pressure = Atmospheric pressure + Gauge pressure
   (c) Charge = Current × time
   (d) Density = Mass × Volume

50. Due to super heating effect,
   (a) work of compressor increases
   (b) rate of turning refrigerant reduces
   (c) power consumption of refrigeration reduces
   (d) control the rate of refrigerant flow

51. The maximum volumetric capacity is
(a) 97% (b) 96%
(c) 95% (d) 85%

52. The possibility of leakage is
(a) less (b) very less
(c) more (d) none of the above

53. It is used to reduce pressure in exploitation system.
(a) Expansion value
(b) Hydrogen
(c) Aqua-ammonia
(d) Pressure-reducing valve

54. Vaporisation of liquid ammonia is done from—
(a) Absorber (b) Generator
(c) Condenser (d) Evaporator

55. The steam pressure in generator is
(a) Very little (b) little
(c) more (d) very much

56. The maximum heat in refrigerant is
(a) Latent heat (b) Specific heat
(c) Sensible heat (d) None of the above

57. The accepted value of avogadro's number is
(a) 1.6×10^{-19} C
(b) 1.6×10^{-19} per gram mole
(c) 6.023×10^{23} C
(d) 6.023×10^{23} per gram mole

58. One horse power equals
(a) 1044 watts (b) 746 watts
(c) 530 watts (d) 230 watts

59. It is the phenomenon of transfer of heat with the actual movement of the particles of the body.
(a) conduction (b) convection
(c) radiation (d) none of the above

60. The temperature of cold storage for grapes is
(a) 34°C – 40°C (b) 42°C – 45°C
(c) 47°C – 49°C (d) None of the above

61. There are .... types of electric charges.
(a) one (b) two
(c) three (d) five

62. The quantity of essential temperature for the transformation of the state of substance is called—
(a) Latent heat (b) Absolute heat
(c) Sensible heat (d) Specific heat

63. Ammonia is soluble in water—
(a) very less (b) less

(c) more (d) very much

64. Leakage is observed from electronic detector by
(a) Light of lamp
(b) Bubble
(c) Colour transformation in tube
(d) Colour transformation of flame

65. Which scale is also called as centigrade scale—
(a) Celsius scale (b) Fahrenheit scale
(c) Reaumer scale (d) None of the above

66. If there were no atmosphere, the average temperature on the surface of the earth would be
(a) lower (b) higher
(c) 0°C (d) same as now

67. Which formula is correct—

(a) $\dfrac{\theta_C - 0}{100} = \dfrac{\theta_F - 32}{180} = \dfrac{\theta_R - 0}{80}$

(b) $\dfrac{\theta_C - 32}{100} = \dfrac{\theta_F - 0}{180} = \dfrac{\theta_R - 0}{80}$

(c) $\dfrac{\theta_C - 0}{100} = \dfrac{\theta_F - 0}{180} = \dfrac{\theta_R - 32}{80}$

(d) None of the above

68. The capacity to do work is
(a) power (b) energy
(c) current (d) voltage

69. The gas which obey gas laws is
(a) Ideal gas (b) Oxygen gas
(c) Hydrogen gas (d) Nitrogen gas

70. This is the method of refrigeration in which heat energy showed be used in place of mechanical energy and the heat of cooling place may be exploited.
(a) dry ice (b) vapour absorption
(c) evaporative (d) liquid gas

71. This is a tank in absorption refrigeration system, in which refrigerant is filled in the form of liquid—
(a) receiver (b) pump
(c) condensor (d) Heat exchanger

72. The pressure of liquid ammonia in evaporator is
(a) 12 kg/cm^2 (b) 9 kg/cm^2
(c) 6 kg/cm^2 (d) 3 kg/cm^2

73. It is used to increase the capacity of exploitation method—
  (a) Heat exchanger (b) Evaporator
  (c) Expansion valve (d) condensor

74. The name of refrigerant with formula C_6H_6 is
  (a) Methane (b) Ethylene
  (c) Propylene (d) Butane

75. The valve is connected in the reciprocating compressor is
  (a) in the piston head
  (b) on the valve plate
  (c) in the cylinder head
  (d) on the top of the shaft

76. Unit without moisture and dust is—
  (a) Hermatic unit (b) Semi-hermatic unit
  (c) Open type unit (d) None of the above

77. By freezing ice on cooling coil—
  (a) Coil gets heated
  (b) Conductor is made
  (c) Insulator is made
  (d) Coil capacity gets increases

78. The diameter of dust particle is—
  (a) 0.001 mm to 0.15 mm
  (b) 0.213 mm to 0.3 mm
  (c) 0.313 mm to 0.333 mm
  (d) None of the above

79. The unit of charge is
  (a) watt (b) ampere
  (c) volt (d) coulomb

80. On the basis of capacity, water coolers are of—
  (a) 2 types (b) 3 types
  (c) 4 types (d) 6 types

81. This gas law was discovered in 1662—
  (a) Boyle's law
  (b) Charle's law
  (c) Gay lussac's law
  (d) Dulong and Petit law

82 A pair of slip rings is used in
  (a) a.c. generator (b) d.c. generator
  (c) a.c. motor (d) d.c. motor

83. The capacity of refrigeration is
  (a) Ton (b) B.T.U.
  (c) C.H.U. (d) Calorie

84. 121°F equals
  (a) 49.5°C (b) 57.5°C
  (c) 84.4°C (d) 87.5°C

85. On mixing more ammonia, weight of solution—
  (a) gets more (b) gets very much
  (c) reduces (d) No effect

86. Refrigerant runs on low pressure in
  (a) Rotary compressor
  (b) Reciprocating compressor
  (c) Centrifugal compressor
  (d) None of the above

87. Gascates are wider in the middle of valve plate and cylinder heard, then
  (a) cooling effect reduces
  (b) refrigerant flow reduces
  (c) speed reduces
  (d) volumetric efficiency reduces

88. The speed of air is
  (a) 1.5 km/sec. (b) 2 km/sec.
  (c) 4 km/sec. (d) 5 km/sec.

89. How many types of ducts—
  (a) 2 (b) 3
  (c) 7 (d) 9

90. The number of springs used normally in one reed is
  (a) 2
  (b) 7
  (c) Nil
  (d) according to size of valve

91. Boiling point of alcohol is
  (a) 40°C (b) 61°C
  (c) 78°C (d) 273°C

92. Perfect gas equation is given by
  (a) $PV = nRT$ (b) $RT = nPV$
  (c) $PT = nRV$ (d) None of the above

93. The instrument used to drill electrically is:
  (a) Poker
  (b) Hand-drill machine
  (c) Electric-drill machine
  (d) None of the above

94. The freezing point of mercury is
  (a) – 70°C (b) –50°C
  (c) –40°C (d) –10°C

95. Cooling coils in refrigeration system:
  (a) Heat produces
  (b) Moisture creates
  (c) makes substance cold
  (d) makes refrigerant cold

96. Temperature suitable for comfortableness of human beings is—
(a) 20°C – 24°C   (b) 24°C – 30°C
(c) 30°C – 36°C   (d) 36°C – 40°C

97. The colour of live wire is—
(a) Blue   (b) Black
(c) Green   (d) Red

98. Which relation is true in a.c.
(a) $\omega = 2\pi T$ (b) $\omega = 2\pi f$
(c) $\omega = \dfrac{2\pi}{f}$ (d) None of the above

99. To remove moisture, fitted between condenser and expansion valve—
(a) vacuum pump   (b) Dehydrator
(c) Harmatic System (d) Hot air sender

100. Halide torch is used for the leakage test of
(a) Freeon-12   (b) SO_2
(c) CO_2 (d) NH_3

101. Air with water vapours is called as
(a) Dew
(b) Humid air
(c) Absolute humidity
(d) Fog

102. Voltmeter is used to measure
(a) electric current
(b) resistance
(c) potential difference
(d) weight

103. The cooling capacity of central air conditioner is
(a) 10,000 – 12,000 B.T.U. per hour
(b) 15,000 – 17,000 B.T.U. per hour
(c) 24,000 – 1,00,000 B.T.U. per hour
(d) 75,000 – 2,00,000 B.T.U. per hour

104. These filters are made of glasswool which have holes and there is sticky substance with holes—
(a) Air fitter   (b) Dried fitter
(c) Electronic fitter (d) Self-changing fitter

105. The main function of air wire is to
(a) remove leakage
(b) remove moisture
(c) tool air
(d) remove dust and smoke

106. When ammonia enters evaporator, temperature reduce to
(a) 0°C   (b) –10°C
(c) –30°C   (d) –50°C

107. The colour of earth wire is
(a) Black   (b) Green
(c) Red   (d) None of the above

108. One unit of B.T.U. equals
(a) 252 calorie   (b) 152 calorie
(c) 136 calorie   (d) 109 calorie

109. Tubes of condenser and evaporator are made of
(a) Iron   (b) Steel
(c) Aluminium   (d) Copper

110. It is the fastest mode of heat transfer—
(a) Conduction   (b) Convention
(c) Radiation   (d) None of the above

111. Which formula is true—
(a) $K.E. = \dfrac{1}{2}\,mv^2$
(b) $P.E. = mgh$
(c) $M.E. = K.E. + P.E.$
(d) All of the above

112 The pressure of atmosphere is called as
(a) Gauge pressure
(b) Atmospheric pressure
(c) Absolute pressure
(d) Atmospheric pressure

113. Condenser is used in—
(a) double pipe type
(b) open type cooler
(c) closed type cooler
(d) Air and water cooled type

114. Clearance volume
(a) has same effect on all compressors
(b) has no effect on compressor capacity
(c) has compressor capacity be affected
(d) has affected compressor speed

115. Four cylinders are connected with compressor
(a) horizontally   (b) 45° angle
(c) 90° angle   (d) vertically

116. It is filled in the copper tubes—
(a) Ammonia   (b) Brian
(c) Freeon-12   (d) Water

117. That temperature which is saturated temperature of air, the moisture present on that

temperature is called—
(a) Dew
(b) Humid air
(c) Absolute humidity
(d) Fog

118. The cooling capacity of room air conditioner is
(a) 4,000 – 36,000 B.T.U. per hour
(b) 36,000 – 40,000 B.T.U. per hour
(c) 24,000 – 1,00,000 B.T.U. per hour
(d) None of the above

119. In this installation of air conditioner, after fitting metal frame on the door, unit is fitted.
(a) window installation
(b) through-the-wall installation
(c) transam installation
(d) None of the above

120. Air washer is used in
(a) Air conditioner   (b) Tank
(c) T.V.   (d) Cooler

121. Refrigerant used in exploit system is
(a) Methyl chloride (b) Ammonia
(c) Ethane   (d) D.D.T.

122. In ice can, air of water comes out from—
(a) Vacuum machine
(b) Ammonia pipe
(c) Centrifugal pump
(d) Blower machine

123. The instrument used to measure the thickness of pipe is
(a) Inside calliper   (b) Outside calliper
(c) Lactometer   (d) Filler Gauge

124. It is the phenomenon of transfer of heat from one part of the body to the another, from particle to particle in the direction of fall of temperature without any actual movement of the particles.
(a) Conduction   (b) Convection
(c) Refraction   (d) Radiation

125. In refrigeration system, it is fixed midway between generator and absorber—
(a) Rectifier   (b) Receiver
(c) Heat exchanger (d) Analyser

126. When oil increases in compressor—
(a) Capacity increases
(b) Capacity decreases
(c) Capacity unaffected
(d) Speed increases

127. On being increase in compressor oil—
(a) Capacity reduces
(b) Capacity increases
(c) Capacity unaffected
(d) None of the above

128. The use of duct in air is—
(a) to heat the air   (b) to cool the air
(c) to purify the air (d) to divide the air

129. The instrument used to measure humidity is called
(a) Thermometer
(b) Animometer
(c) Barometer
(d) Sling Psychrometer

130. It is that kind of machine by which room is cooled in summer and warmed in winter—
(a) Air return
(b) Air outdoor
(c) Air conditioner
(d) Air conditioner plant

131. The number of main factors of air conditioning is—
(a) 2   (b) 3
(c) 4   (d) 5

132. Unit used in summer is—
(a) Heating unit   (b) Cooling unit
(c) Both above   (d) None of (a) and (b)

133. After switching OFF switch, after how much time the switch is made ON
(a) After 2 minutes (b) After 1 minutes
(c) After 45 seconds (d) After 5 seconds

134. The number of switches in switch control is
(a) 3   (b) 5
(c) 6   (d) 8

135. Comfortable air turning rate for man is
(a) 2.5 meter/sec.   (b) 5 meter/sec.
(c) 7.5 meter/sec.   (d) 10 meter/sec.

136. Turning of brian is—
(a) 2 meter per minute
(b) 5 meter per minute
(c) 8 meter per minute
(d) 10 meter per minute

137. Relative humidity for fruits should be—
(a) 50%   (b) 65%
(c) 70%   (d) 85%

138. The boiling point of mercury is
    (a) 357°C   *(b)* 257°C
    (c) 157°C   *(d)* 78°C

139. The work of air filter is
    (a) to lubricate oil
    (b) to remove air from system
    (c) to pure and clean air
    (d) to remove moisture

140. The liquid of the cloth which is put on the bulb of wet bulb thermometer is called
    (a) Cold water   *(b)* Distilled water
    (c) Brian water   *(d)* Moderate water

141. Path of coming and going air is called—
    (a) Inlet   *(b)* Outlet
    (c) Duct   *(d)* Grill

142. In winter relative humidity is
    (a) 40%   *(b)* 60%
    (c) 80%   *(d)* 99%

143. Safety bulb is package unit
    (a) heats air
    (b) prevents air from heating
    (c) prevents pressure beyond limit
    (d) adjust the temperature

144. In air conditioning system, damper is used—
    (a) to control work
    (b) to control moisture
    (c) to control cold air
    (d) to control the entering and existing of air

145. In air conditioning system, air filter is used—
    (a) to remove moisture from system
    (b) to remove air from system
    (c) to remove refrigerant charge besides system
    (d) to purify and clean air

146. Heat pump works—
    (a) only in summer
    (b) only in winter
    (c) in summer and winter
    (d) at any time

147. The place where air conditioner is installed,
    (a) There should be completely dark
    (b) There should be completely light
    (c) There should be shade
    (d) None of the abvoe

148. Vaccant place for turning air is approx.
    (a) 4 meter   *(b)* 3 meter
    (c) 2 meter   *(d)* 1 meter

149. In domestic works, how much capacity package unit are used?
    (a) 20 ton   *(b)* 15 ton
    (c) 10 ton   *(d)* 5 ton

150. Proper installation is made—
    (a) to increase the cost
    (b) to increase the range
    (c) to increase the capactiy
    (d) to increase the efficiency

ANSWERS

1	2	3	4	5	6	7	8	9	10
(d)	*(c)*	*(c)*	*(c)*	*(b)*	*(c)*	*(d)*	*(b)*	*(a)*	*(a)*
11	**12**	**13**	**14**	**15**	**16**	**17**	**18**	**19**	**20**
(d)	*(a)*	*(b)*	*(b)*	*(d)*	*(c)*	*(a)*	*(b)*	*(a)*	*(a)*
21	**22**	**23**	**24**	**25**	**26**	**27**	**28**	**29**	**30**
(b)	*(a)*	*(a)*	*(a)*	*(c)*	*(c)*	*(b)*	*(c)*	*(a)*	*(b)*
31	**32**	**33**	**34**	**35**	**36**	**37**	**38**	**39**	**40**
(d)	*(d)*	*(a)*	*(b)*	*(c)*	*(d)*	*(a)*	*(d)*	*(d)*	*(d)*
41	**42**	**43**	**44**	**45**	**46**	**47**	**48**	**49**	**50**
(c)	*(d)*	*(c)*	*(d)*	*(a)*	*(a)*	*(c)*	*(d)*	*(d)*	*(a)*
51	**52**	**53**	**54**	**55**	**56**	**57**	**58**	**59**	**60**
(c)	*(d)*	*(b)*	*(d)*	*(d)*	*(a)*	*(d)*	*(b)*	*(b)*	*(a)*
61	**62**	**63**	**64**	**65**	**66**	**67**	**68**	**69**	**70**
(b)	*(a)*	*(d)*	*(d)*	*(a)*	*(a)*	*(a)*	*(b)*	*(a)*	*(b)*

71	**72**	**73**	**74**	**75**	**76**	**77**	**78**	**79**	**80**
(a)	*(a)*	*(a)*	*(c)*	*(b)*	*(a)*	*(c)*	*(a)*	*(d)*	*(b)*
81	**82**	**83**	**84**	**85**	**86**	**87**	**88**	**89**	**90**
(a)	*(a)*	*(a)*	*(a)*	*(c)*	*(a)*	*(d)*	*(a)*	*(b)*	*(d)*
91	**92**	**93**	**94**	**95**	**96**	**97**	**98**	**99**	**100**
(c)	*(a)*	*(c)*	*(c)*	*(c)*	*(b)*	*(d)*	*(b)*	*(b)*	*(a)*
101	**102**	**103**	**104**	**105**	**106**	**107**	**108**	**109**	**110**
(b)	*(c)*	*(c)*	*(d)*	*(d)*	*(b)*	*(b)*	*(a)*	*(b)*	*(c)*
111	**112**	**113**	**114**	**115**	**116**	**117**	**118**	**119**	**120**
(d)	*(b)*	*(d)*	*(c)*	*(d)*	*(c)*	*(d)*	*(a)*	*(c)*	*(a)*
121	**122**	**123**	**124**	**125**	**126**	**127**	**128**	**129**	**130**
(b)	*(d)*	*(b)*	*(a)*	*(c)*	*(b)*	*(a)*	*(d)*	*(d)*	*(d)*
131	**132**	**133**	**134**	**135**	**136**	**137**	**138**	**139**	**140**
(c)	*(b)*	*(a)*	*(b)*	*(c)*	*(c)*	*(d)*	*(a)*	*(c)*	*(b)*
141	**142**	**143**	**144**	**145**	**146**	**147**	**148**	**149**	**150**
(c)	*(b)*	*(c)*	*(d)*	*(d)*	*(c)*	*(c)*	*(b)*	*(c)*	*(d)*

———————

4

FITTER

Fitter : A worker who prepares a machine by connecting various components or opens it or repairs it.

Types of fitter:

- *(i)* Machine fitter
- *(ii)* Bench fitter
- *(iii)* Pipe fitter or plumber fitter

Marking Instruments : These are the instruments used for marking the different operations on any job.

Instruments used for marking method:

- *(i)* Marking table
- *(ii)* Surface plate
- *(iii)* Angle plate
- *(iv)* Rule
- *(v)* Scriber
- *(vi)* Punch
- *(vii)* Try-square
- *(viii)* Trammel/divider
- *(ix)* Caliper
- *(x)* Marking block
- *(xi)* V-block etc.

V-Block : This block is a cast-iron made cubical block, in which grooves in the form of 'V' are chopped in upper and lower surfaces.

There are three types of V-block:

1. Ordinary V-block
2. Clamping V-block
3. Magnetic V-block

This block act as base for the marking on the jobs of cylindrical and irregular structure.

File : File is a manual tool of fitter vocation which cuts metal in the form of particles. This is made of high carbon steel, but its tang is kept smooth so that it may not break at the time of using handle.

Main parts of file:

- *(i)* Body
- *(ii)* Tang
- *(iii)* Shoulder
- *(iv)* Heel
- *(v)* Side/edge
- *(vi)* Face
- *(vii)* Toe or tip or point

Classification of file :

- *(i)* **On the basis of length :** Normally the length of file is upto 4", 6", 8", 10", 12", 14", 16", or 18" (100 mm, 150 mm, 250 mm, 300 mm, 350 mm, 400 mm or 450 mm). The length of files 24" to 26" (600 mm to 650 mm) is used in file machine.
- *(ii)* **On the basis of shape :** Flat file, Hand file, Round file, Half round file, Square file, Piller file, Triangular file and Knife-edge file.
- *(iii)* **On the basis of grade :** Rough file, Bastard file, Second cut file, Smooth file and Dead smooth file.
- *(iv)* **On the basis of cut :** Single cut file, Double cut file, Rasp cut file, Spiral cut file and Curved cut file.

Main methods of filing :

- *(i)* **Straight filing :** On the surface of job, drive the file in straight direction is called as straight filing.
- *(ii)* **Cross filing :** On the surface of job, drive the file from one corner to another corner is called cross filing. For this, the worker has to be stand with vice in the angle of 45°.
- *(iii)* **Draw filing :** To make flat accurately to the

surface of job, sometimes having caught job in perpendicular direction on the surface of job, filling is made which is called as draw filing.

Filing machine : In production organisations, filing machine is also used for filing work in large quantity in which 24" to 26" length rectangular files are used.

Chisel : The manual tool which is used for cutting and scratching of metallic or non-metallic substances is called chisel.

Parts of chisel :

(i) Head
(ii) Body
(iii) Point

Chisel is made of carbon steel or crome-venedium steel. Its head is kept smooth and cutting edge is fitted with tamper.

Types of Chisel:

(i) **Hot Chisel :** It is made up of high carbon steel which is used to cut red hot jobs in blacksmith shop. Its cutting angle is 30° and hole is made in its head to catch it.

(ii) **Cold Chisel :** It is made up of carbon steel (0.75% to 1.00% carbon) which is used to cut cold iron and other substances. Its cutting angle is kept from 30° to 70° according to necessity.

Types of chisel on the basis of shape ;

(i) Flat chisel
(ii) Cross-cut chisel
(iii) Round-nose chisel
(iv) Side-cut chisel
(v) Dimond-point chisel
(vi) Cow-mouth chisel

S.No.	Metal	Cutting angle of flat chisel
1	Lead and aluminium	30°
2	Copper	45°
3	Brass	50°
4	Mild Steel	55°
5	Cast iron	60°
6	Tool Steel	65°-70°

Chipping : It is a technique by which we remove metal fold from the surface of job by chisel or hammer.

Scraping : After filing on some job, on its surface up-down fields escape *i.e.* job-surface is not fully plain. The process of making job surface to be plain is said to be scraping.

Types of scraping :

(i) **Flat scrapper :** Its cutting edge is flat but with a light convexity. Its use is made to level the surface of screws slipping on each other.

(ii) **Triangular scrapper :** Its shape is roughly triangular. It is used for scraping the angular parts of the jobs.

(iii) **Half-round scrapper :** Its shape is spherical and is used for scraping of spherical surfaces.

(iv) **Double handled scrapper :** In this type of scrapper, wooden reams are connected on both sides and middle body is fitted scrapper. It is used for scraping flat and spherical surfaces.

Hacksaw : The manual tool to cut metals and other solid substances is called hacksaw. It has two main parts—hacksaw frame and hacksaw blade.

Types of Hacksaw Frame :

(i) Fixed Frame
(ii) Adjustable frame

Parts of Hacksaw Frame :

(i) Frame
(ii) Handle
(iii) Handle clamp and blade holder
(iv) Guide
(v) Blade holder screw
(vi) Wing-nut

Types of hacksaw blade :

(i) **All hard blade :** In this blade, the complete portion is hard in addition to parts with hole.

(ii) **Flexible blade :** The only teeth part of this blade is hard. This blade is used for common use because it can cut small metallic things and it can also make cutting irregular or light spherical surface of job.

Types of hacksaw blade according to teeth per inch:

S.No.	Hacksaw blade	No. of teeths of per inch
1.	Coarse grade	14-18 (25 mm)
2.	Medium grade	20-24 (25 mm)
3.	Fine grade	24-30 (25 mm)
4.	Super fine grade	30-32 (25 mm)

Slitting Saw : The saw which is used to cut grooves in the head of bold and screw, and to cut thin metallic sheets is said to be slitting saw. There is a frame permanently connected in the line of handle in those groove includes a fitted wider blade.

Fret Saw : The saw which is used to cut more depth, a spherical quality hacksaw frame with more width said to be fret saw.

Drill : It is a cutting tool which is connected in drill machine to make holes in metallic and non-metallic substances.

Drills are made up of high speed steel and alloy steel.

Parts of drill :

(i) **Tang :** Back flat surface of drill which is fitted in drill sleave.

(ii) **Shank :** Front cylindrical part of tang which is got hold by machine spindle or drill chak.

(iii) **Neck :** Cylindrical part between shank and body.

(iv) **Body :** Part from neck to point.

Parts in drill body :

(i) Flute
(ii) Margin
(iii) Land/body releif surface
(iv) Point/dead-cube
(v) Cutting lips
(vi) Web

Types of drill :

(i) Flat drill
(ii) Twist drill
(iii) Counter-sink drill
(iv) Pilot drill
(v) Combination drill

Measurement of drill :

(i) **Fractional size :** Normally these drills are made from 1/64 inch to 3 inch in diameter and the diameter of them in the succession of 1/64 inch to 1 inch, 1/64 and rest is increased in the successing of 1/2 inch.

(ii) **Number size :** These drills are made from 1 to 80 number and their diameter increases from large to small number. Number 1 implies 0.228 inch (5.791 mm) and 80 number implies 0.135 inch (0.35 mm).

(iii) **Letter size :** These drills are made from A to Z in 26 size. A implies 0.234 inch (5.944 mm) and Z implies 0.413 inch (10.490 mm).

(iv) **Millimeter Size :** As per ISI marks, these drills are made from 1 mm to 120 mm in diameter. Drill diameter is increased 1 mm to 3 mm in series of 0.05 mm, 3 mm to 14 mm in series of 0.1 mm, 14 mm to 32 mm in series of 0.25 mm, 32 mm to 51 mm in series of 0.55 mm, and 51 mm to 120 mm in series of 1 mm.

Famous types of drill:

(i) Double fluted
(ii) Multi fluted
(iii) Counter boring
(iv) Oil hole
(v) Spirec
(vi) Shell
(vii) Step drill etc.

Cutting speed of drill : The peripheric distance covered in one minute by any point situated on the body of drill is called its cutting speed. It can be shown that

$$\text{C.S.} = \frac{\pi \times \text{diameter of drill (in inch)} \times \text{R.P.M}}{12}$$

foot per minute

or

$$\text{C.S.} = \frac{\pi \times (\text{diameter of drill}) \times \text{R.P.M.}}{1000}$$

meter per minute

Feed of drill : The cutting depth by the drill in one revolution or one minute is called as feed of the drill. It is described in millimeter per revolution or millimeter per minute.

Drill drift : It is a tapered iron-piece which is used to separate sleeve from the spindle of drill machine.

Drill-chuck-key : It is a small tool used to tighten or open the drill in drill chuck. It contains one notchy, toothed tapered wheel and one operating lever.

Tap : Tap is the manual tool used to cut internal threads in the metallic jobs. It is available in the form of a 'set'.

It is made up of high speed steel or alloy steel. Threads are cut on its body and four flutes are cut on its body through which 'chips' come out.

Parts of tap :

- *(i)* **Tang :** The upper most squarel part which is used to run the tap by fitting in handle.
- *(ii)* **Shank :** Cylindrical part of below the tang and, up the body.
- *(iii)* **Body :** Part from shank to tip.

Parts of tap-body :

- *(i)* **Land :** That part of body on which internal threads are cut off.
- *(ii)* **Flute :** Outlet point of cut off chips. Usually there are four cut off flutes in tap.
- *(iii)* **Cutting face :** The front part of land which starts cutting work.
- *(iv)* **Heel :** Rear part of the land.

Types of tap :

(i) According to work:
- *(a)* Hand tap
- *(b)* Extension tap
- *(c)* Master tap
- *(d)* Machine screw tap
- *(e)* Band-shank tap
- *(f)* Spiral fluted tap
- *(g)* Gas tap
- *(h)* Gun tap
- *(i)* Fluteless tap
- *(j)* Stay bolt tap

(ii) According to thread-shape
- *(a)* British Standard Whitworth (S.W.)
- *(b)* British Standard Fine (B.S.F.)
- *(c)* British Standard Pipe (B.S.P.)
- *(d)* British Association (B.A.)
- *(e)* American National Standard (A.N.S.)
- *(f)* Metric International (M.I.)

Hand tap : Internal threads are cut off by turning this tap with hand (with the help of the handle). It has three taps:

- *(i)* **Taper tap :** It contains 8 to 10 threads. It makes 'seat' for another tap.
- *(ii)* **Plug tap :** It contains 3 to 5 threads. It makes threads deep in hole.
- *(iii)* **Bottom tap :** It contain only one thread. It does finishing of threads.

Tapping defects :

- *(i)* Breaking of tap.
- *(ii)* Breaking of thread of ring-side.
- *(iii)* Being defect in the cut-off thread in job.
- *(iv)* Being oversizing of cut-off thread in job.

Reamer : The cutting tool which looks like tap. In this, cutting edges and cutting flutes are made in place of threads. It is used to clean job-holes, to make right measurement and to polish the holes.

It is made of high carbon steel, high speed steel and alloy steel.

Parts of reamer:

- *(i)* **Tang :** Top most square part which after entrapping in handle, reamer is turned.
- *(ii)* **Shank :** Cylindrical part below the tang.
- *(iii)* **Neck :** Smaller diameter part below the shank and above the body. It is also called as 'Recess'.
- *(iv)* **Body :** Part from neck to tip.

Main parts of the reamer body :

- *(i)* Cutting teeth
- *(ii)* Champher angle
- *(iii)* Land
- *(iv)* Flute
- *(v)* Tip

Types of reamer flutes :

- *(i)* **Straight flute :** Flute parallel to the reamer-axis.
- *(ii)* **Helix flute :** Often the reamer flute of diameter more than 10 mm are kept angular *i.e.* kept in helix.
- *(iii)* **Spiral flute :** 'Snake' type flutes are made on taper reamer.

Different types of reamer:

   (i) Hand reamer
  (ii) Machine reamer
 (iii) Shell reamer
 (iv) Adjustable reamer
  (v) Expansion reamer
 (vi) Taper reamer
(vii) Taper pin reamer
(viii) Pillot reamer

Gauge : It is a method used for comparing the same dimensional parts at the time of its construction. It is not a measuring device but a comparing device. It is made of carbon steel, chromium steel and venedium steel.

Classification of gauge :

   (i) **Workshop gauge :** For the manufacturing of components in large quantity, the gauge used by workers in workshop is called workshop gauge.
  (ii) **Inspection gauge :** To inspect jobs and workshop gauge in inspection chamber is called inspection gauge.
 (iii) **Master gauge :** To find out the defect relating measurement created in workshop gauge and inspection gauge is called master gauge.

Types of gauge :

1. Plug gauge
2. Limit gauge
3. Snap gauge
   - Ring gauge
   - Sheet type snap gauge
   - Limit calliper gauge
   - Adjustable snap gauge
4. Radius gauge
5. Feeler gauge
6. Wire gauge
7. Thickness gauge
8. Centre gauge
9. Drill angle gauge
10. Screw-pitch gauge
11. Screw-thread plug gauge
12. Screw-thread ring gauge
13. Roller type thread snap gauge
14. Taper plug gauge
15. Taper ring gauge
16. Telescopic gauge
17. Small hole gauge
18. Bore dial gauge
19. Slip gauge
20. Sine bar
21. Dial test indicator

Jig : The method which is used to guide cutting tool and to get hold. The job for the production of similar components in large quantity is said to be jig.

Types of Jig :

   (i) **Plate type jig :** It is made in the form of 'L'. One locating pin is used on the arm of plate which gets hold the job in the right position. In the back of pin and in other arm of plate, an outlet is left for coming out chopped chips. Thus, job sets in right position and cutting tool finds right way.
  (ii) **Box type jig :** It has two parts: base and cover.

The job is set between two parts in the way as if set in a box. In the part with lid, bush is connected on carbon steel which guides cutting tool. Exit point given in the base for coming out of chips.

Fixture : The method of holding the mechanical process of job is called fixture.

The different techniques of fixtures are—

   (i) Angle plate
  (ii) Parallel blocks
 (iii) Stapped V blocks
 (iv) T-bolt etc.

Jig bushing : The method of get hold of job and to guide cutting tool for the completion of drilling, reaming and taping is called jig bushing.

Template : The method used for the production of similar component in large quantity and to make marking work easy is called template.

Fastener : The process used to connect the two components or different parts of a machine is called fastener.

Methods of fastening :

   (i) **Permanent fastening :** The process to connect the two components or different parts of a machine permanently is called permanent fastening. This act is completed by brazing and gas electric welding. The

fastening of this type is opened after cutting by cutting tools or gas cutters.

(ii) **Semi-permanent fastening :** The process to connect the two components or different parts of a machine by soldering and rivets is called semi-permanent fastening. This fastening is equivalent to permanent but on being necessity, components are separated after cutting rivets by desoldering or chisel or hammer.

(iii) **Temporary fastening :** The process to connect the two components or different parts of a machine using nut-bolt, stud, screw, key etc. This type of fastening is opened and joined easily according to necessity.

Rivet : It is just like a strong headed metallic nail. It is used to connect the parts of two machines, components metallic sheets etc. in semi-permanent form. Rivetted joint is kept on binding from one side by head and other side by the head made from rivets-tail after beating it.

Aluminium, brass and mild steel is used in its manufacturing.

Parts of rivet:

(i) Head
(ii) Body or shank
(iii) Tail

Types of rivet :

(i) Round or cup or snap head rivet
(ii) Pan head rivet
(iii) Pan head with tapered neck rivet
(iv) Flat head rivet
(v) Round countersank head rivet
(vi) Flat countersank head rivet
(vii) Conical heat rivet
(viii) Turbuler rivet etc.

Nut-bolt : It is used to complete the temporary fastening. Entrapping bolt in job-hole, from other side nut is tightened. It is in the form of a rod on whose, atone end, head is made and on the other end, threads are cut off to 1/3 length or to complete length of rod.

Parts of bolt :

(i) Head
(ii) Neck
(iii) Body
(iv) Point

Points to be ponder in context of bolts:

(i) Types of threads-B.S.W., B.S.F, B.S.P, Metric.
(ii) Direction of threads-Right hand, Left hand
(iii) Pitch of threads and threads per inch (T.P.I.)
(iv) Shape of head-square or Hexagonal
(v) Diameter of bolt
(vi) Length of bolt
(vii) Length of threads made on bolt—Half threaded or full threaded
(viii) Metal of bolt—Iron, brass etc.

Types of bolt:

(i) Square head bolt
(ii) Hexagonal head bolt
(iii) Cheese head bolt
(iv) Eye head bolt
(v) Cup head square neck bolt
(vi) Flat countersunk head bolt
(vii) Hook head bolt

Types of nut :

(i) Square nut
(ii) Hexagonal nut
(iii) Flanged nut
(iv) Knurled nut
(v) Wing nut
(vi) Cap nut
(vii) Dome nut
(viii) Capstan nut
(ix) Ring nut

Measurement of square nut :

(i) Distance between two opposite faces $= 1.5\,D + 1$ mm
(ii) Chamfer angle $= 30°$ to $45°$
(iii) Thickness of nut $= 0.8\,D$
(iv) Champher radius $= 2\,D$

Where D is the diameter included depth of the thread of hole in nut.

Measurement of hexagonal nut :

(i) Distance between two opposite faces $= 1.5D + 3$ mm
(ii) Face angle $= 60°$

(iii) Champher angle = 30° to 45°

(iv) Thickness of nut = 0.8 D or 1.0 D

Here, D is the diameter cum depth of the thread of hole in nut.

Stud : Bolt without head is known as stud. Threads are cut on its both ends which are in the form of right hand threads and on other end in the form of left hand threads.

It is used in such places where two or three parts to be tightened together as Automobile Engine Piston–One end of stud is tightened on the base part of the job. Now remaining parts are tightened with nut after entrapping in bolt.

Types of stud:

(i) **Round neck stud :** Its middle part is round.

(ii) **Square neck stud :** Its middle part is in square form which may be tightened or opened using spanner.

(iii) **Stepped neck stud :** Two or three rectangular steps are made in its middle which may be tightened or opened using spanner and one end of stud may be tightened in base upto step.

OBJECTIVE TYPES QUESTIONS

1. Surface plates are—
   - *(a)* two
   - *(b)* three
   - *(c)* four
   - *(d)* six

2. The least count of calliper rule in 'British System' is
   - *(a)* 1/72 inch
   - *(b)* 1/64 inch
   - *(c)* 1/40 inch
   - *(d)* None of the above

3. Try-square is made up of—
   - *(a)* Stainless steel
   - *(b)* Cast iron
   - *(c)* *(a)* and *(b)*
   - *(d)* neither *(a)* nor *(b)*

4. Which one is different from others—
   - *(a)* Hand file
   - *(b)* Round file
   - *(c)* Mill file
   - *(d)* Safe edge file

5. Which file contains 7-8 teeths per centimeter—
   - *(a)* Rough file
   - *(b)* Bastard file
   - *(c)* Smooth file
   - *(d)* Second cut file

6. The length of file is measure from—
   - *(a)* Heel to tang
   - *(b)* Tang to tip
   - *(c)* Heel to tip
   - *(d)* None of the above

7. Out of the following, in which chisel, the cutting angle is 40°—
   - *(a)* Cross-cut chisel
   - *(b)* Side-cut chisel
   - *(c)* Round-cut chisel
   - *(d)* Flat chisel

8. In drill, the cutting speed (in m/minute) for phosphor bronze is—
   - *(a)* 35-50
   - *(b)* 20-35
   - *(c)* 15-45
   - *(d)* 12-25

9. Which one is also same as I.S.I., in context of thread-types—
   - *(a)* B.S.W.
   - *(b)* B.A.
   - *(c)* A.N.S.
   - *(d)* M.I.

10. 'Vernier Bevel Protractor' is a microscopic instrument used to measure—
    - *(a)* density
    - *(b)* distance
    - *(c)* depth
    - *(d)* angle

11. The width of 'gib-head-key' is—
    - *(a)* $\dfrac{\text{diameter of shaft}}{2}$
    - *(b)* $\dfrac{\text{diameter of shaft}}{4}$
    - *(c)* $\dfrac{\text{diameter of shaft}}{6}$
    - *(d)* $\dfrac{\text{diameter of shaft}}{8}$

12. The straight distance between the crest and root of thread is called—
    - *(a)* Major dia
    - *(b)* Minor dia
    - *(c)* Flank
    - *(d)* Pitch line

13. Crest of butress thread is—
    - *(a)* 0.75 × pitch
    - *(b)* 0.125 × pitch
    - *(c)* 0.3707 × pitch
    - *(d)* 0.1375 × pitch

14. In Newall fit system, which one letter represent slack running fit—
    - *(a)* P
    - *(b)* X
    - *(c)* Y
    - *(d)* Z

15. In drill, the portion between neck and point is called as—
    - *(a)* Tang
    - *(b)* Shank
    - *(c)* Body
    - *(d)* None of the above

16. The formula for the diameter of the hole by drill for any tap is given as—
  (a) Drill diameter = Tap diameter + [1.23 × pitch(in mm)]
  (b) Drill diameter = Tap diameter – [1.23 × pitch(in mm)]
  (c) Drill diameter = $\dfrac{7}{8}$ × Tap diameter + $\dfrac{1}{32}$
  (d) Drill diameter = $\dfrac{7}{8}$ × Tap diameter – $\dfrac{1}{32}$

17. Depth of 'British Association' threads is—
  (a) 0.6403 × pitch   *(b)* –0.6 × pitch
  (c) 0.6495 × pitch   *(d)* 0.75 × pitch

18. Match the following :

Iron Alloy			*Iron (in percentage)*
A. Magnetite		I.	Very little
B. Haematite		II.	48
C. Siderite		III.	60-65
D. Pyrite		IV.	70-75

	A	B	C	D
(a)	I	II	III	IV
(b)	I	III	II	IV
(c)	IV	II	III	I
(d)	IV	III	II	I

19. Factor of safety shoud be
  (a) 1-2   *(b)* 2-3
  (c) 3-4   *(d)* 4-5

20. Which one is ferrous metal—
  (a) Steel   *(b)* Pig iron
  (c) Cast iron   *(d)* All of the above

21. In which alloy steel, there is 18% to 22% of tungsten, 0.5% to 1.0% carbon and remaining is iron—
  (a) Tungsten steel   *(b)* Manganese steel
  (c) Carbon steel   *(d)* Nickel steel

22. It is a blue-white coloured, ductile, malleable and good conducting metal and its melting point is 416°C—
  (a) Iron   *(b)* Aluminium
  (c) Nickel   *(d)* Zinc

23. Following remedies are made to prevent corrosion of metals—
  (a) Temporary treatment
  (b) Semi-permanent treatment
  (c) Permanent treatment
  (d) All of the above

24. In case of lubricants, which one is different—
  (a) Liquid   *(b)* Semi-liquid
  (c) Solid   *(d)* Semi-solid

25. Indicated letters of medium grade of grindig wheels are—
  (a) I, J, K, L, M   *(b)* A, B, C, D
  (c) T, U, V, W, X, Y Z *(d)* N, O, P, Q, R, S

26. Unit of energy is—
  (a) Joule   *(b)* Ohm
  (c) Radian   *(d)* Watt

27. Which file contains 20-28 teeths per centimeter—
  (a) Dead smooth file
  (b) Smooth file
  (c) Second cut file
  (d) Bastard file

28. Chisel is made up of—
  (a) Carbon steel
  (b) Crome-Venedium steel
  (c) 'a' or 'b'
  (d) neither 'a' nor 'b'

29. The cutting angle of forged steel in drill is—
  (a) 90°   *(b)* 100°
  (c) 125°   *(d)* 180°

30. In hand tap, tap contains 3 to 5 threads—
  (a) Taper tap   *(b)* Plug tap
  (c) Bottom tap   *(d)* None of the above

31. The least count of vernier calliper is—
  (a) 0.1 mm   *(b)* 0.6 mm
  (c) 0.7 mm   *(d)* None of the above

32. Thread angle for B.S.W. thread is
  (a) 40°   *(b)* 45°
  (c) 50°   *(d)* 55°

33. Independent quantity of carbon in grey-pig iron is
  (a) 0.4%–3.75%   *(b)* 1%–2%
  (c) 92%–95%   *(d)* 4%–6%

34. Tempering temperature of scissor is
  (a) 260°C–270°C   *(b)* 270°C–280°C
  (c) 280°C–290°C   *(d)* 290°C–300°C

35. Bearing housing is made up from—
  (a) Cast Iron and tin
  (b) Brass or zinc
  (c) Iron or manganese
  (d) Cast Iron, brass or zinc

36. In this method, first of all job is cleaned from hydrochloric acid and then dipped it in tin solution. After drying job, it is brightened by rubbing it with wooden-dust—
 (a) Tinning (b) Galvanising
 (c) Electroplating (d) Corrosion

37. Which content is used for the machining of brass jobs—
 (a) Water (b) Mineral oil
 (c) Kerosene oil (d) Engine oil

38. In the context of lubricants, combustion point implies—
 (a) The minimum temperature for any lubricant on which the same can be poured from one pot to another and the same starts freezing on lesser temperature
 (b) The temperature of any lubricant at which it starts evaporating
 (c) The temperature of any lubricant at which oil vapours start burning
 (d) None of the above

39. Which sign indicates machine finish—
 (a) M (b) f
 (c) Δ (d) X

40. Example of natural abrasive is—
 (a) Silicon Carbide (b) Aluminium Oxide
 (c) Diamond (d) All of the above

41. How many types of try-squares
 (a) two (b) four
 (c) five (d) six

42. In which chisel, cutting angle and forging angle are equal to 30°—
 (a) Flat chisel
 (b) Round-nose chisel
 (c) Cow-mouth chisel
 (d) Side-cut chisel

43. The length of normal hacksaw blade is—
 (a) 10 inch (b) 12 inch
 (c) 14 inch (d) 18 inch

44. The cutting speed (in metre/minute) for mild steel in drill is—
 (a) 12–25 (b) 20–35
 (c) 15–45 (d) 20–35

45. It is used for making jewellery—
 (a) Antimony (b) Chromium
 (c) Platinum (d) Yellow brass

46. Which solder is different out of the following—
 (a) Tin-smith solder (b) Plumber solder
 (c) Electric solder (d) Silver solder

47. How many types of thrust bearings
 (a) 2 (b) 6
 (c) 7 (d) 8

48. In this method, lubricant oil is kept on some height than machine and it is supplied to various components of machine through oil-hole, cotton-wide, pipe etc. on the principle of gravitation
 (a) Gravitational feed of lubrication
 (b) Splash feed of lubrication
 (c) Force feed of lubrication
 (d) None of the above

49. Match the following:
 A. Gear oil I. Range : 80–250 S.A.E.
 B. Fat oil II. Range : 80–500 S.U.S. at 100° F
 C. Refrigeration oil III. Acquired from pig fat
 D. Engine oil IV. Used as oil

	A	B	C	D
(a)	I	II	III	IV
(b)	I	III	II	IV
(c)	III	I	II	IV
(d)	II	I	III	IV

50. Description of any grinding wheel is indicated by KA 36 H 6V, it contains 6 as—
 (a) Kind of brand
 (b) Number of manufacturer
 (c) Shape of grains
 (d) Construction

51. How many types of power saw—
 (a) 3 (b) 5
 (c) 6 (d) 8

52. Following activities are mainly done on Lathe Machine—
 (a) Facing (b) Partnening
 (c) Drilling (d) All of the above

53. When two bevel gears, power is forwarded at right angle, then they called as—
 (a) Spur gear (b) Meter gear
 (c) Worm gear (d) Hypoid gear

54. Soldering is processesed almost on the follow-

ing temperature—
(a) 3000°C   (b) 300°C
(c) 30°C   (d) 10°C

55. Which one is also called as odd leg calliper
(a) Inside calliper   (b) Outside calliper
(c) Jenny calliper   (d) None of the above

56. Match the following:

Metal	*Cutting angle of flat chisel*
A. Copper	I. 60°
B. Brass	II. 55°
C. Mild steel	III. 50°
D. Cast Iron	IV. 45°

	A	B	C	D
(a)	I	II	III	IV
(b)	I	III	II	IV
(c)	IV	II	III	I
(d)	IV	III	II	I

57. Which relation is correct for the least count of metric micrometer—
(a) Least count = Pitch of spindle + No. of parts of thimble
(b) Least count = Pitch of spindle – No. of parts of thimble
(c) Least count = Pitch of spindle × No. of parts of thimble
(d) Least count $= \dfrac{\text{Pitch of spindle}}{\text{No. of parts of thimble}}$

58. In context of threads, helix angle is—
(a) Lead × circumference on pitch dia
(b) Lead ± circumference on pitch dia
(c) Lead/circumference on pitch dia
(d) None of the above

59. Taper for B.S.P. threads—
(a) $\dfrac{3}{4}$ inch per foot   (b) $\dfrac{4}{3}$ inch per foot
(c) $\dfrac{1}{2}$ inch per foot   (d) 2 inch per foot

60. In Newall fit system, common running fit is indicated by letter—
(a) X   (b) P
(c) W   (d) Y

61. Out of the following which is non-ferrous metal—
(a) Tin   (b) Zinc
(c) Antimony   (d) All of the above

62. How many types is iron mainly—
(a) 2   (b) 4
(c) 5   (d) 9

63. Speed of blade in reciprocating power saw machine—
(a) 20 to 100 strokes per minute
(b) 40 to 170 strokes per minute
(c) 80 to 200 strokes per minute
(d) None of the above

64. This part is established on bad-wedge (in the form of 'H'), on which tool post and apron on the front—
(a) Saddle   (b) Compound slide
(c) Too-post   (d) Cross-slide

65. It is also named as centering chuck—
(a) Two jaws chuck   (b) Three jaws chuck
(c) Four jaws chuck   (d) Magnetic chuck

66. Match the following:

A. S.U.D.	I. American System
B. R.S.	II. British System
C. D.E.	III. German System
D. S.A.E.	IV. Indian System

	A	B	C	D
(a)	I	II	III	IV
(b)	II	I	IV	III
(c)	I	II	IV	III
(d)	IV	III	II	I

67. It is a cutting process which is used to level the surface of any job—
(a) Honing   (b) Grinding
(c) Scraping   (d) Lapping

68. In the context of 'Lathe Machine'
(a) Cutting speed $= \dfrac{\pi \times \text{R.P.M.}}{1000}$ metre/______

(b) Cutting speed $= \dfrac{\pi \times \text{Diameter (in mm)} \times \text{R.P.M.}}{1000}$ metre/______

(c) Cutting speed $= \dfrac{\pi \times 360 \times \text{Diameter (in mm)}}{\text{R.P.M.}}$ metre/______

(d) Cutting speed $= \dfrac{\pi \times \text{R.P.M.} \times \text{Diameter}}{360}$ metre/minute

69. What type of threads are cut in water pipe and its fittings—
    (a) I.S.P.   *(b)* C.S.P.
    (c) B.S.P.   *(d)* P.S.P.

70. The least count of metric-micrometer is—
    (a) 0.1 mm   *(b)* 0.01 mm
    (c) 0.001 mm   *(d)* 0.0001 mm

71. Callipers are made up of—
    (a) Wood   *(b)* Steel
    (c) Carbon steel   *(d)* Copper

72. Which one is also known as rat tail file—
    (a) Flat file   *(b)* Round file
    (c) Square file   *(d)* Piller file

73. Out of the following, which chisel has forging angle of 25°
    (a) Flat chisel
    (b) Cross-cut chisel
    (c) Round-nose chisel
    (d) Side-cut chisel

74. In drill, the cylindrical part between shunk and body is called as
    (a) Tang   *(b)* Neck
    (c) Flute   *(d)* None of the above

75. In drill, the cutting angle for mild steel is—
    (a) 90°   *(b)* 100°
    (c) 125°   *(d)* 180°

76. How to measure the least count of metric vernier calliper—
    (a) Least count = One portion of main scale + one portion of vernier scale
    (b) Least count = One portion of main scale − one poriton of vernier scale
    (c) Least count = One portion of main scale ± one portion of vernier scale
    (d) None of the above

77. The least count of micrometer is—
    (a) 0.001 cm   *(b)* 0.005 cm
    (c) 0.01 cm   *(d)* None of the above

78. Which drill is also known as central drill
    (a) Pilot drill
    (b) Combination drill
    (c) Counter sink drill
    (d) None of the above

79. Match the following :

Hacksaw blade	*Teeths per inch*
A. Fine grade	I. 14–18
B. Medium grade	II. 20–24
C. Coarse grade	III. 24–30
D. Super fine grade	IV. 30–32

	A	B	C	D
(a)	I	II	III	IV
(b)	I	III	II	IV
(c)	III	I	II	IV
(d)	III	II	I	IV

80. Formula for velocity ratio of gear train—
    (a) $N_1 . T_2 = N_2 . T_1$ *(b)* $N_1 . N_2 = T_1 . T_2$
    (c) $N_1 . T_1 = N_2 . T_2$ *(d)* None of the above

81. It is used to connect shaft with gear is the starting position of clutch machine—
    (a) Cone clutch   *(b)* Multiplate clutch
    (c) Air clutch   *(d)* Friction clutch

82. The ends of cylindrical jobs made from strong sheets, setting opposite each other, is called joint (made from soldering and brazing)—
    (a) Grooved joint
    (b) Edged joint
    (c) Paned-down joint
    (d) Roofing joint

83. Match the following :

A. Tinmann Jenny	I. For making holes in the sheet
B. Shearing machine	II. For making word, number, design etc. on sheet
C. Engraving machine	III. For cutting sheets
D. Punching machine	IV. For preparing ridge in sheet for wiring

	A	B	C	D
(a)	I	II	III	IV
(b)	IV	III	II	I
(c)	IV	III	I	II
(d)	I	II	IV	III

84. Cast-iron pipe is used in—
    (a) Aeroplanes
    (b) Domestic water line
    (c) Electric wiring
    (d) None of the above

85. Normally case hardening is done for the steel in which there is—
    (a) Carbon   *(b)* Low-carbon
    (c) High-carbon   *(d)* High-chromium

86. For H.S.S. hardening, soft material is first heated and then made cold in the following:
(a) Acid   (b) Water
(c) Air   (d) Oil

87. Twist drill has lip-angle of
(a) 112°   (b) 118°
(c) 146°   (d) 150°

88. Sheet cutting from hacksaw, tooth pitch of blade should be—
(a) Maximum   (b) Minimum
(c) a or b   (d) Neither a nor b

89. Match the following :

A. Stapped Pulley — I. Third pulley used between driver pulley and driven pulley for keeping belt in pulling position.

B. Jockey Pulley — II. On this flat phase type pulley flat belt made of rubber, canvass or leather is driven.

C. Round Pulley — III. On this pulley, many stapps are made having different diameters.

D. Split Pulley — IV. This pulley contains are phase and one hub. It can be tightened on the shaft having small or large diameter.

	A	B	C	D
(a)	I	II	III	IV
(b)	III	I	II	IV
(c)	I	III	IV	II
(d)	II	III	I	IV

90. This pipe is used in underground water line—
(a) Cast-iron pipe
(b) P.V.C. pipe
(c) Cement-concrete pipe
(d) All of the above

91. 'Lathe bad' is made of—
(a) M.S.   (b) N.S.
(c) C.I.   (d) H.C.S.

92. If the zero of vernier scale in British vernier calliper with any low temperature of 0.001 inch, measurement of main scale shows 4.85 inch, and Ninth part of vernier is in the straight line of main scale, then the measurement will be—
(a) 0.009 inch   (b) 4.841 inch
(c) 4.859 inch   (d) 5.859 inch

93. One micron is equal to
(a) 10^{-3} m   (b) 10^{-6} m
(c) 10^{-9} m   (d) 10^{-12} m

94. Which method is used in fixture—
(a) Angle plate   (b) T-bolt
(c) Parallel blocks   (d) All of the above

95. The standard width of plane washer is—
(a) 0.1 (diameter of bolt)
(b) 0.15 (diameter of bolt)
(c) 1.5 (diameter of bolt)
(d) 2 (diameter of bolt)

96. How many types of tolerance—
(a) 2   (b) 3
(c) 4   (d) 7

97. In this fit, male and female parts are made easily slippy on each other. In this fit plus (+) is kept allowance and its value is kept low—
(a) Running fit   (b) Clearance fit
(c) Sliding fit   (d) Ringing fit

98. If the shape of hole is 0.60 ± 0.02, then its tolerance is—
(a) + 0.02   (b) + 0.01
(c) 0.58   (d) 0.04

99. Special vernier callipers are of following types
(a) 2   (b) 4
(c) 5   (d) 7

100. It is used to measure the thickness of paper—
(a) Paper gauge micrometer
(b) Blade type micrometer
(c) Sheet metal micrometer
(d) Tube micrometer

101. It is often with a square or hexagonal head, built in with washer cap screw—
(a) Set screw   (b) Wooden screw
(c) Shoulder screw   (d) Collar head screw

102. How many types are fits in B.S.S.
(a) 7   (b) 11
(c) 19   (d) 21

103. The quality of a metal due to which it gets a figure accordingly on twisting is called—
(a) Brittleness   (b) Toughness
(c) Tenacity   (d) Malleability

104. Match the following :

Thread		*Depth*
A. A.N.S.	I.	$0.6495 \times$ pitch
B. Butress	II.	$0.75 \times$ pitch
C. Acme	III.	$0.5 \times$ pitch $+ 0.002$ inch
D. B.A.	IV.	$-0.6 \times$ pitch

	A	B	C	D
(a)	I	II	III	IV
(b)	I	III	II	IV
(c)	III	I	II	IV
(d)	III	II	I	IV

105. In this system, scarfs are made on the ends of round or flat rods. By entangling the scarfs of two rods each other, forge welding V done called as—
(a) Lap forge welding
(b) Butt-forge welding
(c) Split forge welding
(d) Angle forge welding

106. By this method, after forge welding of two pieces of rods each other, total length of rod is increased—
(a) Lap forge welding
(b) Butt forge welding
(c) Split forge welding
(d) Angle forge welding

107. This is a tool with micro-wire which is used to clean nozzle welding torch—
(a) Cylinder key   *(b)* File
(c) Spanner   *(d)* Tip cleaner

108. The tool for measuring depth of welding work done in any job is said to be—
(a) Cylindrical key   *(b)* Welding torch
(c) Weld gauge   *(d)* Wire brush

109. How much temperature can be acquired in the fire of Oxi-LPG flame—
(a) 3100°C–3300°C   *(b)* 2700°C–2800°C
(c) 2400°C–2700°C   *(d)* 1800°C–2300°C

110. In long jobs, welding in little distance, to join metal pieces primarily, is said to be—
(a) Filler rod   *(b)* Root-gap
(c) Tacking   *(d)* Clamping

111. Metal rod or wire used to fill up the joints of job in gas welding work is said to be—
(a) Filler rod   *(b)* Root-gap
(c) Tacking   *(d)* Clamping

112. How many types of electrodes on the basis of flux coating—
(a) Two   *(b)* Three
(c) Six   *(d)* Seven

113. After heating any metallic piece, making holes in it by punch or hammer is said to be—
(a) Marking   *(b)* Cutting
(c) Punching   *(d)* Drifting

114. With the help of this tool, roundness is created in job—
(a) Flatter   *(b)* Swage
(c) Drift   *(d)* Cone

115. At 1100°C temperature, colour of mild steel is
(a) Red   *(b)* Yellow
(c) White   *(d)* Dull cherry red

116. After heating any metallic piece, to widen the diameter of hole present in it, is said to be—
(a) Marking   *(b)* Cutting
(c) Punching   *(d)* Drifting

117. This tool is used to give ring type shape to metal pieces—
(a) Flatter   *(b)* Swage
(c) Drift   *(d)* Cone

118. The boring tool which is used to wider the holes already made in hot metal piece—
(a) Flatter   *(b)* Swage
(c) Drift   *(d)* Cone

119. In forging, it is done for falling down ash—
(a) Pocker   *(b)* Sprinker
(c) Swoop   *(d)* Shovel

120. This machine vice is used to bind the large jobs on machine—
(a) Plane machine vice
(b) Flenged machine vice
(c) Vertical machine vice
(d) Universal machine vice

121. Adjustable snap gauge is made in the shape of—
(a) A   *(b)* C
(c) T   *(d)* U

122. The parts of rivet are
(a) Head   *(b)* Body
(c) Tail   *(d)* All of the above

123. In forging, it is used to set coal properly—
(a) Pocker   *(b)* Sprinker
(c) Swoop   *(d)* Shovel

124. In this method, after heating a piece of red hot metallic-sheet, desired shape is acquired by beating from hand hammer—
  (a) Hand forging (b) Machine forging
  (c) Drop forging (d) None of the above

125. In forging, it is used for pouring coal in furnace—
  (a) Pocker (b) Sprinker
  (c) Swoop (d) Shovel

126. The shape of this spanner is just like 'G' letter—
  (a) Hook spanner (b) Box spanner
  (c) Monkey spanner (d) Allen key spanner

127. This vice machine is used to bind the small jobs on machine—
  (a) Plane machine vice
  (b) Flenged machine vice
  (c) Vertical machine vice
  (d) Universal machine vice

128. The handle used in eye-hole of hammer is—
  (a) Peen (b) Wedge
  (c) Handle (d) Pole

129. This hammer is used to draw out nails from furniture wooden packing etc.—
  (a) Sledge hammer (b) Soft hammer
  (c) Mallet (d) Claw hammer

130. Gun metal contains copper—
  (a) 5% (b) 10%
  (c) 20% (d) 85%

131. Hacksaw blade are available in following length:
  (a) 50–100 mm (b) 100–150 mm
  (c) 150–200 mm (d) 200–300 mm

132. Files are made of—
  (a) Carbon tool steel
  (b) Low-carbon steel
  (c) High-carbon steel
  (d) None of the above

133. During welding process, job is got held by—
  (a) Earth clamp (b) Job clamp
  (c) Cable connector (d) Wire brush

134. 'Tera' means—
  (a) 10^3 (b) 10^6
  (c) 10^9 (d) 10^{12}

135. 'Nano' means—
  (a) 10^{-3} (b) 10^{-6}
  (c) 10^{-9} (d) 10^{-12}

136. Number of threads in tapper tap are—
  (a) Only 1 (b) 3 to 5
  (c) 5 to 8 (d) 8 to 10

137. The coming out way for chopped chips in the body of tap—
  (a) Land (b) Cutting face
  (c) Chips way (d) Flute

138. Which tap is also called as 'T-shaped handle'—
  (a) Solid tap handle
  (b) Adjustable tap handle
  (c) Jaw type handle
  (d) None of the above

139. Number of threads in bottom tap are—
  (a) only 1 (b) 3 to 5
  (c) 5 to 8 (d) 8 to 10

140. Its shunk is parallel and tapered. In parallel shunk reamer, parallel flutes are cut off—
  (a) Hand reamer (b) Shell reamer
  (c) Pilot reamer (d) Machine reamer

141. This reamer can be used only by machine. Slot is cut on its shunk for entrapping if into machine arber—
  (a) Hand reamer (b) Shell reamer
  (c) Pilot reamer (d) Machine reamer

142. Blade of this screw driver has four flutes—
  (a) Standard screw driver
  (b) Offset screw driver
  (c) Philips screw driver
  (d) Rachit screw driver

143. 985 litres equals
  (a) 4.54 gallon (b) 14.5 gallon
  (c) 50.6 gallon (d) 216.96 gallon

144. 1 ton (metric) equals
  (a) 2000 pound (b) 2100 pound
  (c) 2240 pound (d) 2340 pound

145. 1 kilogram force equals
  (a) 4.17 Newton (b) 9.81 Newton
  (c) 14.5 Newton (d) 15.7 Newton

146. In which length, half-round file is available—
  (a) 50–100 mm (b) 100–400 mm
  (c) 400–500 mm (d) 500–700 mm

147. This file is used to cut metals in large quantity—
  (a) Bastard file (b) Smooth file
  (c) Rough file (d) Second cut file

148. This file is used for semi-finishing work—
  (a) Bastard file (b) Smooth file
  (c) Rough file (d) Second cut file

149. At the time of chipping, how many millimetre cut should not be taken in one time—
  (a) 3 mm (b) 5 mm
  (c) 6 mm (d) 8 mm

150. In drill, '1' number means—
  (a) 0.0135 inch (b) 0.0102 inch
  (c) 0.228 inch (d) 0.425 inch

ANSWERS

1	2	3	4	5	6	7	8	9	10
(b)	(b)	(c)	(b)	(a)	(c)	(a)	(b)	(d)	(d)
11	**12**	**13**	**14**	**15**	**16**	**17**	**18**	**19**	**20**
(b)	(c)	(b)	(b)	(c)	(b)	(b)	(d)	(c)	(d)
21	**22**	**23**	**24**	**25**	**26**	**27**	**28**	**29**	**30**
(a)	(d)	(d)	(b)	(a)	(a)	(b)	(c)	(c)	(b)
31	**32**	**33**	**34**	**35**	**36**	**37**	**38**	**39**	**40**
(a)	(d)	(a)	(a)	(d)	(a)	(b)	(c)	(b)	(c)
41	**42**	**43**	**44**	**45**	**46**	**47**	**48**	**49**	**50**
(a)	(b)	(b)	(b)	(c)	(d)	(a)	(a)	(b)	(d)
51	**52**	**53**	**54**	**55**	**56**	**57**	**58**	**59**	**60**
(a)	(d)	(b)	(b)	(c)	(d)	(d)	(c)	(a)	(d)
61	**62**	**63**	**64**	**65**	**66**	**67**	**68**	**69**	**70**
(d)	(c)	(c)	(a)	(b)	(a)	(c)	(b)	(c)	(b)
71	**72**	**73**	**74**	**75**	**76**	**77**	**78**	**79**	**80**
(c)	(b)	(a)	(b)	(d)	(b)	(a)	(b)	(d)	(c)
81	**82**	**83**	**84**	**85**	**86**	**87**	**88**	**89**	**90**
(d)	(b)	(b)	(d)	(b)	(b)	(b)	(b)	(b)	(d)
91	**92**	**93**	**94**	**95**	**96**	**97**	**98**	**99**	**100**
(c)	(c)	(b)	(d)	(b)	(a)	(c)	(d)	(a)	(a)
101	**102**	**103**	**104**	**105**	**106**	**107**	**108**	**109**	**110**
(c)	(d)	(c)	(a)	(a)	(c)	(d)	(c)	(b)	(c)
111	**112**	**113**	**114**	**115**	**116**	**117**	**118**	**119**	**120**
(a)	(a)	(c)	(b)	(b)	(d)	(d)	(c)	(a)	(b)
121	**122**	**123**	**124**	**125**	**126**	**127**	**128**	**129**	**130**
(d)	(d)	(c)	(a)	(d)	(a)	(a)	(c)	(d)	(d)
131	**132**	**133**	**134**	**135**	**136**	**137**	**138**	**139**	**140**
(b)	(c)	(b)	(d)	(c)	(d)	(d)	(c)	(a)	(d)
141	**142**	**143**	**144**	**145**	**146**	**147**	**148**	**149**	**150**
(b)	(c)	(d)	(c)	(b)	(b)	(c)	(a)	(a)	(c)

5

WELDING

Welding : The welding is a process through which two same or different metals are joined with or without filler rod on pressurising or without pressurising the metals at the right temperature. The welding is a permanent joint and different metals like alloy steel, carbon steel, copper, brass, nickel, cast-iron, bronze, Monal metal, aluminium etc. can be joined. The filler metal is used to fill the blank space created in joints during the welding.

Methods of Welding:

(i) **Fusion/Non-Pressure Welding :** In this method both the ends of metals are melted so that they could mix in each other. The blank space between the metals is filled by the filler-metal on melting it, on cooling the joints complete. There is a no need of pressure in it that is why it is called non-pressure welding.

This welding is of four types:

   (a) Arc Welding   *(b)* Gas Welding

   (c) Thermit Welding   *(d)* Forge Welding

(ii) **Plastic/Pressure Welding :** In this method both the edges of different metals are heated just below to their melting point and then put some pressure to join the both metals. There is no need of filler metal in this method.

This welding is also of four types:

(a) Resistance Welding

(b) Pressure Gas Welding

(c) Forge Welding

(d) Thermit Welding

Instruments Used as Fire Extinguisher in Workshops :

   (i) **Foam Type :** Fire spreads from flammable oil fat or spirit is extinguished in it.

   (ii) **CO_2 Gas Type :** Fire spreads through electric equipments is extinguished by it.

  (iii) **B.C.F (or C.T.C) Type :** Fire spreads through electricity and flammable liquids is extinguished by it.

  (iv) **Fire Blanket :** It is a woolen cloth, which can be wrapped around the body in case a person gets fire and then rolling the body at the ground he/she can get control on fire.

Use of Precautionatory Equipments While Welding:

1. Helmet and Hand Shield
2. Portable welding screen
3. Gloves/Apron
4. Leg Guard
5. Torch light
6. Electrode Carrier
7. Hydrolic back pressure value
8. Safety Belts
9. Safety valves and
10. Goggels

First-Aid : It is a primary treatment, for an accidental patient, which is given before getting the doctor's check up or treatment.

The following things are found in a first-aid box:

   (i) Pain-reliever tablets

   (ii) Small slates of wood

  (iii) Dettol

  (iv) Sterite cotton

   (v) Cloth

  (vi) Triangular cloth

 (vii) Safety pin

(viii) Burnol

  (ix) Tincture Benzene

   (x) Tincture Iodine

(xi) Bandage

(xii) Mercury chrome etc.

Joint Made from Forge Welding :

(i) **"LAP" or "SCARF" Weld Joint :** In this process, slanted shape is given to the ends after heating they are put on each other and then joined. A slope is given to the slanted part so that melted layer could come out easily.

(ii) **'Bat' Weld Joint :** In this process both the edges are joined on putting them before each other and this type of joint make an angle of 90° with the length.

(iii) **'T' Weld Joint :** This joint looks like '⊥' *i.e.*, upward down position of English alphabet 'T'. Here one end putting in the middle of other and then joined so that it makes an angle of 90°.

(iv) **'V' or 'Splice' Weld Joint :** In this, an end is make the shape of 'V' and other end is welded after putting it inside the first one.

(v) **Gas Welding :** It was started in AD 1895. When oxygen and acetelene are mixed and burnt, the flames appeared whose temperature reaches upto 3140°C. Gas welding is done through this flame.

In Gas welding, copper ferrous and non-ferrous metals, aluminium, brass etc are joined. This is a fusion welding method.

There are two types of gas welding:

(i) **Low Pressure Gas Welding :** In this method, acetelene is used after preparing it in low pressure acetelene generator.

(ii) **High Pressure Gas Welding :** In this method acetelene gas is used from the cylinder where the pressure is 15.5 kg/cm^2 and the gas is in liquid state.

The pressure of oxygen in both above methods is 125 kg/cm^2. It (pressure) is in compressed form.

Arc Welding : In this method an arc is created between metals and electrode to heat the metals at their welding temperature. The temperature is about 3600–4000°C at arc or electric flame. This heat melts the metals and electrode. Melted metals when cools after mixing in each other there becomes a strong joint.

Main Methods of Arc Welding:

(i) Carbon arc welding

(ii) Mettalic arc welding

(iii) Inert gas arc welding

(iv) Sub-merged arc welding

(v) Atomic Hydrogen arc welding

Electron Beam Welding : In this method of welding heat is created, on focussing of high energy electron beam on the welding place or point. When electrodes strike at high speed to the metals then their energy convert into heat energy and this heat is so strong that it can melt the metal easily. This method is used to weld from a thin metal to 50 mm thick metal. It is useful to weld refractory the metals like tungsten, columbium, mollybdenum and tentalum.

Gases Used in Welding : Gases are used in welding so that a flame could be created on mixing the gases with the help of which welding is done.

1. Oxygen : On the basis of weight, on earth, 21% oxygen in 50% air and 89% oxygen in water is found. The oxygen was discovered by Joseph Prestley at the end of eighteenth century and the usage of oxygen started in 1892 for industrial purposes. This gas is stored in the strong steel cylinder and these cylinder do not have any joint.

The pressure of oxygen in cylinder is 150 kg/cm^2. The oxygen cylinders are used in following sizes:

(a) Big Size (6.8 m^3 O$_2$)

(b) Medium Size (3.5 m^3 O$_2$)

(c) Small Size (2.25 m^{3}O$_2$)

Generally we use the 6 m^3 size's cylinder, which contains about 8 kg oxygen. This oxygen gas liquefied at the pressure of 120 to 140 kg/cm^2.

2. Acetelene : Acetelene (C$_2$H$_2$) is a flammable, gas which was discovered in 1836. The methods of making acetelene gas are:

(a) **In Direct Contact of Carbon and Hydrgen :** In this method an electric arc of two carbon electrodes in a hydrogen medium, is created. Due to this reason hydrogen and carbon together makes acetelene, methane and ethane gases.

(b) **From Breaking of Natural Gas :**

$$2CH_4 \quad \rightarrow \quad C_2H_2 \quad + \quad 3H_2$$
(Methane)   (Acetelene)   (Hydrogen)

(c) **From Calcium Carbide :**

$$CaC_2 + 2H_2O \rightarrow Ca(OH)_2 + C_2H_2$$
(Calcium Carbide)(Water)   (Lime)   (Acetelene)

The equipment which is used to generate acetelene is known as Acetelene Generator. It can be divided as follows:

(a) On the basis of generating the Gas power.

(b) On the basis of structure.

(c) On the basis of burning of carbide or pouring of water.

(d) On the basis of power to drop carbide.

(e) On the basis of gas pressure.

(f) On the basis of usable method.

Acetelene Purifier: It is generally used to purify the acetelene gas obtained from acetelene generators, and it is fitted between the generator and water seal.

3. Hydrogen : It is used to weld and cut the soft metals like magnesium, aluminium and lead. This gas is filted in the steel's cylinders of the pressure of 14 kg/cm². The burning temperature of this gas is about 3090°C.

Following are the main methods of making hydrogen gas :

(a) **On passing** electricity in water, hydrogen is deposited at cathode and oxygen is deposited at anode.

(b) **By Reaction of metals with water :**

$$2\,Na + 2\,H_2O \rightarrow 2\,NaOH + H_2$$
(Sodium) (Water)   (Sodium   (Hydrogen)
                  Hydroxide)

(c) **Bash Method :**

$$C + H_2O \xrightarrow{1000°C} CO + H_2$$
(Coke) (Vapour)   (Carbon (Hydrogen)
                  monoxide)

Water Gas
$$\downarrow +H_2O \text{ (Vapour)}$$
$$CO_2 + 2H_2O$$
(Carbon dioxide)   (Water)

(d) **Lane Method :**

$$2\,Fe + 4\,H_2O \rightarrow Fe_3O_4 + 4H_2$$
(Iron)   (Vapour) (Iron oxide) (Hydrogen)

4. Retart Gas : This gas is a mixture of many inflammable gases which are obtained from the breaking of oil temperature. When one kg fuel oil is heated at the temperature of 720°C to 740°C, about 0.35 to 0.4 m³ retart gas forms.

5. Refinery Oil Gas : This gas forms as a bi-product in the oil refinery industries. Its structure changes as we use it because faster vaporising material vaporises early.

6. Natural Gas : It is a mixture of hydrocarbons and is obtained naturally in oil-wells. It is colourless and odourless.

7. Coke Oven (or Bi-product) Gas : This gas forms at the time of distillation of coal. This gas is obtained as a bi-product with other products from coal.

8. Propane and Butane : This gas is obtained in 23 kg & 33 kg steel cylinders in oil refinery industries. The critical temperature is high and critical pressure is low of these gases.

9. Petrol and Kerosine Gas : Petrol and Kerosine are converted into vapour forms after heating and these are used in welding.

10. Argon Gas : This gas is using as a shielding medium from a long time. Its boiling point is 155.7°C and electric arc is more permanent in it.

11. Helium Gas : This gas is used as a shielding medium for welding the metals like aluminium, magnesium and copper. Its boiling point is –452°F and it is lighter than air.

12. Carbon dioxide : At normal temperature, CO_2 is non-reactive gas but when temperature increases it converts into oxygen and carbon monoxide.

Instruments Used in Gas Welding :

1. Oxygen Cylinder
2. Acetelene Cylinder
3. Torch Lighter
4. Hoddge pipe
5. Hydraulic back pressure valve (as water seal)
6. Pressure Regulator
7. Welding rod and flux
8. Keys and Clips
9. Apron and Gloves
10. Acetelene Generator
11. Saftey Valve
12. Gas Purifier
13. Welding table
14. Blow pipe

15. Trolly
16. Welding Goggles
17. Wire brushes etc.

Neutral Flame : When acetelene and oxygen burns in equal quantity then neutral flame creates. Its temperature is 3200°C.

Carborising Flame : The quantity of acetelene is more in this flame. There appears a white angle in between the internal angle and outer part, which is known as acetelene feather. Its temperature is about 3100°C.

This flame is used for nickel and monil metal welding and soldering of silver, it is also used for layering of hard material.

Oxidising Flame : The quantity of oxygen in this flame is more and the length of internal angle is less than the length of neutral flame. It's color is blue and shape is of sharp angle. Its temperature is about 3300°C. This flame is used only for brass welding.

Soft Flame : It's velocity is not more than 10 to 15 m/second. Such type of flame is used in welding. The weld metal moves and spreads easily before it.

Hard Flame : It's velocity is much more than 100 meter per second. It spreads and bursts the melted metal that is why welding is not possible with it.

Detonation : The velocity of this flame is just little more than 100 m/s and it is not useful in welding.

Breaking of Flame : It means flame does not burns at the tip but ahead of it. The reason behind it is that gases supplies at the high pressure which can be mend by using regulators at the working pressure of gas.

Popping : It is a defect of flame which means there comes a sound of Pit-pit from welding torch. It is because of shortage of supply of gas.

Property of a Good Weld :

1. There should not be any blow hole inside weld.
2. No cracking in weld.
3. The welding metal should not be prominent.
4. Breath of welding must be equal.

Techniques of Gas Welding:

1. In flat position
2. Vertical Welding
3. Over-Head Welding and
4. Lindey-Welding

More Penetration : In this defect, the metal flows at other side when metal is melted highly which is result of high temperature of flame (which is due bigger size of tip as compared to the width of plate). To overcome on this defect we need a tip of accurate size and a right speed.

Incomplete Penetration : Sometimes edges of base metals do not melts because of low temperature of flame, due to which it's filler does not join with the metals. Another reason for this defect is improper preparations of edges of joints. This defect can be reduced or corrected by preparing of edges properly and using of right size of tip.

Welding Joint : The place which is used to join two parts of metal through Gas or Arch welding is known as 'welding joint'.

These are of five types :

1. Lap Joint : Single fillet, Double fillet, Single lap, Double lap and Flagened single lap.

2. Butt Joint : Open flaged, Closed flaged, Open upset, Closet upset, Open square, Closed square, Open single 'V', Closed single 'V', Open double 'V', Closed double 'V', Open single bevel, Closed single bevel, Open double bevel, Closed double bevel, Open single '∪', closed single '∪', open double '∪', closed double '∪', Open single 'J', Closed Single 'J', Open double 'J', Closed double 'J', Open strand and closed strand.

3. Edge Joint

4. Corner's Joint : Flush type, Half open, full open.

5. T-Joint : Single fillet, Double fillet, Single bevel, Double bevel, Single 'J', Double 'J'.

Filler Rod/Welding Rod : It's main function is to provide extra metal to fill the blank space of joint. It is obtained in the shape of roll and a rod of one meter length of circular and square shape. It sells according to the weight.

There are two types of filler rod :

1. Metallic Rod : To weld at the job of iron generally steel rod is used. The quantity of carbon is more in it than the base metal.

2. Non-Metallic Rod : Non-metal are those in which iron is not found. De-oxidising or fluxing agents are found in it.

The selection of welding rod depends upon

following elements—

1. Working part of metal

2. At using place

3. Height of working part

Name of a Few Filler Rod :

1. Drawn-Manganese Rod

2. Drawn-Copper Rod

3. Drawn-Brass Rod

4. Drawn-Aluminium Rod

5. Super-Silicon Cast Iron Rod

6. Cast-Aluminium Rod

7. Mild Steel (Copper Coated) Rod

8. Venedium Steel Rod

9. Low-Carbon Steel Rod

10. Chrome-Venedium Steel Rod

11. Stay Light Rod

Flame Cutting : It is a chemical method of cutting the metals. For which heat of oxy-acetelene gas is used. The principle of cutting the hot metal through flame depends upon the burning of oxygen from the speed of jet. In this method, metal is heated upto dark red and then releasing in the form of oxygen jet due to which the metal burns without melting. With the help of this straight, curved and circular and outer of every shape and to put holes internal cutting can be done. This method is used to make ships, mineral industries, boilers, trains, bridges and building and especially to demolish them.

Solder : It is mainly an alloy of tin and lead. The melting point of tin is 232°C and lead is 327°C. When both are mixed in the ratio of 63 and 37 then this melting point becomes 183°C. Generally/Frequently usable solders are:

1. Electric solder

2. Best Tin-Man solder

3. Plumber solder

4. Normal solder

There should be following properties of a good solder:

1. The melting point of solder should be less than the joining metals near about 60°C to 70°C.

2. It has a property to wet the other metals efficiently.

3. It should not have any problem when it is in liquid state.

4. It should be able to make a mixture with the mixed metals.

Flux : Flux protects the melted solder and base of metal from oxidisation. They pulls the dissolved oxides outside.

They are found in the form of powder, paste and liquid. Flues which are generally used are : *acid of salt, Zinc-chloride, or cut acid, Biroju, tello and nausadar)*

The selection of flux depends upon following:

1. Method of soldering

2. Shape of joint

3. Types of main metal

4. Solder which is used

5. Rates/prices of flux

6. To remove the flux which remains after soldering

Brazing : It is a permanent joint, which does not open on heating once applied. Therefore it is called hard solder. In this soldering borax is used in the form of flux. There should be a temperature of more than 600°C for this method.

The following are the methods of brazing:

1. Blow pipe brazing

2. Torch brazing

3. Electric brazing

4. Furnace brazing

5. Dip brazing

The best fire for brazing is the fire of wood coal.

Molecule : It is the smallest particle of an element which contains all the virtues of that element.

Atom : It is the smallest particle of molecule. Atoms are made up of the following paricles:

1. Proton : These are positively charged particles.

2. Neutron : Neutrons are those atoms which have no electric charge. They have equal number of electrons and protons and both have electric charge same and opposite and can neutralize to each other.

Neutron has no electric charge.

3. Electron : These are negatively charged.

Single Face Supply : There are two wires in this supply where one phase is hot and other is neutral. There is a difference of 230 volt between them.

Transformer : It is an electric instrument which is used to convert low voltage and high ampere current

into high voltage and low ampere current.
Transformation Ratio

$$= \frac{\text{No. of coils in primary winding}}{\text{No. of coils in secondary winding}}$$

$$= \frac{\text{Primary voltage}}{\text{Secondary voltage}} = \frac{\text{Secondary current}}{\text{Primary current}}$$

There are two windings in it:

1. Primary Winding : To which coil, electric supply is given, is called as primary winding (electric).

2. Secondary Winding : To which coil, supply is taken is called as secondary winding.

There are two types of transformers:

1. Step-Up Transformer : This transformer up the voltage.

2. Step Down Transformer : This transformer down the voltage.

3. Welding Estimation : This is a process through which we counts the expenditure before weldings. Material cost, labour cost and over-head cost affects the welding.

Operating Factor : It is the ratio of burning of arc and total time taken in joint. In a good welding shop the operative factor is 50% and in field it's quantity may be 20%.

Cost of Energy in Welding Estimation:

$$\text{Cost of energy} = \left(\frac{\text{Arc Voltage} \times \text{Current}}{1000} \right) \times \left(\frac{\text{time of burning of arc}}{60} \right) \times \left(\frac{\text{current}}{\text{efficiency of machine}} \right)$$

OBJECTIVE TYPE QUESTIONS

1. Cast Iron is pre-heated at the temperature:
   (a) 500°C *(b)* 400°C
   (c) 350°C *(d)* 300°C
2. Which of the following is called as non-pressure welding—
   (a) Autogeneous welding
   (b) Fusion Welding
   (c) Gas Welding
   (d) Plastic Welding
3. The flame is right for pre-heating—
   (a) Oxy-hydrogen *(b)* Oxy-propane
   (c) Oxy-butane *(d)* Oxy-acetelene
4. To make this gas oxygen and acetelene are mixed in equal quantity—
   (a) Neutral Flame
   (b) Oxidising Flame
   (c) Carborising Flame
   (d) None of the above
5. Plates can be welded in leftend technique—
   (a) Less than 2 mm height plates
   (b) More than 2 mm height plates
   (c) Less than 5 mm height plates
   (d) More than 5 mm height plates
6. The following temperature can be obtained from the oxy-acetelene flame:
   (a) 3100°C to 3300°C
   (b) 2700°C to 2800°C
   (c) 2400°C to 2700°C
   (d) 1800°C to 2300°C
7. Splatter is used in—
   (a) Soldering *(b)* Brazing
   (c) Welding *(d)* All of the above
8. Machine is used for arc welding—
   (a) Rectifier *(b)* A.C. Transformer
   (c) D.C. Generator *(d)* All of the above
9. The temperature of oxy-hydrogen flame—
   (a) 2000°C *(b)* 3000°C
   (c) 2800°C *(d)* 2500°C
10. At which volts arc welding method can be completed—
    (a) 10 to 40 volts *(b)* 40 to 100 volts
    (c) 100 to 160 volts *(d)* 160 to 200 volts
11. The gas is generally leaks from—
    (a) Hoddge pipe
    (b) Welding torch
    (c) Joint of hoddge and torch
    (d) None of the above
12. The part which puts the job at the right place is–
    (a) Pin *(b)* Lugs
    (c) Cup and Cone *(d)* All of the above
13. Which colour is found in oxidizing flame—
    (a) Red *(b)* Green
    (c) Light blue *(d)* Dark blue

14. Slag or outer non-metal particles when remain inside weld-metal is known as—
(a) Slug Inclusion   *(b)* Spatter
(c) Under-cut   *(d)* Porosity

15. Hydrogen is stored at—
(a) 10 kg/cm² pressure
(b) 11 kg/cm² pressure
(c) 14 kg/cm² pressure
(d) None of the above

16. On the basis of expenditure, electrodes are—
(a) Two types   *(b)* Five types
(c) Seven types   *(d)* Nine types

17. Water to Carbide method is used to make—
(a) Acetelene   *(b)* Oxygen
(c) Hydrogen   *(d)* None of the above

18. When torch flame is forwarded towards 'bead' and filler rod runs backward to torch flame then it is callcd—
(a) Leftward Welding
(b) Arc Welding
(c) Rightward Welding
(d) None of the above

19. The oxygen gas liquefies at the pressure—
(a) 140 kg/cm²   *(b)* 240 kg/cm²
(c) 260 kg/cm²   *(d)* None of the above

20. In this test, a small part of job is tested after cutting and after the cut part is repaired—
(a) Gamma-ray test
(b) Magnetic test
(c) Destructive test
(d) Semi-destructive test

21. Pre-heat makes job before welding or brazing—
(a) Strong   *(b)* Hard
(c) Porous   *(d)* Crackless

22. The joints are inspected—
(a) After welding
(b) Before welding
(c) At the time of welding
(d) All of the above

23. The pipe which is attached to the acetelene cylinder is of—
(a) Green colour   *(b)* Red colour
(c) Blue colour   *(d)* Black colour

24. With the help of this test overlapping of weld metal, root penetration of fillet joint and fusion can be identified—
(a) Hardness test   *(b)* Fillet Rotcher test
(c) Nick-break test   *(d)* Freeband test

25. The maximum temperature of neutral flame of oxy-acetelene is—
(a) 1050°C   *(b)* 2000°C
(c) 2800°C   *(d)* 3250°C

26. This sign is used to describe starting weld signs afterward—
(a) Starting weld sign
(b) Mark of arrow
(c) Complement sign
(d) Symbolic line

27. Welding method is used to join—
(a) Same-metals
(b) Two different metals
(c) Two same or different metals
(d) None of the above

28. The meaning of $\widehat{K}$ is—
(a) Stud
(b) Field welding
(c) No. of spots or projection
(d) Double bevel butt

29. Which of the following welding is done at the highest temperature—
(a) Arc welding   *(b)* Braze welding
(c) Brazing   *(d)* Soldering

30. The cost of welding depends upon—
(a) Cost of material
(b) Cost of Labour
(c) Cost of over-head
(d) All of the above

31. D.A. cylinder is put always in—
(a) Horizontal position
(b) Vertical position
(c) Bending position
(d) All of the above

32. All the metals which are used in welding comes under it—
(a) Material cost   *(b)* Labour cost
(c) Over head cost *(d)* All of the above

33. The first digit of electro-coding shows
(a) Types of flux
(b) Welding position
(c) Tension capacity
(d) Direction of welding

34. The type of joint is shown at reference line by—
(a) 'A'   (b) 'R'
(c) 'O'   (d) '→'

35. Lap joint is used for—
(a) Upto 3 mm thick plates
(b) Less than 2 mm thick plates
(c) More than 3 mm thick plates
(d) All of the above

36. Ferrous-material is—
(a) Cast Iron   (b) Brass
(c) Bronze   (d) None of the above

37. Weldability depends upon—
(a) Methods of welding
(b) Metal
(c) Both of the above
(d) None of the above

38. ⏢ is name of—
(a) Bend   (b) Seem
(c) Plug   (d) Spot

39. Generally length of electrodes is—
(a) 250 mm   (b) 350 mm
(c) 300 mm   (d) 450 mm

40. In ⏚ name of complement sign is—
(a) Single-μ-butt   (b) Single-bevel-butt
(c) Chipping finish   (d) Fillet

41. The third digit of electro-coding shows—
(a) Types of flux
(b) Direction of welding
(c) Tensile strength
(d) None of the above

42. Copper is—
(a) Wrought iron   (b) Alloy steel
(c) Carbon steel   (d) None of the above

43. For which welding neutral flame is right—
(a) Brass   (b) Aluminium
(c) Manganese   (d) Chromium

44. The pitch of weld is shown on reference line from—
(a) 'A'   (b) '0'
(c) 'P'   (d) 'O'

45. Which is not used in Gas welding—
(a) Oxygen Gas
(b) Flux
(c) Coated electrode

(d) Filler rod

46. The current for arc in A.C. welding is used—
(a) By Rectifier
(b) By D.C. generator
(c) By A.C. generator
(d) By transformer

47. Which measures in weld Gauge—
(a) Machine current
(b) Weld beed
(c) Diameter of electrodes
(d) Direction of welding

48. The eye should be washed in case of arc-eye-
(a) From water
(b) From Fresh Water (10 milli litre)
(c) From Sodium-bi-carbonate (3.4 g)
(d) (b) and (c)

49. Welding of following is done from Inert gas arc welding—
(a) Stainless steel
(b) Magnesium
(c) Alloy
(d) All of the above

50. The colour of metals converts from yellow to white at—
(a) 900°C temperature
(b) 1100°C temperature
(c) 1300°C temperature
(d) 1500°C temperature

51. Non-Ferrous material is—
(a) Cast iron   (b) Brass
(c) Mild steel   (d) None of the above

52. 'π' is symbol of—
(a) Double bevel butt
(b) Stud
(c) Square butt
(d) Double 'U' butt

53. Gas welding regulators are used in—
(a) Single stage
(b) Double stage
(c) Both of the above
(d) None of the above

54. The name of weld sign '◺' is—
(a) Single 'U' butt
(b) Single bevel butt
(c) Chipping finish
(d) Fillet

55. The flame which forms from the mixing of oxygen and acetelene in equal proportion is—
(a) Neutral　　　　(b) Carborising
(c) Oxidisation　　(d) Oxidising

56. In this method, same metals are joined with the help of same metallic filler rod
(a) Hetrogeneous welding
(b) Autogeneous welding
(c) Both of the above
(d) None of the above

57. The maximum temperature of oxy-acetelene flame is at—
(a) Near the torch tip
(b) In between the flame
(c) Equal at every place
(d) Out of flame

58. Gas welding is used to join—
(a) Copper　　　　(b) Aluminium
(c) Brass　　　　　(d) All of the above

59. Tungsten electrode used in Atomic hydrogen arc welding is—
(a) One　　　　　(b) Two
(c) Three　　　　(d) Five

60. The instrument used to extinguish the fire in workshops is—
(a) Foam type
(b) Carbon dioxide Gas type
(c) C.T.C or B.C.F. type
(d) All of the above

61. The temperature of arc is—
(a) 1550°C　　　　(b) 3500°C
(c) 2400°C　　　　(d) 2000°C

62. The iron-metal on which welding can be done is—
(a) Carbon steel　　(b) Alloy steel
(c) Wrought iron　　(d) All of the above

63. Mechanical energy is converted into electric energy by—
(a) Generator　　　(b) Television
(c) Transistor　　　(d) Motor

64. Which of the following is carbon-steel—
(a) Low carbon steel
(b) Medium carbon steel
(c) High carbon steel
(d) All of the above

65. Electric energy is converted into mechanical energy by—
(a) Television　　　(b) Generator
(c) Electric Motor　(d) Transistor

66. The name of the sign '*' is—
(a) Bend　　　　　(b) Seem
(c) Plug　　　　　(d) Spot

67. Which is done at the lowest temperature—
(a) Welding　　　　(b) Brazing
(c) Soldering　　　(d) Braze welding

68. Under this cost, the expenditure on workers who are working on weldings is calculated—
(a) Material cost　　(b) Labour cost
(c) Over-head cost　(d) None of the above

69. Electric current is measured by—
(a) Voltmeter　　　(b) Galvanometer
(c) Motor　　　　　(d) Rectifier

70. The paint colour of aceteline cylinder is—
(a) Brown-Green　　(b) Red
(c) Black　　　　　(d) None of the above

71. Electrode in argon arc welding is made from—
(a) Copper　　　　(b) Babbit Metal
(c) Tungsten　　　(d) Aluminium

72. It is the ratio of burning of arc and total time to complete the joint—
(a) cost of welding estimation energy
(b) Operating factor
(c) Quantity of electrode Material
(d) None of the above

73. The electric arc was discovered in—
(a) 1802　　　　　(b) 1810
(c) 1818　　　　　(d) 1800

74. The temperature at which centigrade and fahrenheit is equal is—
(a) 40°C　　　　　(b) 73°C
(c) 173°C　　　　(d) 273°C

75. Electricity is supplied by—
(a) Motor Generator
(b) Transformer
(c) Rectifier
(d) All of the above

76. Generally the length of hoddge pipe is—
(a) 5 meter　　　　(b) 10 meter
(c) 15 meter　　　(d) 20 meter

77. The reason for fluctuation in arc is—
(a) Change in flow
(b) Change in resistance

(c) Change in voltage
(d) All of the above

78. The chemical formula of acetelene is—
(a) C_2H_4 *(b)* C_2H_6
(c) C_2H_2 *(d)* C_3H_6

79. The acronym for L.P.G. is—
(a) Low-pressure gas
(b) Liquefied petroleum gas
(c) Lightening Pressure Gauge
(d) None of the above

80. The gas filled in D.A. cylinder is—
(a) Butane Gas   *(b)* Marsh Gas
(c) Acetone Gas   *(d)* All of the above

81. The unit of current is
(a) Volt   *(b)* Ampere
(c) Bar   *(d)* Pascal

82. The colour of gas welding goggles is—
(a) Yellow   *(b)* Brown-Green
(c) Black   *(d)* Light Brown

83. The outer defects in welding—
(a) Crator-spattor   *(b)* Crack
(c) Porosity   *(d)* All of the above

84. Which method is used in arc cutting—
(a) Metallic arc welding
(b) Carbon arc cutting
(c) Plasma arc cutting
(d) All of the above

85. The melting point of electric solder is—
(a) 100°C   *(b)* 150°C
(c) 200°C   *(d)* 250°C

86. The quantity of carbon in medium-carbon steel is—
(a) 0.1 to 0.3%   *(b)* 0.3 to 0.5%
(c) 0.3 to 0.8%   *(d)* 0.8% to 1.2%

87. Flux is obtained in—
(a) Powder Form   *(b)* Liquid Form
(c) Solid Form   *(d)* Gaseous Form

88. The colour of copper is—
(a) Dark brown   *(b)* Black
(c) Brown-black   *(d)* Red

89. The name of weld sign $\overline{V}$ is—
(a) Single 'U' butt
(b) Single bevel butt
(c) Chipping Finish
(d) Fillet

90. The Formula of drug is—
(a) drug = Leg × thickness of plate
(b) drug = Leg/thickness of plate
(c) drug = Leg × thickness of plate × 100
(d) drug = $\dfrac{\text{Leg}}{\text{thickness of plate}} \times 100$

91. The meaning of sign 'XXX' is—
(a) Bend   *(b)* Seem
(c) Plug   *(d)* Spot

92. In this method, both the edges are melted so that the metals of both edges could mix and the blank space of joint is filled with the melted filler metal on calling the joint completes or fillet
(a) Plastic Welding
(b) Fusion Welding
(c) Welding Resistance
(d) Pressure Gas Welding

93. The permanent fasteners are—
(a) Rivetting   *(b)* Welding
(c) Cotton-pin   *(d)* *(a)* and *(b)*

94. The reason of catching fire in welding work-shops—
(a) Smoking
(b) Storage of inflammable material
(c) Due to sparking in faulty wires
(d) All of the above

95. Which is used in D.C. welding—
(a) D.C. Generator
(b) Rectifier
(c) Both of the above
(d) None of *(a)* and *(b)*

96. In this method, a strong flow of electric current is passed in welding metals due to which the metals heated upto plastic condition and after that on applying pressure both the parts are joined—
(a) Atomic welding
(b) Resistance welding
(c) Butt Welding
(d) Flash Welding

97. This welding method is used to weld a thin metallic sheet to 50 mm thick metal—
(a) Electron beam welding
(b) Atomic welding

(c) Thermit welding
(d) Projection welding

98. Electron-beam welding is useful to weld the following metals—
(a) Mollybdenum   *(b)* Tentalum
(c) Columbium   *(d)* All of the above

99. The quantity of nitrogen in air is—
(a) 1%   *(b)* 21%
(c) 78%   *(d)* 99%

100. The chemical formula of Iron oxide is—
(a) Fe_2O_3 *(b)* FeO_2
(c) Fe_3O_2 *(d)* Fe_3O_4

ANSWERS

1	2	3	4	5	6	7	8	9	10
(d)	*(b)*	*(d)*	*(a)*	*(c)*	*(a)*	*(b)*	*(d)*	*(c)*	*(b)*
11	**12**	**13**	**14**	**15**	**16**	**17**	**18**	**19**	**20**
(c)	*(d)*	*(d)*	*(a)*	*(c)*	*(a)*	*(a)*	*(c)*	*(a)*	*(d)*
21	**22**	**23**	**24**	**25**	**26**	**27**	**28**	**29**	**30**
(d)	*(d)*	*(b)*	*(b)*	*(d)*	*(c)*	*(c)*	*(d)*	*(a)*	*(d)*
31	**32**	**33**	**34**	**35**	**36**	**37**	**38**	**39**	**40**
(b)	*(a)*	*(a)*	*(a)*	*(a)*	*(a)*	*(c)*	*(c)*	*(d)*	*(c)*
41	**42**	**43**	**44**	**45**	**46**	**47**	**48**	**49**	**50**
(b)	*(b)*	*(d)*	*(c)*	*(c)*	*(d)*	*(b)*	*(d)*	*(d)*	*(c)*
51	**52**	**53**	**54**	**55**	**56**	**57**	**58**	**59**	**60**
(b)	*(c)*	*(c)*	*(d)*	*(a)*	*(b)*	*(b)*	*(d)*	*(b)*	*(d)*
61	**62**	**63**	**64**	**65**	**66**	**67**	**68**	**69**	**70**
(b)	*(d)*	*(a)*	*(d)*	*(c)*	*(d)*	*(c)*	*(b)*	*(b)*	*(d)*
71	**72**	**73**	**74**	**75**	**76**	**77**	**78**	**79**	**80**
(a)	*(b)*	*(a)*	*(a)*	*(d)*	*(a)*	*(b)*	*(c)*	*(b)*	*(c)*
81	**82**	**83**	**84**	**85**	**86**	**87**	**88**	**89**	**90**
(b)	*(b)*	*(d)*	*(d)*	*(d)*	*(b)*	*(a)*	*(d)*	*(b)*	*(d)*
91	**92**	**93**	**94**	**95**	**96**	**97**	**98**	**99**	**100**
(b)	*(b)*	*(d)*	*(d)*	*(c)*	*(b)*	*(a)*	*(d)*	*(c)*	*(d)*

6

PLUMBING

Plumbing : The technique through which pipe lines are lay down, joined, opened and taken to branch line is known as plumbing.

Qualities of a good plumber :

1. He must have the knowledge of modern tools used in plumbing.
2. He must have the knowledge of sanitary-fittings
3. A plumber should be an efficient worker.
4. He should have the complete knowledge of casting iron pipe and pipe fittings.
5. He must also know the job of fitter only then he can do fittings properly as efficiently.

Tools For Plumbing :

1. Steel Rule : This tool is used to take direct measurement i.e measurement can be read directly on it. It is made up of stainless steel or spring steel. It is of different sizes, which can be of 150 mm, 300 mm or 600 mm measuring.

2. Outside Calliper : By this indirect measuring tool i.e. the outside's measurement is taken and its working points are bent towards inside so they could not rubbed easily. After taking measurement, from this tool, its open measurement is checked by the the steel rule.

3. Inside Calliper : By this indirect measuring tool, the internal measurement is taken. It is also made up of mild-steel and its working points are bent towards outside and its case are hard.

4. Divider : It is used for drawing 150 mm circles or arcs. It is used to divide a straight line into equal parts. Its both arms are pointed and straight towards the end. It is of three kinds :

(a) spring type

(b) form type

(c) needle point type.

5. Straight Edge : This tool is used to draw lines. It is used to check the level of the surface. This tool is about made up of steel. It's length is 100 mm to 1000 mm.

6. Spirit Level : This tool is used to check the levelling of joined lines. It can also be used to check the level of machines base. The spirit is filled in it and air bubbles are passed in it. When the surface is plain the air bubble is in between. When this air bubble is little below or above and the place where the bubble is considered above (high).

7. Plumb Bob : This tool is used to check the vertical pipe-line. It is made up of steel or brass. Its face point is conical, whose angle is of 60°. There is a hole in the upper end of this tool to use it and a thread is put into this whole.

8. Steel Taper Rule : This tool is used to measure a long distance. There is a steel's flexible rule in it. Its length is of six foot. It can be used to measure the rough surface.

9. Steel Tape : This tool is used to measure a very long distance. Its length is of 25 feet to 100 feet. Besides steels is made up of canvas and clothes. The length of pipe is measured by it easily.

10. Try-Square : It is also known as *triangular zone*. It is made up of stock cast iron, wood, aluminimum and steel, and blade is made up of stainless steel, spring steel or alloy steel. Its size is taken from the length of blade. It is of 3 inch or 75 mm to 12 inch or 300 mm. It is used to check the pipe line at the angle of 90°.

11. Scriber : This tool is made up of steel's thin wire. Its diameter is of 3 mm. Its end is sharp and pointed. Its point is grinded at the angle of 15° to 5°. This tool is used for marking i.e. used to draw a line on the surface of the metal. It is of 3 types.

(a) simple scriber

(b) improved scribes

(c) Adjustable scriber.

12. Jenny/Hermofrodite Calliper : It is a marking tool. It is used to draw parallel line on the surface of a metal in the fitting shops. The shape of this tool is such that its one arm is sharply pointed at the one end and other arm is bent at the angle of 90° from the front and end of 10 mm radius.

13. Punch : This marking tool is mainly used to mark at the surface of the metal or to strengthen the lines. It is made up of high carbon steel rod and its length is about 100 mm.

It is of the following types :

(a) Dot Punch   (b) Centre Punch

(c) Prick Punch   (d) Solid Punch

(e) Hollow Punch

14. Rivet Set : While riveting, it is used to lay the sheets. It is hollow from inside and it is also made up of high steel carbon. Its hole is 1/64" inch bigger than rivet.

15. Rivet Snap : This is used to make the second head while doing reveting. Its mouth is semi-circled from the front.

16. Rivet Dollies : It is also used to provide base under the rivet head while doing riveting. Its shape is also like the rivet snap.

17. Hammer : It is used to give blow forging, bending, chipping and riveting is performed by it on blowing.

18. Vernier Calliper : It is precission instrument, which is used to measure the size of job from outside, inside. Depth and diameter is also measured by it. It's size is about 150 mm to 1200 mm.

19. Wire Gauge : This gauge is used to check the height of wire, sheet and thickness of pipe. It is not rectangular or spherical shape. It has different standards. Generally S.W.G.(Standard Wire Gauge) gauge is used.

20. Snip : It is a hand-cutting tool. It is used to cut the thin sheets or Rods. It is a sort of scissor which is made up of high carbon steel. It's sharpness is grind at the angle of 80° and it's size is 300 mm. It is of two types.

(a) Straight snip (b) Bent snip

21. Shear : It is also a snip but its size is bigger than 300 mm. This tool is used to cut the 6 mm thick sheets and 12 mm diameter's rod. It is also made up of high carbon steel and it is also of two types :

(a) Stock shear   (b) Block shear

22. Hacksaw : It is an important cutting tool by which a metal can be cut easily. It has two important parts :

(a) Frame   (b) Blade

23. Chisel : It is also a hand-cutting tool which is used where cutting through file and hacksaw is difficult. It is made up of high carbon steel which contains 0.75% to 0.85% carbon.

This sheets, "rod" etc are cut into two parts and wall is cut by it to fit the pipes. It is mainly of two parts.

(a) Cold set   (b) Hot set

24. File : This tool is used to rub the smaller particles of a metal. It is made up of high carbon steel, and apart from tang, its other part is hard and temper. There are teeths on its face (i.e. surface) which are actually cutting edges used to cut (rub) the metal. It has following parts – Tang, Heel, soulder face, site, tip/point.

25. Drill : The tool which is used to make a hole is known as drill. It is made up of high carbon steel and high speed steel. Drill are hard and temper.

There are mainly three types of drill:

(a) Flat drill   (b) Twist drill

(c) Carbide bit twist drill.

26. Drill Machine : The drill is tied in this machine and then it is used. It is mainly of two types:

(a) Portable drill machine

(b) Stationary drill machine

27. Tap : By this tool, screwing is done inside any cylindrical hole. The process of cutting screwings by this tool is known as tapping. It can be used either manually or machinically. It is made up of high carbon steel and high speed steel. It has the following parts – Tang, Shank, Body Flutes, Land, Cutting edge and Heel.

28. Die : The die is used for screwing on outside of a rod, shaft or pipe. It is made up of high carbon steel and high speed steel. Die-stock is used to hold it. It is of the following types :

(a) Round split die *(b)* Adjustable die
(c) Die nut *(d)* Die plate
(e) pipe die and *(f)* acron etc.

29. Saw : It is used to cut the wood. When saw is pulled towards the cutter's side only then the cutting of wood(s) starts. Blade and handle are its two main parts.

Type of Saw

(a) Rip saw
(b) Key hole saw
(c) Cross-cut saw
(d) Compass saw.
(e) Panel shaw
(f) Curve cutting saw
(g) Tenon saw
(h) Copying saw
(i) Dovetail saw
(j) Bow-saw/frame saw.

Fastening : The parts are joined or tied in this method. The sources in engineering industry which are used to join the different machine parts are called fasteners.

The following methods are used to join the parts of machine –

(i) Temporary fastening
(ii) Semi permanent fastening
(iii) Permanent fastening

Pipe : It is a hollow cylindrical piece which is used for carrying any liquid or gaseous material from one place to another. The pipe which has a diameter less than 12 mm is known as a tube.

Classifications of Pipe : The classification of pipes is done as following :

1. On the basis of metal or Material : Steel pipe, plastic pipe, rubber pipe, cast iron pipe, wrought iron pipe, brass pipe, cement pipe, stoneware etc

2. On the basis of size : Round pipe and square pipe

3. On the basis of width : Conduit pipe

4. On the basis of work : Water pipe, gas pipe, oil pipe and furniture pipe

5. On the basis of production : Pipes made after moulding, pipes made by drilling, pipes made by welding, drawn pipe, extrusion pipe made in cold condition through rolling.

6. On the basis of Performance : Standard, Heavy and extra heavy

7. On the basis of joint : Threaded pipe, flanged pipe, collar pipe, socket and spigot joint.

Pipe Joints : The process of joining the pipes is known as pipe joints. After joining the pipes one after another there forms a pipeline. For example socket spigot joints for cast iron pipes, welding for steel pipes, flanges joints or riveting is done, or on putting screwing at the ends of the pipes, these pipes are joined by sockets

Pipe joints are of the following types :

(i) Socket or spigot goints
(ii) Flange joints
(iii) Thread pipe joint
(iv) Knuckle joint
(v) Expansion joints
(vi) Lead pipe joints
(vii) Asbestos cement pipe joints.

Features of PVC Pipes :

(i) They are not affcted by rust
(ii) These pipes are very light weight
(iii) It can tolerate the pressure of water upto 2.5 kg/cm^3 10 kg/cm^3.
(iv) P.V.C. pipes are bad conductors of electricity.
(v) P.V.C. pipe's life is long.

Limitations of P.V.C :

(i) These pipes become soft at high temperature.
(ii) These pipes cannot be used at high pressure.
(iii) These pipes cannot be make of bigger diameter.
(iv) P.V.C. cannot be used far a long span.
(v) It has maximum expansion temperature.

Water : It is a natural element without which one cannot image about life. The water is used for the following purposes :

(i) It is a natural fire extinguisher.
(ii) Water is used for drinking, cooking, bathing, washing etc.
(iii) Water is used for vapour-power.
(iv) To grow the crops, water is used
(v) It is also used in different machines and industries.

The basic resources of water are rain-water, snow (glacier etc).

There are two different categories of source of water :

1. Source of Surface Water : The water which is found on the surface of earth is known as surface water sources. e.g. rivers, ponds, lakes, etc.

2. Source of Ground Water : The water which is obtained from under ground sources are called source of groundwater e.g. springs, wells, tubewells hand pumps etc.

Pure Waters : Pure water contains two parts of hydrogen and one part of oxygen. It has following properties

(i) Colourless

(ii) Odourless

(iii) Sweet taste

(iv) No living organisms (like bacteria etc.)

Hardness of Water : Due to this property of water, froth does not appear in the water even after an excess use of soaps/detergents. This hardness in water comes in the presence of carbonate, sulphate and chlorides compounds of calcium and magnesium. There are two types of hardness in water :

1. Permanent hardness : Dissolving sulphates of calcium and magnesium creates hardness in water.

2. Temporary hardness : Presence of bi-carbonates of calcium and magnesium is responsible for temporary hardness of water.

To Make Bacteria Free Water : The following techniques are used to make drinkable water :

(i) Gravity technique

(ii) Pumping technique

(iii) Double technique

Three Methods of Water Heating : Water can be boiled or heated through gas, oil, soft coke, steam coal, wood fuel, electricity and solar energy. The heat is given through following three methods in any material

(i) Radiation

(ii) Convection

(iii) Conduction

The supply of hot water is done through following methods :

(i) Tank system

(ii) Cylinder system

(iii) Tank and cylinder system.

Valve : The valve is used in water tank or water reservoir to control the flowing of water, besides it to release air from the pipes, these valves are used. Valve are of following types

(i) Sluice valve

(ii) Pressure releif valve

(iii) Air releif valve and

(iv) Check valve.

Water Meter : The quantity of water which is used in houses is measured by water meter. The capacity of measuring water per hour is different. For example, 15 mm's size meter can measure 2000 litre water per hour, and 15000 litre water per hour can be measured by the 50 mm size meter. These days the quantity of water is measured in litre and kilolitres

$$1 \text{ kilolitre} = 100 \text{ litre}$$
$$1 \text{ gallon} = 4.546 \text{ litre}$$

Following are the qualities of a good meter :

(i) Its reading should be in readable condition

(ii) It should be made of good quality metal

(iii) Its all joints should be leak proof.

(iv) It can be fitted on pipeline easily

(v) It must have minimum cost expenditure

(vi) There must be a seal in it so that it could not be tempered

(vii) The life line of water meter should be long

(viii) It should be able to take the water reading efficiently.

Sanitary System And Sanitation : The arrangement which are made to keep a city clean and disease free, are called sanitory system. The word 'sanitary' is taken from sanitation. The sanitary plants are divided into three categories :

(i) collection plant

(ii) treatment plant

(iii) disposal plant

In today's industrial area, different types of sanitary fittings are done in the houses for proper cleanliness. Sanitary fitting is divided into two main categories :

2. Ablation Fittings : The clean water comes into such fittings and passed out in clean form after using. For example, sink wash basin, Bath tubs etc.

3. Soil Fittings : With the help of such fittings, the dirty water of houses, and faecal water is passed through them. For example; water closet; urinals, and slope sink etc.

Drainage : It is ametion through which all the waste after use water is passed like, the dirty water of wash basin, kitchen, bathroom, house, hotels water or rain water etc falls in the sewer. The house's water closet and, faecal/urinal water do not come in them. The drain is open and nowadays in cities water from kitchen, hotels etc is supplied to them directly. It is known as water ground drainage system. Cast iron and stoneware pipes are used for this purpose.

1. Open Drain : The open channel which are constructed along with the boundary of houses, or bath side of road are called open drain. According to their shape or cross-section, these are of following types:

(i) Semi-circled

(ii) 'V' shaped

(iii) 'U' shaped and

(iv) Rectangular.

2. Under Ground Drain : This drainage system is used in houses or hotels or in kitchens to pass out the water from them to outside channels or sewers.

OBJECTIVE TYPE QUESTIONS

1. The characterstic of an efficient plumber
   (a) he should have the knowledge of sanitary fittings
   (b) he should have the knowledge of modern tools
   (c) a plumber should be an efficient worker
   (d) All of the above

2. Which of the following is done at lowest temperature?
   (a) Soldering   *(b)* Braze welding
   (c) Welding   *(d)* Brazing

3. Which of the following statement is true?
   (i) The joints in soldering are not as strong as of brazing
   (ii) The solder's joints affected less from rust comparatively.
   (iii) The melting point of a complement metal in soldering is greater than 427°C but less than the main metal. While the melting point of complement metal in brazing is less than 427°C
   (iv) Both in soldering and brazing two different metals are joined.
   (a) *(i)*, *(ii)*, *(iii)* and *(iv)*
   (b) *(i)*, *(ii)* and *(iii)*
   (c) *(i)*, *(ii)* and *(iv)*
   (d) *(i)* and *(ii)*

4. The melting point of plumber solder is
   (a) 192°C   *(b)* 205°C
   (c) 70°C   *(d)* 304°C

5. Due to this property metals are converted into liquid state after melting and then they can be moulded
   (a) Stiffness   *(b)* Refractoriness
   (c) Fusibility   *(d)* Weldability

6. Circles and arcs of 150 mm radius are drawn by it and a line can also be divided into equal parts by it.
   (a) Outside calliper *(b)* Inside calliper
   (c) Straight Edge   *(d)* Divider

7. It is used to make holes in the metal at both hot and cold state. While making holes in cold jobs, a nut is put under the job and then hammer is hit on it to make a hole :
   (a) Prick punch   *(b)* Solid punch
   (c) Hollow punch   *(d)* Dot punch

8. The work is done through hitting the hammer
   (a) Riveting   *(b)* Bending
   (c) Chipping   *(d)* All of the above

9. This hammer is used in black smithy
   (a) Soft hammer   *(b)* Mallet
   (c) Hand hammers   *(d)* Sledge hammer

10. It is a hand cutting tool which is used to cut the thin sheets or rods.
    (a) Snip   *(b)* Wire gauge
    (c) Vernier calliper *(d)* Hammer

11. Its cutting point is bent from the body to one site and it is used to make square groove as key-chains.
    (a) Diamand point chisel
    (b) Cross-cut chisel
    (c) Size cut chisel
    (d) Cow-Mouth chisel

12. It is made up of by round high carbon steel rod heated in a furnace and forged. It is mostly used in carpenter's shop.
   (a) Flat drill   *(b)* Twist drill
   (c) Carbide bit   *(d)* All of the above

13. The Tap bigger than 1/4 inch tapper sank is called –
   (a) Gas Tap   *(b)* Machine screw tap
   (c) Machine Tap   *(d)* Gun Tap.

14. The act of drawing point, arc and angle parallel lines and center point etc at the surface of a metal according to drawing is called –
   (a) Hacksawing   *(b)* Chipping
   (c) Filing   *(d)* Marking

15. It is a light yellow colour wood which is used to make furnitures, to colour the leather and it is also used to make the handles of the tool.
   (a) Nut   *(b)* Devdar
   (c) Kell   *(d)* Acacia

16. What are the different types of iron are –
   (a) 3   *(b)* 4
   (c) 5   *(d)* 6

17. The quantity of copper in forging brass is
   (a) 2%   *(b)* 30%
   (c) 40%   *(d)* 68%

18. The root and crest of these screwing are semi-circled and these are used in lead-bottles of railway coupling.
   (a) Knuckle thread *(b)* Buttrace thread
   (c) Worm thread   *(d)* Acme thread.

19. The quantity of iron particles in red haematite is –
   (a) 40% to 50%   *(b)* 50% to 60%
   (c) 47% to 70%   *(d)* 70% to 90%

20. Which of the following is done at highest temperature –
   (a) Soldering   *(b)* Brazing
   (c) Arc welding   *(d)* Braze welding

21. There are 14 to 16 teeths per square centimeter in this file –
   (a) Rough file   *(b)* Bastard file
   (c) Second cut file *(d)* Dead smooth file

22. The drawbacks of these acarbonic flux is that if after soldering they are not washed completely or properly then they can damage the joints –
   (a) Corrosive flux
   (b) Normal flux
   (c) Non-corrosive flux
   (d) None of the above

23. Due to this property, the metals can tolerate the sudden shocks and blows –
   (a) Stiffness   *(b)* Plasticity
   (c) Fusibility   *(d)* Impact Resistance

24. Which of the following punches have different shapes –
   (a) Dot Punch   *(b)* Hollow Punch
   (c) Centre Punch   *(d)* Prick Punch

25. The hand tap less than the 1/4 inch diameter is known as –
   (a) Master tap   *(b)* Extension tap
   (c) Band sank tap *(d)* Machine screw tap

26. The act of cutting screwings in the internal hole made by the drill is called –
   (a) Tapping   *(b)* Reaming
   (c) Hacksawing   *(d)* Chipping

27. How many types of steel is generally found –
   (a) 2   *(b)* 3
   (c) 4   *(d)* 5

28. The Non-ferrous metal is –
   (a) Iron   *(b)* Steel
   (c) Gold   *(d)* None of the above

29. The quantity of nickel in nickel silver is –
   (a) 10%   *(b)* 30%
   (c) 40%   *(d)* 60%

30. How many types of screws are there –
   (a) Two   *(b)* three
   (c) Four   *(d)* Five

31. The outer drawback of welding is –
   (a) Porosity   *(b)* Crack
   (c) Crator spatter *(d)* All of the above

32. The hammers are generally made from –
   (a) Copper   *(b)* Iron
   (c) Cast-steel   *(d)* None of the above

33. Necessary heat resistance or induction is obtained by this method through heating and it is the fast method for brazing –
   (a) Electric brazing
   (b) Furnace brazing
   (c) Blowpipe brazing
   (d) Torch brazing

34. The following material is liquid –
    (a) Oxygen   (b) Mercury
    (c) Hydrogen   (d) Carbon
35. In our country, iron and ore are found in enough quantity –
    (a) Bihar   (b) Madhya Pradesh
    (c) Madras   (d) All of the above
36. This tool is used to draw lines on metals and level of surface is also checked by it –
    (a) Steel rule   (b) Divider
    (c) Straight edge   (d) Spirit level
37. This chisel is also known as cap chisel –
    (a) Cross-Cut chisel
    (b) Flat chisel
    (c) Round nose chisel
    (d) Cow mouth chisel
38. This saw is used to lock. It has a handle like the file :
    (a) Compass saw   (b) Bow saw
    (c) Copying   (d) Key hole saw
39. How many types of washer are there?
    (a) Two   (b) Three
    (c) Four   (d) Five
40. This pipe is also known as "Hume pipe" –
    (a) R.C.C pipe   (b) Rubber pipe
    (c) P.V.C pipe   (d) PVDC pipe
41. It is a small piece of pipe and screwing is done outside it and it is used to join two pipes –
    (a) Flange   (b) Cross
    (c) Plug   (d) Nipple
42. The quality of a good meter is –
    (a) upper loss should be minimum in it.
    (b) reading should be clear (readable condition)
    (c) all its joints must be leak proof
    (d) all of the above
43. The colour of acetyline cylinder is
    (a) Red   (b) Marroon
    (c) Black   (d) None of the above
44. The quantity of bronze in the plumber solder is –
    (a) 34%   (b) 40%
    (c) 60%   (d) 66%
45. It is also known as load-stone –
    (a) Sideright   (b) Magnetite
    (c) Red haematite   (d) Brown haematite

46. Due to this property, the metal creates hurdle in bending under outer pressure.
    (a) Stiffness arc   (b) Plasticity
    (c) Fusibility   (d) Impact resistance
47. The Innert gas arc welding is done to weld –
    (a) Alloy   (b) Magnesium
    (c) Stainless steel   (d) All of above
48. This harmmer is used to make channels grooves etc. in the sheets –
    (a) Straight Pen hammer
    (b) Cross Pen hammer
    (c) Ball Pen hammer
    (d) All of the above
49. The necessary temperature for Brazing is –
    (a) $600°C$
    (b) Less than $600°C$
    (c) More than $600°C$
    (d) $0°C$
50. It is a measuring tool which is used to take direct measures i.e., the reading of measure is just taken directly on it –
    (a) Steel rule   (b) Straight Edge
    (c) Plumb bob   (d) Spirit level
51. Its point is grind from $25°$ to $30°$ and it is used to strengthen the lines on the thin sheets –
    (a) Dot Punch   (b) Prick Punch
    (c) Solid Punch   (d) Hollow Punch
52. The sharpened edge of this chisel is circular and it's cutting angle is like a pen –
    (a) Diamand point chisel
    (b) Cow-Mouth chisel
    (c) Size-cut chisel
    (d) Rond Nose-chisel
53. The body of this tap is formed into 3 part –
    (a) Master tap   (b) Machine tap
    (c) Stay bolt tap   (d) Gun tap
54. It is used for the screw whose dimeter is less than 3 mm.
    (a) Round split Die   (b) Pipe Die
    (c) Die plater   (d) Acron die
55. The frame of this saw is made up of wood and the length of blade which is fitted into it is 300 mm to 400 mm
    (a) Copieng saw   (b) Bow Saw
    (c) Hole saw   (d) Pannel saw
56. The act of making hole in a metal is called –
    (a) Fitting   (b) Punching

(c) Tapping   *(d)* Drilling

57. It is a light-weight wood which is used to make the goods for games –
(a) Mulberry   *(b)* Mango
(c) Padtal   *(d)* Kail

58. How many types of plain carbon steels are found?
(a) Two   *(b)* Three
(c) Four   *(d)* Seven

59. It is a very good-conductor of elecricity, which is used to make electricity cables and parts of aeroplane –
(a) Nickel Silver   *(b)* Gun Metal
(c) Bronze   *(d)* Duralumin

60. The full form of B.S.P.T. is –
(a) British standard Plumbing Thread
(b) British Sanitary & Plumbing Thread
(c) British Sanitary & Pipe Thread
(d) British Standard Pipe Thread

61. On the basis of work, pipe are of following kinds –
(a) Two types   *(b)* Three types
(c) Four types   *(d)* Seven types

62. R.C.C pipe has the following properties –
(a) They are rust free
(b) They can be made of bigger diameter easily
(c) Have a long life
(d) All of the above

63. It is used to lay down the pipe lines in all (four) directions and there are internal screwing on its all ends –
(a) Cross   *(b)* Flanges
(c) Bend   *(d)* Albow

64. The part where the water flows, after coming out from the impellar of the pump, its cross-section is equal at every where –
(a) Turbine pipe
(b) Volute pump
(c) Reciprocating pump
(d) Hydrochloric Ram

65. In Argon-arc welding, the electrode is made up of –
(a) Tungsten   *(b)* Copper
(c) Babit Metal   *(d)* Aluminimum

66. This tool is used to check the vertical pipe line–
(a) Steel rule   *(b)* Straight Edge
(c) Plumb Bob   *(d)* Steel taprule

67. The number of tungsten electrode used in Atomic hydrogen arc–welding –
(a) One   *(b)* Two
(c) Three   *(d)* Four

68. This hammer is used to make corners in the sheet metal –
(a) Ball Pen hammer
(b) Straight pen hammer
(c) Cross pen hammer
(d) All of the above

69. The number of flutes in it are comparatively more than normal tap, as a result it has more cutting edges thus makes much accurate screwings –
(a) Hand Tap
(b) Machine Tap
(c) Extension Tap
(d) Master Tap

70. It is a modern die which is used for screwing on rod which is fitted in some hole as groove–
(a) Die nut   *(b)* Pipe die
(c) Acron die   *(d)* Rount split die

71. The method through which the lines are strengthen on the surface of metal –
(a) Fitting   *(b)* Threading
(c) Punching   *(d)* Reaming

72. The limitation of P.V.C pipe is –
(a) These pipes can not used for a long span
(b) Their relative multiplicant is high
(c) They cannot be make of bigger diameter
(d) All of the above

73. The open end of the pipe is closed by this –
(a) Nipple   *(b)* Socket
(c) Cross   *(d)* Plug

74. Which is used for low lift –
(a) Centrifugal pump
(b) Reciprocating pump
(c) Turbine pump
(d) None of the above

75. In this method, spellter is melted into a hold and added so much flux that about 25 mm flux layer swims then joint on dipping in it is completed –
(a) Electric Brazing   *(b)* Dip Brazing
(c) Furnace Brazing   *(d)* Torch Brazing

76. This punch is used to make holes in the thin sheets and leather etc. A plate of wood is put below the sheet or leather to use it –
(a) Prick punch   *(b)* Solid punch
(c) Centre punch   *(d)* Hollow punch

77. Magnetite is found in –
(a) Ranchi   *(b)* Gaya
(c) Kolkata   *(d)* Chennai

78. Due to this property a metal can be lengthened on spreaded after breaking it –
(a) Toughness   *(b)* Malleability
(c) Ductility   *(d)* Hardness

79. Its cutting edge is of 'V' shape. It is used to make corners of 'V' Groove, square groove etc.
(a) Size cut chisel
(b) Round nose chisel
(c) Diamand point chisel
(d) Flat chisel

80. Smooth file contains –
(a) 10 – 12 teeths/sq cm
(b) 14 – 16 teeths/sq cm
(c) 20 – 24 teeths/sq cm
(d) 28 – 35 teeths/sq cm

81. There are prominent teeths on its face which is of triangular shape and used to cut the wood, lead and some soft metals –
(a) Single cut file   *(b)* Double cut file
(c) Rasp cut file   *(d)* Spiral cut file

82. In how many categories a sanitary station is divided
(a) Two   *(b)* Three
(c) Five   *(d)* Seven

83. Due to this property a metal spreads here and there after a blow –
(a) Brittleness   *(b)* Toughness
(c) Malleability   *(d)* Hardness

84. Hammer which is made up of wood is called –
(a) Sledge hammer   *(b)* Soft Hammer
(c) Mallet   *(d)* Hand hammer

85. Before welding or brazing, pre-heat makes the job –
(a) Crackless   *(b)* Hard
(c) Porous   *(d)* Strong

86. The quantity of iron in pig iron is –
(a) 92%   *(b)* 92.5%
(c) 93%   *(d)* 93.5%

87. Such cuts are circular and are made up of complete spherical shape on the surface of file–
(a) Single cut fits   *(b)* double cut file
(c) Spiral cut files   *(d)* Rasp cut file

88. It is spiral fluted tap from the front and is used to cut chips easily –
(a) Gun tap   *(b)* Stay belt tap
(c) Bend sank tap   *(d)* None of the above

89. The process of cutting screws on the outer side of pipe by the die, is called –
(a) Marking   *(b)* Reaming
(c) Threading   *(d)* Punching

90. The colour of this tree is light yellow-brown. We get Tarpeen oil and Biroja from this tree and it is affected quickly by the white –
(a) Cheed   *(b)* Padtal
(c) Sagwaan   *(d)* Sheesham

91. Which of the following is called Graphite –
(a) Free-carbon   *(b)* Combined carbon
(c) Grey cast iron   *(d)* Pig iron

92. Ferrous metal is –
(a) Aluminium   *(b)* Copper
(c) Lead   *(d)* Steel

93. 6% tin is found in –
(a) Naval Brass   *(b)* Cartidge Brass
(c) Red Brass   *(d)* Yellow Brass

94. It is used to join the two pipes at different angles and there are internal scrawing at its ends –
(a) Nipple   *(b)* Plug
(c) Band   *(d)* Elbow

95. Such types of bacterias need oxygen to live and these are used to purify the sewage –
(a) Anaerobic bacteria
(b) Aerobic bacteria
(c) Both of the above
(d) None of the above

96. Gas welding regulator is used
(a) Single stage   *(b)* Double stage
(c) Both of above   *(d)* None of the above

97. The selection of flux depends upon –
(a) types of original metal
(b) shape of joint
(c) on the usable solder
(d) All of the above

98. Its point is at 90° angle and it is used to drill (to make the mark darken) so that point can be

easily set –
(a) Centre punch   (b) Dot punch
(c) Hollow punch   (d) Solid punch

99. This chisel is used to cut the sheets into chisel spherical shape and making round holes –
(a) Diamond point chisel
(b) Cow-mouth chisel
(c) Size cut chisel
(d) Round-nose chisel

100. Which metal is joined with the method of –
(a) Two same metals
(b) Two different metals
(c) Two same or different metals
(d) None of the above

101. It is also known as safe edge-file
(a) Hand file   (b) Square file
(c) Triangular file   (d) Flat file

102. The number of teeths in a rough file –
(a) 8 – 10 per sq cm
(b) 10 – 12 per sq cm
(c) 14 – 16 per sq cm
(d) 20 – 24 per sq cm

103. Make the right match –

A. Stud	I. ⊥		
B. Double V butt	II. X̂		
C. Single J butt	III. ◣		
D. Fillet	IV. Û		

	A	B	C	D
(a)	I	II	III	IV
(b)	I	II	IV	III
(c)	II	I	IV	III
(d)	II	IV	I	III

104. Its point is grind at 60° angle, it is used only to make the line darken/strengthen.
(a) Centre punch   (b) Dot punch
(c) Prick punch   (d) Solid punch

105. The hammer of big size is called
(a) Sledge hammer   (b) Mallet
(c) Soft hammer   (d) Hand hammer

106. It is also known as 'Gunia'.
(a) Scriber   (b) Try-square
(c) Steel tap   (d) Plumb bob

107. Use of neutral flame for welding is absolutely right for
(a) Manganese   (b) Chromium
(c) Iron   (d) Gold

108. Weldability depends upon –
(a) Method of welding
(b) On metal
(c) Both of (a) and (b)
(d) None of the above

109. This file contains 10 to 12 teeths per square centimeter –
(a) Rough file   (b) Bastard file
(c) Second cut file   (d) Smooth file

110. It is used in those places where chances of gas or liquid leakages are more –
(a) Machine Tap   (b) Gun Tap
(c) Gas Tap   (d) Stag-Belt Tap

111. It is a combined form of Rip-saw and cross-cut saw –
(a) Pannel saw   (b) Dove tail saw
(c) Compass saw   (d) Curve cutting saw

112. When two parts are fitted at the centre or one part is constant and other is sliding, this relation is called –
(a) Tapping   (b) Reaming
(c) Threading   (d) Fitting

113. These are fitted in between two pipes at a small distance so that they can be opened if pipeline has some problems. Two pipes can be joined by it –
(a) Union   (b) Cap
(c) Plug   (d) Socket

114. The sanitary fitting which is used to stop the entering of poisonous smells of sewers or drains into the houses is called –
(a) Trap   (b) Water seal
(c) Bent pipe   (d) Cone cap cowl

115. This pipe is also known as delivery pipe because gas is supplied to gas holder through this –
(a) Inspection hole   (b) Main valve
(c) Inlet pipe   (d) Stand pipe

116. Which of the following does not use in welding.
(a) Coated electrode (b) Filler rod
(c) Flux   (d) Oxygen Gas

117. The quantity of silicon in grey-pig is –
(a) 0.20%   (b) 2.50%
(c) 2.80%   (d) 3.00%

118. Due to this property a metal can tolerate many

blows without breaking –
(a) Brittleness   (b) Toughness
(c) Malleability   (d) Hardness

119. It is a sort of hexagonal or square nut but fluetes are cut into it and is used to clean the old screwings –
(a) Die nut   (b) Pipe Die
(c) Die plate   (d) Adjustable die

120. The process of shorten the width (height) of a metal through chisel is called –
(a) Punching   (b) Drilling
(c) Chipping   (d) Riveting

121. In medium pitch blade number of teeths per cm is
(a) 8   (b) 10
(c) 14   (d) 16

ANSWERS

1	2	3	4	5	6	7	8	9	10
(d)	(a)	(c)	(a)	(c)	(d)	(b)	(d)	(d)	(a)
11	**12**	**13**	**14**	**15**	**16**	**17**	**18**	**19**	**20**
(c)	(a)	(c)	(d)	(d)	(d)	(d)	(a)	(c)	(c)
21	**22**	**23**	**24**	**25**	**26**	**27**	**28**	**29**	**30**
(c)	(a)	(d)	(b)	(d)	(a)	(a)	(c)	(b)	(c)
31	**32**	**33**	**34**	**35**	**36**	**37**	**38**	**39**	**40**
(d)	(c)	(a)	(b)	(b)	(c)	(a)	(d)	(b)	(a)
41	**42**	**43**	**44**	**45**	**46**	**47**	**48**	**49**	**50**
(d)	(d)	(b)	(d)	(b)	(a)	(d)	(a)	(c)	(a)
51	**52**	**53**	**54**	**55**	**56**	**57**	**58**	**59**	**60**
(b)	(d)	(c)	(c)	(b)	(d)	(a)	(b)	(d)	(d)
61	**62**	**63**	**64**	**65**	**66**	**67**	**68**	**69**	**70**
(b)	(d)	(a)	(a)	(a)	(c)	(b)	(c)	(d)	(c)
71	**72**	**73**	**74**	**75**	**76**	**77**	**78**	**79**	**80**
(c)	(d)	(d)	(a)	(b)	(d)	(b)	(b)	(c)	(c)
81	**82**	**83**	**84**	**85**	**86**	**87**	**88**	**89**	**90**
(c)	(b)	(a)	(c)	(a)	(c)	(c)	(a)	(c)	(a)
91	**92**	**93**	**94**	**95**	**96**	**97**	**98**	**99**	**100**
(a)	(d)	(a)	(c)	(b)	(c)	(d)	(a)	(b)	(c)
101	**102**	**103**	**104**	**105**	**106**	**107**	**108**	**109**	**110**
(a)	(a)	(b)	(b)	(a)	(b)	(b)	(c)	(b)	(c)
111	**112**	**113**	**114**	**115**	**116**	**117**	**118**	**119**	**120**
(a)	(d)	(a)	(a)	(c)	(a)	(b)	(b)	(a)	(c)
121									
(b)									

7

FORGER, HEAT TREATMENT, BLACK SMITHY

Forging : The act of heating to steel and wrought iron upto red-hot and then beating them by a hammer to combine or moulding into some specific shape and size is known as forging.

When this act is done by hand through a hand hammer then it is known as Hand Forging or Black Smithy.

Significance of Forging :

1. Parts prepared by this method takes less time to machine.
2. The wastage of metal is very less by this method.
3. Internal structure of the metal becomes pure by this method.
4. It takes comparatively less time which further decrease the cost of parts.

Limitations of Forging :

1. If any parts remain longer in the furnace, it (metal) could burn.
2. The metals which becomes brittle on heating cannot be forged.

Types of Forging :

1. Hand Forging
2. Machine Forging
3. Drop Forging

Instruments Used in Black Smithy

1. Forge or Furnace
2. Anvil
3. Different types of tongs
4. Swage Block and Stand
5. Cold Set Chisel
6. Gauge
7. Hardie
8. Fullers Top & bottom
9. Swage Rounding Top & bottom
10. Flatter
11. Hot Set Chisel
12. Square Punch
13. Round Punch
14. Drifts
15. Water Pot
16. Hammer and Sledge hammer
17. Set hammer
18. Cone
19. Bick Iron
20. Leg Vice

Difference Between Chisel and Drift

Chisel : It is used to cut Hot and Cold metals. It is made up of high carbon steel. Cold set is used to cut the cold-metals while Hard Set is used to cut the hot metals.

Drift : It is like a taper pin which is taper on both sides from the center. It is also made up of high carbon steel. It is used to increase the diameters of holes or tapering the holes. It is used after the punching.

Difference Between Drilling and Punching

Punching	Drilling
1. This method is used in both hot and cold metals.	1. This method is used only in cold metals.

2. The holes made by punching are of different shapes.	**2.** Only cylindrical holes are made by this method.
3. The holes made by this method are accurate and pure.	**3.** The holes made by this method are much accurate than punching.
4. No Machine is used in punching	**4.** Drilling machine is used here.

Temperature for Forging :

Metals which are to be Temperature
Forged *(in degree centigrade)*
Wrought Iron 860°C – 1340°C
Mild Steel 815°C – 1290°C
Medium Carbon Steel 760°C – 1250°C
High Carbon Steel 760°C – 1140°C
Copper, Brass & Bronze 540°C – 900°C
Magnesium &
Aluminium Alloy 320°C – 480°C

Heat Treatment :

Heat treatment is a method by which internal structure of a metal can be converted after doing it hot and cold and then its mechanical properties can be altered accordingly.

It is used for the following reasons:

1. To increase the hardness of metal.
2. To soft the hard metal so that machining can be done on it (metal).
3. To protect metal from rusting.
4. To strengthen its tensile strength and mechanical properties after doing some internal changes in it.
5. To overcome the defects in its internal structure which appears due to working in hot and cold conditions.
6. To harden the cutting tools so that they can cut to other metals.

Following Important Structure are Done Through Heat-Treatment

1. **Ferrite :** It is a structure of pure iron, in which quantity of carbon is very low. It is very soft and ductile.

2. **Cementite :** Mixturing of carbon in iron is known as cementite. It is very hard and brittle.
3. **Pearlite :** It is a mixture of ferrite and cementite. It contains 88% ferrite and 12% cementite. It is very strong.
4. **Austenite :** To obtain this structure steel is heated to upper critical temperature. After that its internal structure changes completely. It is hard but not brittle.
5. **Martenisite :** It is also a mixture of carbon and iron. For this steel of Austenite structure is being cold immediately and converted into another structure which is known as Martenisite structure. It is also very hard and brittle.
6. **Troostite :** If steel of Martenisite structure is again heated upto 400°C then we obtained Troostite structure. It is very very hard. Machining is very difficult on this steel structure. It can easily tolerate the vibrations.
7. **Sorbite :** It is a mixture of Ferrite and Cementite. This structure is obtained by heating the steel upto 700°C and then we to tempering on it and when it cool down then we get the sorbite structure. It is strong and ductile.

Lower Critical Point : When steel is being heated, its temperature increases slowly and when temperature reaches upto 723°C then after this temperature, there starts a gradual change in its internal structure. Thus the point (of temperature) on which steels internal temperature changes, is known as lower critical point.

Upper Critical Point : When steel is being heated more than its lower critical point, as the temperature increases, the internal structure of steel changes gradually and when its internal structure changes completely, means when iron and carbon intermixed in the hard form then changes which were taking place stop. This temperature point where changes stop, is known as upper critical point.

Critical Range : The difference between lower critical temperature and upper critical temperature is known as critical range. The internal structure of steel changes at this particular range.

Name of Heat Treatment Techniques :

1. Normalising
2. Annealing
3. Hardening
4. Tempering
5. Case Hardening
6. Cyaniting
7. Nitriding
8. Flame Hardening
9. Induction Hardening

Matter : All those things are called matter which can be felt by out sensories. For example, book, Iron, Table, Chair, Wood etc. Anything which occupies space and has mass and creates obstacle is known as matter.

On the basis of physical states, all the matter can be classified into three groups : Solids, Liquids & Gases.

(i) **Solids :** They have a definite shape and a definite volume *e.g.* Carbon, Wood, Iron etc.

(ii) **Liquids :** They have definite volume but not the definite shape. *e.g.* Milk, Mercury, Oil etc.

(iii) **Gases :** Neither have definite volume nor the definite shape. *e.g.* Hydrogen, Oxygen etc.

Classification of Matter :

1. Elements : An element is a substance which cannot be split up into two or more simpler substances by the usual physical or chemical methods, which has different virtues than the original substances. *e.g.* Carbon, Sulphur and Oxygen etc.

2. Compounds : A Compound is a substance made up of two or more elements chemically combined in a fixed proportion by weight *e.g.* salt (sodium chloride), washing soda, water (H_2O) etc.

3. Mixtures : A mixture is a substance which consists of two or more elements or compounds not chemically combined together. *e.g.* Air, Water Vapour, Juice etc.

Solder : It is an alloy which is used for joining two metal surfaces. It is an alloy of tin and lead. The melting point of tin is 232°C while the melting point of lead is 327°C. When we mix them at the ratio of 63 to 37, then melting point becomes 183°C.

Following are generally used solder :

1. Electric solder
2. Best Tinman solder
3. Plumber solder
4. Normal solder

Heat : It is a special type of energy which can works.

Source of heat : Sun, Fuel and Electricity.

Temperature : It tells about the intensity of heat in a thing.

Measuring Units of Heat :

Calorie : It is that quantity of heat, which increase the temperature of 1 gram water upto 1°C. Specific heat of water is 1.

$$1 \text{ calories} = 1 \text{ gm} \times 1°C$$
$$= 4.2 \text{ Joule}$$

Joule is smaller unit of heat.

The bigger unit of heat is kilo calorie

1 Kilo calories = 1000 Calories.

Unit of Temperature : Temperature is measured by thermometers. There are three measurements of temperature.

1. Centrigrade or Celsius
2. Fahrenheit
3. Reaumer

The relationship among above three thermometers is $\dfrac{C}{5} = \dfrac{F-32}{9} = \dfrac{R}{4}$

Quantity of Heat : Anything whose mass is m and specific heat is S, if it's temperature is increased upto $t°C$, the quantity of heat in that thing is

$$Q = m \times s \times t \text{ Calorie}$$

OBJECTIVE TYPE QUESTIONS

1. In this method, a portion of metal is heated until it becomes red and after that beated by power hammer and given a desired shape.
   - (a) Hand Forging
   - (b) Machine Forging
   - (c) Drop Forging
   - (d) None of the above

2. Instrument which does not use in Black Smithy
   - (a) Hardie
   - (b) Swage
   - (c) Chisel
   - (d) Swoop

3. Match the following :
   A. Swoop   I. To put coal into the furnace
   B. Sprinker   II. To drop the ash into ground
   C. Poker   III. Shower to cease fire
   D. Showel   IV. To set the coal correctly

	A	B	C	D
(a)	I	II	III	IV
(b)	I	II	IV	III
(c)	IV	III	II	I
(d)	IV	III	I	II

4. Square, pointed and launching part of anvil is known as :
   (a) Hardie hole   (b) Punch hole
   (c) Tail   (d) Beak

5. It is rectangular, hard head stack, which is inserted on Anvil's hardie's hole and is used as a base to cut the hot metal's part.
   (a) Spring   (b) Drift
   (c) Hardie   (d) Swage

6. On heating a metal part and putting it on the anvil and then increasing its length by beating the hammer is called
   (a) Drifting   (b) Punching
   (c) Setting Down   (d) Drawing Out

7. Forging temperature for carbon steel is
   (a) 100°C to 400°C
   (b) 800°C to 1300°C
   (c) 900°C to 1150°C
   (d) 1150°C to 1700°C

8. In this method, the total length of a rod is increased by Forge Weld by joining two portions of the rod.
   (a) Ring Forge Welding
   (b) Butt Forge Welding
   (c) Slit Forge Welding
   (d) Lap Forge Welding

9. The reason of doing Annealing is :
   (a) To make a metal part soften as it can be used in machining.
   (b) To mend the electric and magnetic properties of a metal part.
   (c) To bring out the bubbles from the piece of metal.
   (d) All of the above.

10. The quantity of carbon in medium carbon steel is
    (a) 0.12% to 0.25% (b) 0.25% to 0.5%
    (c) 0.5% to 0.9%   (d) 0.9% to 1.5%

11. The Annealing temperature for the tool steel is
    (a) 875°C to 975°C (b) 815°C to 840°C

(c) 760°C to 780°C (d) 780°C to 810°C

12. In this method, piece of metals are heated just below the lower critical point (approx. 700°C) and then cool down gradually in the ash of the furnace.
    (a) Process Annealing
    (b) Complete Annealing
    (c) Spherodice Annealing
    (d) None of the above

13. The process through which the hardness and brittleness of a piece of metal is decreased known as:
    (a) Annealing   (b) Tempering
    (c) Normalising   (d) Hardening

14. The colour of the Axe's convex surface is—
    (a) Brown   (b) Blue
    (c) Dark Brown   (d) Violet

15. The tempering temperature of normal cutter is
    (a) 220°C to 230°C (b) 230°C to 235°C
    (c) 235°C to 240°C (d) 240°C to 250°C

16. The carborising time for insertion of carbon upto 0.8 mm to 1.2 mm depth is
    (a) 4 to 5 hours   (b) 6 to 7 hours
    (c) 7 to 10 hours   (d) 8 to 12 hours

17. The quantity of copper in Brass is
    (a) 88%   (b) 75% to 95%
    (c) 63% to 67%   (d) 17% to 37%

18. The colour of *Kharad's* tool used to cut the copper is
    (a) Light Red   (b) Dark Red
    (c) Khaki   (d) Indigo (sky blue)

19. It is a bearing tool which is used to widen the already made hole in a hot piece of metal.
    (a) Swage   (b) Flatter
    (c) Spring   (d) Drift

20. At the following temperature, the colour of soft iron is yellow.
    (a) 1000°C   (b) 1100°C
    (c) 1200°C   (d) 1300°C

21. To increase the diameter of the hole present in a piece of hot metal is known as
    (a) Bending   (b) Drifting
    (c) Punching   (d) Marking

22. The Annealing temperature for the soft steel is
    (a) 875°C to 975°C (b) 840°C to 940°C
    (c) 760°C to 780°C (d) both (a) & (b)

23. In this method, hardness of tool steel is lesser and its ductility and .... is bit increased.
    (a) Process Annealing
    (b) Complete Annealing

(c) Spherodice Annealing
(d) None of the above

24. In this method, hard steel plate is heated with job in the furnace. After that job and plate is drawn out from the furnace and desired portion of job is touched with plate and heated again.
(a) Single heat tempering
(b) Double heat tempering
(c) Lead bath tempering
(d) Sand bath tempering

25. The tempering temperature of stone cutter tool and scissors is
(a) 240°C to 250°C   *(b)* 250°C to 260°C
(c) 260°C to 270°C   *(d)* 270°C to 280°C

26. The main method of case hardening processing is
(a) Cyaniding   *(b)* Annealing
(c) Normalising   *(d)* Tempering

27. This stack is used to make spherical shapes :
(a) Half moon stack *(b)* Convex stack
(c) Hatchet stack   *(d)* Beak horn stack

28. In this method, marks of hammer and mellit are removed.
(a) Drawing   *(b)* Spinning
(c) Flanishing   *(d)* Piercing

29. Two edges are joined at the angle of 90° in this joining process.
(a) Cap joint   *(b)* Cup joint
(c) Flanged joint *(d)* Lap joint

30. The number of screwing is done on $\frac{1}{2}$ inch to $\frac{3}{4}$ inch diameter's pipe.
(a) 19 screwing/inch
(b) 14 screwing/inch
(c) 11 screwing/inch
(d) 7 screwing/inch

31. It is created by a blower which sucks air from atmosphere and sents this air with pressure in the furnace
(a) Force draft   *(b)* Induced draft
(c) Natural draft   *(d)* None of the above

32. The calorific value of this forge fuel is 10,000 kcal per kg:
(a) Coal Gas   *(b)* Liquid Fuel
(c) Coke   *(d)* Coal

33. It is used to hold narrow rectangular section's jobs
(a) Flat clip   *(b)* Flat bar clip
(c) Side bit clip *(d)* Belt clip

34. Which one is ferrous metal:
(a) soft iron   *(b)* ductile iron
(c) tool steel   *(d)* all of the above

35. This steel is made up of mild-steel and to protect it from the rust it is covered with a layer of nickel.
(a) Black sheet   *(b)* Bright sheet
(c) Tin sheet   *(d)* G.I. sheet

36. The approximate gravity of forged aluminium is
(a) 2.56   *(b)* 2.57
(c) 6.71   *(d)* 7.217

37. The colour of king spril spring is
(a) Red   *(b)* Dark red
(c) Little red   *(d)* Sky blue

38. The quantity of lead in a fuse wire is:
(a) 48%   *(b)* 50%
(c) 55%   *(d)* 57%

39. The prominent colour of Black Smith's tool is
(a) Violet   *(b)* Dark Violet
(c) Brown   *(d)* Dark Brown

40. The process by which a piece of metal is converted to its original position is called
(a) Tempering   *(b)* Annealing
(c) Normalising   *(d)* Hardening

41. It is used to give a shape of ring to a piece of metal.
(a) Cone   *(b)* Drift
(c) Spring   *(d)* Tongs

42. The colour of mild steel at 1000°C is
(a) Red   *(b)* Light Cherry Red
(c) Dark Cherry Red   *(d)* Yellow

43. The tempering temperature for Haxa and Spring is
(a) 280°C to 300°C *(b)* 270°C to 280°C
(c) 260°C to 270°C *(d)* 250°C to 260°C

44. The hole in the face of Anvil to make holes in jobs is called
(a) Hardie Hole   *(b)* Rinch Hole
(c) Beek   *(d)* Base

45. To lesser the length of a piece of metal on heating it and beating by a hammer after putting on Anvil–
(a) Bending   *(b)* Drawing out
(c) Jumping   *(d)* Marking

46. The aim of heat treatment is
(a) To make soften or hard of a piece of metal.
(b) To make a piece of metal usable for machine.
(c) To make a piece of metal frictionless.
(d) All of the above

47. The process through which a piece of metal's internal tension is reduced, known as:
 (a) Tempering   (b) Annealing
 (c) Normalising   (d) Hardening

48. The Annealing temperature for medium carbon steel is:
 (a) 760°C to 780°C   (b) 815°C to 840°C
 (c) 840°C to 940°C   (d) 875°C to 975°C

49. In this method, on heating a job to its tempering temperature and then dipped into the melted lead. Which reduced the job's temperature and then cooled in the presence of air.
 (a) Single heat tempering
 (b) Double heat tempering
 (c) Lead Bath Tempering
 (d) Sand Bath Tempering

50. The tempering temperature of scrapper and surgery tools is—
 (a) 220°C to 230°C
 (b) 230°C to 240°C
 (c) 240°C to 250°C
 (d) 250°C to 260°C

51. It is an iron sheet on which a layer of zinc is applied—
 (a) Black sheet   (b) Bright sheet
 (c) Tin sheet   (d) G.I. sheet

52. This stack is used to give base to the squared edges—
 (a) Rectangular stack
 (b) Square stack
 (c) Convex stack
 (d) Hatchet stack

53. In this, the cusps of a sheet are removed by Mallit's strokes—
 (a) To make straight   (b) Flanishing
 (c) Spinning   (d) Drawing

54. This joint is used to join the pipes—
 (a) Flaged joint   (b) Cap joint
 (c) Cup joint   (d) Lay out

55. The Non-Ferrous metal is—
 (a) Carbon steel   (b) Bronze
 (c) Ductile Iron   (d) Alloy steel

56. The specific gravity of silver is—
 (a) 11.4   (b) 13.598
 (c) 2.56   (d) 6.71

57. The quantity of tin in gun metal is—
 (a) 2%   (b) 10%
 (c) 57%   (d) 88%

58. The prominent colour of milling cutter, chaser, rimer and drill is—
 (a) Brown   (b) Dark brown
 (c) Violet   (d) Earthy yellow

59. In this process, piece of metals are heated a little more than their upper critical point (about 850°C) and then they are cooled upto 600°C to 700°C in the water and after this temperature they are cooled intermittently and in last they are left to cool into the air—
 (a) Process Annealing
 (b) Complete Annealing
 (c) Spherodice Annealing
 (d) None of the above

60. The quantity of carbon in high carbon steel is—
 (a) Less than 0.12%
 (b) 0.25% to 0.5%
 (c) 0.5% to 0.9%
 (d) 0.9% to 1.5%

61. The prominent colour of normal cutter and drill is—
 (a) Earthy yellow   (b) Light yellow
 (c) Violet   (d) Blue

62. It is used to join the length of two different sizes of pipes.
 (a) Sockets   (b) Reducing sockets
 (c) Bend   (d) Albow

63. This stack is used to catch the bending, leveling and to catch other supports is—
 (a) Horse head stack (b) Funnet stack
 (c) Creazing stack   (d) Pipe stack

64. In this joint, the edges are first bent in the shape of hook and then using a separate sheet they are completed in two different joints—
 (a) Cam joint   (b) Cap joint
 (c) Lap joint   (d) Seem joint

65. The screwing done on the pipes of 3/4 inch diameter and more is—
 (a) 19 screwing/inch
 (b) 14 screwing/inch
 (c) 11 screwing/inch
 (d) 7 screwing/inch

66. The quantity of carbon is coke is—
 (a) 50 to 75%   (b) 60%
 (c) 80%   (d) 88%

67. This punch is used to make holes in sheets
 (a) Pin punch   (b) Solid punch
 (c) Center punch   (d) Dot punch

68. The width of a marking table is kept—

(a) 1 to $1\frac{1}{2}$ meter   (b) $1\frac{1}{2}$ to 2 meter

(c) 2 to $2\frac{1}{2}$ meter   (d) $2\frac{1}{2}$ to 3 meter

69. This file is of less width's rectangular cross-section—
(a) Flat file   (b) Hand file
(c) Piller file   (d) Triangular file

70. Liquid material is—
(a) Oxygen   (b) Gold
(c) Mercury   (d) Carbon

71. The first product made up of mineral iron—
(a) Cast Iron   (b) Pig Iron
(c) Carbon Steel   (d) Alloy Steel

72. In this method, on heating the job to its upper critical point, its cutting edge is dipped into the water or oil for 2 to 3 times and then cooled—
(a) Single heat tempering
(b) Double heat tempering
(c) Lead bath tempering
(d) Sand bath tempering

73. The quantity of copper in phospher bronze is—
(a) 0.5%   (b) 7.9%
(c) 56.6%   (d) 92%

74. The relative gravity of brass is—
(a) 7.409   (b) 7.852
(c) 7.217   (d) 7.3

75. This coke is used on wash basins—
(a) Plug cokes   (b) Bib cokes
(c) Pillar coke   (d) None of the above

76. These are the zinc layered alternative furrows and ridges sheets of iron which are used for roofing on houses
(a) Black sheet   (b) Tin sheet
(c) G.I. sheet   (d) G.I. corrugated sheet

77. The quantity of carbon in tool steel is
(a) less than 0.12% (b) 0.25% to 0.5%
(c) 0.5% to 0.9%   (d) 0.9% to 1.5%

78. It is a finishing tool which is used to level the job's surface and to make "stop" in jobs.
(a) Flatter   (b) Hardie
(c) Chisel   (d) Cone

79. The stand used to establish the Anvil is called—
(a) Base   (b) Face
(c) Beek   (d) Tail

80. The finishing of edges and corners of job, which is made up of a piece of metal, is called—
(a) Setting down   (b) Drawing out
(c) Drifting   (d) Punching

81. The forging temperature of mild iron is—
(a) 100°C to 400°C
(b) 800°C to 1300°C
(c) 900°C to 1150°C
(d) 1150°C to 1700°C

82. In this method, the scarfs are made at the ends of the spherical and rectangular rods and Forge Welding is done after embedding the scarfs of two rods in each other.
(a) Lap Forge Welding
(b) Butt Forge Welding
(c) Ring Forge Welding
(d) Angle Forge Welding

83. The method of Annealing process is—
(a) Process Annealing
(b) Complete Annealing
(c) Spherodice Annealing
(d) All of the above

84. The Annealing temperature of high carbon steel is—
(a) 875°C to 975°C (b) 815°C to 840°C
(c) 780°C to 810°C (d) 760°C to 780°C

85. The aim of Hardening is—
(a) To make an increment in the life, working capacity and capability of a piece of metal.
(b) To make a piece of metal anti-frictional.
(c) To make steel harden so that it can be used to out other metals.
(d) All of the above.

86. It is fitted among the pipelines so that it can control the quantity of material passing through pipelines.
(a) Stop valves   (b) Plug
(c) Nipple   (d) Flange

87. This stack is used to provide base to the narrow and deep edges.
(a) Square Stack   (b) Half Moonstack
(c) Hatchet Stack   (d) Pipe Stack

88. The length of marking table is kept—

(a) 1 to $1\frac{1}{2}$ meter   (b) $1\frac{1}{2}$ to 2 meter

(c) 2 to $2\frac{1}{2}$ meter   (d) $2\frac{1}{2}$ to 3 meter

89. This chisel is used to clean the right angles surfaces—
    (a) Flat chisel
    (b) Cow mouth chisel
    (c) Round nose chisel
    (d) Side cutting chisel

90. A particular shine of metals is called—
    (a) Tension   *(b)* Ductility
    (c) Luster   *(d)* Conductivity

91. The quantity of iron in Grey Pig iron is—
    (a) 92%   *(b)* 92.5%
    (c) 93%   *(d)* 70%

92. This zone forms above the combustion zone and its environment is reducing—
    (a) Reduction zone   *(b)* Melting zone
    (c) Pre-heating zone   *(d)* Stack zone

93. This steel is used in spring, big die and in drop forgings
    (a) Dead Mild steel
    (b) Mild steel
    (c) Medium carbon steel
    (d) High carbon steel

94. The quantity of chromium in venedium steel is—
    (a) 1.5%   *(b)* 5%
    (c) 12.5%   *(d)* 4.5%

95. It is obtained after heating the martensite upto 400°C
    (a) Austenite   *(b)* Pearlite
    (c) Troostite   *(d)* Sorbite

96. The melting point of this solder is 192° C
    (a) Electric solder
    (b) Normal solder
    (c) Plumber solder
    (d) Best Tinman's solder

97. This process is done at 350°C—
    (a) Soldering   *(b)* Brazing
    (c) Welding   *(d)* All of the above

98. These are used to join the thin sheets—
    (a) Pen head
    (b) Counter sunk head
    (c) Flat head
    (d) Tapper Neck Pen head

99. The diameter of tap drill is
    (a) $\dfrac{\text{diameter of tap}}{2 \times \text{diameter of screwing}}$
    (b) diameter of tap $+2 \times$ diameter of screwing
    (c) diameter of tap $-2 \times$ diameter of screwing
    (d) diameter of tap $\pm 2 \times$ diameter of screwing

100. The temperature at which any liquid becomes solid
    (a) Melting point   *(b)* Boiling point
    (c) Freezing point   *(d)* Vaporing point

ANSWERS

1	2	3	4	5	6	7	8	9	10
(b)	*(d)*	*(c)*	*(c)*	*(c)*	*(d)*	*(c)*	*(c)*	*(d)*	*(b)*
11	**12**	**13**	**14**	**15**	**16**	**17**	**18**	**19**	**20**
(c)	*(a)*	*(b)*	*(c)*	*(b)*	*(c)*	*(c)*	*(c)*	*(d)*	*(b)*
21	**22**	**23**	**24**	**25**	**26**	**27**	**28**	**29**	**30**
(b)	*(d)*	*(c)*	*(b)*	*(c)*	*(a)*	*(b)*	*(c)*	*(b)*	*(b)*
31	**32**	**33**	**34**	**35**	**36**	**37**	**38**	**39**	**40**
(a)	*(b)*	*(b)*	*(d)*	*(c)*	*(a)*	*(c)*	*(a)*	*(b)*	*(c)*
41	**42**	**43**	**44**	**45**	**46**	**47**	**48**	**49**	**50**
(a)	*(c)*	*(a)*	*(b)*	*(c)*	*(d)*	*(b)*	*(b)*	*(c)*	*(a)*
51	**52**	**53**	**54**	**55**	**56**	**57**	**58**	**59**	**60**
(d)	*(a)*	*(a)*	*(a)*	*(b)*	*(a)*	*(b)*	*(a)*	*(b)*	*(c)*
61	**62**	**63**	**64**	**65**	**66**	**67**	**68**	**69**	**70**
(b)	*(b)*	*(a)*	*(b)*	*(c)*	*(c)*	*(b)*	*(a)*	*(c)*	*(c)*
71	**72**	**73**	**74**	**75**	**76**	**77**	**78**	**79**	**80**
(b)	*(a)*	*(d)*	*(d)*	*(c)*	*(d)*	*(d)*	*(a)*	*(a)*	*(a)*
81	**82**	**83**	**84**	**85**	**86**	**87**	**88**	**89**	**90**
(b)	*(a)*	*(d)*	*(c)*	*(d)*	*(a)*	*(a)*	*(c)*	*(d)*	*(c)*
91	**92**	**93**	**94**	**95**	**96**	**97**	**98**	**99**	**100**
(b)	*(a)*	*(c)*	*(d)*	*(c)*	*(c)*	*(a)*	*(c)*	*(c)*	*(c)*

8

MISCELLANEOUS

AMPLIFIERS

One of the most important functions of electronic circuitry is amplification. A device by means of which amplification is affected is known as amplifier or an amplifier may be defined as a device that increases the voltage, current or power of an input signal with the aid of vacuum tubes or transistors by furnishing the additional power from a separate power source.

In the description of a vacuum tube amplifier, it is assumed that the a.c. component of the plate current is proportional to the input signal voltage. This shows that the amplified output voltage is proportional to the input signal. If the signal amplitude is doubled or tripled, the amplitude of output also gets doubled or tripled respectively. Thus, we can say that the vacuum tube amplifier is a linear device. This is only possible provided the characteristic curve of the tube is linear.

Classification of Amplifiers

Amplifiers are classified in ways descriptive of their character and properties. They are commonly classified in five ways:

(1) According to use (2) According to circuits (3) In terms of their frequency range of operation (4) According to portion of the cycle during which plate current flows (5) According to the range of frequencies amplified compared with central frequency.

(1) *According to use to which they are subjected*
    (a) Voltage amplifier   *(b)* Power amplifier

(2) *According to circuit*
    (a) Single stage amplifiers,
    (b) Cascade amplifiers.

(3) *In terms of frequency range of operation*
    (a) Audio frequency amplifiers,
    (b) Video frequency amplifiers,
    (c) Intermediate frequency amplifiers,
    (d) Radio frequency amplifiers.

(4) *According to the operation*

Another means of classifying amplifiers are by the duration of the conduction period in relation to one cycle of the input signal. In this respect, circuits are divided into four categories.

    (a) Class A   *(b)* Class AB
    (c) Class B   *(d)* Class C

Types of amplification (i) Voltage amplification *(ii)* Current amplification *(iii)* Power amplification *(iv)* Power sensitivity.

OSCILLATORS

An oscillator uses a transistor or vacuum tube in a circuit to generate an a.c. output. The oscillator circuit is basically an amplifier.

Oscillator function is similar to a vacuum tube amplifier. In either case d.c. power is supplied from the plate supply source and this results in alternating wave signal from across the output terminals. In amplifiers, however, the frequency, waveform and magnitude of the generated alternating power is governed by the controlling a.c. voltage from an external source applied to the control rid of the amplifier tube. In oscillators, on the other hand, frequency, waveform and magnitude of the a.c. voltage generated depends only on the tube and associated circuit, and no external controlling voltage is required.

The principle of oscillations is that the electrons acquire kinetic energy from the plate supply source and the tube with its associated circuit converts their kinetic energies into the alternating field energy at the output terminals. In this way, the tube in oscillator converts the d.c. power into a.c. power. Here we shall discuss a simplified theory of oscillations by considering a circuit of pure inductance and capacitance.

POWER SUPPLIES

A power supply converts the a.c. input of the 50 Hz power line to d.c. output voltage. Actually, power supply needed for the amplifiers in electronic equipment and several other equipments.

The power supply system includes the following sections:

1. Rectifier section 2. Filter section 3. Regulation system 4. Bleeder resistor.

We shall now describe the different sections. The rectifier section consists of two vacuum diodes (if full wave rectifier) or only one diode (if half wave rectifier) along with a transformer. The performance of half wave and full wave rectifiers has been discussed in the previous articles.

(TELEVISION)

TELEVISION

It is a process of mass communication which enables us to see video images at a distance.

TELEVISION TRANSMITTER

Figure shows the simplified block diagram of a television transmitter. The video signals obtained from camera tube are applied to a number of video amplifier stages. Synchronising generator produces sets of pulse to operate the system at appropriate timing. The horizontal synchronising pulses are applied to horizontal direction saw-tooth generator.

GENERAL PRINCIPLE OF IMAGE TRANSMISSION

The instrument, which responds to the light intensities reaching it from the illuminated object and converts the fluctuations in brightness of light (dark portions of the object surface reflect small light while brighter portions reflect a greater amount of light) it receives into corresponding electrical variations, can serve the purpose of image transmissions. Such a device is called 'pick-up instruments'. These electrical variations called video signal after amplitude modulation are transmitted by the antenna in

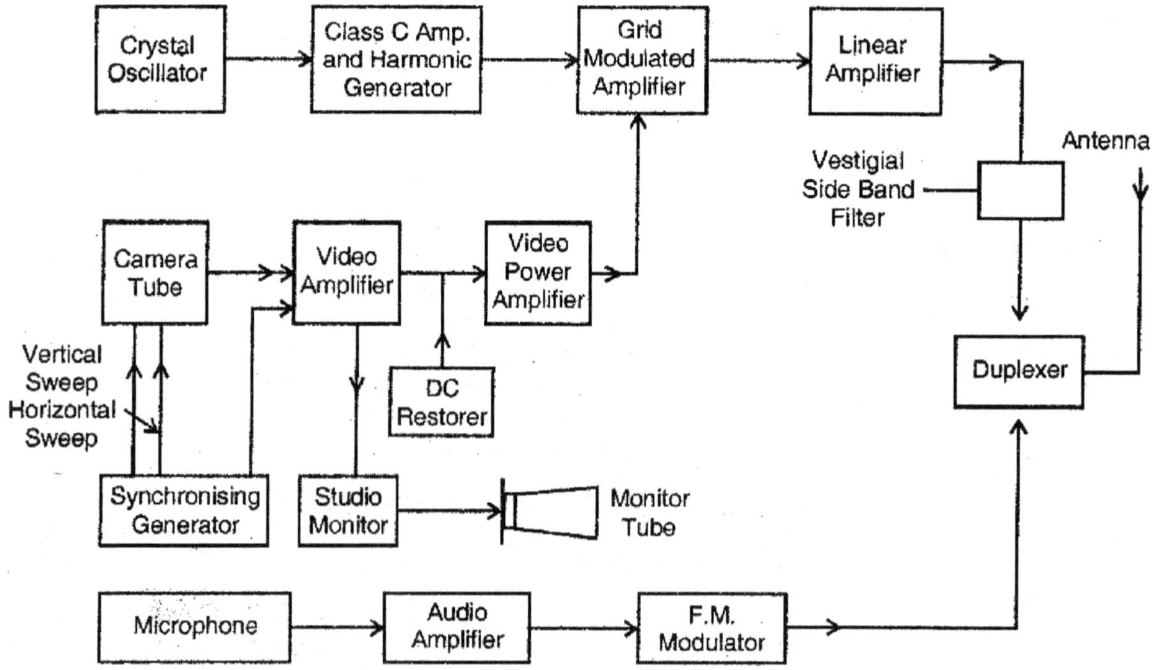

conventional fashion. At the receiver, video signal after demodulation is applied to a suitable device for reproducing the corresponding light intensity variations so as to depict the basic structure of the transmitted picture. A photo-sensitive device tan fulfil such a function in image transmission system as microphone serve in sound-transmission system.

The conversion of an optical image into a set of corresponding voltage impulses is performed in steps. The whole scene, at the transmitter is broken into many small pictures of varying brightness and then these pictures are viewed instantaneously in a definite sequence by the pick up system—the process being called as scanning, to produce corresponding electrical signal for transmission after modulation. In television 25 complete images are scanned and transmitted per second. Each image undergoes 625 lines scanning sequence to provide a desired degree of image detail. The whole process of image transmission can be stated in brief as follows:

(i) Optical image of the object of scene is focussed, by means of an optical lens system on a photo-sensitive plate contained in a camera tube.

(ii) The image is scanned by a cathode ray beam which is deflected either magnetically or electrostatically so that it traverses the photosensitive plate in an ordered sequence.

(iii) Due to scanning, electrical variations corresponding to the brightness of the scanned element are produced. This video signal after modulation is transmitted.

Television transmitter sends out two separate r.f. carriers over a single antenna. One carrier is frequency-modulated by sound (audio signal), while the other is amplitude-modulated by the picture information on the video signal.

A set of pulse-called synchronising pulses, is also transmitted with the video signal to keep the scanning sequence at the receiver in step with that at the transmitter.

RECEPTION OF SIGNALS

At the television receiver both audio and video signals are picked up by the receiver antenna and then subjected to heterodyne action by the conventional super-heterodyne receiving circuits. After suitable amplification by the r.f. amplifier, both signals are applied to video detector. This detector separates audio I.F. signal from video I.F. signal, and then demodulates video signal. Audio I.F. signal after separation is sent to frequency demodulation circuit.

Video signal is applied to a cathode ray picture tube for the image reproduction. The synchronising pulses are applied to beam deflecting circuits of the tube to keep picture scanning at the screen in step with that at the transmitter camera tube.

The following points are important in television system:

(1) Pick up instrument (2) Image scanning sequence (3) Scanning synchronisation (4) Television transmitter (5) Television receiver (6) Vestigial side band transmission.

COLOUR TELEVISION

If the reproduction in colour is desired, some means of transmission information regarding the colour content of the original scene must be found. A number of different colours can be formed by the combination of three coloured light. Experience has indicated that colours red, blue and green when combined with each other in various proportions, will produce a wider range of colours than any other combination of colours.

RADIO COMMUNICATION

RADIO COMMUNICATION

Radio communication can be defined as the interchange of symbols, signals, intelligence between two or more points, employing electromagnetic waves as the medium of transmission.

The Spectrum of Electromagnetic Waves

The electromagnetic waves cover a wide range of frequencies or wavelengths. They are classified as follows:

(1) *Radio Frequency Wave.* They have frequency range from a few c/s upto 10^9 c/s and are generated by electronic devices, mainly oscillating circuits.

(2) *Microwaves.* The frequency range is from 10^9 c/s to 3×10^{11} c/s and are generated by elecronic

devices as klystron and magnetron.

(3) *Infra red Spectrum.* The frequency range is from 3×10^{11} c/s upto 4×10^{14} c/s and are produced by molecules and hot bodies. These waves find various applications in industry, astronomy, medicine etc.

(4) *Light and Visible Spectrum.* The frequency is from 4×10^{14} c/s upto 8×10^{14} c/s and are produced by atoms and molecules as a result of internal adjustment in the motion of their components, principally that of the electrons.

(5) *Ultraviolet Rays.* The frequency range is from 8×10^{14} c/s to about 3×10^{17} c/s and are produced by atoms and molecules in electric discharges.

(6) *X-rays.* The frequency range is from 3×10^{17} c/s upto 5×10^{19} c/s and are produced by the inner, or more tightly bound electrons in atoms.

(7) *Gamma Rays.* The frequency range is from 3×10^{18} c/s upto more than 3×10^{22} c/s and are of nuclear origin. They are produced by many radioactive substances.

High Frequencies

For radio communication, wide range of frequencies is required in order to impart appreciable amount of intelligence to the electrical system in the communication process.

Modulation Methods

There are standard methods used to transmit the intelligence at radio frequencies. Some characteristic of the wave is varied in accordance with the information to be transmitted.

One way of modulation is termed as *amplitude modulation.* In this process, the amplitude of the carrier is varied in accordance with the amplitude and frequency of the modulating signal. Frequency of carrier remains constant.

Another way of modulation is to alter the frequency of the carrier for the purpose of intelligence transmission, termed as *frequency modulation.*

Reception of Radio Signals

The first step in reception of radio signals is to abstract signal energy at micro level from the radio wave passing the receiving point. This however is for a frequency band around the target signal frequency. The second step is to select the wanted signal and discriminate the signal of other frequencies. The ability is called *selectivity* and is achieved by tuning of resonant circuit used in receiving system.

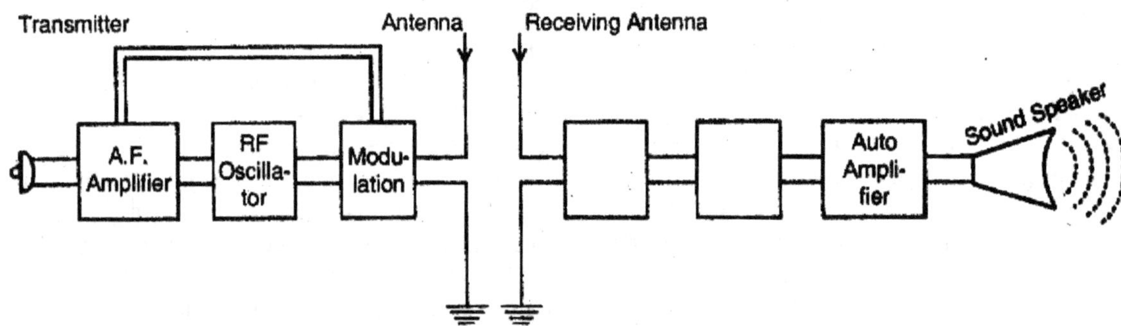

The third step is to recover the original modulating signal from the modulating wave. This process is called *detection.*

General Picture of Radio Transmission and Reception

Figure gives a clear picture of the steps involved at the transmitting and receiving stages.

The first step at the transmitter is to convert audible sound waves into electrical impulses by microphone. The impulses are then amplified by audio amplifier. For the transmission of these impulses, modulation is performed.

The carrier wave 550 k.c. is generated by r.f. oscillator. The output of modulator is applied to a transmitting antenna. The modulated carrier wave is thus sent out into space by the antenna.

At the receiver a voltage is induced in the antenna when the latter cuts these electromagnetic waves radiated by the transmitting antenna. The proper frequency is chosen by means of tuner.

COMPUTER CONCEPTS

COMPUTER

It is a device for automatically carrying out a *program of instructions.*

Task of Computer

The computer's task can be divided into three categories.

1. Arithmetic operations
2. Comparison operations
3. Storage and retrieval operations.

Computer Systems

On basis of processing speed, computer can be divided into four categories:

1. Super computers
2. Main frames
3. Mini computers
4. Micro computers.

Software

Programs and series of programs are referred to as **software**. Some programs direct the computer in its own internal operations. Other programs are written to solve users problems. These are referred to as application programs and latter one's are called system software.

Hardware

Hardware consists of the actual physical components of the computer. The three basic components of a computer system are: a central processing unit, a primary storage unit and peripheral devices.

Super Computers

These are the fastest, most powerful and most expensive computers which are available at present.

For most business application, the extremely high-speed processing capabilities of a super computer are not necessary. For such a purpose, any main frame is adequate.

TYPES OF COMPUTERS

There are two different types of computers: (1) Digital, (2) Analogue.

(1) *Digital Computer.* The **automatic digital computer** was invented in 1833 by Charles Babbage (1791-1871), a British mathematician. A **digital computer** is so called because it uses a series of digits to represent all types of information. The binary digits, 0 and 1, also called bits, are used almost exclusively.

(2) *Analogue Computers.* The analogue computer has high gain direct coupled amplifier, known as operational amplifier, abbreviated as op amp.

An actual op amp may have gain of about 10^6 to 10^8 on dc, which may reduce to 10^4 to 10^5 at 1 Hz, staying constant to about 10 Hz and thereafter decreasing linearly with frequency at 20 dB per decade. The input impedance may be 10 kΩ to 10^6 MΩ and output impedance may be few ohms only.

In contrast to digital computers, analogue computers use the values of continuously varying physical quantities to represent information. For example, the angles of displacement of minute and hour hands round a clock face constitute an analogue method of representing time, whereas digital clocks use decimal digits.

Although all computers have the above overall purpose, they differ in structure from one to another. They mostly contain the same basic components interconnected in similar ways.

GLOSSARY OF TERMS

Address. Number given to a memory location for identification.

Algorithm. A set of well defined rules or processes for the solution of a problem in a finite number of steps.

Analogue. A term relating to the representation of data by means of continuously variable physical quantities.

Batch. A set of transactions awaiting processing.

B.C.D. Binary Coded Decimal

Bit. Binary digit, 0 or 1 on the binary scale.

C.P.U. Central Processing Unit.

Disc. Direct Access Storage Device.

File. A series of records.

Hardware. The machinery of the computer, CPU and peripherals seen by naked eye.

I.A.S. Instant access store, alternative name for memory.

Jump. Capability of altering the sequence of processing depending on the result of a test.

Memory. Part of the CPU used for storing data and programs.

Micro Computer. Very small computer with single CPU and with limited facilities.

Mini Computer. Computers of intermediate size and processing speed between a micro computer and a main frame.

Program. Set of instructions to the computer.

System Analysis. A study of the way in which a procedure is carried out.

Terminal. The device for communicating with a computer.

V.D.U. Visual Display Unit.

Verifying. Processing of checking data when it has been punched entered into a computer/device.

TELEPHONY AND TELEPRINTER

COMMUNICATION

By communication we mean the exchange of information. Any thing to which some meaning or sense can be attributed may be defined as **information.** A written message, a word, a picture are all examples of **information.** The ancient Greek, word *tele* means *far.* Thus we can say, telecommunication means communication over long distance. In the modern age, telecommunication includes only the electrical signals of long distance communication.

These days, the vast field of telecommunication includes telegraphy, telephony, fascimile, television, telemetering, radar and satellite communication. All these systems employ some form of electric signalling to carry the information. The instrument where the information is processed for signalling is known as **transmitter,** and the instrument where the signal is converted into the original information is called **receiver.** The information is carried from transmitter to receiver through a **channel.** If the channel is in the form of a transmission line, the whole system is called the **line communication.** On the other hand if the channel is merely an open space, the whole system is called **Radio** or **Wireless communication.**

Telegraphy and Telephony are two branches of line communication. The telegraphy means writing information at far off distances. Telegraphy was invented by Morse in 1844.

Telegraph information consists of letters, figures and punctuation marks such as full stop, comma etc. Each of these is called a **character.** The complete set of these characters is called a **signal code** or simply a **code.** Thus a code is defined as a coherent system of rules serving some particular object or purpose.

Morse Code

When Morse code is used on an ordinary land lines or on radio circuits, the duration of a dash signal is three times the duration of a dot signal and the duration of space between signal elements is equal to the time period of a dot element. The dot and dash signals are thus represented by lines, the length representing the character; the latter being three times that representing the former.

Morse code for land line system can be used for a.c. signal current or d.c. signalling by using **current on** for marking and **current off** for spacing. For double current d.c. signalling positive potential can be used for spacing and negative for marking. The total duration of the signal combination is not the same for each character. The longest is the numeral 0 which has a total duration 19 times that of the shortest character E.

Cable Code

This is a special form of Morse code extensively employed in **submarine cable telegraphy.** There are two types of code used these days. (1) Normal Cable Code, (2) Double Current Cable Code.

Telephone Exchanges

The function of a telephone exchange is to interconnect four-wire line so as to permit a call to be established correctly. If both the dialing and the called subscribers are connected to the same exchange, it merely has to interconnect them. In case the wanted subscriber is connected to some other exchange, the calling subscriber must be routed progressively and correctly, so that his call may eventually reach the wanted number. There has been basically three generations of exchanges.

(i) Strowger type *(ii)* Cross bar exchange *(iii)* Processor controlled exchange.

Traffic Engineering

This is the branch of engineering which is related to measuring such traffic and its fluctuations and growth, as well as optimum traffic routing arrangements. This applies to telephones also.

Baudot Telegraph System

Baudot system uses 5-unit CCITT code No. 1. Thus each character is represented by a combination of five positive and negative impulses and this combination impulse is sent and received by means of brush arms moving over metallic arcs or quadrants each divided into five segments.

Baudot Distributor. Distributor is a most important part of Baudot system and each Baudot station is provided with its own distributors. It consists of three sets of segmented rings and three sets of continuous rings. In Guad-Baudot system there are four quadrants in each segment ring, each quadrant having five segments insulations from one another.

Teleprinter

Machines utilizing the start-stop principle are known as **teleprinter.** There are two types of **teleprinters**—electro-mechanical and electronics. The electro-mechanical teleprinters manufactured by the Hindustan Teleprinters, Chennai are now being replaced by electronic teleprinters using micro-processors and digital memory devices. The mechanical parts of electronic teleprinter have been reduced to the barest minimum and that too confined to the printer unit only.

There are various methods to employ start-stop telegraphy. The most popular method widely used is a teleprinter. Teleprinter is a electro-mechanical device by means of which message can be sent and received on a piece of paper in typical forms as in an ordinary type-writer machine. In an actual teleprinter the rotating burst and metal rings are replaced by cam and levers.

EXERCISE

1. In case of the probability of the message to reach successfully is 1 in 16, then the information will be at least of length
   (a) 4 bits   *(b)* 3 bits
   (c) 7 bits   *(d)* 13 bits

2. Which of the following section plays significant role for sensitivity and selectivity?
   (a) IF   *(b)* Mixer
   (c) Detector   *(d)* None of these

3. Audio frequency range lies between
   (a) 30 MHz and 250 MHz
   (b) 20 Hz and 20 k MHz
   (c) 50 MHz and 500 MHz
   (d) 35 Hz and 45 k MHz

4. De-emphasis circuit is used
   (a) for de-emphasising high frequency component
   (b) prior to modulation
   (c) both *(a)* and *(b)*
   (d) none of the above

5. SHF could be used for
   (a) satellite communication
   (b) FM radio broadcasts
   (c) both *(a)* and *(b)*
   (d) none of the above

6. The frequency tolerancy for the RF carrier in the standard AM radio broadcast band is
   (a) +20 Hz   *(b)* +35 Hz
   (c) +75 Hz   *(d)* d+150 Hz

7. In which of the following frequency bands are the standard AM radio broadcast stations?
   (a) HF   *(b)* MF
   (c) UHF   *(d)* None of these

8. A monostable multivibrator can be used to generate
   (a) sweep   *(b)* sinusoidal
   (c) both *(a)* and *(b)*   *(d)* none of the above

9. Excessive hum in a power supply could be due to
   (a) capacitor   *(b)* defective rectifier
   (c) both *(a)* and *(b)*   *(d)* none of the above

10. For the transmission of message to distant parts of the globe, sound waves are first converted into electrical signals with the help of
    (a) mechanical energy
    (b) electrical energy

(c) microphone
(d) none of the above

11. A colour camera is
    (a) a combination of three or four monochrome cameras with optical accessories
    (b) vidicon camera
    (c) both *(a)* and *(b)*
    (d) none of the above

12. In TV if there is no brightness but sound is normal, the trouble could be in
    (a) horizontal oscillator
    (b) vertical oscillator
    (c) both *(a)* and *(b)*
    (d) none of the above

13. Equalizing pulses in TV are sent during
    (a) vertical blanking
    (b) horizontal blanking
    (c) both *(a)* and *(b)*
    (d) none of the above

14. In a TV receiver which stage is not necessary for producing horizontal output?
    (a) Horizontal APC *(b)* Damper
    (c) both *(a)* and *(b)* *(d)* None of the above

15. The sound signal in video composite signal of TV is
    (a) FSK   *(b)* AM
    (c) FM   *(d)* None of these

16. TV broadcasting system in India is as per CCIR
    (a) system X   *(b)* system B
    (c) system A   *(d)* system I

17. In R.F. characteristics, ratio of effective radiated power of vision and sound is
    (a) 4 : 3   *(b)* 5 : 1
    (c) 3 : 2   *(d)* 2 : 3

18. Image orthicon is a sensitive tube and is capable of handling a wide range of
    (a) light values *(b)* contrast
    (c) both *(a)* and *(b)* *(d)* none of the above

19. Video signal is composed of camera signal carrying
    (a) information
    (b) receiver

(c) picture information
(d) none of the above

20. A F.M. transmitter is used for the purpose of
    (a) audio signal
    (b) transmission
    (c) audio signal transmission
    (d) none of the above

21. In ground wave propogation the absorption of waves
    (a) decreases with frequency
    (b) increases with frequency
    (c) both *(a)* and *(b)*
    (d) none of the above

22. The ionosphere consists of
    (a) positive charge layer
    (b) negative charge layer
    (c) both *(a)* and *(b)*
    (d) none of the above

23. Virtual height of an ionospheric layer is ..... the heat height
    (a) less than   *(b)* equal to
    (c) more than   *(d)* none of these

24. When power ratios are expressed in dBm, the reference power is
    (a) 1 mW   *(b)* 3 mW
    (c) 2 mW   *(d)* 5 mW

25. The effect of transit-time noise is significant in
    (a) HF   *(b)* LF
    (c) both *(a)* and *(b)* *(d)* none of these

26. The first step of radio transmitter is to convert audible sound waves into
    (a) electrical waves
    (b) magnetic waves
    (c) electrical impulses by microphone
    (d) both *(a)* and *(b)*

27. The proper frequency is chosen by means of
    (a) sound   *(b)* tuner
    (c) both *(a)* and *(b)* *(d)* none of these

28. When antenna conductor cuts the electro-magnetic flux of the wave, voltage is
    (a) increased   *(b)* induced
    (c) constant   *(d)* none of these

29. In frequency modulation, the amplitude for the carrier is kept essentially
   (a) variable   (b) constant
   (c) zero   (d) none of these

30. Modulation methods are used to transmit the intelligence at
   (a) signal
   (b) frequencies
   (c) radio frequencies
   (d) none of these

31. Machine language is different
   (a) for some computer
   (b) for each kind of computer c.p.u.
   (c) both (a) or (b)
   (d) none of the above

32. Every operation that the computer is capable of performing is indicated by a specific
   (a) code   (b) language
   (c) binary code   (d) none of these

33. Machine language is also called
   (a) language
   (b) machine
   (c) binary representation
   (d) none of the above

34. The supervisor program is the major component of the
   (a) system
   (b) operating system
   (c) all system
   (d) language

35. When the computer is first turn on, the supervisor program is the ..... to be used.
   (a) last program   (b) first program
   (c) middle program   (d) none of the above

36. A job is a unit of work to be processed by the
   (a) CPU   (b) ALU
   (c) TD   (d) memory

37. The supervisor schedules the order of input and
   (a) other operations
   (b) a few operations
   (c) output operations
   (d) none of the above

38. COBOL is a
   (a) language program
   (b) machine program
   (c) high-level program
   (d) none of the above

39. Disk and tape drives are commonly used
   (a) hard copy
   (b) soft copy
   (c) secondary storage devices
   (d) none of the above

40. Which of the following computer is currently the smallest and least costly computer
   (a) Super computer
   (b) Micro computer
   (c) both (a) and (b)
   (d) none of the above

41. The essential components of teleprinter are
   (a) 2   (b) 3
   (c) 4   (d) 5

42. Machines utilizing the start-stop principle are known as
   (a) teleprinters   (b) Baudot system
   (c) signal   (d) none of these

43. In teleprinter the operator is not required to remember
   (a) unit   (b) the codes
   (c) board   (d) none of these

44. The study of Baudot system is helpful in understanding the working of
   (a) telephones
   (b) teleprinters
   (c) traffic engineering
   (d) both (b) and (c)

45. Baudot Distributor is the most important part of Baudot system and each Baudot station is provided with its own
   (a) codes   (b) distributors
   (c) both (a) and (b) (d) none of these

46. Telegraph signals are formed by making changes in the electrical condition of
   (a) a system   (b) a circuit
   (c) the lines   (d) none of these

47. ..... distinct source of distortion have been recognised

(a) Four   (b) Five

(c) Three   (d) Six

48. Depending upon the manufacturer a teleprinter transmitter may be of the type/types

(a) Multiple contact type

(b) Individual contact type

(c) Single contact type

(d) All (a), (b) and (c)

49. Which type of speaker is used in telephone receivers?

(a) Fixed coil type   (b) Coaxial type

(c) Tweeter type   (d) None of these

50. Telegraphy was invented in

(a) 1857   (b) 1873

(c) 1844   (d) 1790

ANSWERS

1	2	3	4	5	6	7	8	9	10
(a)	(a)	(b)	(a)	(a)	(a)	(b)	(a)	(a)	(c)
11	**12**	**13**	**14**	**15**	**16**	**17**	**18**	**19**	**20**
(a)	(a)	(a)	(a)	(c)	(b)	(b)	(c)	(c)	(c)
21	**22**	**23**	**24**	**25**	**26**	**27**	**28**	**29**	**30**
(b)	(b)	(c)	(a)	(a)	(c)	(b)	(b)	(b)	(c)
31	**32**	**33**	**34**	**35**	**36**	**37**	**38**	**39**	**40**
(b)	(c)	(c)	(b)	(b)	(a)	(c)	(c)	(c)	(b)
41	**42**	**43**	**44**	**45**	**46**	**47**	**48**	**49**	**50**
(c)	(a)	(b)	(b)	(b)	(b)	(c)	(d)	(a)	(c)

ARITHMETICAL AND NUMERICAL ABILITY

NUMBER SYSTEM

1. There are four numbers A, B, C and D. Average of the first three i.e., A, B and C is 15 and that of B, C and D is 16. If the last number, i.e., D is 19, then the first number is—
   A. 15
   B. 16
   C. 17
   D. 18

2. Of the three numbers, the first is twice the second and thrice the third. If the average of three is 22, the three numbers are—
   A. 12, 18, 36
   B. 18, 12, 36
   C. 36, 12, 18
   D. 36, 18, 12

3. If a person is standing on the sixth number in the queue from both the ends, the total persons in the queue are—
   A. 9
   B. 11
   C. 12
   D. 13

4. A number 'x' when multiplied by 5 and added to three times its own gives 64, the number is—
   A. 8
   B. 12
   C. 14
   D. 18

5. A number which when multiplied by 11 is as much above 180 as it was originally below it. The number is—
   A. 25
   B. 30
   C. 40
   D. 45

6. The sum of a number and its reciprocal is thrice the difference of the number and its reciprocal. Find the number.
   A. $\sqrt{2}$
   B. $\sqrt{3}$
   C. $\sqrt{5}$
   D. $\sqrt{7}$

7. A boy was asked to find $\dfrac{7}{9}$ of a fraction. He made a mistake of dividing the fraction by $\dfrac{7}{9}$ and so got an answer which exceeded the correct answer by $\dfrac{8}{21}$. Find the correct answer.
   A. $\dfrac{2}{3}$
   B. $\dfrac{5}{7}$
   C. $\dfrac{7}{12}$
   D. $\dfrac{7}{15}$

8. There are 408 boys and 312 girls in a school, which are to be divided into equal sections of either boys or girls alone. Find the maximum number of boys or girls that can be placed in a section. Also find the total number of sections thus formed.
   A. 10, 20
   B. 24, 30
   C. 24, 40
   D. 30, 30

9. The sum of all possible two-digit number formed from three different one-digit natural numbers, when divided by the sum of the original three numbers is equal to—
   A. 11
   B. 18
   C. 22
   D. 36

10. There are four prime numbers written in ascending order. The product of the first three is 385 and that of the last three is 1001. The last number is—
    A. 19
    B. 17
    C. 13
    D. 11

11. If the number 357 ★ 25 ★ is divisible by both 3 and 5, then the missing digits in the unit's place and thousandth place respectively are—
    A. 0, 4
    B. 5, 4
    C. 5, 6
    D. 0, 6

12. The difference between two numbers is 1365. When the larger number is divided by the smaller one, the quotient is 6 and the remainder is 15. The smaller number is:

A. 360   B. 295
C. 270   D. 240

13. When a number is divided by 31, the remainder is 29. When the same number is divided by 16, what will be the remainder?
A. 15   B. 13
C. 11   D. Data inadequate

14. In dividing a number by 585, a student applied the method of short division. He divided the number successively by 5, 9 and 13 (factor of 585) and got the remainders 4, 8 and 12. If he had divided the number by 585, the remainder would have been:
A. 584   B. 292
C. 144   D. 24

15. When a number divided by 6 leaves a remainder 3. When the square of the same number is divided by 6, the remainder is:
A. 3   B. 2
C. 1   D. zero

ANSWERS

1	2	3	4	5	6	7	8	9	10
B	D	B	A	B	A	C	B	C	C

11	12	13	14	15
C	C	D	A	A

SOME SELECTED EXPLANATORY ANSWERS

1. $\dfrac{A+B+C}{3} = 15,$

or, $A + B + C = 15 \times 3 = 45$ ... (i)

$\dfrac{B+C+D}{3} = 16,$

or $B + C + D = 48$ ... (ii)

$D = 19$

$\therefore\ B + C + 19 = 48$

or, $B + C = 48 - 19 = 29$

But, $A + B + C = 45$

Putting the value of $B + C = 29$ in the above equation (i), we get $A + 29 = 45$

$\therefore\ A = 45 - 29 = 16.$

2. Let the third number $= x$

$\therefore$ First number $= 3x$

Second number $= \dfrac{3x}{2}$

$\therefore \dfrac{1}{3}\left[x + 3x + \dfrac{3x}{2}\right] = 22 \Rightarrow \dfrac{11}{2}x = 66$

$\Rightarrow x = \dfrac{66 \times 2}{11} = 12 = $ Third number,

$12 \times 3 = 36 = $ First number,

$\dfrac{12 \times 3}{2} = 18 = $ Second number.

3. If the person is standing at sixth number in the queue from both sides, that means there are five persons ahead and five persons behind him. Hence, total number of persons in the queue is $5 + 1 + 5 = 11.$

4. $5 \times x + 3x = 64 \qquad \Rightarrow 8x = 64$

$\therefore \qquad x = \dfrac{64}{8} = 8.$

5. Let the number is x

$\therefore \qquad 180 - x = 11x - 180$

$\Rightarrow \qquad 180 + 180 = 11x + x$

$\Rightarrow \qquad\qquad 360 = 12x,$

$\Rightarrow \qquad\qquad x = \dfrac{360}{12} = 30.$

6. Let the no. $= x$ then its reciprocal $= \dfrac{1}{x}$

By the question, $\left(x + \dfrac{1}{x}\right) = 3\left(x - \dfrac{1}{x}\right)$

$\Rightarrow \qquad \dfrac{x^2+1}{x} = \dfrac{3(x^2-1)}{x}$

$\Rightarrow \qquad x^2 + 1 = 3x^2 - 3$

$\Rightarrow \qquad 3x^2 - x^2 = 3 + 1$

$\therefore \qquad x = \sqrt{2}.$

7. Let the required fraction $= x$

then, by the question $\quad x \div \dfrac{7}{9} - x \times \dfrac{7}{9} = \dfrac{8}{21}$

$\Rightarrow \qquad x \times \dfrac{9}{7} - \dfrac{7x}{9} = \dfrac{8}{21}$

$\Rightarrow \qquad \dfrac{32x}{63} = \dfrac{8}{21}$

$\Rightarrow \qquad x = \dfrac{8}{21} \times \dfrac{63}{32} = \dfrac{3}{4}$

Hence, the correct answer $= \dfrac{3}{4} \times \dfrac{7}{9} = \dfrac{7}{12}.$

8.
```
    312) 408(1
         312
      96) 312 (3
          288
          24) 96 (4
              96
              ×
```

$\therefore$ Maximum number of girls or boys that can be placed in a section $= 24$ and total

number of such section $= \dfrac{408}{24} + \dfrac{312}{24}$

$= 17 + 13 = 30$

9. Let three different one digit natural numbers be x, y and z.

Then, sum of all possible two digits numbers

$= (10x + y) + (10y + x) + (10x + z)$
$\qquad + (10z + x) + (10y + z) + (10z + y)$
$= 22x + 22y + 22z = 22 (x + y + z)$

Hence, required number $= 22$.

10. Let four prime numbers be a, b, c and d respectively.

Now, $\dfrac{abc}{bcd} = \dfrac{385}{1001} \qquad \Rightarrow \dfrac{c}{d} = \dfrac{5}{13}$

Hence, $a = 5$ and $d = 13$

11. 357 ★ 25 ★

For divisible by 5, the last digit must be either 0 or 5.

If last digit is 0, then other required digit will be 2 or 5 or 8

Hence, the numbers are (0, 2) or (0, 5) or (0, 8)

If last digit is 5, then other required digit will be 0 or 3 or 6 or 9

Hence, the numbers are (5, 0) or (5, 3) or (5, 6) or (5, 9)

So, correct option is (c).

12. Here, $(x + 1365) = 6x + 15$

$\Rightarrow 5x = 1350$

$\therefore \quad x = \dfrac{1350}{5} = 270$

Hence, the smaller number $= 270$.

13. The number $= 31x + 29$.

Here, given data is inadequate.

14.

```
    5 | a
    9 | b – 4
   13 | c – 8
      | 1 – 12
```

Now, $\quad c = 13 \times 1 + 12 = 25$

$b = 9c + 8 = 9 \times 25 + 8 = 233$

$a = 5b + 4 = 5 \times 233 + 4$
$\qquad\qquad\qquad = 1165 + 4 = 1169$

$1169 = 585 \times 1 + 584$

Hence, required remainder $= 584$.

15. The number $= 6x + 3$

Now, $(6x + 3)^2 = 36x^2 + 36x + 9$
$\qquad\qquad\quad = (36x^2 + 36x + 6) + 3$
$\qquad\qquad\quad = 6(6x^2 + 6x + 1) + 3$

Hence, required remainder $= 3$.

LCM AND HCF

1. The L.C.M. and H.C.F. of two numbers are 4284 and 32 respectively. If one of the numbers is 204, the other is
   A. 672
   B. 576
   C. 676
   D. 572

2. Two numbers are in the ratio of 8 : 15. If their H.C.F. is 4, the numbers are
   A. 32 and 60
   B. 16 and 30
   C. 80 and 150
   D. 64 and 120

3. The greatest number that will divide 366, 513 and 324 leaving the same remainder in each case is
   A. 21
   B. 18
   C. 27
   D. 42

4. The L.C.M. of two numbers is 45 times their H.C.F. If the sum of the L.C.M. and the H.C.F. of these two numbers is 1150 and one of the numbers is 125, then the other number is
   A. 256
   B. 225
   C. 250
   D. 255

5. The H.C.F. and the L.C.M. of two numbers are 50 and 250 respectively. On dividing one of these numbers by 2, 50 is obtained as quotient. The numbrs are
   A. 100, 125
   B. 80, 100
   C. 125, 100
   D. 200, 250

6. Three bells ring respectively at an interval of 15 seconds, 20 seconds and 24 seconds. If they ring continuously for 12 minutes then how many times, during this period, will they ring together?
   A. 2 times
   B. 6 times
   C. 5 times
   D. 3 times

7. If the sum of two numbers is 55 and the H.C.F. and L.C.M. of these numbers are 5 and 120 respectively. Find the sum of their reciprocals.
   A. $\dfrac{120}{11}$
   B. $\dfrac{11}{120}$
   C. $\dfrac{601}{55}$
   D. $\dfrac{55}{601}$

8. The LCM of two numbers is 48. The numbers are in the ratio of 2 : 3. The sum of the numbers is
   A. 64
   B. 40
   C. 32
   D. 28

9. Find the greatest number that will divide 43, 91 and 183 so as to leave the same remainder in each case.
   A. 13
   B. 9
   C. 7
   D. 4

10. The greatest possible length which can be used to measure exactly the length 7m, 3m 85cm, 12m 95 cm is
    A. 42 cm
    B. 35 cm
    C. 25 cm
    D. 15 cm

11. A, B and C start at the same time in the same direction to run around a circular park. A completes a round in 252 seconds, B in 308 seconds and C in 198 seconds, all starting at the same point. After what time will they meet again at the starting point?
    A. 46 minutes 12 seconds
    B. 45 minutes
    C. 42 minutes 36 seconds
    D. 26 minutes 18 seconds

12. Which of the following has most numbers of divisors?

    A. 182   B. 176

    C. 101   D. 99

13. Which is of the following is a co-primes?

    A. (23, 92)   B. (21, 35)

    C. (18, 25)   D. (16, 62)

14. Let N be the greatest number that will divide 1305, 4665 and 6905, leaving the same

remainder in each case. Then find the sum of the digits in N.

    A. 8   B. 6

    C. 5   D. 4

15. The greatest number which one dividing 1657 and 2037 leaves remainder 6 and 5 respectively, is:

    A. 305   B. 235

    C. 127   D. 123

ANSWERS

1	2	3	4	5	6	7	8	9	10
A	A	A	B	A	B	B	B	D	B

11	12	13	14	15
A	B	C	D	C

SOME SELECTED EXPLANATORY ANSWERS

1. 1st number × 2nd number = LCM × HCF

∴   204 × 2nd number = 4284 × 32

∴   2nd number $= \dfrac{4284 \times 32}{204} = 672$

∴   2nd number = 672

2. Let the numbers be $8x$ and $15x$

$$8x = 2 \times 2 \times 2 \times x$$
$$15x = 3 \times 5 \times x$$

∴ LCM of $8x$ and $15x = 2 \times 2 \times 2 \times x \times 3 \times 5$
$$= 120x$$

Now, 1st number × 2nd number = HCF × LCM

$\Rightarrow$ $8x \times 15x = 4 \times 120x$

$\Rightarrow$ $120x^2 = 4 \times 120x$

$\Rightarrow$ $x = 4$

∴   Numbers are $8 \times 4 = 32$ and $15 \times 4 = 60$

3. Difference between 366 and 513 = 513 − 366
$$= 147$$

and difference between 513 and 324
$$= 513 - 324 = 189$$

∴ HCF of 147 and 189

```
       147) 189 (1
            147
       × 42) 147 (3
            126
       × 21) 42 (2
             42
              ×
```

∴ The required largest number is 21.

4. LCM of the two numbers = 45 × HCF

and   LCM + HCF = 1150

$\Rightarrow$ 45 × HCF + HCF = 1150

$\Rightarrow$ HCF(45 + 1) = 1150

$\Rightarrow$ $HCF = \dfrac{1150}{46} = 25$

∴   LCM = 45 × 25 = 1125

∵ 1st number × 2nd number = LCM × HCF

∴ 125 × 2nd number = 1125 × 25

∴   2nd number $= \dfrac{1125 \times 25}{125} = 225.$

5. According to the condition of the problem, 50 is obtained on dividing one of the numbers by 2

∴ One of the numbers = 50 × 2 = 100

Now, 1st number × 2nd number = LCM × HCF

∴   100 × 2nd number = 250 × 50

∴   2nd number $= \dfrac{250 \times 50}{100} = 125$

Hence, numbers are 100 and 125.

6. LCM of 15, 20 and 24

5	15,	20,	24
4	3,	4,	24
3	3,	1,	6
	1,	1,	2

LCM = 5 × 4 × 3 × 2 = 120

$\because$ 12 minutes = 12 × 60 = 720 seconds

$\therefore$ Number of times the bells will ring together during 12 minutes

$$= \frac{720}{120} = 6 \text{ times.}$$

7. Let the number be x and y.

Then, $x + y = 55$;

$xy = $ HCF × LCM = 5 × 120

$\therefore$ Sum of their reciprocals

$$= \frac{1}{x} + \frac{1}{y} = \frac{x+y}{xy} = \frac{55}{5 \times 120} = \frac{11}{120}.$$

8. Let the two numbers be $2x$ and $3x$;

their LCM = $6x$

Now, $6x = 48$ $\therefore$ $x = 8$

Hence, the numbers are 2 × 8, 3 × 8 = 16, 24

Their sum = 16 + 24 = 40.

9.

```
   2240) 3360 (1          1120) 5600 (5
         2240                   5600
   1120 ) 2240 (2                 ×
          2240
            ×
```

Hence, N = HCF of 3360,

2240 and 5600 = 1120

Sum of digits in N = 1 + 1 + 2 + 0 = 4.

10. 7m = 700 cm;

3m 85 = 385 cm;

12m 95cm = 1295 cm

```
   385) 700 (1
        385
   315) 385 (1
        315
        70) 315 (4
            280
            35 ) 70 (2
                 70
                  ×
   35) 1295 (37
       105
       245
       245
        ×
```

Hence, required length = HCF of 700 cm, 385 cm, 1295 cm = 35 cm.

11.

2	252,	308,	198
2	126,	154,	99
3	63,	77,	99
3	21,	77,	33
7	7,	77,	11
11	1,	11,	11
	1,	1,	1

Hence, LCM = 2 × 2 × 3 × 3 × 7 × 11 = 2772

Hence, A, B, C will meet again at the starting point after 2772 sec. = 46 min 12 sec.

12.

Numbers	Their divisors
182	→ 1, 2, 7, 13, 14, 26, 91 and 182
176	→ 1, 2, 4, 8, 16, 22, 44, 88 and 176
101	→ 1 and 101
99	→ 1, 3, 9, 11, 33 and 99

Therefore, 176 has the most number of divisors.

13. HCF of 23 and 92 = 23

HCF of 21 and 35 = 7

HCF of 18 and 25 = 1

HCF of 16 and 62 = 2

Hence, 18 and 25 are co-prime numbers.

14. N = HCF of (4665 – 1305),

(6905 – 4665) and (6905 – 1305)

= HCF of 3360, 2240 and 5600 = 112

Sum of digit of 1 + 1 + 2 = 4.

15. Required number = HCF of (1657 – 6) and

(2037 – 5) = HCF of 1651 and 2032 = 127.

```
   1651) 2032 (1
         1651
         381) 1651 (4
              1524
              127) 381 (3
                   381
                    ×
```

AVERAGE

1. One-third of a certain journey was covered at the rate of 25 km per hour, one-fourth at the rate of 30 km per hour and the rest at the 50 km per hour. What is the average speed per hour for whole journey?

   A. $33\dfrac{1}{3}$ kmph

   B. $44\dfrac{1}{4}$ kmph

   C. $22\dfrac{1}{2}$ kmph

   D. 33 kmph

2. A batsman has a certain average of runs for 16 innings. In the 17th innings, he makes a score of 85 runs thereby increasing his average by 3. What is the average after the 17th inning?
   A. 33 runs B. 34 runs
   C. 37 runs D. 36 runs

3. The average of 6 observations is 12. A new seventh observation is included and the new average is decreased by 1. The seventh observation is
   A. 1 B. 3
   C. 5 D. 6

4. The average age of 30 students in a class is 12 years. The average age of a group of 5 of the students is 10 years and that of another group of 5 of them is 14 years. The average age of the remaining students is
   A. 8 years B. 10 years
   C. 12 years D. 14 years

5. Out of the three given numbers, the first number is twice the second and thrice the third. If the average of three numbers is 121, what is the difference between the first and third number?
   A. 144 B. 77
   C. 99 D. 132

6. If the average marks of three batches of 55, 60 and 45 students is 50, 55 and 60, then average marks of all the students is:
   A. 55 B. 54
   C. 54.68 D. 55.68

7. The average of 8 numbers is 20. The average of first two numbers is $15\dfrac{1}{2}$ and that of the next three is $21\dfrac{1}{3}$. If the sixth number is less than the seventh and eighth numbers by 4 and 7 respectively, then the eighth number is:
   A. 27 B. 25
   C. 22 D. 18

8. A pupil's marks were wrongly entered as 83 instead of 63. Due to that the average marks for the class got increased by half. What is the number of pupils in the class?
   A. 73 B. 40
   C. 40 D. 10

9. A cricketer whose bowling average is 12.4 runs per wicket takes 5 wickets for 26 runs and thereby decreases his average by 0.4. The number of wickets taken by him till the last match was:
   A. 85 B. 80
   C. 72 D. 64

10. The average weight of a class of 24 students is 35 kg. If the weight of the teacher is included, the average rises by 400 g. What is the weight of the teacher?
    A. 55 kg B. 53 kg
    C. 50 kg D. 45 kg

11. Nine men went to a hotel. Eight of them spent Rs. 3 for each over their meals and the ninth spent Rs. 2 more than the average expenditure of all the nine. What is the total money spent by them?

A. Rs. 29.25   B. Rs. 29.50
C. Rs. 29   D. Rs. 30

12. The average age of 24 students in a class is 10. If the teacher's age is included, the average increases by one. The age of the teacher is

A. 25   B. 30
C. 35   D. 40

13. The average of 5 consecutive even numbers A, B, C, D and E is 34. What is the product of B and D?

A. 1152   B. 1368
C. 1224   D. 1088

14. The average of 50 numbers is 30. If two numbers, 35 and 40 are discarded, then the average of the remaining numbers is nearly:

A. 29.68   B. 29.27
C. 28.78   D. 28.32

15. The average monthly salary of 20 employees of an organisation is Rs. 1500. If the manager's salary is added, then the average salary increases by Rs. 100. Find the manager's monthly salary?

A. Rs. 4800   B. Rs. 3600
C. Rs. 2400   D. Rs. 2000

ANSWERS

1	2	3	4	5	6	7	8	9	10
A	C	C	C	D	C	B	B	A	D

11	12	13	14	15
A	C	A	A	B

SOME SELECTED EXPLANATORY ANSWERS

1. Let the total distance covered during journey = 60 km

$\frac{1}{3}$ of the distance covered during journey

$$= 60 \times \frac{1}{3} = 20 \text{ km}$$

$\frac{1}{4}$ of the distance covered during journey

$$= \frac{1}{4} \times 60 = 15 \text{ km}$$

∴ The distance covered during the rest of journey = 60 − (20 + 15) = 25 km

Time taken to cover 20 km at 25 km/h

$$= \frac{20}{25} \text{ hours} = \frac{4}{5} \text{ hour}$$

Time taken to cover 15 km at 30 km/h

$$= \frac{15}{30} \text{ hours} = \frac{1}{2} \text{ hour}$$

Time taken to cover 25 km at 50 km/h

$$= \frac{25}{50} \text{ hours} = \frac{1}{2} \text{ hour}$$

Total time taken $= \frac{4}{5} + \frac{1}{2} + \frac{1}{2}$

$$= \frac{9}{5} \text{ hours}$$

Hence average speed per hour $= 60 \div \frac{9}{5}$

$$= \frac{60 \times 5}{9} = \frac{100}{3} \text{ km / h}$$

$$= 33\frac{1}{3} \text{ km / h}$$

2. Average increase in the score of 17 innings = 3 runs

Total increase in the score of 17 innings = 3 × 17 = 51 runs

∴ His average of 16 innings = 85 − 51 = 34 runs

Hence, average after the 17th innings
$$= 34 + 3 = 37 \text{ runs}$$

3. Seventh observation $= (7 \times 11 - 6 \times 12) = 5$

4. Let, the required average age be x
Then, $5 \times 10 + 5 \times 14 + 20 \times x = 30 \times 12$
$$\Rightarrow \qquad 20x = 360 - 120$$
$$\Rightarrow \qquad 20x = 240$$
$$\Rightarrow \qquad x = 12$$

5. Let the three numbers be x, $\dfrac{x}{2}$ and $\dfrac{x}{3}$ respectively,

Now, $\dfrac{1}{3}\left(x + \dfrac{x}{2} + \dfrac{x}{3}\right) = 121$

$$\Rightarrow \quad \dfrac{11x}{6} = 121 \times 3$$

$$\therefore \quad x = \dfrac{121 \times 3 \times 6}{11} = 198$$

Hence, required difference $= x - \dfrac{x}{3} = \dfrac{2x}{3}$

$$= \dfrac{2}{3} \times 198 = 132$$

6. Required average Marks

$$= \dfrac{55 \times 50 + 60 \times 55 + 45 \times 60}{55 + 60 + 45} = \dfrac{8750}{160} = 54.68$$

7. Let the sixth, seventh and eighth numbers are x, $x + 4$ and $x + 7$.
Sum of last three numbers

$$= 8 \times 20 - (2 \times \dfrac{31}{2} + 3 \times \dfrac{64}{3})$$

$$\Rightarrow x + x + 4 + x + 7 = 160 - 95$$
$$\Rightarrow 3x + 11 = 65$$
$$\Rightarrow 3x = 54 \qquad \therefore \ x = 18$$
New eighth number $= x + 7 = 18 + 7 = 25$

8. Let the total number of pupils in the class be x; then,

$$\dfrac{83 - 63}{x} = \dfrac{1}{2} \qquad \Rightarrow \dfrac{20}{x} = \dfrac{1}{2} \qquad \therefore \ x = 40$$

9. Let the number of wickets taken by him be x till the last match.

Then, $\dfrac{x \times 12.4 + 26}{x + 5} = 12$

$$\Rightarrow \ 12.4x + 26 = 12x + 60$$

$$\Rightarrow 0.4x = 34 \quad \therefore \ x = \dfrac{340}{4} = 85$$

10. Let the weight of the teacher be x kgs, then

$$\dfrac{24 \times 35 + x}{25} = 35.4$$

$$\Rightarrow \ 840 + x = 885 \qquad \therefore \quad x = 45 \text{ kgs}$$

12. Age of the teacher $= (25 \times 11 - 24 \times 10)$ years
$$= 35 \text{ years}$$

13. Let 5 consecutive even numbers A, B, C, D and E be x, $x + 2$, $x + 4$, $x + 6$ and $x + 8$ respectively.

Now, $\dfrac{x + x + 2 + x + 4 + x + 6 + x + 8}{5} = 34$

$$\Rightarrow 5x + 20 = 170$$
$$\Rightarrow 5x = 150 \qquad \therefore \ x = 30$$
Then, $\ B = x + 2 = 30 + 2 = 32$;
$D = x + 6 = 30 + 6 = 36$
Hence, their product $= 32 \times 36 = 1152$

14. The average of remaining 48 numbers

$$= \dfrac{50 \times 30 - (35 + 40)}{48} = \dfrac{1500 - 75}{48}$$

$$= \dfrac{1425}{48} = 29.68$$

15. Let manager's salary be Rs. x, then

$$\dfrac{20 \times 1500 + x}{21} = 1600$$

$$\Rightarrow \ 30{,}000 + x = 33600$$
$$\therefore \ x = \text{Rs. } 3600$$

PROBLEMS BASED ON AGES

1. The ratio of ages of A and B is 3 : 11. After 3 years the ratio becomes 1 : 3. What are the ages of A and B?
   A. 9 years, 33 years
   B. 10 years, 40 years
   C. 9 years, 27 years
   D. None of these

2. Two years ago, the ratio of Ram's and Mohan's age was 3 : 2 and at present 7 : 5. What are their present ages?
   A. 14 years, 10 years
   B. 15 years, 10 years
   C. 13 years, 9 years
   D. None of these

3. The ages of Samir and Saurabh are in the ratio of 8 : 15 respectively. After 9 years the ratio of their ages will be 11 : 18. What is the difference between their ages in years?
   A. 20 years
   B. 21 years
   C. 22 years
   D. 24 years

4. The present age of father is 34 years more than that of his son. 12 years ago, father's age was 18 times the age of his son. The present age of son in years is:
   A. 12
   B. 14
   C. 16
   D. 18

5. A mother is 25 years older than her daughter. Five years ago, the age of the mother was 6 times the age of the daughter. What is the present age of mother?
   A. 25 years
   B. 29 years
   C. 32 years
   D. 35 years

6. The difference between the present ages of P and Q is 4 years. The ratio of their ages after 5 years will be 9 : 8. The present age of P is:
   A. 24 years
   B. 30 years
   C. 32 years
   D. None of these

7. Ten years ago, the age of Divya was half of the age of Namrata. If the ratio of present ages of both is 3 : 4, the sum of their present ages is:
   A. 35 years
   B. 30 years
   C. 25 years
   D. 18 years

8. The ratio between the present ages of A and B is 5 : 3 respectively. The ratio between A's age 4 years ago and B's age 4 years hence is 1 : 1. The ratio between A's age 4 years hence and B's age 4 years ago is:
   A. 4 : 1
   B. 3 : 1
   C. 2 : 1
   D. 1 : 3

9. Ram got married 8 years ago. His present age is $\frac{6}{5}$ times his age at the time of marriage. Ram's sister was 10 years younger to him at the time of his marriage. What is the present age of Ram's sister?
   A. 40 years
   B. 38 years
   C. 36 years
   D. 32 years

10. A father said to his son, "I was as old as you are at present at the time of your birth." If the father's age is 38 years now. Five years ago the age of son was:
    A. 38 years
    B. 33 years
    C. 19 years
    D. 14 years

ANSWERS

1	2	3	4	5	6	7	8	9	10
A	A	B	B	D	D	A	B	B	D

13

SOME SELECTED EXPLANATORY ANSWERS

1. Let the ages of A and B be $3x$ and $11x$ years; then

$$\frac{3x+3}{11x+3} = \frac{1}{3} \quad \Rightarrow \quad 9x + 9 = 11x + 3$$

$$\Rightarrow 2x = 6 \qquad \therefore \quad x = 3$$

Hence, their present age, $3x = 3 \times 3 = 9$ years; $11x = 11 \times 3 = 33$ years

2. Let the present ages of Ram and Mohan are $7x$ and $5x$ years; then

$$\frac{7x-2}{5x-2} = \frac{3}{2} \quad \Rightarrow \quad 14x - 4 = 15x - 6$$

$$\therefore \quad x = 2$$

Hence, their present ages : $7 \times 2 = 14$ years and $5 \times 2 = 10$ years

3. Let the present ages of Samir and Saurabh are $8x$ and $15x$ years respectively; then

$$\frac{8x+9}{15x+9} = \frac{11}{18} \quad \Rightarrow \quad 144x + 162 = 165x + 99$$

$$\Rightarrow 21x = 63 \quad \therefore \quad x = 3$$

Hence, difference of their ages $= 15x - 8x = 7x$ $= 7 \times 3 = 21$ years

4. Let the present ages of father and his son be $x + 34$ and x years respectively; then

$18(x - 12) = x + 34 - 12$

$\Rightarrow 18x - 216 = x + 22$

$\Rightarrow 17x = 238 \qquad \therefore \ x = 14$

Hence, present age of his son $= 14$ years

5. Let the present ages of mother and her daughter are $(x + 25)$ and x years respectively; then

$6(x - 5) = x + 25 - 5$

$\Rightarrow \quad 6x - 30 = x + 20$

$\Rightarrow \qquad 5x = 50 \qquad \therefore \ x = 10$

Hence, the age of the mother $= 10 + 25$ $= 35$ years

6. Let the present ages of P and Q be $(x + 4)$ and x years;

then, $\dfrac{x+4+5}{x+5} = \dfrac{9}{8} \quad \Rightarrow \quad 8x + 72$ $= 9x + 45 \qquad \therefore \ x = 27$

Hence, present age of P $= 27 + 4 = 31$ years

7. Let the present ages of Divya and Namrata are $3x$ and $4x$ years respectively; then

$$\frac{3x-10}{4x-10} = \frac{1}{2}$$

$\Rightarrow \quad 6x - 20 = 4x - 10$

$\Rightarrow \qquad 2x = 10 \quad \therefore \ x = 5$

Hence, sum of their ages $= 3x + 4x = 7x$ $= 7 \times 5 = 35$ years

8. Let the present ages of A and B are $5x$ and $3x$ years respectively; then,

$$\frac{5x-4}{3x+4} = 1 \quad \Rightarrow \quad 5x - 4 = 3x + 4$$

$\Rightarrow 2x = 8 \qquad \therefore \quad x = 4$

Hence, their present ages are 20 years and 12 years.

So, required ratio $= (20 + 4) : (12 - 4)$ $= 24 : 8 = 3 : 1$

9. Let the present age of Ram be x years; then

$$\frac{x}{x-8} = \frac{6}{5} \quad \Rightarrow \quad 5x = 6x - 48$$

$\therefore \quad x = 48$

Hence, present age of Ram's sister $= 48 - 10 = 38$ years.

10. Let the age of father was x years at the time of his son's birth, then present age of father and his son will be $2x$ and x years,

Now, $\quad 2x = 38 \qquad \therefore \quad x = 19$ years

Hence, 5 years ago the age of son was $19 - 5$ $= 14$ years

CHAIN RULE

1. A fort has provision for 50 days. After 15 days a reinforcement of 150 men arrives and the provision now lasts 25 days. How many men were there in the fort?
   A. 300
   B. 225
   C. 275
   D. 200

2. In a fort there is provisions for 40 days for 275 persons. If after 16 days 125 persons leave the fort for how many more days the provisions will last?
   A. 35 days
   B. 44 days
   C. 45 days
   D. 53 days

3. 60 men could complete a work in 250 days. They worked together for 200 days. After that the work had to be stopped for 10 days due to bad weather. How many more men should be engaged to complete the work in time?
   A. 20
   B. 18
   C. 15
   D. 10

4. A contractor undertook to complete a project in 90 days and employed 60 men on it. After 60 days, he found that $\frac{3}{4}$ of the work has already been completed. How many men can he discharge so that the project may completed exactly on time?
   A. 15
   B. 20
   C. 30
   D. 40

5. A flagstaff 17.5 m high casts a shadow of length 40.25 m. The height of the building, which casts a shadow of length 28.75m under similar condition will be:
   A. 21.25 m
   B. 17.5 m
   C. 12.5 m
   D. 10 m

6. If 5 men or 9 women can do a piece of work in 19 days, then 3 men and 6 women will do the same work in how many days?
   A. 21
   B. 18
   C. 15
   D. 12

7. A certain number of men can finish a piece of work in 100 days. If there were 10 men less, it will take 10 days more for the work to be finished. How many men were there originally?
   A. 110
   B. 100
   C. 82
   D. 75

8. Some persons can do a piece of work in 12 days. Two times the number of such persons will do half of that work in:
   A. 12 days
   B. 3 days
   C. 6 days
   D. 4 days

9. 2 men and 7 boys can do a piece of work in 14 days; 3 men and 8 boys can do the same in 11 days. Then 8 men and 6 boys can do three times of this work in
   A. 30 days
   B. 4 days
   C. 21 days
   D. 18 days

10. If 3 men or 6 boys, working 7 hours a day can do a piece of work in 10 days; how many days will it take to complete a piece of work twice as large with 6 men and 2 boys working together for 8 hours a day?

    A. 9
    B. $8\frac{1}{2}$
    C. $7\frac{1}{2}$
    D. $6\frac{1}{2}$

11. If 15 men can do a certain amount of work in 20 days working 8 hours a day, in how many days will 10 men do three times the work working 6 hours a day?

   A. 120 days   B. 70 days
   C. 100 days   D. None of these

12. 40 men consume 60 kgs of rice in 15 days, then in how many days will 30 men consume 12 kgs of rice?

   A. 9 days   B. $6\dfrac{1}{4}$ days

   C. 4 days   D. $3\dfrac{1}{4}$ days

13. 56 men can complete a piece of work in 24 days. In how many days can 42 men complete the same piece of work?

   A. 48   B. 32
   C. 20   D. 16

14. Running at the same constant rate, 6 identical machines can produce a total of 270 bottles per minute. At this rate, how many bottles could 10 such machines produce in 4 minutes?

   A. 1400   B. 1600
   C. 1800   D. 2000

15. 400 persons, working 9 hours a day complete $\dfrac{1}{4}th$ of the work in 10 days. The number of additional persons, working 8 hours a day, required to complete the remaining work in 20 days, is:

   A. 275   B. 250
   C. 675   D. 200

ANSWERS

1	2	3	4	5	6	7	8	9	10
B	B	C	B	C	C	A	B	C	C

11	12	13	14	15
A	C	B	C	C

SOME SELECTED EXPLANATORY ANSWERS

1.

Days	Men
35↑	x ↓
25	$x + 150$

$$\Rightarrow \frac{x+150}{x} = \frac{35}{25} \qquad \Rightarrow 1 + \frac{150}{x} = \frac{35}{25}$$

$$\Rightarrow \frac{150}{x} = \frac{10}{25}$$

$$\therefore x = \frac{25}{10} \times 150 = 375$$

Required number of men = 375 – 150 = 225

2.

Persons	Days
275↑	24 ↓
150	x

$$\Rightarrow \frac{x}{24} = \frac{275}{150} \qquad \therefore x = \frac{275}{150} \times 24 = 44 \text{ days}$$

3.

Days	Men
50↑	60 ↓
40	x

$$\Rightarrow \frac{x}{60} = \frac{50}{40} \qquad \therefore x = \frac{50}{40} \times 60 = 75 \text{ men}$$

Hence, number of additional men = 75 – 60
$$= 15$$

4.

Work	Days	Men
$\dfrac{3}{4}$ ↓	60 ↑	60 ↓
$\dfrac{1}{4}$	30	x

$$\Rightarrow \frac{x}{60} = \frac{60}{30} \times \frac{1/4}{3/4}$$

$$\therefore x = \frac{60}{30} \times \frac{1}{3} \times 60 = 40 \text{ days}$$

Hence, number of men to be discharged
$$= 60 – 40 = 20$$

5.

Shadow (m)	Object (m)
40.25 ↓	17.5 ↓
28.75 ↓	x ↓

$$\Rightarrow \quad \frac{x}{17.5} = \frac{28.75}{40.25}$$

$$\therefore \quad x = \frac{28.75 \times 17.5}{40.25} = 12.5 \text{ m}$$

6. 5 men $\equiv$ 9 women

$$\therefore \quad 3 \text{ men} = \frac{9}{5} \times 3 = \frac{27}{5} \text{ women}$$

Hence, 3 men and 6 women $= \dfrac{27}{5} + 6$

$$= \frac{57}{5} \text{ women}$$

Women	Days
9 ↑	19 ↓
$\dfrac{57}{5}$ ↑	x ↓

$$\Rightarrow \quad \frac{x}{19} = \frac{9 \times 5}{57}$$

$$\therefore \quad x = \frac{9 \times 5}{57} \times 19 = 15 \text{ days}$$

7.

Days	Men
100 ↑	x ↓
110 ↑	$x - 10$ ↓

$$\Rightarrow \quad \frac{x-10}{x} = \frac{100}{110} \qquad \Rightarrow \quad 110x - 1100 = 100x$$

$$\Rightarrow \quad 10x = 1100 \qquad \therefore \quad x = 110$$

Hence, initially the number of men $= 110$

8.

Work	Persons	Days
1 ↓	x ↑	12 ↓
$\dfrac{1}{2}$ ↓	$2x$ ↑	a ↓

$$\Rightarrow \quad \frac{a}{12} = \frac{x}{2x} \times \frac{1}{2} \qquad \therefore \quad a = \frac{1}{4} \times 12 = 3 \text{ days}$$

9. Here, 14×2 men $+ 14 \times 7$ boys $\equiv 11 \times 3$ men $+ 11 \times 8$ boys

$$\Rightarrow 28 \text{ men} + 98 \text{ boys} \equiv 33 \text{ men} + 88 \text{ boys}$$

$$\Rightarrow 5 \text{ men} = 10 \text{ boys} \quad \therefore \quad 1 \text{ man} = 2 \text{ boys}$$

Then, 2 men and 7 boys $\equiv$ 4 boys + 7 boys

$$= 11 \text{ boys}$$

& also, 8 men and 6 boys $\equiv$ 16 boys + 6 boys

$$= 22 \text{ boys}$$

Work	Boys	Days
1 ↓	11 ↑	14 ↓
3 ↓	22 ↑	x ↓

$$\Rightarrow \quad \frac{x}{14} = \frac{11}{22} \times \frac{3}{1}$$

$$\therefore \quad x = \frac{1}{2} \times 3 \times 14 = 21 \text{ days}$$

12.

Men	Rice (kgs)	Days
40 ↑	60 ↓	15 ↓
30 ↑	12 ↓	x ↓

$$\Rightarrow \quad \frac{x}{15} = \frac{12}{60} \times \frac{40}{30}$$

$$\therefore \quad x = \frac{12}{60} \times \frac{40}{30} \times 15 = 4 \text{ days}$$

14.

Machines	Time (minutes)	Bottles
6 ↓	1 ↓	270 ↓
10 ↓	4 ↓	x ↓

$$\Rightarrow \quad \frac{x}{270} = \frac{4}{1} \times \frac{10}{6}$$

$$\therefore \quad x = \frac{4 \times 10}{6} \times 270 = 1800 \text{ bottles}$$

15.

Work	Hours	Days	Persons
$\dfrac{1}{4}$ ↓	9 ↑	10 ↑	400 ↓
$\dfrac{3}{4}$ ↓	8 ↑	20 ↑	x ↓

$$\Rightarrow \quad \frac{x}{400} = \frac{10}{20} \times \frac{9}{8} \times \frac{3/4}{1/4}$$

$$\therefore \quad x = \frac{1}{2} \times \frac{9}{8} \times 3 \times 400 = 675$$

Hence, number of additional persons

$$= 675 - 400 = 275$$

TIME AND DISTANCE

1. Starting from a point at a speed of 4 km/hr a man reaches at a cerain place and returns back to the point from where he had started journey on bicycle at the speed of 16 km/hr. His average speed during the entire journey will be :
   A. 6.4 km/h
   B. 8.4 km/h
   C. 5.4 km/h
   D. 10 km/h

2. A motorist covers a certain distance at a average speed of 48 km/h in 45 minutes. What speed in km/h he must maintain to cover the same distance in 30 minutes?
   A. 66 km/h
   B. 79 km/h
   C. 80 km/h
   D. 72 km/h

3. A policeman saw a thief at a distance of 200 m. The policeman and the thief started running at the same time. If the policeman runs at a speed of $4\frac{1}{6}$ m per second and the thief at a speed of $3\frac{1}{3}$ m per second, after what time the policeman will catch the thief?
   A. 12 min
   B. 10 min
   C. 9 min
   D. 4 min

4. A monkey wants to climb up a glazed pole. He climbs 12 metres in 1 minute and then he slips back 3 metres in the next minute. If the pole is 63 metre high, how long does he take to climb at the top of the pole?
   A. $11\frac{1}{4}$ min
   B. $12\frac{1}{2}$ min
   C. $12\frac{3}{4}$ min
   D. $14\frac{3}{4}$ min

5. The distance between two stations A and B is 300 km. A train leaves the station A with a speed of 40 km/hr. At the same time another train departs from the station B with a speed of 50 km/hr. How much time will these two trains take to cross each other?
   A. 3 hrs 40 min
   B. 3 hrs 20 min
   C. 2 hrs 20 min
   D. 3 hrs 45 min

6. Nilesh goes to school from his village at the speed of 4 km/hr and returns from school to village at the speed of 2 km/hr. If he takes 6 hours in all, then what is the distance between the village and the school?
   A. 8 km
   B. 6 km
   C. 5 km
   D. 4 km

7. By increasing the speed of the bus by 10 km/hr the time of journey for 72 km is reduced by 36 minutes. What was the original speed of the bus?
   A. 30 km/hr
   B. 35 km/hr
   C. 40 km/hr
   D. 45 km/hr

8. A train covers a distance in 50 minutes, if it runs at a speed of 48 km/hr on an average. The speed at which the train must run to reduce the time of journey to 40 minutes will be:
   A. 70 km/hr
   B. 60 km/hr
   C. 55 km/hr
   D. 50 km/hr

9. A certain distance is covered by a vehicle at a certain speed. If half of this distance is covered by another vehicle in double the time, the ratio of the speeds of the two vehicles is:
   A. 4 : 1
   B. 1 : 4
   C. 2 : 1
   D. 1 : 2

10. A is faster than B. A and B each walk 24 km. The sum of their speeds is 7 km/hr and sum of times taken by them is 14 hours. What is the speed of A?
    A. 7 km/hr
    B. 5 km/hr
    C. 4 km/hr
    D. 3 km/hr

ANSWERS

1	2	3	4	5	6	7	8	9	10
A	D	D	C	B	A	A	B	A	C

SOME SELECTED EXPLANATORY ANSWERS

1. Average speed during the entire journey

$$= \frac{2xy}{x+y} = \frac{2 \times 4 \times 16}{4+16} = \frac{8 \times 16}{20} = 6.4 \text{ km/hr.}$$

2. Let required speed be x km/hr; then

$$x \times \frac{1}{2} = 48 \times \frac{3}{4} \quad \therefore \quad x = 48 \times \frac{3}{4} \times 2$$

$$= 72 \text{ km/hr}$$

3. Suppose the policeman will catch the thief after t seconds

then, $\left(\dfrac{25}{6} - \dfrac{10}{3}\right) t = 200 \Rightarrow \dfrac{5}{6} t = 200$

$$\therefore t = \frac{200 \times 6}{5} = 240 \text{ sec} = 4 \text{ min.}$$

4. The monkey climbs 12 metres in 1 minute and then he slips back 3 metres in the next minute
$\therefore$ The monkey climbs in the first 2 minutes
$= 12 - 3 = 9$ metres
$\therefore$ In the first 12 minutes the monkey climbs
$= 9 \times 6 = 54$ metres
Remaining height of the pole to be covered by the monkey $= 63 - 54 = 9$ metre
$\therefore$ The monkey will climb the height of 9 metres in the 13th minute
$\because$ The monkey climbs 12 metres in 1 minute

$\therefore$ The monkey will climb 9 metres in $\dfrac{1}{12} \times 9$

$= \dfrac{3}{4}$ minute

$\therefore$ Time spent in climbing at the top of the

pole $= \left(12 + \dfrac{3}{4}\right)$ minutes $= 12\dfrac{3}{4}$ minutes

5. The two trains are moving in the opposite directions

$\therefore$ Relative speed = 40 + 50 = 90 km/hr.

$\therefore$ Time taken to cross each other $= \dfrac{300}{90} = 3\dfrac{1}{3}$

hours or, 3 hours 20 minutes.

6. Let x km be the distance between village and the school; then

$$\frac{x}{4} + \frac{x}{2} = 6 \qquad \Rightarrow \frac{3x}{4} = 6$$

$$\therefore \quad x = \frac{6 \times 4}{3} = 8 \text{ km}$$

8. Let x km/hr be the required speed of the train; then

$$x \times \frac{40}{60} = 48 \times \frac{50}{60}$$

$$\therefore \quad x = \frac{48 \times 50}{40} = 60 \text{ km/hr}$$

9. Let x km/hr and t hr be the certain speed and certain time.

Then, ratio of their speeds $= \dfrac{x}{t} : \dfrac{x}{2 \times 2t} = 1 : \dfrac{1}{4}$

$= 4 : 1$

10. Let speeds of A and B are x_1 and x_2 km/hr and times taken by them are t_1 and t_2 hrs, then
$$x_1 + x_2 = 7 \text{ km/hr} \qquad \text{...(i)}$$
$$t_1 + t_2 = 14 \text{ hrs} \qquad \text{...(ii)}$$

Now, $\dfrac{24}{x_1} + \dfrac{24}{x_2} = 14 \Rightarrow \dfrac{24(x_1 + x_2)}{x_1 x_2} = 14$

$$\therefore \quad x_1 x_2 = \frac{24 \times 7}{14} = 12$$

Then, $x_1 - x_2 = \sqrt{(x_1 + x_2)^2 - 4 x_1 x_2}$

$$= \sqrt{(7)^2 - 4 \times 12} = 1 \quad \text{...(iii)}$$

Solving *(i)* and *(iii)* we get $x_1 = 4$ km/hr

TIME AND WORK

1. A and B working together complete a work in 35 days. If A takes 60 days to complete it, how long would B alone take to complete it?
   A. 64 days
   B. 72 days
   C. 81 days
   D. 84 days

2. A few children working together can do a piece of work in 18 days. If the number of children employed on the work is made double, how long would they take to complete half of the work?

   A. $4\dfrac{1}{2}$ days
   B. $2\dfrac{1}{3}$ days

   C. $8\dfrac{3}{4}$ days
   D. $6\dfrac{1}{2}$ days

3. 10 men or 18 boys can do a piece of work in 15 days. In how many days would 25 men and 15 boys complete the same work working together?

   A. $5\dfrac{1}{2}$ days
   B. $4\dfrac{1}{2}$ days

   C. $6\dfrac{2}{3}$ days
   D. $2\dfrac{1}{3}$ days

4. A cistern is filled by a tap in $3\dfrac{1}{2}$ hours. Due to a leak in the bottom of the cistern, it takes half an hour longer to fill the cistern. If the cistern is full, how long will it take the leak to empty it?
   A. 28 hours
   B. 29 hours

   C. $31\dfrac{1}{3}$ hours
   D. 38 hours

5. A is twice as good a workman as B and thrice as good a workman as C. If C alone can do a piece of work in 24 days, how long would the three persons take to finish the work working together?

   A. $3\dfrac{3}{11}$ days
   B. $4\dfrac{4}{7}$ days

   C. $4\dfrac{4}{11}$ days
   D. $3\dfrac{4}{11}$ days

6. If 3 men and 5 women can do a piece of work in 8 days and 2 men and 7 boys can do the same work in 12 days. Find the number of boys, the work done by whom can equate the work done by 10 women.
   A. 19 boys
   B. 21 boys
   C. 23 boys
   D. 15 boys

7. 8 men alone can complete a piece of work in 12 days. 4 women alone can complete the same piece of work in 48 days and 10 children alone can complete the piece of work in 24 days. In how many days can 10 men, 4 women and 10 children together complete the piece of work?
   A. 6
   B. 8
   C. 10
   D. 15

8. A works twice as fast as B. If B can complete a piece of work independently in 12 days. Find in how many days A and B together can complete the work?
   A. 8 days
   B. 6 days
   C. 4 days
   D. 18 days

9. A contractor undertook to complete a project in 90 days and employed 60 men on it. After 60 days, he found that $\dfrac{3}{4}$ of the work has already been completed. How many men can he discharge so that the project may be completed exactly on time?

A. 15   B. 20
C. 30   D. 40

10. A can do a piece of work in 25 days and B can do it in 20 days. They work together for 5 days and then A goes away. In how many days will B finish the remaining work?

A. 33 days   B. 20 days
C. 11 days   D. 10 days

ANSWERS

1	2	3	4	5	6	7	8	9	10
D	A	B	A	C	B	A	C	B	C

SOME SELECTED EXPLANATORY ANSWERS

1. (A + B)'s 1 day's work = $\dfrac{1}{35}$

and also, A's 1 day's work = $\dfrac{1}{60}$

Hence, B's 1 day's work = $\dfrac{1}{35} - \dfrac{1}{60} = \dfrac{5}{420} = \dfrac{1}{84}$

So, B will do the whole work in 84 days.

3. 10 men $\equiv$ 18 boys

$25 \text{ men} \equiv \dfrac{18}{10} \times 25 = 45 \text{ boys}$

Hence, 25 men + 15 boys = 45 + 15 = 60 boys
Now, 18 boys can do a piece of work in 15 days.
Hence, 60 boys will do a piece of work in

$\dfrac{15 \times 18}{60} = \dfrac{9}{2}$ days $= 4\dfrac{1}{2}$ days.

4. In 1 hour $\dfrac{2}{7}$ cistern is filled by the tap.

Hence, in $\dfrac{1}{2}$ hour $\dfrac{2}{14} = \dfrac{1}{7}$ cistern is filled by the tap.

So, $\dfrac{1}{7}$ cistern is emptied by the leakage in 4 hours.

So, 1 cistern will be emptied by the leakage in 28 hours.

6. Here, (3 men + 5 women) × 8
$\equiv$ (2 men + 7 boys) × 12

$\Rightarrow$ 40 women $\equiv$ 84 boys

$\therefore$ 10 women $\equiv \dfrac{84}{40} \times 10 = 21$ boys

Hence, work done by 10 women
= work done of 21 boys.

7. B's 1 day's work = $\dfrac{1}{4} - \dfrac{1}{12} = \dfrac{2}{12} = \dfrac{1}{6}$

Hence, B alone will complete the work in 6 days.

8. Ratio of efficiency of A and B = 2 : 1
Then, ratio of their time taking = 1 : 2
Hence, if B can complete the work in 12 days, then A in 6 days.

Now, (A + B)'s 1 day's work = $\dfrac{1}{6} + \dfrac{1}{12} = \dfrac{3}{12} = \dfrac{1}{4}$

So, A and B together can complete the work in 4 days.

9. After 60 days remaining work = $1 - \dfrac{3}{4} = \dfrac{1}{4}$

In 60 days $\dfrac{3}{4}$ work has been done by 60 men

In 30 days $\dfrac{1}{4}$ work will be done by

$60 \times \dfrac{4}{3} \times \dfrac{1}{4} \times \dfrac{60}{30} = 40$ men.

Hence, required number of men = 60 – 40 = 20 (which are to be discharged).

BOATS AND STREAMS

1. A boat goes 6 km upstream and back to the starting point in 2 hours. If the current of the stream runs at the rate of 4 km/hr, find the speed of the boat in still water.
   A. 6 km/hr
   B. 8 km/hr
   C. 10 km/hr
   D. 12 km/hr

2. A boat covers 24 km upstream and 36 km downstream in 6 hours, while it covers 36 km upstream and 24 km downstream in 6½ horus. Find the speed of the current.
   A. 2 km/hr
   B. 4 km/hr
   C. 6 km/hr
   D. 8 km/hr

3. A man can row 5 km/hr in still water and the speed of the stream is 1.5 km/hr. He takes an hour when he travels upstream to a place and back again to the starting point. How far is the place from the starting point?
   A. 2.275 km
   B. 3.5 km
   C. 1.5 km
   D. None of these

4. The speed of a boat in still water is 6 km/hr and the speed of the stream is 1.5 km/hr. A man rows to a place at a distance of 22.5 km and comes back to the starting point. Find the total time taken by him.
   A. 8 hours
   B. 10 hours
   C. 12 hours
   D. 4 hours

5. A boat covers 20 km downstream and 6 km upstream in 3 hours, while it covers 30 km downstream and 12 km upstream in 5 hours. What is the speed of boat in still water?
   A. 6 km/hr
   B. 8 km/hr
   C. 10 km/hr
   D. 12 km/hr.

6. Samir can travel 12 miles downstream in a certain river in 6 hours less than it takes him to travel the same distance upstream. But when he could double his rowing rate for his 24-mile round trip, the downstream 12 miles would then take only one hour less than the upstream 12 miles. Find the speed of the current in miles/hour.
   A. $2\frac{2}{3}$
   B. $2\frac{1}{3}$
   C. $1\frac{2}{3}$
   D. $1\frac{1}{3}$

7. A boat takes 6 hours to travel from place M to N downstream and back from N to M upstream. If the speed of the boat in still water is 4 km/hr; what is the distance between two places?
   A. 6 kms
   B. 8 kms
   C. 12 kms
   D. Data inadequate

8. A man can row upstream at 8 km/hr and downstream at 13 km/hr. The speed of the stream is:
   A. 2.5 km/hr
   B. 4.2 km/hr
   C. 5 km/hr
   D. 10.5 km/hr

9. A man's speed with the current is 15 km/hr and the speed of the current is 2.5 km/hr. The man's speed against the current is:
   A. 12.5 km/hr
   B. 10 km/hr
   C. 9 km/hr
   D. 8.5 km/hr

10. A motorboat, whose speed is 15 km/hr in still water goes 30 km downstream and comes back in a total of 4 hours 30 minutes. What is the speed of the stream (in km/hr)?
    A. 10
    B. 6
    C. 5
    D. 4

ANSWERS

1	2	3	4	5	6	7	8	9	10
B	A	A	A	B	B	D	A	B	C

SOME SELECTED EXPLANATORY ANSWERS

1. Let the speed of a boat in still water = x km/hr; then

$$\frac{6}{x-4}+\frac{6}{x+4}=2 \quad \Rightarrow \quad \frac{2x}{x^2-16}=\frac{1}{3}$$

$$\Rightarrow x^2-6x-16=0$$
$$\Rightarrow (x-8)(x+2)=0$$

Hence, the speed of the boat = 8 km/hr.

2. Let x km/hr and y km/hr be the speeds of the boat in still water and the speed of the current respectively, then

$$\frac{24}{x-y}+\frac{36}{x+y}=6 \Rightarrow \frac{4}{x-y}+\frac{6}{x+y}=1 \quad ...(i)$$

And, $\quad \dfrac{36}{x-y}+\dfrac{24}{x+y}=\dfrac{13}{2} \quad\quad ...(ii)$

Solving these two equations, we get
$$x+y=12; \; x-y=8$$

Hence, $y=\dfrac{1}{2}(12-8)=2$ km/hr.

3. Let required distance be x km, then

$$\frac{x}{5-1.5}+\frac{x}{5+1.5}=1 \Rightarrow \frac{x\times2}{7}+\frac{x\times2}{13}=1$$

$$\Rightarrow 40x=91 \quad\quad \therefore x=91/40=2.275 \text{ km}$$

4. Required time period $=\dfrac{22.5}{6+1.5}+\dfrac{22.5}{6-1.5}$

$$=\frac{45}{15}+\frac{45}{9}=8 \text{ hours.}$$

5. Let x km/hr and y km/hr be the speed of boat in still water and speed of current respectively; then

$$\frac{20}{x+y}+\frac{6}{x-y}=3 \quad\quad ...(i)$$

and also, $\quad \dfrac{30}{x+y}+\dfrac{12}{x-y}=5$

$$\Rightarrow \frac{15}{x+y}+\frac{6}{x-y}=\frac{5}{2} \quad\quad ...(ii)$$

Solving equations *(i)* & *(ii)*, we get $x+y=10$ and $x-y=6$

Since, $x=\dfrac{1}{2}(10+6)=8$ km/hr.

6. Let x km/hr and y km/hr be the speed of rowing in still water and speed of the current respectively; then

$$\frac{12}{x-y}-\frac{12}{x+y}=6 \quad \Rightarrow \quad \frac{24y}{x^2-y^2}=6$$

$$\Rightarrow x^2=y^2+4y \quad\quad ...(i)$$

Again, $\quad \dfrac{12}{2x-y}-\dfrac{12}{2x+y}=1$

$$\Rightarrow \frac{24y}{4x^2-y^2}=1 \quad \Rightarrow x^2=\frac{y^2+24y}{4} \quad ...(ii)$$

From equations (i) and (ii), we get

$$y^2+4y=\frac{y^2+24y}{4} \quad \Rightarrow 3y^2=8y$$

$$\therefore \quad y=\frac{8}{3}=2\frac{1}{3} \text{ miles/hr.}$$

8. The speed of the stream $=\dfrac{1}{2}(13-8)=\dfrac{5}{2}$

$$=2.5 \text{ km/hr.}$$

9. The man's speed in still water
$$=15-2.5=12.5 \text{ km/hr}$$
Hence, the men's speed against the current
$$=12.5-2.5=10 \text{ km/hr}$$

10. Let speed of the stream be x km/hr, then

$$\frac{30}{15+x}+\frac{30}{15-x}=4\frac{1}{2} \Rightarrow \frac{30\times30}{225-x^2}=\frac{9}{2}$$

$$\Rightarrow \frac{200}{225-x^2}=1 \quad\quad \Rightarrow x^2=225-200$$

$$\Rightarrow x^2=25 \quad\quad \therefore \quad x=5 \text{ km/hr.}$$

ALLIGATION OR MIXTURE

1. A shopkeeper buys 26 kgs of milk @ Rs. 16 per kg. He also buys from another source an inferior quality of milk @ Rs. 10 per kg. How much quantity of the latter should he buy to mix it with the former so that he can sell the mixture @ Rs. 14 per kg without making any loss?
   A. 13 kgs
   B. 12 kgs
   C. 14 kgs
   D. 16 kgs

2. Two vessels A and B contain mixture of milk and water in the ratio 4 : 1 and 9 : 11 respectively. They are mixed in the ratio of 3 : 2. Find the ratio of milk : water in the resulting mixture.
   A. 34 : 16
   B. 33 : 17
   C. 16 : 34
   D. 17 : 33

3. A shopkeeper has 50 kgs of rice. He sells a part of it at 20% profit and the rest at 40% profit. If he gains 25% on the whole, find the quantity of each part.
   A. 12.5 kgs and 37.5 kgs
   B. 37.5 kgs and 12.5 kgs
   C. 23.5 kgs and 21.5 kgs
   D. 21.5 kgs and 23.5 kgs

4. A man bought a certain quantity of sugar for Rs. 8000. He sells one-fourth of it at 20% loss. At what per cent profit should he sell the remainder stock so as to make an overall profit of 20%?
   A. 20%
   B. 30%
   C. 35%
   D. 40%

5. Rs. 675 was divided among 75 boys and girls. Each boy gets Rs. 20 whereas a girl gets Rs. 5. Find the number of boys and girls.
   A. 20, 55
   B. 15, 60
   C. 25, 50
   D. 30, 45

6. A vessel contains mixture of liquids A and B in the ratio 3 : 2. When 20 litres of the mixture is taken out and replaced by 20 litres of liquid B, the ratio changes to 1 : 4. How many litres of liquid A was there initially present in the vessel?
   A. 12 litres
   B. 18 litres
   C. 24 litres
   D. 22 litres

7. A container is full of milk. One-third of milk is taken out of it and replaced by same quantity of water. Then again one-third of the mixture is taken out of it and replaced by the same quantity of water. The process is repeated 4 times. If 16 litres of milk is left in the container at the end of 4th operation, find the capacity of the container.
   A. 76 litres
   B. 81 litres
   C. 82 litres
   D. 85 litres

8. The cost of type-I rice is Rs. 15 per kg and type-II is Rs. 20 per kg. If both type I and type II are mixed in the ratio of 2 : 3, then find the price per kg of the mixed variety.
   A. Rs. 19.50
   B. Rs. 19
   C. Rs. 18.50
   D. Rs. 18

9. In what ratio must a grocer mix two varieties of tea worth Rs. 60 a kg and Rs. 65 a kg so that by selling the mixture at Rs. 68.20 a kg he may gain 10%?
   A. 4 : 5
   B. 3 : 5
   C. 3 : 4
   D. 3 : 2

10. A vessel contains 80 litres of milk. 16 litres of milk was taken out of the vessel and replaced by water. Then 16 litres of mixture was withdrawn and again replaced by water. The operation was repeated for third time. How much milk is now left in the vessel?

A. 96.40 litres   B. 50.36 litres

C. 40.96 litres   D. 32.76 litres

ANSWERS

1	2	3	4	5	6	7	8	9	10
A	B	B	B	A	B	B	D	D	C

SOME SELECTED EXPLANATORY ANSWERS

1.

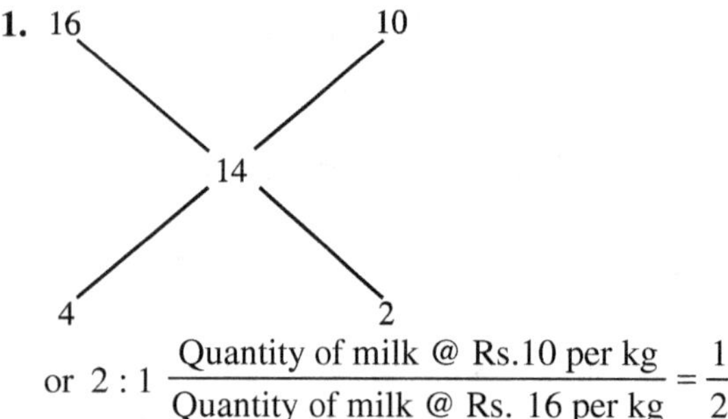

or 2 : 1

$$\frac{\text{Quantity of milk @ Rs.10 per kg}}{\text{Quantity of milk @ Rs. 16 per kg}} = \frac{1}{2}$$

So, quantity of milk @ Rs. 10 per kg. $= \dfrac{26}{2}$

$= 13$ kgs.

2. Fraction is

	Milk	*Water*
A :	$\dfrac{4}{5}$	$\dfrac{1}{5}$
B :	$\dfrac{9}{20}$	$\dfrac{11}{20}$

$(3A + 2B) = $ A and B : $\left(\dfrac{12}{5}+\dfrac{9}{10}\right)$ $\left(\dfrac{3}{5}+\dfrac{11}{10}\right)$

$\dfrac{33}{10}$ $\dfrac{17}{10}$

So, Ratio of milk : water in the resulting mixture $= 33 : 17$.

3.

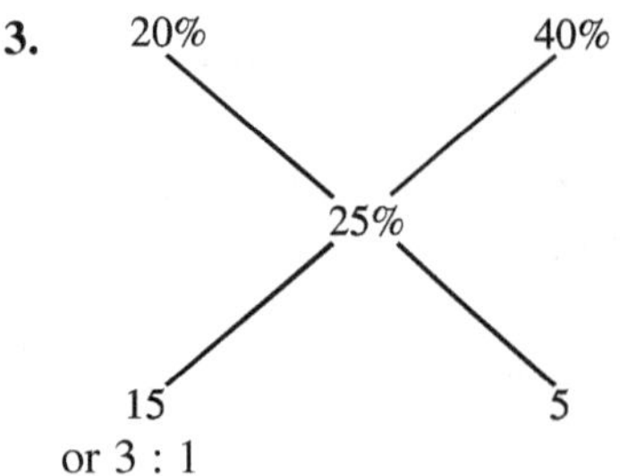

or 3 : 1

Quantity sold at 20% profit $= \dfrac{3}{3+1} \times 50$

$= 37.5$ kgs.

Quantity sold at 40% profit $= (50 - 37.5)$

$= 12.5$ kgs.

4. Let the remainder stock be sold at $x\%$ profit.

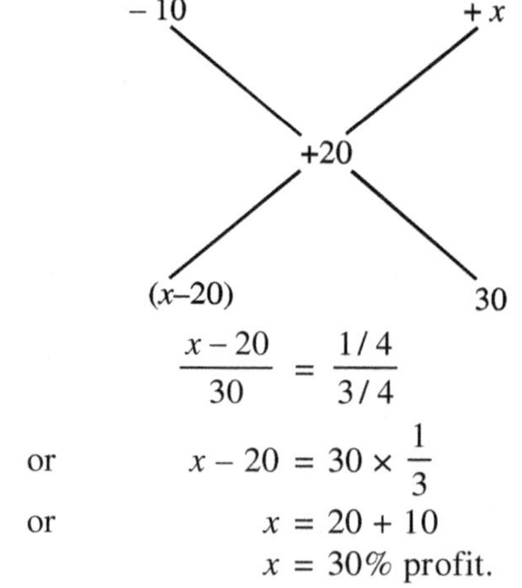

$$\frac{x - 20}{30} = \frac{1/4}{3/4}$$

or $\quad x - 20 = 30 \times \dfrac{1}{3}$

or $\quad x = 20 + 10$

$x = 30\%$ profit.

5. Average money per head (boy or girl)

$$= \text{Rs. } \frac{675}{75} = \text{Rs. } 9$$

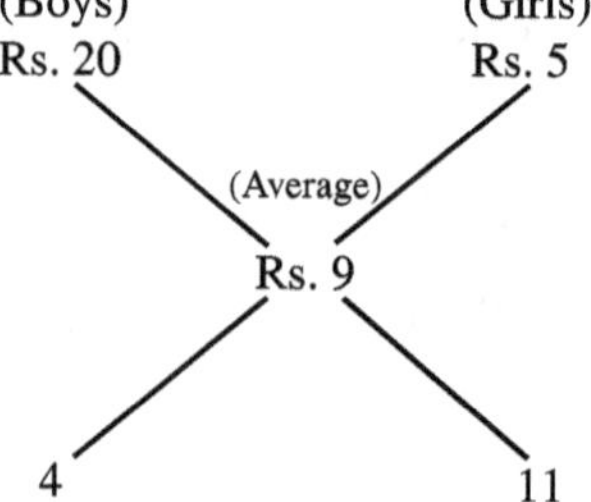

$$\text{Number of boys} = \frac{4}{4+11} \times 75 = 20$$

$$\text{Number of girls} = \frac{11}{4+11} \times 75 = 55.$$

6. % of liquid B initially present in the vessel

$$= \frac{2}{3+2} \times 100 = 40\%$$

% of liquid B finally present in the vessel

$$= \frac{4}{1+4} \times 100 = 80\%$$

The second solution is liquid B which is being mixed and it has 100% liquid B.

80% of liquid B present in the resultant mixture may be taken as average percentage. So, using rule of alligation on liquid B per cent, we can write,

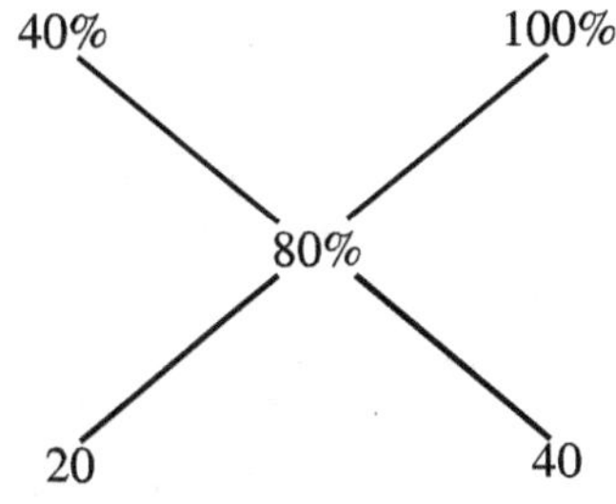

or   1 : 2

The ratio of liquid left in the vessel to liquid B being mixed = 1 : 2

Since the quantity of liquid B being mixed is 20 litres, the quantity of liquid left in the vessel is 10 litres.

Therefore, the total quantity of liquid initially present in the vessel

$$= 10 + 20 = 30 \text{ litres}$$

$$\text{Quantity of liquid A} = \frac{3}{2+3} \times 30$$

$$= 18 \text{ litres.}$$

7. Let capacity of the container be x litre; then

$$x(1 - 1/3)^4 = 16 \quad \Rightarrow \quad x\left(\frac{2}{3}\right)^4 = 16$$

$$\Rightarrow x \times \frac{16}{81} = 16 \qquad \therefore \quad x = 81 \text{ litres}$$

8. Let the price per kg of mixed variety be Rs. x; then

By the rule of alligation,

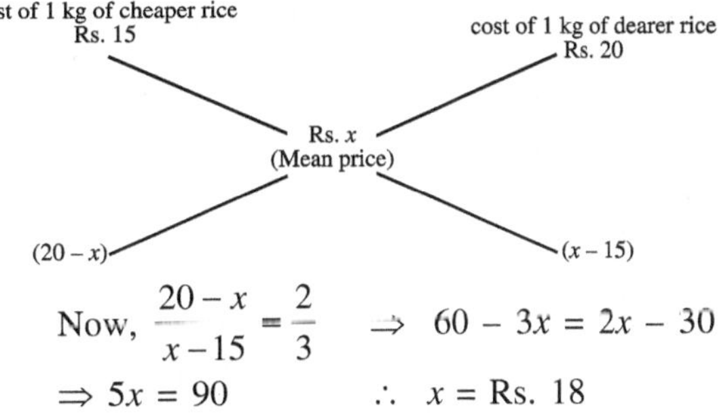

$$\text{Now, } \frac{20-x}{x-15} = \frac{2}{3} \quad \Rightarrow \quad 60 - 3x = 2x - 30$$

$$\Rightarrow 5x = 90 \qquad \therefore \quad x = \text{Rs. } 18$$

9. S.P. of 1 kg mixture = Rs. 68.20, Gain % = 10%

$$\text{Hence, C.P. of 1 kg mixture} = \frac{100}{110} \times \text{Rs. } 68.20$$

$$= \text{Rs. } 62$$

By the rule of alligation

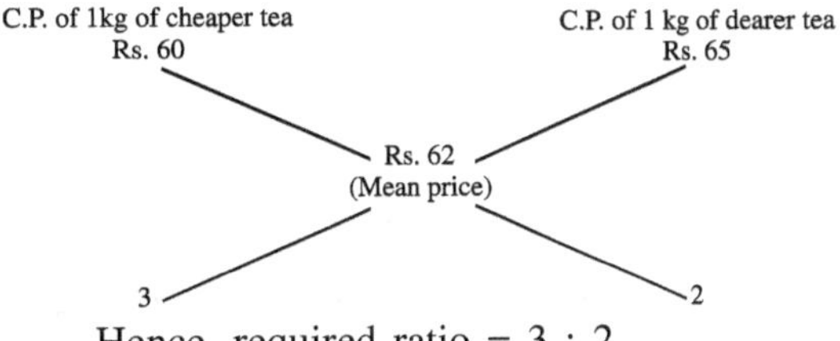

Hence, required ratio = 3 : 2

10. Amount of milk left $= 80\left(1 - \dfrac{16}{80}\right)^3$

$$= 80\left(\frac{4}{5}\right)^3$$

$$80 \times \frac{64}{125} = 40.96 \text{ litres.}$$

PERCENTAGE

1. A student who secures 20% marks in an examination fails by 30 marks. Another student who secures 32% gets 42 marks more than those required to pass. The percentage of marks required to pass is:
   A. 20
   B. 25
   C. 28
   D. 30

2. In a college election, a candidate secured 62% of the votes and is elected by a majority of 144 votes. The total number of votes polled is:
   A. 600
   B. 800
   C. 925
   D. 1200

3. In an organisation, 40% of the employees are matriculates, 50% of the remaining are graduates and the remaining 180 are postgraduates. How many employees are graduates?
   A. 360
   B. 240
   C. 300
   D. 180

4. The population of a village is 4500. $\frac{5}{9}$ th of them are males and rest females. If 40% of the males are married, then the percentage of married female is :
   A. 35
   B. 40
   C. 50
   D. 60

5. A's income is 10% more than B's. How much per cent is B's income is less than A's?
   A. 10%
   B. 7%
   C. $9\frac{1}{11}\%$
   D. $6\frac{1}{2}\%$

6. If the price of a television set is increased by 25%, then by what percentage should the new price be reduced to bring the price back to original level?
   A. 15%
   B. 20%
   C. 25%
   D. 30%

7. In an election one of the two candidates gets 40% votes and loses by 100 votes. Total number of votes is :
   A. 500
   B. 400
   C. 600
   D. 1000

8. The gross income of a person is Rs. 20000. 10% of his income is exempted from income tax and his net income is Rs. 19100. The rate of income tax is :
   A. 3%
   B. 2%
   C. 4%
   D. 5%

9. The owner of a cell phone shop charges his customer 32% more than the cost price. If a customer paid Rs. 6600 for the cell phone, then what was the cost price of the cell phone?
   A. Rs. 5000
   B. Rs. 5500
   C. Rs. 5800
   D. Rs. 6100

10. If the cost of pins reduced by Rs. 4 per dozen, 12 more pins can be purchased for Rs. 48. The cost of pins per dozen after reduction is:
    A. Rs. 8
    B. Rs. 12
    C. Rs. 16
    D. Rs. 20

11. In an examination 80% of the students passed in Mathematics and 70% passed in English, while 10% students failed in both the subjects. If 360 students passed in both the subjects, find the total number of students who appeared in the examination.
    A. 400
    B. 600
    C. 630
    D. 640

12. Electric tax is increased by 20% and its consumption is decreased by 20%. The change in the expenditure is:
    A. 4% decrease
    B. 4% increase
    C. 5% decrease
    D. 5% increase

13. The selling price of certain commodity was reduced by 25%. As a result of it, the sales increased by 30%. What was the effect of it on cash collected by daily sales?
A. 2.5% decrease
B. 2.5% increase
C. 5% decrease
D. 5% increase

14. The wheat sold by a grocer contained 10% low quality wheat. What quantity of good quality wheat should be added to 150 kgs of wheat so that the percentage of low quality wheat becomes 5%?

A. 50 kgs
B. 85 kgs
C. 135 kgs
D. 150 kgs

15. Nilam spends 15% of her monthly income on household expenses. She spends 17% of the monthly income in travelling and 6% on medical expenses and saves the rest Rs. 15,500. What is her monthly income?
A. Rs. 20,000
B. Rs. 25,000
C. Rs. 30,000
D. Rs. 35,000

ANSWERS

1	2	3	4	5	6	7	8	9	10
B	A	D	C	C	B	A	D	A	B

11	12	13	14	15
B	A	A	D	B

SOME SELECTED EXPLANATORY ANSWERS

1. $\quad$ 20% of $x + 30 = 32\%$ of $x - 42$

$\Rightarrow \quad$ 12% of $x = 72$

$\Rightarrow \quad x = \dfrac{72 \times 100}{12} = 600$

Pass Mark $= 20\%$ of $600 + 30 = 150$

Pass percentage $= \left(\dfrac{150}{600} \times 100\right)\% = 25\%$

2. (62% of $x - 38\%$ of x) $= 144$

$\Rightarrow$ 24% of $x = 144 \quad \Rightarrow \quad x = \dfrac{144 \times 100}{24} = 600$

3. $\quad$ Matriculates $= \dfrac{40}{100}x = \dfrac{2x}{5}$

Remaining $= \left(x - \dfrac{2x}{5}\right) = \dfrac{3x}{5}$

Graduates $= \dfrac{50}{100} \times \dfrac{3x}{5} = \dfrac{3x}{10}$

Remaining $= \dfrac{3x}{5} - \dfrac{3x}{10} = \dfrac{3x}{10}$

Now, $\dfrac{3x}{10} = 180$

$\therefore \ x = \dfrac{10 \times 180}{3} = 600$

$\therefore$ Graduates $= \dfrac{3 \times 600}{10} = 180$.

4. Males $= \left(\dfrac{5}{9} \times 4500\right) = 2500$

Females $= 2000$

$\therefore \quad$ Married males $= \dfrac{40}{100} \times 2500 = 1000$

and married females $= 1000$

$\therefore$ Percentage of married females

$= \left(\dfrac{1000}{2000} \times 100\right)\% = 50\%$.

5. Required percentage $= \left[\dfrac{10}{(100 + 10)} \times 100\right]\%$

$= 9\dfrac{1}{11}\%$.

6. Required reduction $= \dfrac{25}{100 + 25} \times 100 = 20\%$.

7. Out of 100, difference in votes = $(60 - 40) = 20$

20% of $x = 100$

$$\therefore x = \frac{100 \times 100}{20} = 500.$$

8. Gross income = Rs. 20000

Income exempted from income tax = 10% of gross income

$\therefore$ Income on which income tax is chargeable

$= (100 - 10\%) = 90\%$ of gross income

$$= 20000 \times \frac{90}{100} = \text{Rs. } 18000$$

$\therefore$ Total income tax paid on

$$= \text{Rs. } 20000 - \text{Rs. } 19100$$
$$= \text{Rs. } 900$$

$\therefore$ Rate per cent of income tax $= \dfrac{900}{18000} \times 100$

$$= 5\%$$

9. Let cost price of the cell phone be Rs. x; then

$$x + \frac{32}{100} \times x = 6600 \quad \Rightarrow \quad \frac{132x}{100} = 6600$$

$$\therefore x = \frac{100 \times 6600}{132} = \text{Rs. } 5000.$$

10. Let reduced price by Rs. x per dozen, then

$$\frac{48}{x} - \frac{48}{x+4} = 1 \quad \Rightarrow \quad \frac{48 \times 4}{x^2 + 4x} = 1$$

$$\Rightarrow \quad x^2 + 4x - 192 = 0$$
$$\Rightarrow \quad (x + 16)(x - 12) = 0$$
$$\therefore \qquad\qquad x = \text{Rs. } 12.$$

11. Here, percentage of students failed in Mathematics and English be 30% and 20% respectively.

Percentage of students failed either one or both subjects = $30 + 20 - 10 = 40\%$

Hence, percentage of pass students = $100 - 40$
$$= 60\%$$

Now, $60\% = 360$

$$\therefore 100\% = \frac{360}{60} \times 100 = 600.$$

12. Let initially electric tax is Rs. 100 and consumption = 100 units

Decrease in consumption
$$= 100 \times 100 - 120 \times 80 = \text{Rs. } 400$$

Hence, decrease percentage $= \dfrac{400 \times 100}{100 \times 100} = 4\%.$

13. Let the selling price of a commodity be Rs. 100 and number of sales = 100 units

Decrease in daily cash = $100 \times 100 - 75 \times 130$
$$= \text{Rs. } 250$$

Hence, decrease percentage

$$= \frac{250 \times 100}{100 \times 100} = 2.5\%.$$

14. Let x kg of good wheat be added; then

$$\frac{10}{100} \times 150 = \frac{5}{100}(150 + x)$$

$$\Rightarrow 150 + x = 300 \quad \therefore \quad x = 150 \text{ kg.}$$

15. Let her monthly income be Rs. x; then

$$x - \left(\frac{15}{100} \times x + \frac{17}{100} \times x + \frac{6}{100} \times x \right) = 15{,}500$$

$$\Rightarrow x - \frac{38x}{100} = 15500 \quad \Rightarrow \quad \frac{62x}{100} = 15500$$

$$\therefore \quad x = \frac{15500 \times 100}{62} = \text{Rs. } 25000.$$

PROFIT AND LOSS

1. Ashok bought 25 kg of rice at the rate of Rs. 6 per kg and 35 kg of rice at the rate of Rs. 7 per kg. He mixed the two and sold the mixture at the rate of Rs. 6.75 per kg. What was his gain or loss in the transaction?
   A. Rs. 16 gain
   B. Rs. 16 loss
   C. Rs. 10 gain
   D. None of these

2. Profit after selling a commodity for Rs. 425 is same as loss after selling it for Rs. 355. The cost of the commodity is :
   A. Rs. 285
   B. Rs. 390
   C. Rs. 295
   D. Rs. 400

3. Ram bought 4 dozen apples at Rs. 12 per dozen and 2 dozen at Rs. 16 per dozen. He sold all of them to earn 20%. At what price per dozen did he sell the apples?
   A. Rs. 14.40
   B. Rs. 16.00
   C. Rs. 16.80
   D. Rs. 16.20

4. At what price must Kantilal sell a mixture of 80 kg sugar at Rs. 6.75 per kg with 120 kg at Rs. 8 per kg to gain 20%?
   A. Rs. 7.50 per kg
   B. Rs. 8.20 per kg
   C. Rs. 8.35 per kg
   D. Rs. 9 per kg

5. A person bought an article and sold it at a loss of 10%. If he had bought it for 20% less and sold it for Rs. 55 more, he would have had a profit of 40%. The C.P. of the article is :
   A. Rs. 200
   B. Rs. 225
   C. Rs. 250
   D. None of these

6. A dealer sold a machine to a shopkeeper at 20% profit. The shopkeeper sold the machine to a customer so as to get 25% profit for himself. The difference between the selling price of the dealer and that of the shopkeeper was found to be Rs. 129. What is the initial price of the machine?
   A. Rs. 410
   B. Rs. 420
   C. Rs. 430
   D. Rs. 440

7. A man bought a horse and cart. If he sold the horse at 10% loss and the cart at 20% gain he would not loss anything. If he sold the horse at 5% loss and the cart at 5% gain he would lose Rs. 10 in the bargain. What did he pay for each?
   A. Rs. 400, Rs. 200
   B. Rs. 300, Rs. 300
   C. Rs. 250, Rs. 350
   D. Rs. 350, Rs. 250

8. The marked price of a radio is 20% more than its cost price. If a discount of 10% is given on the marked price, the gain percentage is:
   A. 8
   B. 10
   C. 12
   D. 15

9. A dishonest dealer sells his goods at the cost price and still earns a profit of 60% by underweight. What weight does he use for a kg?
   A. 625 gms
   B. 750 gms
   C. 800 gms
   D. 850 gms

10. A man sells two horses for Rs. 990 each. On one he gains 10% and the other he loses 10%. What is his total percentage of gain or loss in the transaction?
    A. 1% gain
    B. 1% loss
    C. 2% gain
    D. 2% loss

ANSWERS

1	2	3	4	5	6	7	8	9	10
C	B	B	D	C	C	A	A	A	B

SOME SELECTED EXPLANATORY ANSWERS

1. C.P. of 60 kg mixture = Rs. $(25 \times 6 + 35 \times 7)$
= Rs. 395
S.P. of 60 kg mixtire = Rs. (60×6.75)
= Rs. 405
$\therefore$ Gain = Rs. $(405 - 395)$
= Rs. 10

2. Let C.P. = Rs. x
Then, $425 - x = x - 355 \Rightarrow 2x = 780$
$\therefore$ x = Rs. 390

3. C.P. of 6 dozen apples = Rs. $(12 \times 4 + 16 \times 2)$
= Rs. 80

$\therefore$ S.P. = Rs. $\left(\dfrac{120}{100} \times 80 \right)$

= Rs. 96

$\therefore$ S.P. per dozen = Rs. $\left(\dfrac{96}{6} \right)$ = Rs. 16

4. C.P. of 1 kg sugar = $\dfrac{80 \times 6.75 + 120 \times 8}{200}$

= Rs. 7.50

$\therefore$ S.P. of 1 kg = Rs. $\left(\dfrac{120}{100} \times 7.50 \right)$

= Rs. 9 per kg

5. Let C.P. = Rs. x,

then S.P. = $\dfrac{90}{100} \times x$ = Rs. $\dfrac{9x}{10}$

Now, when C.P. = Rs. $\dfrac{80x}{100}$ = Rs. $\dfrac{4x}{5}$;

then S.P. = $\dfrac{140}{100} \times \dfrac{4x}{5}$ = Rs. $\dfrac{28x}{25}$

But, $\dfrac{28x}{25} - \dfrac{9x}{10} = 55 \Rightarrow \dfrac{11x}{50} = 55$

$\therefore$ x = Rs. 250

6. Let the initial price = Rs. x; then C.P. for dealer

$= \dfrac{120}{100} \times x$ = Rs. $\dfrac{6x}{5}$

Again, C.P. for shopkeeper $= \dfrac{125}{100} \times \dfrac{6x}{5}$

$=$ Rs. $\dfrac{3x}{2}$

Now, $\dfrac{3x}{2} - \dfrac{6x}{5} = 129 \Rightarrow \dfrac{3x}{10} = 129$

$\therefore$ $x = \dfrac{10 \times 129}{3}$ = Rs. 430

7. Here, 10% C.P. of horse = 20% C.P. of cart;
Hence, C.P. of horse = $2 \times$ C.P. of cart;
Let C.P. of cart and horse be Rs. x and Rs. $2x$
respectively; then,

$\dfrac{5}{100} \times 2x - \dfrac{5}{100} \times x = 10 \Rightarrow \dfrac{1}{20} x = 10$

$\therefore x = 200$
Hence, C.P. of a cart = Rs. 200 and C.P. of a
horse = 2×200 = Rs. 400

8. Let C.P. be Rs. 100; then marked price
= Rs. 120

Since, S.P. = $\dfrac{90}{100} \times 120$ = Rs. 108

$\therefore$ Profit = $108 - 100$ = Rs. 8, Hence, gain = 8%.

9. Required weight = $\dfrac{100}{160} \times 1000$ = 625 gms.

10. Here, loss % = $\left(\dfrac{10}{10} \right)^2$ = 1%.

SIMPLE INTEREST

1. A lent a sum of Rs. 1250 to B at a certain rate of interest for 3 years and a sum of Rs. 1500 to C at the same rate of interest for 2 years. If he was paid total Rs. 258.75 as interest in both cases, find the rate of interest at which money was lent by him.

   A. $4\frac{1}{6}\%$

   B. $6\frac{1}{4}\%$

   C. $2\frac{1}{7}\%$

   D. $3\frac{5}{6}\%$

2. A invested Rs. 5000 at a certain rate of simple interest and Rs. 4000 for the same period at 1% higher rate of interest. If the interest in both cases is same, the former rate of interest is :

   A. 3%
   B. 4%
   C. 6%
   D. 5%

3. If a certain sum of money at simple interest amounts to Rs. 1900 in 3 years and to Rs. 2050 in 5 years, the rate per cent per annum is :

   A. 4½%
   B. 3½%
   C. 2½%
   D. 5¼%

4. A certain sum of money lent out on simple interest amounts to Rs. 1760 in 2 years and to Rs. 2000 in 5 years. Find the sum.

   A. Rs. 1650
   B. Rs. 1500
   C. Rs. 1580
   D. Rs. 1600

5. Out of the sum of Rs. 1550, a part was lent out at 5% p.a. simple interest and the remaining at 8% p.a. simple interest. If the total interest in both cases after 3 years is Rs. 300, the sum of money lent out at 8% p.a. simple interest was:

   A. Rs. 760
   B. Rs. 775
   C. Rs. 750
   D. Rs. 780

6. If simple interest on a certain sum of money for 4 years at 5% p.a. is same as the simple interest on Rs. 840 for 10 years at the rate of 4% p.a., the sum of money is:

   A. Rs. 1780
   B. Rs. 1660
   C. Rs. 1680
   D. Rs. 1620

7. What equal instalment of annual payment will discharge a debt which is due as Rs. 848 at the end of 4 years at 4% per annum simple interest?

   A. Rs. 200
   B. Rs. 212
   C. Rs. 225
   D. Rs. 250

8. Madhavi lent Rs. 5000 to Kamla for 5 years and Rs. 3000 to Vimla for 4 years. Find the rate of interest, if Madhavi gets an interest of Rs. 600 in the end.

   A. 1.62%
   B. 2.5%
   C. 3%
   D. 4%

9. A sum of money doubles itself in 7 years at simple interest. In how many years it will become four fold?

   A. 10 years
   B. 14 years
   C. 21 years
   D. 35 years

10. An amount doubles itself at the end of 8 years with a certain rate of simple interest. What will be the total simple interest on Rs. 8000 at that rate at the end of 4 years?

    A. Rs. 2000
    B. Rs. 4000
    C. Rs. 6000
    D. None of these

ANSWERS

1	2	3	4	5	6	7	8	9	10
D	B	A	D	C	C	A	A	C	B

32

SOME SELECTED EXPLANATORY ANSWERS

1. $\dfrac{1250 \times R \times 3}{100} + \dfrac{1500 \times R \times 2}{100} = 258.75$

$\Rightarrow 6750\ R = 25875$

$\therefore \qquad R = \dfrac{25875}{6750} = \dfrac{23}{6} = 3\dfrac{5}{6}\%$

2. Here, $\dfrac{5000 \times R \times T}{100} = \dfrac{4000 \times (R+1) \times T}{100}$

$\Rightarrow 5R = 4R + 4 \qquad \therefore \quad R = 4\%$

3. Simple interest for 2 years
$\qquad$ = Rs. 2050 – Rs. 1900 = Rs. 150

$\therefore$ Simple interest for 1 year = Rs. $\dfrac{150}{2}$

$\qquad\qquad\qquad\qquad = $ Rs. 75

Since simple interest for 3 years = Rs. 75 × 3
$\qquad\qquad\qquad\qquad\qquad = $ Rs. 225

$\therefore \qquad$ Principal = Rs. 1900 – Rs. 225
$\qquad\qquad\qquad = $ Rs. 1675

Hence, $\quad$ Rate $= \dfrac{75 \times 100}{1675 \times 1} = 4\frac{1}{2}\%$

4. Interest for 3 years = Rs. 2000 – Rs. 1760
$\qquad\qquad\qquad = $ Rs. 240

$\therefore$ Interest for 1 year = Rs. $\dfrac{240}{3} = $ Rs. 80

And interest for 2 years = Rs. 80 × 2 = Rs. 160
$\therefore$ Principal = Rs. 1760 – Rs. 160 = Rs. 1600

5. Let Rs. x and Rs $(1550 - x)$ were lent out at 8% and 5% respectively; then

$\dfrac{x \times 8 \times 3}{100} + \dfrac{(1550 - x) \times 5 \times 3}{100} = 300$

$\Rightarrow 24x + 23250 - 15x = 30000$

$\Rightarrow 9x = 6750 \quad \therefore \quad x = \dfrac{6750}{9} = $ Rs. 750

6. Here, $\dfrac{P \times 5 \times 4}{100} = \dfrac{840 \times 4 \times 10}{100} \Rightarrow 5P = 8400$

$\therefore P = \dfrac{8400}{5} = $ Rs. 1680

7. Let equal instalment be Rs. x; then

$x + \dfrac{x \times 4 \times 3}{100} + x + \dfrac{x \times 4 \times 2}{100} + x$

$\qquad\qquad\qquad + \dfrac{x \times 4 \times 1}{100} + x = 848$

$\Rightarrow 4x + \dfrac{24x}{100} = 848 \quad \Rightarrow \dfrac{106x}{25} = 848$

$\therefore \ x = \dfrac{848 \times 25}{106} = $ Rs. 200

8. $\dfrac{5000 \times R \times 5}{100} + \dfrac{3000 \times R \times 4}{100} = 600$

$\Rightarrow \qquad 250\ R + 120\ R = 600$
$\Rightarrow \qquad\qquad\qquad 370R = 600$

$\therefore \qquad\qquad\qquad R = \dfrac{600}{370} = 1.62\%$

9. Let principal be Rs. x; then amount = Rs. $2x$,
Hence, I = $2x - x = $ Rs. x.

$R = \dfrac{x \times 100}{x \times 7} = \dfrac{100}{7}\%$ p.a.

Now, amount = Rs. $4x$; then I = $4x - x$
$\qquad\qquad\qquad\qquad = $ Rs. $3x$

Hence, T $= \dfrac{3x \times 100}{x \times \dfrac{100}{7}} = \dfrac{3 \times 100 \times 7}{100} = 21$ years

10. Let principal = Rs. x; then amount = Rs. $2x$;
I = $2x - x = $ Rs. x

$R = \dfrac{x \times 100}{x \times 8} = \dfrac{25}{2}\%$

Again, $\qquad$ I $= \dfrac{8000 \times 25 \times 4}{100 \times 2} = $ Rs. 4000

———

COMPOUND INTEREST

1. The compound interest on a certain sum of money invested for 3 years at 5% per annum is Rs. 1891.50. What will be the simple interest on the same sum at the same rate for 2 years?
   A. Rs. 1700
   B. Rs. 1200
   C. Rs. 1500
   D. Rs. 2100

2. A sum of money lent out at a certain rate of simple interest amounts to Rs. 6600 in 2 years and to Rs. 6900 in 3 years. What will be the compound interest on the same sum of money if lent out at the same rate for 2 years?
   A. Rs. 605
   B. Rs. 715
   C. Rs. 615
   D. Rs. 595

3. A man deposits Rs. 1200 in a bank on the 1st day of each year. If the bank pays 5% per annum compound interest on deposited sum of money, what will be the amount to his credit on the 10th day of the second year?
   A. Rs. 2560
   B. Rs. 2460
   C. Rs. 2370
   D. Rs. 2860

4. If the difference between compound and simple interest on a certain sum of money for 3 years at 5% per annum is Rs. 244, the sum is :
   A. Rs. 40000
   B. Rs. 25000
   C. Rs. 30000
   D. Rs. 32000

5. A man purchased a sewing machine for Rs. 5000. If due to sustained use value of this sewing machine depreciates by 6% annually, find its value after 3 years.
   A. Rs. 3775.67
   B. Rs. 4152.92
   C. Rs. 4250.25
   D. Rs. 4356.25

6. Find the sum on which the difference between compound and simple interest for 3 years at 10% per annum will be Rs. 868.
   A. Rs. 29500
   B. Rs. 27625
   C. Rs. 28500
   D. Rs. 28000

7. Samir invested Rs. 15000 at the rate of interest 10% p.a. for 1 year. If the interest compound six months. What amount will Samir get at the end of the year?
   A. Rs. 16,500
   B. Rs. 16525.50
   C. Rs. 16537.50
   D. Rs. 18,150

8. The compound interest on a certain sum for 2 years at 10% per annum is Rs. 525. The simple interest on the same sum for double the time at half the rate per cent per annum is:
   A. Rs. 800
   B. Rs. 600
   C. Rs. 500
   D. Rs. 400

9. The least number of complete years in which a sum of money put at 20% compound interest will be more than doubled is:
   A. 6
   B. 5
   C. 4
   D. 3

10. On a sum of money, the simple interest for 2 years is Rs. 660, while the compound interest is Rs. 696.30, the rate of interest being the same in both cases. Find the rate of interest.
    A. Rs. 12%
    B. 11%
    C. 10%
    D. 9%

ANSWERS									
1	2	3	4	5	6	7	8	9	10
B	C	B	D	B	D	C	C	C	B

SOME SELECTED EXPLANATORY ANSWERS

1. Here, $1891.50 = P\left[\left(1+\dfrac{5}{100}\right)^3 - 1\right]$

$\Rightarrow \quad 1891.50 = P\left[\left(\dfrac{21}{20}\right)^3 - 1\right]$

$\Rightarrow \quad 1891.50 = P\left(\dfrac{1261}{8000}\right)$

$\therefore P = \dfrac{1891.50 \times 8000}{1261} = $ Rs. 12000

Now, $\text{S.I.} = \dfrac{12000 \times 5 \times 2}{100} = $ Rs. 1200

2. Here, 1 year's S.I. = Rs. 6900 – Rs. 6600
= Rs. 300

$\therefore$ 2 year's S.I. = 300 × 2 = Rs. 600

$\therefore$ Principal = Rs. 6600 – Rs. 600
= Rs. 6000

Hence, $\text{Rate} = \dfrac{600 \times 100}{6000 \times 2} = 5\%$

$\therefore \quad \text{C.I.} = 6000\left[\left(1+\dfrac{5}{100}\right)^2 - 1\right]$

$= 6000\left[\left(\dfrac{21}{20}\right)^2 - 1\right] = \dfrac{6000 \times 41}{400} = $ Rs. 615

3. Required amount $= 1200\left(1+\dfrac{5}{100}\right) + 1200$

$= 1200 \times \dfrac{21}{20} + 1200 = 1260 + 1200 = $ Rs. 2460

4. Here, $P\left[\left(1+\dfrac{5}{100}\right)^3 - 1\right] - \dfrac{P \times 5 \times 3}{100} = 244$

$\Rightarrow P \times \dfrac{1261}{8000} - \dfrac{3P}{20} = 244 \Rightarrow P \times \dfrac{61}{8000} = 244$

$\therefore \quad P = \dfrac{244 \times 8000}{61} = $ Rs. 32000

5. Here, value of the machine after 3 years

$= 5000\left(1-\dfrac{6}{100}\right)^3 = 5000 \times \dfrac{47}{50} \times \dfrac{47}{50} \times \dfrac{47}{50}$

= Rs. 4152.92.

6. Here, $P\left[\left(1+\dfrac{10}{100}\right)^3 - 1\right] - \dfrac{P \times 10 \times 3}{100} = 868$

$\Rightarrow P \times \dfrac{331}{1000} - \dfrac{3P}{10} = 868$

$\Rightarrow P \times \dfrac{31}{1000} = 868 \quad \therefore \quad P = \dfrac{868 \times 1000}{31}$
$= $ Rs. 28000

7. $A = 15000\left(1+\dfrac{5}{100}\right)^2 = 15000 \times \dfrac{441}{400}$

$= $ Rs. 16537.50

8. Here, $P\left[\left(1+\dfrac{10}{100}\right)^2 - 1\right] = 525$

$\Rightarrow P\left[\dfrac{121}{100} - 1\right] = 525 \Rightarrow P \times \dfrac{21}{100} = 525$

$\therefore \quad P = \dfrac{525 \times 100}{21} = $ Rs. 2500

Hence, required S.I. $= \dfrac{2500 \times 5 \times 4}{100} = $ Rs. 500

9. Here, $P\left(1+\dfrac{20}{100}\right)^n > 2P \Rightarrow \left(\dfrac{6}{5}\right)^n > 2$

Hence, if $n = 4$ then, $\left(\dfrac{6}{5}\right)^4 = \dfrac{1296}{625} > 2$

So, $n = 4$ years

10. Here, S.I. for 1 year = Rs. 330
Since, simple interest of Rs. 330 for 1 year
= 696.30 – 660 = Rs. 36.30

Hence, required rate $= \dfrac{36.30 \times 100}{330 \times 1} = \dfrac{3630}{330}$
$= 11\%$

AREA AND PERIMETER

1. If side of a square is reduced by 50%, its area will be reduced by
   A. 50%
   B. 75%
   C. 80%
   D. 60%

2. If each side of a square is doubled, its area will become
   A. double
   B. four times
   C. three times
   D. eight times

3. Three sides of a triangle are in the ratio of 17 : 15 : 8. If the perimeter of this triangle is 40 m, find its area
   A. 50 sq. m.
   B. 49 sq. m.
   C. 60 sq. m.
   D. 69 sq. m.

4. If the length of a rectangle is increased by 20% and width is decreased by 15%, then its area
   A. decreases by 4%
   B. increases by 2%
   C. decreases by 2%
   D. increases by 3%

5. If the length of a rectangle is increased by 20%, then by how much per cent its breadth must be decreased so as to keep its area unaltered?
   A. 25%
   B. $8\dfrac{1}{3}\%$
   C. $16\dfrac{2}{3}\%$
   D. 20%

6. The ratio of length and breadth of a rectangular plot is 71 : 61 respectively. The area of the plot is 17324 m². What is perimeter of the plot?
   A. 264 m
   B. 284 m
   C. 528 m
   D. 614 m

7. If the length and breadth of a rectangular field are increased, the area increases by 50%. If the increase in length was 20%, by what percentage was the breadth increased?
   A. 20%
   B. 25%
   C. 30%
   D. 40%

8. The length and breadth of a varandah is 40 m and 15 m respectively. How many stone slabs of size 6 decimetre × 5 decimetre each are needed in flooring it:
   A. 1000
   B. 2000
   C. 3000
   D. 4000

9. The circumference of a circular plot is 396 m. What is the area of the circular plot?
   A. 9,446 m²
   B. 9,856 m²
   C. 12,474 m²
   D. 18,634 m²

10. If the sides of an equilateral triangle are increased by 20%, 30% and 50% respectively to form a new triangle, the increase in the perimeter of the equilateral triangle is:
    A. 25%
    B. $33\dfrac{1}{3}\%$
    C. 50%
    D. 100%

ANSWERS

1	2	3	4	5	6	7	8	9	10
B	B	C	B	C	C	B	B	C	B

SOME SELECTED EXPLANATORY ANSWERS

1. Area of the square $= x^2$ sq. m.

   Side of the new square $= x - 50\%$ of $x = \dfrac{x}{2}$ m

   $\therefore$ Area of the new square $= \left(\dfrac{x}{2}\right)^2 = \dfrac{x^2}{4}$ sq. m.

   $\therefore$ Reduction in area of the square $= x^2 - \dfrac{x^2}{4}$

   $$= \dfrac{3x^2}{4} \text{ sq. m.}$$

   $\therefore$ Percentage reduction $= \dfrac{3x^2/4}{x^2} \times 100 = 75\%$

2. Area of the square $= x^2$ sq. m

   Now, area of the new square $= (2x)^2 = 4x^2$ sq. m

   Hence, it is clear that if side of a square is doubled, its area becomes four times.

3. Suppose sides of the triangle are $17x$ m, $15x$ m and $8x$ metres

   $\therefore$ Perimeter $= 17x + 15x + 8x = 40x$

   Now, $40x = 40$

   $\Rightarrow x = 1$ m

   Therefore, the sides are $17 \times 1 = 17$ m, $15 \times 1 = 15$ m and $8 \times 1 = 8$ m

   $\because (17)^2 = (15)^2 + (8)^2,$

   i.e., it is a right angled triangle

   $\therefore$ Area of the right angled triangle

   $$= \dfrac{1}{2} \times 8 \times 15 = 60 \text{ sq.m.}$$

4. Area of the rectangle $= xy$ sq. metre

   Area of the new rectangle $= \dfrac{120}{100} x \times \dfrac{85}{100} y$

   $$= 1.020 \, xy \text{ sq. metre}$$

   $\therefore$ Increase in the area $= 1.02 \, xy - xy$

   $$= .02 \, xy \text{ sq. m.}$$

   $\therefore$ Percentage increase $= \dfrac{.02xy}{xy} \times 100 = 2\%$

5. Area of the rectangle $= xy$

   On reducing the breadth by $A\%$ and increasing the length by 20%

   Length of the new rectangle $= \dfrac{120x}{100} x = 1.2x$

   Breadth of the new rectangle $= y - A\%$ of y

   $$= y\left(1 - \dfrac{A}{100}\right)$$

   $\therefore$ Area of the new rectangle $= 1.2x \times y\left(1 - \dfrac{A}{100}\right)$

   Now, $xy = 1.2 \, xy\left(1 - \dfrac{A}{100}\right) \Rightarrow 1 = 1.2\dfrac{(100 - A)}{100}$

   $\Rightarrow \qquad 1.2\,A = 120 - 100$

   $\therefore \qquad A = \dfrac{20}{1.2} = 16\dfrac{2}{3}\%$

6. Let length and breadth of a rectangle be $71x$ and $61x$ m; then

   $71x \times 61x = 17324 \Rightarrow x^2 = \dfrac{17324}{71 \times 61} = 4$

   $\therefore \qquad x = 2$

   Hence, length $= 71 \times 2 = 142$ m; breadth

   $$= 61 \times 2 = 122 \text{ m}$$

   Since, perimeter $= 2(142 + 122) = 2 \times 264$

   $$= 528 \text{ m}$$

7. Here, $20 + x + \dfrac{20 \times x}{100} = 50 \Rightarrow x + \dfrac{x}{5} = 30$

   $\Rightarrow \dfrac{6x}{5} = 30 \qquad \therefore x = \dfrac{5 \times 30}{6} = 25$

   Hence, breadth was increased by 25%

8. Required number of stone slabs $= \dfrac{40 \times 15}{\dfrac{6}{10} \times \dfrac{5}{10}}$

   $$= \dfrac{40 \times 15 \times 100}{6 \times 5} = 2000$$

9. Radius of circular plot $= \dfrac{396 \times 7}{2 \times 22} = 63$ m

   Area of the circular plot $= \dfrac{22}{7} \times 63 \times 63$

   $$= 12{,}474 \text{ m}^2$$

VOLUME AND SURFACE AREA

1. If a solid sphere of 3 cm radius is melted and recast into a right circular cone whose base radius is same as that of the sphere, the height of the cone will be
   A. 8 cm
   B. 12 cm
   C. 6 cm
   D. 5 cm

2. Diameter of a roller is 2.4 m and it is 1.68 m long. If it takes 1000 complete revolutions once over to level a field, the area of the field is
   A. 12672 sq. m
   B. 12671 sq. m
   C. 12762 sq. m
   D. 11768 sq. m

3. If each edge of a cube is increased by 10%, then by how much per cent will the surface area of this cube be increased?
   A. 21%
   B. 18%
   C. 15%
   D. 20%

4. Height and base radius of a solid cylinder are 14 m and 4 m respectively. It is melted and recast into a solid cone of the same base radius as that of the cylinder, what will be the height of the cone?
   A. 21 m
   B. 42 m
   C. 48 m
   D. 54 m

5. A room is in the form of a cube of side 10 m. How many bales of cotton can be kept in it if each bale covers 5 cu m space?
   A. 100
   B. 175
   C. 200
   D. 225

6. Three cubes having side 2 cm, 3 cm and 4 cm respectively are melted together to form a new cube. The side of the new cube will be
   A. 3.526 cm
   B. 4.628 cm
   C. 4.626 cm
   D. 4.528 cm

7. If base diameter of a cylinder is increased by 50%, then by how much per cent its height must be decreased so as to keep its volume unaltered?
   A. 45.56%
   B. 55.56%
   C. 50.16%
   D. 62.33%

8. The surface area of a cube is 600 sq. m. Its diagonal is
   A. $10\sqrt{3}$ cm
   B. $5\sqrt{3}$ cm
   C. $4\sqrt{2}$ cm
   D. $10\sqrt{2}$ cm

9. The base diameter of a conical tomb is 28 m and its slant height is 50 m. Find the cost of white washing its curved surface at the rate of 80 paise per sq. m?
   A. Rs. 1860
   B. Rs. 1760
   C. Rs. 1950
   D. Rs. 1875

10. The volume of a cuboid is 1120 cu cm and its height is 5 cm while the length and the breadth of the cuboid are in the ratio 8 : 7. The length of this cylinder exceeds the breadth by
    A. 4 cm
    B. 2 cm
    C. 7 cm
    D. 5 cm

ANSWERS

1	2	3	4	5	6	7	8	9	10
B	A	A	B	C	C	B	A	B	B

SOME SELECTED EXPLANATORY ANSWERS

1. Volume of the cone = Volume of the sphere

$$\therefore \quad \frac{1}{3}\pi(3)^2 \times h = \frac{4}{3}\pi \times 3^3 \Rightarrow h = 12 \text{ cm}$$

Hence, height of the cone = 12 cm.

2. Surface area of the roller = $2\pi rh$

$$= 2 \times \frac{22}{7} \times 1.2 \times 1.68 = 12.672 \text{ sq. m}$$

In one complete revolution, the roller covers 12.672 sq. m.

$\therefore$ It will cover in 1000 revolutions
$$= 12.672 \times 1000 = 12672 \text{ sq. m}$$

Hence, area of the field = 12672 sq. m.

3. Percentage increase in the surface area of the cube $= \left(x + y + \dfrac{xy}{100} \right)\%$

$$= \left(10 + 10 + \frac{10 \times 10}{100} \right)\% = 21\%.$$

4. Here,

volume of the cone = Volume of the cylinder

$$\Rightarrow \quad \frac{1}{3}\pi r^2 \times \text{height} = \pi r^2 \times 14$$

$$\therefore \qquad \text{Height} = 14 \times 3 = 42 \text{ m}$$

Thus, height of the cone = 42 m.

5. Volume of the cubical room = $(10)^3$
$$= 1000 \text{ cu m}$$

Number of cotton bales which can be placed in the room

$$= \frac{\text{Volume of the room}}{\text{Volume of each cotton bale}} = \frac{1000}{5} = 200.$$

6. Volume of the new cube = $2^3 + 3^3 + 4^3$
$$= 8 + 27 + 64 = 99\text{cu cm}$$

$\therefore$ Side of the new cube = $\sqrt[3]{99}$ = 4.626 cm.

7. Change in the volume of the cylinder

$$= \left(x + y + (-z) + \frac{xy + y(-z) + (-zx)}{100} + \frac{xy(-z)}{100^2} \right)\%$$

Since volume of the cylinder remains unchanged.

$$\therefore \qquad \text{Change} = 0\%$$

$$\text{Now,} \left(50 + 50 + (-z) + \frac{50 \times 50 - 50z - 50z}{100} + \frac{50 \times 50 \times (-z)}{100^2} \right) = 0$$

$$\therefore \quad 100 - z + 25 - z - .25z = 0$$

$$\Rightarrow 2.25z = 125 \Rightarrow z = \frac{125}{2.25} = 55.56$$

$\therefore$ Height of the cylinder should be decreased by 55.56%.

8. Here, $\qquad 6 \times (\text{side})^2 = 600$
$$\Rightarrow \qquad \text{side}^2 = 100$$
$$\Rightarrow \qquad \text{side} = \sqrt{100} = 10 \text{ cm}$$

$\therefore$ Diagonal of the cube$= \sqrt{3} \times \text{side}$
$$= \sqrt{3} \times 10$$
$$= 10\sqrt{3} \text{ cm.}$$

9. Area of the curved surface of the cone

$$= \frac{22}{7} \times \frac{28}{2} \times 50 = 2200 \text{ sq. m.}$$

$\therefore$ Cost of white washing at 80 paise per sq. m

$$= 2200 \times \frac{80}{100} = \text{Rs. } 1760.$$

10. Suppose the length and the breadth of the cuboid are $8x$ cm and $7x$ cm

$\therefore$ Here, $\quad 8x \times 7x \times 5 = 1120$

$$\Rightarrow x^2 = \frac{1120}{280} = 4 = (2)^2 \quad \Rightarrow \quad x = 2$$

$\therefore$ Length of the cuboid $= 8 \times 2 = 16$ cm
Breadth of the cuboid $= 7 \times 2 = 14$ cm

Hence, it is clear that length of the cuboid exceeds the breadth by 2 cm.

AREA AND PERIMETER

1. The length of a plot is four times its breadth. A playground measuring 1200 square metres occupies a third of the total area of the plot. What is the length of the plot, in metres?
   A. 20
   B. 30
   C. 60
   D. None of these

2. The width of a rectangular hall is $\frac{3}{4}$ of its length. If the area of the hall is 300 m², then the difference between its length and width is:
   A. 3 m
   B. 4 m
   C. 5 m
   D. 15 m

3. The length and breadth of a rectangular piece of land are in ratio of 5 : 3. The owner spent ₹ 3000 for surrounding it from all the sides at ₹ 7.50 per metre. The difference between its length and breadth is:
   A. 50 m
   B. 100 m
   C. 150 m
   D. 200 m

4. A room 8 m × 6 m is to be carpeted by a carpet 2 m wide. The length of carpet required is:
   A. 12 m
   B. 36 m
   C. 24 m
   D. 48 m

5. The length of a rectangle is increased by 60%. By what per cent would the width have to be decreased to maintain the same area?
   A. $37\frac{1}{2}\%$
   B. 60%
   C. 75%
   D. 120%

6. A man walked 20 m to cross a rectangular field diagonally. If the length of the field is 16 m, the breadth of the rectangle is:
   A. 4 m
   B. 16 m
   C. 12 m
   D. Cannot be determined

7. If the ratio of the areas of two squares is 9 : 1, the ratio of their perimeters is:
   A. 9 : 1
   B. 3 : 1
   C. 3 : 4
   D. 1 : 3

8. The perimeter of both, a square and a rectangle are each equal to 48 m and the difference between their areas is 4 m². The breadth of the rectangle is:
   A. 10 m
   B. 12 m
   C. 14 m
   D. None of these

9. Area of a square with side x is equal to the area of a triangle with base x. The altitude of the triangle is:
   A. $\frac{x}{2}$
   B. x
   C. $2x$
   D. $4x$

10. If only the length of the rectangular plot is reduced to $\frac{2}{3}$rd of its original length, the ratio of original area to reduced area is:
    A. 2 : 3
    B. 3 : 2
    C. 1 : 2
    D. None of these

11. If the radius of a circle be reduced by 50%, its area is reduced by:
    A. 25%
    B. 50%
    C. 75%
    D. 100%

12. The perimeter of a rhombus is 52 m while its longer diagonal is 24 m. Its other diagonal is:
    A. 5 m
    B. 10 m
    C. 20 m
    D. 28 m

13. The circumference of a circle is 352 m, then its area in m² is:
    A. 9856
    B. 8956
    C. 6589
    D. 5986

ANSWERS

1	2	3	4	5	6	7	8	9	10
D	C	A	C	A	C	B	A	C	B

11	12	13
C	B	A

SOME SELECTED EXPLANATORY ANSWERS

1. Area of the plot = $3 \times 1200 = 3600$ m^2
   Let breadth be x m. Then length = $4x$ m
   According to the question,
   $4x \times x = 3600 \Rightarrow x^2 = 900 \Rightarrow x = 30$
   Hence, length of the plot = $4 \times 30 = 120$ m.

2. Let length be x m, then breadth = $\dfrac{3x}{4}$ m

   Area of the hall = $x \times \dfrac{3x}{4} = \dfrac{3x^2}{4}$

   According to the question,

   $\dfrac{3x^2}{4} = 300 \Rightarrow x^2 = 400 \Rightarrow x = 20$

   Length = 20 m and breadth = $\dfrac{3}{4} \times 20 = 15$ m

   Difference = $20 - 15 = 5$ m

3. Let length = $5x$ m and breadth = $3x$ m
   Perimeter of rectangle = $2(5x + 3x) = 16x$ m

   But perimeter = $\dfrac{\text{Total cost}}{\text{Rate}} = \dfrac{3000}{7.50} = 400$ m

   Now, $16x = 400 \Rightarrow x = 25$
   length = $5x = 5 \times 25 = 125$ m
   breadth = $3x = 25 \times 3 = 75$ m
   Difference = $125 - 75 = 50$ m

4. Length of the carpet = $\dfrac{8 \times 6}{2} = 24$ m.

7. Let the areas of the squares be $(9x^2)$ m^2 and (x^2) m^2
   Then, their sides are $3x$ m and x m respectively

   Ratio of their perimeters = $\dfrac{12x}{4x} = 3 : 1$

9. According to the question,

   $$x^2 = \frac{1}{2} \times x \times h$$

   $\Rightarrow \qquad h = \dfrac{2x^2}{x} = 2x$

10. Let length = x and breadth = y

    New length = $\dfrac{2}{3}x$

    $\therefore \dfrac{\text{Original area}}{\text{Reduced area}} = \dfrac{xy}{\dfrac{2}{3}xy} = \dfrac{3}{2} = 3 : 2$

11. Original area = πr^2, New area = $\pi \left(\dfrac{r}{2}\right)^2 = \dfrac{\pi r^2}{4}$

    Reduction in area = $\pi r^2 - \dfrac{\pi r^2}{4} = \dfrac{3\pi r^2}{4}$

    Reduction per cent = $\dfrac{3\pi r^2}{4} \times \dfrac{1}{\pi r^2} \times 100 = 75\%$

12. Side of rhombus = $\dfrac{52}{4} = 13$ m

    In $\triangle ABM$,
    $x^2 = (13)^2 - (12)^2$
    $x^2 = 169 - 144$
    $x^2 = 25$
    $\Rightarrow \quad x = 5$ m
    $\therefore$ Another diagonal
    $\qquad = 2 \times 5 = 10$ m

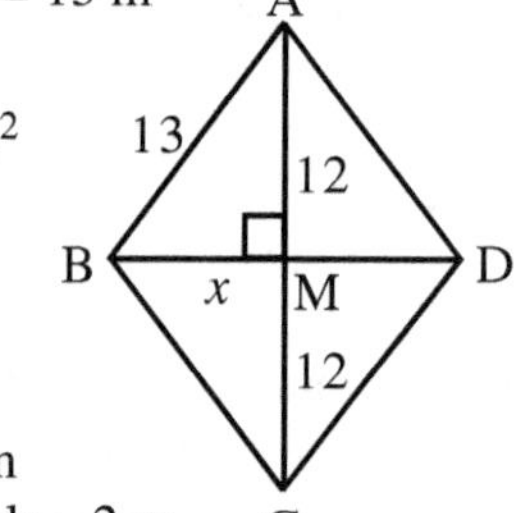

13. Circumference of a circle = $2\pi r$

    $\Rightarrow \qquad 352 = 2 \times \dfrac{22}{7} \times r$

    $\Rightarrow \qquad r = \dfrac{352 \times 7}{44} = 56$ m

    Area of circle = $\pi r^2 = \dfrac{22}{7} \times 56 \times 56$

    $\qquad = 9856$ m^2